1987

UNDERSTANDING HOSPITAL FINANCIAL MANAGEMENT

Second Edition

Allen G. Herkimer, Jr., Ed.D., FHFMA, CMPA
Southwest Texas State University
San Marcos, Texas

AN ASPEN PUBLICATION®
Aspen Publishers, Inc.

1986

Rockville, Maryland
Royal Tunbridge Wells

Library of Congress Cataloging in Publication Data

Herkimer, Allen G.
Understanding hospital financial management.

"An Aspen publication."
Includes bibliographies and index.
1. Hospitals—Business management. 2. Hospitals—Finance. I. Title. [DNLM: 1.
Economics, Hospital—United States. 2. Financial Management. 3. Hospital
Administration—United States. WX 157 H548u]
RA971.3.H47   1986   362.1'1'0681   86-14181
ISBN: 0-87189-392-4

Editorial Services: Marsha Davies

Library of Congress Catalog Card Number: 86-14181
ISBN: 0-87189-392-4

Printed in the United States of America

1 2 3 4 5

To Fay

Table of Contents

Preface to First Edition

Over the past few years there have been a great number of state and federal bills introduced by legislators recommending the establishment of hospital budget, cost review, and rate-setting regulatory devices or agencies. States that have passed these bills into law, such as Arizona, New York, Maryland, Massachusetts, Oregon, Connecticut, and Washington, have seen their regulatory agencies or commissions experience only limited success in holding down costs. The federal government is continually seeking new ideas to restrain the rate of increase in health care costs. Such mechanisms as health service agencies, professional standards review organizations, utilization review committees, incentive reimbursement programs, health maintenance organizations, prospective payment plans, cost limitations, rate ceilings, and *lessor of cost or charges* have either been tried or written into law for the primary purpose of containing and/or restraining the cost of health care.

In the health care environment today, there are five basic weaknesses in any of these external regulatory approaches.

First, the fact that an external agency is trying to control health care institutional operations immediately creates an atmosphere of negativism within the institution. In this setting, one entity tries to close loopholes while the other looks for ways to keep them open, or opens new ones. In the end, everyone has lost sight of the primary objective. The primary purpose of the health care institution has been obscured.

Second, most external regulatory programs are institutionalized, or oriented toward controlling facility costs with little, if any, effort toward controlling the costs caused by the private physician and other related individuals and/or groups. Until more attention is directed toward controlling the physician-generated costs, health care costs will continue to escalate regardless of the constraints placed upon the institutions by the regulatory agencies.

Third, most of the external regulatory agencies utilize a negative, or penalty, approach to controlling health care costs. In effect, these programs tend to discourage the cost-efficient and high quality health care facility. The result can only be the creation of low motivated internal management and a mediocre overall quality of health care.

Fourth, the public and the physicians are continually requesting and expecting the most sophisticated health care technology, as well as many varieties of health care services. Such demands upon the health care industry along with the normal inflationary trend, plus the fact that the health care industry is labor intensive, make the cost of operating a health care institution rise. Until the patient and the physician are willing to assume more responsibility for controlling health care costs, these costs will continue to escalate just as fast as the Consumer Price Index does, if not faster.

Finally, there is no suitable quantitative or qualitative measurement device available to the external regulatory agencies, or to internal health care management, that can be used to evaluate accurately the services a patient receives. Presently, the health care industry is restricted by misleading measurement tools such as cost per patient day to analyze health care costs between institutions and from one period to another.

The solution to the control of health care costs must come from effective and enlightened management within the institution, not from external regulatory agencies. External agencies can only control the amount of reimbursement the health care facility receives for its services; they cannot control the costs to the institution that generate those services. Cost control must be started and maintained by the health care institution's own management team.

At present, there is no book designed specifically to assist the health care department manager, his supervisors, and other nonaccountant professionals to do a more effective financial management job. This fact has always concerned me, because I emphatically believe that the department manager and his peers are the first-line financial managers of a health care institution. Further, I believe that top health care institutional management should expect these individuals to run their respective departments as if they were running their own businesses. Moreover, their departments should contribute a specific net margin to the operations of the entire facility. Nothing short of these expectations should be tolerated.

Many times individuals have been promoted to department manager or supervisor because they possess high technical skill levels, such as medical technologists, radiology technicians, registered nurses, plant engineers, dieticians or physical therapists. Unfortunately, the Peter Principle usually takes over because many of these highly skilled technical individuals possess virtually no knowledge of health care financial management. They have been promoted to their level of incompetence.

Certainly financial management is one of the primary responsibilities of a department manager or supervisor. But *effective* financial management is another matter entirely, and is critical to profitability and productivity.

It is my opinion that in order to control health care costs, an institution's department managers and their supervisors must first know the origins of costs and how they change under varying conditions. Therefore, one of the primary goals of this book is to acquaint the department manager, supervisor, and other nonaccountant health care professionals with the basic techniques of health care financial management.

Another goal of this book is to stimulate the readers' interest in health care financial management and to motivate them to pursue further education in this area.

Further, I hope to encourage readers to implement the management techniques presented here, so that they will become more effective health care professionals. Effective health care cost control starts at the top in each department of the institution.

Top management, such as the board of trustees and administration, cannot control health care costs. They can only establish policies that encourage cost effectiveness and create an environment of cost awareness.

I hope this book will stimulate the readers to perform constructive, corrective action within their respective departments and to use one of management's most important tools . . . IMAGINATION. Only then can health care institutions require fewer external regulations to achieve our mutual objectives: effective cost control for better health care for our nation's citizens.

Allen G. Herkimer, Jr.

Preface to Second Edition

A prospective payment system (PPS) instead of a retrospective payment system.

Diagnosis-related groups (DRGs) instead of an à la carte method of determining payments.

A competitive market environment instead of a tightly regulated market environment.

Cash flow motivation instead of bottom-line motivation.

These changes only partially reflect the dynamics of hospital financial management. In fact, the term hospital is rapidly being replaced by the term "health system." To survive these and future environmental changes in the hospital industry, management must understand that hospitals are not immune to the consequences of ineffective management. They must adopt an aggressive and creative posture.

The days of "protective custody" are over. The Darwinian concept of "survival of the fittest" should serve as the benchmark for hospital financial managers' future decisions. Creative and effective hospital financial management is the key to the hospital's survival.

For this type of financial management, the hospital needs to have as heads of its operations a risk-oriented Chief Executive Officer (CEO) and Chief Financial Officer (CFO) who spend a considerable amount of time on strategic planning and marketing in order to place their hospital in the most favorable market position. To accomplish this task, they must depend on the expertise of their subordinates—the people who must carry on the day-to-day operations of the facility in a cost-efficient manner.

Control of hospital costs must come from enlightened management within the institution, not from external regulatory agencies. External agencies can control only the amount of cash payments the hospital receives for its services; they cannot control the costs the hospital incurs to generate those services. The hospital's own management team must initiate and maintain cost and productivity control.

The CEO and the CFO alone cannot control a hospital's costs or productivity. They can serve only as catalysts. Only the department manager of each responsibility center can control departmental cost and productivity; the manager is on the "firing line," where cost and productivity begin and end.

This book is intended to help the hospital department manager and other nonaccountant professionals understand the mechanics of hospital financial management. Department managers have not always been recognized as active and essential members of the hospital's financial management team, yet they are the first-line financial managers of the organization. Further, top management should expect department managers to run their departments as if they were running their own businesses, which might include building in incentives for rewarding the effective and penalizing the inefficient. Moreover, their departments should contribute a specific net margin to the operations of the entire organization. Nothing less can be tolerated.

Medical technologists, radiology technicians, registered nurses, plant engineers, dieticians, physical therapists, or physicians are frequently promoted to department manager or supervisor positions because they possess high-level technical skills. Unfortunately, the Peter Principle usually takes over because many of these highly skilled technical individuals possess virtually no knowledge or experience in financial management, much less hospital financial management. They have been promoted to their levels of incompetence.

Financial management is certainly one of the primary responsibilities of a hospital department manager or supervisor. But *effective* financial management is another matter entirely; it is critical to the hospital's survival, as it ensures the hospital's productivity and profitability.

In order to control hospital costs, the institution's department managers and their supervisors must know and understand where costs originate and how each reacts and changes under varying economic conditions and volume. One of the primary goals of this book, therefore, is to acquaint the reader with the basic principles and techniques of hospital financial management.

Another goal is to stimulate the reader's interest in hospital financial management and to motivate each reader to pursue further education in this area.

Further, the author hopes that readers will be encouraged to implement the management techniques presented here so that they will become more effective hospital professionals. Effective hospital cost control starts at the top of every institution's departments.

The health of the hospital is primary; the health of the patient depends upon the hospital's condition. Without a financially sound and therefore healthy hospital, neither patients nor their physicians can receive the quality of health care that they expect and to which they are entitled. The board of trustees and administration cannot control the financial viability required; they can only establish policies and create a healthy working environment that encourages cost effectiveness and cost awareness. Only this kind of environment can deliver quality health care services.

Allen G. Herkimer, Jr.,
Ed.D., FHFMA, CMPA

Acknowledgments

I imagine that the thoughts of a book's author are somewhat similar to those of a movie producer. Both have experienced the thrill of conceiving and developing an idea into a tangible, meaningful end product or service; both have received acclaim and recognition as originator, director, and presenter. It is even more thrilling and gratifying when the originator is asked to recast and develop a second edition. But both know that their creations could not exist without the support and contributions of many individuals behind the scenes.

There are two anonymous groups to whom I express my heartfelt gratitude and recognition. The first group is composed of the many health care professionals and students with whom I have had the good fortune and privilege to work and socialize during my nearly 30 years in the health care industry. These individuals have contributed immeasurably to my knowledge of hospital (health care) financial management; they provided a forum for a never-ending exchange of ideas and concepts that has stimulated me to write this book.

The second group is composed of present-day health care managers: department managers, chief financial officers, chief executive officers, and health administration students who are no longer satisfied to be just glorified technicians or bookkeepers but are persons who see their roles expanding to those of creative and effective health care resource managers. These individuals are continually striving for excellence; they are the health care financial managers and leaders of tomorrow. I have sincere faith in their ability and desire to help this nation's health care institutions to perform efficiently and effectively with a minimum of governmental intervention and control.

Specific individuals and organizations have allowed me to include in this text material that I believe has made a substantial impact on the health care industry. Their contributions are as follows:

- *Will Bishop*, Director of Finance, the California Hospital Association and the three California chapters of the Hospital Financial Management Association. I have included some illustrations from their *Budget Manual*. As expressed in the Foreword of the manual: "This document is not copyrighted in order to encourage its use for the benefit of the health care industry."
- *Gordon L. Briggs*, Director of Publications and Marketing of the College of American Pathologists (CAP), who "expressed delight" to hear that I was making reference to CAP's Workload Recording Method for Clinical Laboratories and including portions in Appendix A.
- *Darwin W. Schlag, Jr.*, National Health Care Partner, Laventhol & Horwath, for permitting me to include in Appendix B the "Listing of DRGs Weighting Factor and Related Data" and the "Cumulative Frequencies of DRGs," which represents information accumulated by Laventhol & Horwath from the HCFA Bureau of Data Management and Strategy report (June 21, 1982) of 20 percent sample discharges by diagnosis.
- *Lorna Small*, one of my health administration students at California State University, Northridge, for allowing me to include her case study of game planning in Chapter 4.

I am grateful to my wife, Fay, for her continued belief that I could corral my thoughts into a book and for her willingness to spend lonely evenings while I wrote in my study.

Finally, I wish to acknowledge Aspen Publishers, Inc., for its willingness to risk investment in a project that I believe in: namely, that the health care industry, through knowledgeable managers and directors, can manage itself effectively and efficiently.

Chapter 1

The Evolution of Health Care Financial Management

Once I participated in a meeting of chief financial health care officers from across the United States. At issue was whether this group would endorse a major change in the recording and reporting system used to measure health care productivity quantitatively. Many individuals expressed various doubts, but one individual brought the meeting back on course by observing that, "in all probability, the wheel as we know it now was not originally perfectly round."

Similarly, the health care industry has also gone through many evolutionary phases, from the era of philanthropic and community supported institutions through the heavily government-controlled era. Presently, the industry is entering a brand new type of development—the competitive marketplace with its diagnosis-related groups (DRGs), prospective payment systems (PPSs), and competitive medical plans (CMPs). Accordingly, the financial management of these institutions has changed.

For a moment, let us go back to the turn of the century and examine the evolution of health care financial management and specifically, accounting systems. During the first half of the twentieth century, the accounting systems were actually scorekeeping and bookkeeping systems. Records were usually maintained on a cash basis with relatively little concern for costs, as long as there was sufficient money available either from gifts, donations, or charges to patients. Third party guarantors were few. There was little recognized need or concern for any sophisticated management reporting and control system. The primary concern was the patient—patient health care—with an oblivious attitude toward the health of the health care facility.

By mid-century, the accrual accounting system was being installed in most hospitals, and the bookkeepers had to become accountants.

In 1966, when Medicare was introduced into the nation's health care facilities, the accountant's role, and the accounting system, needed expansion and sophistication. The accountant became a controller. For the first time in many health care facilities, as a result of the Medicare-mandated cost finding process, health care facilities were able to calculate the total (direct and allocated) costs for a specific revenue-producing department. Prior to Medicare, the majority of the health care facilities were concerned only with direct departmental costs, and rates were frequently set based not on costs but in relation to charges or rates in a neighboring health care facility or on what management thought might be an appropriate rate.

However, these demands and regulations were not all bad. Up until Medicare, few of this nation's health care institutions had used cost finding as a management tool to determine a department's total costs. Neither, for that matter, had they used cost finding to determine the cost or charge (price) for individual departmental service. In 1972, Public Law 92-603 required all hospitals to generate at least a one-year operating budget and a three-year capital expenditure plan. Even then, budgeting was relatively new to most hospitals. The federal government, through its Medicare regulations, literally mandated a more effective and informative financial management information system.

It is unfortunate that these demands were mandated by an external force, and designed only to meet the government's need-to-know requirements, instead of internal management's need-to-know decision-making information needs. This is a sad commentary upon the aged health care industry, which had refused to mature as other industries responded to the changing times. Internal management has found many benefits from the results of these mandated requirements such as cost finding, budgeting, and market assessment. Until 1966, the combined governmental programs represented a relatively small proportion of health care purchases. Blue Cross and commercial insurance carriers were the most significant purchasers of health care services representing sixty to seventy percent, while the self-pay purchasers represented only about ten to twenty percent, depending upon the geographical location of the health care facility.

Under the 1967 Amendments to the Act, incentive reimbursement was introduced into health care financial management. Incentive reimbursement experiments were encouraged in order to motivate cost efficiency while maintaining or improving quality in the provision of health care services.

It was not until approximately 1970 that some health care facilities and third party reimbursement agencies such as Medicare and Blue

Cross began to think about prospective reimbursement based upon future costs. Until this time, most health care facilities had been paid for services based upon retrospective costs (discussed later) generating from the institution's general accounting system. Figure 1–1 illustrates the evolution of health care financial management and related accounting systems.

Under the 1972 Amendments to the Act, demonstration projects were promoted using prospective reimbursement as the central motivating tool to encourage more effective internal health care management. In the meantime, as more of the nation's population became eligible for benefits, the government was becoming the most dominant purchaser of health care service. The key words are "retrospective" and "prospective." Under the retrospective reimbursement system, *historical* financial and statistical data are used to determine the rate of reimbursement. Under the prospective reimbursement or payment plan, *future,* or projected, financial and statistical data are used.

Most of the prospective payment systems were paid on a per-diem or per-patient-day basis *until October 1, 1983.* On this date, the Medicare program began paying hospitals on a per-case or diagnosis-related group (DRG) basis. Presently, the federal government is promoting prospective payment on a capitation (per person) basis. This method, sometimes referred to as the health maintenance organization (HMO) system, pays for most health care services a person would require over a period of time, whether the patient/member uses the service or not.

The fact that future financial and statistical data are required accelerates the changes in health care financial management. This brings up the question, "What is Health Care Financial Management?"

Figure 1–1 Evolution of Health Care Financial Management

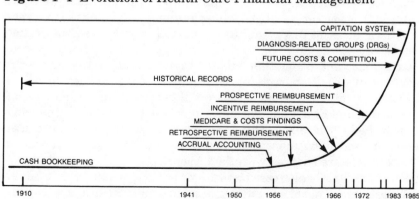

HEALTH CARE FINANCIAL MANAGEMENT DEFINED

Webster defines "to manage" as "to direct or carry on business or affairs; to make and keep submissive; to treat with care, to achieve one's purpose." It also uses such words as "handle, control and contrive" to further define "manage."[1] In another dictionary, Webster includes such definitions as "to succeed in accomplishing, to continue and to alter by manipulation."[2]

Seawell defines the health care financial management objective as being "to plan and control the activities and affairs of the (institution) so that its purpose is achieved at reasonable costs to the community." He further states that, at the very least, this objective includes the long-run realization of revenues equal to costs. He concludes by saying that this minimum (break-even) financial performance must be attained because it is necessary to the continued existence of the institution and, therefore, to the institution's continued ability to provide needed health care services.[3] In its simplest terms, this means "make a profit, or else."

Some of the key words in these definitions are:

- control
- manipulate
- succeed
- continue
- plan
- achieve

In this work, the author has defined health care financial management as "the art of manipulating health care resources, i.e., labor, supplies, and capital, to ensure financial viability so that the health care institution can meet its immediate and long range objectives." Anything short of this would be considered mismanagement or malmanagement.

It is important to note that only the word institution was included in the definition. "Department" was omitted because occasionally a department or some of its services will become obsolete and/or nonproductive and be discontinued. It is important to stress the continuation of the health care institution even, at times, at the expense of an underutilized department: delivery room, nursery, maternity, etc.

Those who are charged with the responsibility of the financial management of their health care institution should remember that a health care institution must be healthy in order to furnish health care. For this reason alone, *I place the health of the health care institution ahead of the health of the patient.* Without a healthy institution, organizationally and financially, the employees of the health care institution will suffer, and individual patients will be deprived of quality health care because of inadequate health care resources to treat their needs.

HEALTH CARE FINANCIAL MANAGER IDENTIFIED

The financial manager of a health care institution is usually associated with the title of Director of Fiscal Services; Vice President, Fiscal Affairs; Controller; or with a myriad of other "financial" titles.

Health care financial management is becoming increasingly complex with the establishment of federal and state rate regulating agencies: the peer review organizations (PRO), prevailing charge profile (PCP), customary charge profile (CCP), preferred provider organizations (PPO), certificate-of-need regulations, budgeting requirements for medical and technological advances, and labor relations problems. Each one of these external forces has a direct impact upon a health care institution's financial viability and each requires the close attention of a health care financial manager.

These external forces, coupled with the public and governmental critics who are constantly demanding more restraint and control of health care costs, have made the financial management of a health care institution more than a one-person show.

The health care industry is a complex business, ever changing and exceptionally dynamic. More promising is the fact that the health care environment is approaching that of the natural marketplace environment.

Accordingly, the day of the bookkeeper with the green eyeshade is over. The traditional health care accountant-controller and the traditional health care department head have become obsolete. No single individual can possibly handle the entire financial management responsibility of a health care institution.

There is only one logical and reasonable approach to health care financial management: shared responsibility or management by involvement.

It is impossible for chief financial officers of any health care institutions to control costs—they can only assist, direct, and monitor the direction of the control of the costs. They cannot increase productivity— they can only provide the financial management tools, such as budgets and performance standards, to measure and evaluate productivity.

Only department managers and their supervisors can control costs and elevate the level of production. It is the department managers and their supervisors who have the day-to-day contact through which health care resources are either economically utilized or haphazardly wasted. These individuals are the true financial managers.

In reality, financial managers have the responsibility to make appropriate decisions and effectively manipulate the use of health care resources to assure the financial viability of their institutions. Within the parameters of this definition, the Executive Housekeeper, the Head Nurse, the Admitting Supervisor, the Plant Engineer, the Food Service Manager, as well as the Chief Financial Officer are all financial managers. With the Chief Executive Officer, the Board of Trustees, the physicians, and the patients, they are all involved in the health care financial management process. They are all responsible for producing continuous, quality health care in the institution's service area at the most reasonable cost possible.

As with the accountants in green eyeshades, traditional department *heads* are also obsolete. They should be classified as department *managers*. They no longer excel in just special technical capabilities; they are managers who are responsible for their institution's investment in the health care resources used by their respective departments. Individuals who hold these positions should no longer be referred to as "Department Heads." If they are not managers, it is the responsibility of the institution's CEO and/or the CFO to train and develop them into managers. They should be recognized managers of finance, of people, of resources, and of equipment, and should be held accountable for these assets. This recognition is not only important from top management perspective, but from the department managers themselves.

MANAGEMENT BY INVOLVEMENT

Management by Involvement is divided into a two-phase program. The first phase is called the Strategic Team Planning (STP) stage, during which the organization's team members will initiate, interpret, review, and establish a set of objectives and priorities.

The second phase is the Budgetary Operating Control (BOC) portion which generates organization financial and production standards through a budgetary and industrial (management) engineering program, compares actual expenses to the budget, and initiates corrective measures for any unfavorable variances.

When properly implemented and conducted, these concepts will help to develop a working team which can increase efficiency in production and can assure sufficient quality to perpetuate operations. Both of these concepts will be discussed in considerable detail in Chapter 4.

The basic premise behind Management by Involvement is to train and develop members of the management hierarchy in the health care institution's overall operations. The training is accomplished by having management staff actively participate in the institution's budget-planning, problem-solving and decision-making processes as well as its operational functions. This management development technique serves to motivate department managers and their supervisors to exert full energies toward the success of any plan, because they have been involved in the designing of the plan.

Maier cites results from various studies which show the benefits of a participative approach. He concludes that: "Psychologically the participative approach adds up to sound motivation; clarification of attitude differences; security of group membership; constructive social pressure; prevention or removal of misunderstanding; good communication; and respect for human dignity."[4]

Perhaps the greatest problem relating to the development of managers is that the success of the Management by Involvement program is contingent upon the caliber of top management. As they are trained for positions of greater responsibility, department managers and supervisors are likely to emulate many of the characteristics and practices of their superiors. Ineffective top management can inhibit the development of effective managers in an organization. Bad habits that are picked up along the way will eventually become the incompetence of those who advance to top management.

Furthermore, if an organization suffers from poor management, the need for devoting formal attention to the management development program may not be recognized.[5] Since management development is needed for all managers and not just for an elite group of management trainees, Management by Involvement offers unique methods of continuing education. The key ingredients to Management by Involvement, then, are:

- participation
- responsibility
- teamwork

MANAGEMENT INFORMATION AND ACCOUNTING

A health care financial manager's greatest responsibility is to make appropriate decisions. Appropriate and considered decisions can be made only with timely, accurate, relevant, and adequate knowledge of the issue at hand. This information may be either quantitative or qualitative in nature. Management accounting is an indispensable tool for furnishing this kind of management information. Basically, management accounting and management information are not usually intended for anyone but the health care institution's management team. Very briefly, management accounting's primary purposes are to provide internal reporting to managers for use in

- Planning and controlling current operations
- Making special decisions and in formulating long-range strategic plans.[6]

Peter Drucker defined management accounting as the use of analysis and information as the foundation for managerial decision making. He includes management accounting as one of seven conceptual foundations to the management boom. The other conceptual foundations are:

- productivity
- decentralization
- personnel management
- manager development
- marketing
- long-range planning[7]

Horngren tells us that the management process is a series of decisions aimed at some objective or set of objectives. Accounting systems for management decision making and implementation are the means for data accumulation, interpretation, and reporting that are tailored to aid the management process.[8]

Management accounting has been referred to as the "IT"—the best of management tools because it features two ingredients which are not customarily used in general accounting procedures. These ingredients are:

I—Imagination in forecasting events both in financial and statistical language.

T—Timely reporting and analysis on a prospective (before-the-fact) basis.

IT—IT is a management tool which assists department managers and their supervisors to estimate where they and their departments are headed.[9]

COMPARISON OF MANAGEMENT ACCOUNTING AND GENERAL ACCOUNTING

The following is a comparative analysis of management accounting and general accounting.[10]

Management Accounting	General Accounting
• future events, statistical and financial data.	• historical events, statistical and financial data.
• tries to forecast "where a department is headed."	• tells "where a department has been."
• subject to internal analysis and auditing.	• subject to external surveillance and auditing.
• estimated calculations, assumptions and projections.	• exact records and facts.
• utilizes imagination with the risk of being wrong or *nearly* right.	• routine in nature, stating and recording facts with no risk to accuracy.
• subject to management's interpretation and assumptions.	• governed by external policies and regulations.
• prospective in nature on a "before-the-fact" basis.	• retrospective in nature on an "after-the-fact" basis.

Both management and general accounting principles are essential to any management information system. The precise information generated by the general accounting system serves as the foundation for the management (information) accounting system. However, general accounting is concerned only with the operating revenues and costs of a department, whereas management accounting is concerned with other types of costs. These other costs (as well as revenues) will be discussed in Chapter 3.

The key to management information and accounting is that the data must communicate what the users need to know in the format and/or the media they can understand in order to assist them in becoming effective department managers and supervisors. The key words here are

- user
- need-to-know
- format

The challenge is to develop a *management information* system between the reporter and user, and to furnish only the key indices the user needs to know to manage the responsibility center effectively and efficiently.

PROFITABILITY AND PRODUCTIVITY STUDY

Management reporting is meant to be a working tool for all levels of management. Frequently, the department manager and his supervisors are not finance or numbers oriented. For this reason, the format of a management report does not need to be limited to columns of numbers as illustrated in the Profitability & Productivity (P&P) study of an

Table 1–1 Profitability & Productivity Study of an Intravenous Therapy Department for the Five-Year Period from 19x1 through 19x5

	19x1	19x2	19x3	19x4	19x5
Net revenue	$57,152	$48,652	$65,637	$79,443	$81,776
Net expense	47,957	55,465	51,041	54,567	54,790
Net profit or (loss)	9,195	(6,813)	14,596	24,876	26,986
Units of service procedures	10,781	14,689	14,709	17,351	18,089
Average number of employees	4.2	3.0	2.5	2.4	2.6
Net revenue per employee	13,608	16,217	26,255	33,010	31,452
Net expense per employee	11,418	18,488	20,416	22,736	21,073
Units of service per employee	2,567	4,896	5,884	6,230	6,957
Net revenue per unit of service	5,722	3,721	4,896	5,089	5,091
Net expense per unit of service	4,448	3,776	3,470	3,145	3,029

Figure 1–2 Profitability & Productivity Study per Employee for the Five-Year Period Ending 19x5

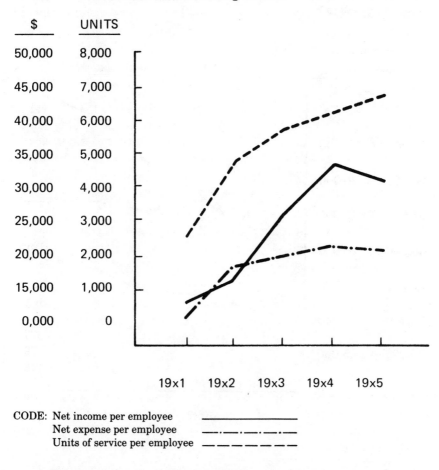

CODE: Net income per employee

Net expense per employee

Units of service per employee

intravenous therapy department in Table 1–1. It may be expressed in charts and graphs as illustrated in Figures 1–2 and 1–3.[11] Management reports are virtually useless if the user cannot interpret what the reporter is trying to convey. Experience has shown that the best method of designing a management report is for the reporter to work with the user during the design process. The objective is to use the simplest language. Charts and graphs as illustrated in Figures 1–2 and 1–3 are frequently the most effective format.

Figure 1–3 Profitability & Productivity Study of an Intravenous Therapy Department for the Five-Year Period Ending 19x5

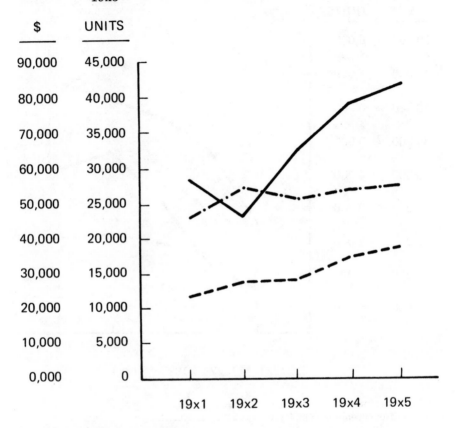

CODE: Net income per department
       Net expense per department
       Units of service per department

NEED-TO-KNOW INFORMATION

The need-to-know type of financial management information assumes a pyramid structure as illustrated in Figure 1–4.[12] Top management "needs to know" management information that is primarily concerned with the overall operations of the health care institution. The Statement of Condition (or Balance Sheet) and Statement of Operations (or Profit and Loss) may be supplemented with an Executive Highlight

Figure 1–4 Need-to-Know Pyramid of Health Care Financial
Management Information

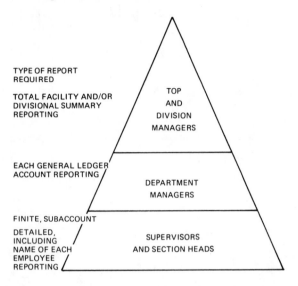

Report, which would include such information as net profit or loss from
operations, day's revenue of uncollected accounts receivable, outstanding balances on loans and accounts payable, and patient volume
(Exhibit 1–1). Division managers need to know the net operating margin of the departments they are responsible for (Exhibit 1–2). Therefore,
an abbreviated, concise report is all that is required at this level of
management.

Department managers should be aware of the overall operation of the
department, therefore they require more detailed information than the
division managers. Usually a departmental financial report will record
each general ledger account charged to a respective department.
Depending upon the size of the department and the number of departmental supervision and section heads, management information
reports should be sufficiently detailed to reflect each budgeted employee
and each line item charged to the respective department or responsibility center. As far as employee cost control is concerned, the payroll
report that is generated for each pay period usually presents sufficient
timely information for department managers or their supervisors and
section heads to analyze labor efficiency adequately. As for other
expenses, a department management report should be similar to the one
in Exhibit 1–3. Management information reports should *not* be limited

Exhibit 1–1 Executive Highlight Report for the _____ Month Period Ending _____, 19___

MEMORIAL HOSPITAL
ANYTOWN, U.S.A.

EXECUTIVE HIGHLIGHT REPORT
FOR THE _____ MONTH PERIOD ENDING _____, 19___

	Current Month			Description	Year to Date		
	Actual	Plan	Percentage variance		Actual	Plan	Percentage variance
	$	$	%	Net inpatient revenue	$	$	%
				Net outpatient revenue			
				Net patient expense			
				Net patient profit (loss)			
				Net nonpatient revenue/expense			
	$	$	%	Net operating profit (loss)	$	$	%
				Net Operations Cash Final			
	$	$	%	Beginning cash balance	$	$	%
				Net cash receipt			
				Less: net cash disbursements			
				Ending cash balance			
				Plus: other cash reserves			
	$	$	%	Total cash on hand	$	$	%
				Patient Volume			
				Inpatient Days			
			%	Nonmaternity and pediatric			%
				Maternity			
			%	Total adult and pediatric			%
			%	Newborn			%
				Inpatient Discharges			
			%	Nonmaternity and pediatric			%
				Maternity			
			%	Total adult and pediatric			%
			%	Newborn			%
				Outpatient Visits			
			%	Private referred			%
				Clinics			
				Emergency service			
			%	Total outpatient visits			%

Exhibit 1–1 continued

	Previous Year	Current Year	
	Amount	Amount	Percentage change
Patient Accounts Receivable			
Gross inpatient accounts receivable	$_____	$_____	_____ %
Gross outpatient accounts receivable	_____	_____	_____
Gross patient accounts receivable	_____	_____	_____
Less: Reserved for bad debts	_____	_____	_____
Net inpatient accounts receivable	$_____	$_____	_____ %
Net outpatient accounts receivable	$_____	$_____	_____ %
Number of days inpatient revenue uncollected	_____	_____	_____
Number of days outpatient revenue uncollected	_____	_____	_____
Accounts and Notes Payable			
Trade payables	_____	_____	_____
Short-term notes payable	_____	_____	_____
Long-term notes payable	_____	_____	_____
Number of days trade payable unpaid	$_____	$_____	_____ %

Exhibit 1-2 Divisional Summary of Operations—Nursing Services, for the _____ Month Period Ending _____, 19____

MEMORIAL HOSPITAL
ANYTOWN, U.S.A.

DIVISIONAL SUMMARY OF OPERATIONS—NURSING SERVICES
FOR THE _____ MONTH PERIOD ENDING _____, 19____

Direct Expense Analysis

	Current Month			Open to Date		
	Actual	Plan	Percentage Variance	Actual	Plan	Percentage Variance
Revenue Producing Departments						
Medical/Surgical Intensive Care	$	$	%	$	$	%
Coronary Care						
Medical/Surgical Acute						
Pediatric Acute						
Maternity						
Nursery						
Total Revenue Producing Departments	$	$	%	$	$	%
Non-Revenue Producing Departments						
Nursing Administration	$	$	%	$	$	%
Inservice Education-Nursing						
Total Non-Revenue Producing Departments	$	$	%	$	$	%

Revenue and Expense Analysis - (Year to Date Only)

Department	1 Gross charges to patients	2 Direct expense	3 Overhead expense	4 Total expense (2+3=4)	5 Gross operating margin 1-4=5	6 Allowances from gross charges	7 Net operating margin 5-6=7	8 Planned net operating margin	9 Percentage variance 8:7=9
Medical/Surgical Intensive Care	$	$	$	$	$	$	$	$	%
Coronary Care									
Medical/Surgical Assets									
Pediatric Assets									
Maternity									
Nursery									
Total Nursing Service	$	$	$	$	$	$	$	$	%

Exhibit 1–3 Departmental Operating Statement—Radiology, for the _____ Month Period Ending, _____, 19____

MEMORIAL HOSPITAL
ANYTOWN, U.S.A.

DEPARTMENTAL OPERATING STATEMENT – RADIOLOGY
FOR THE _____ MONTH PERIOD ENDING, _____, 19___

	Current Month			Description	Year to Date		
	Actual	Plan	Percentage variance		Actual	Plan	Percentage variance
				Production Volume			
	$	$	%	Inpatient relative value units	$	$	%
	$	$	%	Outpatient relative value units	$	$	%
				Total relative value units			
				Gross Charges to Patient			
	$	$	%	Inpatient	$	$	%
	$	$	%	Outpatient	$	$	%
				Total gross charges to patient			
				Direct Expenses			
				Salaries and wages			
	$	$	%	Radiologists and assts.	$	$	%
				Registered techs.			
				Technicians			
				Aides and orderlies			
				Students and trainees			
				Residents			
				Chief technician			
				Secretarial			
				Clerical			
	$	$	%	Total salaries and wages	$	$	%
				Purchased Services			
	$	$	%	Radiologist fees	$	$	%
				Other purchased service			
	$	$	%	Total purchased service	$	$	%

Exhibit 1–3 continued

	Current Month			Year to Date		
	Actual	Plan	Percentage variance	Actual	Plan	Percentage variance
Supplies and Expenses						
Printed forms and stationery	$	$	%	$	$	%
Stationery						
Films						
Developing chemicals						
Other supplies						
Uniforms and gowns						
Dues and subscriptions						
Repairs and maintenance						
Travel						
Miscellaneous						
Total supplies and expenses	$	$	%	$	$	%
Capital Expenses						
Equipment rentals	$	$	%	$	$	%
Depreciation						
Total capital expenses	$	$	%	$	$	%
Total direct expense	$	$	%	$	$	%
Gross operating margin	$	$	%	$	$	%
Percent of gross charges to patients	$	$	%	$	$	%
Direct Cost Per Relative Value Unit						
Salaries and wages	$	$	%	$	$	%
Purchased services						
Supplies and expenses						
Capital expenses						
Total direct cost per R.V.U.	$	$	%	$	$	%
Productivity						
Hours paid	$	$	%	$	$	%
R.V.U. per hours paid	$	$	%	$	$	%
Overhead (estimate)	$	$	%	$	$	%
Net profit (or loss)	$	$	%	$	$	%

Exhibit 1–4 Departmental Exception Report—Dietary, for the _____ Month Period Ending _____, 19_____

MEMORIAL HOSPTIAL
ANYTOWN, U.S.A.

DEPARTMENTAL EXCEPTION REPORT - DIETARY
FOR THE _____ MONTH PERIOD ENDING _____ 19__

Current month			Description	Year to Date		
Actual	Plan	F/U*		Actual	Plan	F/U
$2.81	$2.00					
$2.81	$2.50	U	Salary, food and supply Cost per meal	$2.45	$2.50	—
$1.35	$1.15	U	Food and supply cost per meal	$1.20	$1.15	U
$4.19	$4.10	—	Total meals served per patient day	$4.20	$ .10	—
$2.57	$2.50	—	Total meals served per person hours	$2.45	$2.50	U
$3.75	$3.63	U	Average hourly salary	$3.50	$3.63	—

*Note: F = favorable, U = unfavorable; record only a U if data is unfavorable. Leave blank if favorable.

to these routine (monthly) reports. Reports can be designed for one-time, single purpose use such as a cost/benefit analysis of a capital investment, or as an exception type of report illustrated in Exhibit 1–4.

In summary, it is obvious that in the health care industry, financial management can become a fine art. Department managers and their supervisors must exercise precise psychological perception and skillful diplomacy in order to manipulate people and other health care resources effectively to achieve the desired end product. In the health care industry, the end product is quality patient care delivered in the most effective and efficient method possible.

REFERENCES

1. Editors, *The New Merriam Webster Pocket Dictionary* (New York: G. & C. Merriam Co., 1971), p. 302.
2. *Webster's Seventh New Collegiate Dictionary* (Springfield, Mass.: G. & C. Merriam Co., 1963), p. 513.

3. L. Vann Seawell, *Hospital Financial Accounting Theory and Practice* (Chicago, Ill.: Hospital Financial Management Association, 1975), p. 14.

4. Norman R. F. Maier, *Psychology in Industry* (Boston, Mass.: Houghton Mifflin Co., 1965), 3rd edition.

5. Ibid.

6. Allen G. Herkimer, Jr., *How Accounting Will Serve the Manager of the Future* (Chicago, Ill.: Hospital Financial Management Association, 1972).

7. Peter Drucker, *Management: Tasks, Responsibilities and Practices* (New York: Harper & Row, 1974), p. 27.

8. Charles T. Horngren, *Cost Accounting A Managerial Emphasis* (Englewood Cliffs, N.J.: Prentice-Hall, Inc., 1972), p. 154.

9. Allen G. Herkimer, Jr., *How Accounting Will Serve the Manager of the Future* (Chicago, Ill.: Hospital Financial Management, 1972).

10. Ibid.

11. Allen G. Herkimer, Jr., *Concepts in Hospital Financial Management* (Paradise Valley, Ariz.: Alfa Associates, 1970), 1st edition, pp. 125–126.

12. Ibid., p. 5.

Organization Structure— Fundamental Principles of Sound Health Care Financial Management

If you were to survey a group of management consultants to determine why a business—any business—fails, you would probably find a combination of the following reasons for each failure:

- poor operational results and goals not achieved
- poor communication
- duplication of effort
- insufficient revenue
- sluggish cash flow
- operational losses
- wrong management decisions
- operating on a crises basis
- low employee morale
- high employee turnover
- low employee production

While these may be some reasons why businesses have failed, they are really only symptoms. They are actually caused by more generic organizational problems such as:

- poor organizational structure design
- inadequate, untimely and inaccurate management information systems
- ineffective revenue and accounts receivable control

- few or no formalized long-range plans
- unrealistic, if any, employee production standards

Davidson tells us that "a good reorganization plan ought to include preventive maintenance devices—for example, constant monitoring of organizational effectiveness and attention to the organizational impact of proposed laws that would be genuine reform."[1]

Managerial problems such as low productivity, unobtained goals, poor cash flow, high employee turnover, or poor employee motivation may be the most apparent. Frequently, when one digs in to find what is causing a particular problem—such as disgruntled employees—one will find that the problem is only a symptom of something more generic in nature.

Without question, the generic problem that causes the greatest management inefficiencies and low production is a poorly designed organizational structure.

There's an old Greek saying that the fish always starts smelling at the head. The fish's head must know the direction in which it is going because the body will blindly follow whichever direction the head points at a particular time. This philosophy can be applied in all walks of life. The key to successful management is to organize yourself before you try to organize your subordinates.

ORGANIZE YOURSELF FIRST

The critical rule in organizing yourself is to be honest with yourself. Honestly appraise your own strengths and weaknesses. Know what you know, and know that you know it; know what you don't know and know that you don't know it.

It has been said that good managers can leave the business for a month and have it run as well while they are gone as it does while they are present.

Obviously, the manager could not leave for an extended period of time without effective and responsible subordinates to carry on the operations. But who hired these effective subordinates? Who trained them and developed them into a cohesive working team? The answer is, of course, that the team was developed by the manager who can confidently take the long vacation or the business trip.

Mangers are only as good as their subordinates. And it is the management expertise that molds the subordinates into an efficient, productive working team.

CHARACTERISTICS OF A SUCCESSFUL MANAGER

If the health care industry is to assume its managerial responsibility, it must adopt a more businesslike attitude in its day-to-day operations. Responsive and effective management from all levels of the organization, especially the department manager level, is an absolute requirement if the desired quality health care is to be maintained at a reasonable cost.

What are some of the characteristics of an effective manager?

Perhaps the most important characteristic is the ability to manage and cope with change. In fact, the effective department manager or supervisor must be able to:

- respond positively to change
- produce change
- capitalize on change

In a dynamic industry such as the health care industry, one's ability to manage and manipulate change will be the greatest asset of an effective manager.

Other important characteristics include:

- self and professional confidence
- "now" attitude
- positive flexibility

The effective department manager or supervisor must know what the plans are, what the expected results are, and what strategies are to be used to obtain these results. Generally, secure decisions will be in harmony with the desired results. Effective department managers or supervisors must be confident! But, they must also be able to recognize an inappropriate decision, admit it, and take appropriate corrective measures.

This confidence shows that the institution's objectives do, in fact, exist; that the department's objectives coincide; and that the objectives are communicated to the appropriate individuals in the department. All the members of the team must know and accept their jobs and responsibilities and be prepared to exercise initiative in making decisions required to implement the appropriate plans and strategies.

The effective department managers or supervisors must take the *"now"* attitude in the decision-making process. They must face each issue as it occurs and not procrastinate. Supervisors should make every decision as if their institution's life depended upon it.

Positive flexibility enables the effective department manager or supervisor to look at an issue and see it as an opportunity and a challenge instead of a problem. It is the ability to cope with change and adjust to an organization's life cycle. The life cycle of organizations can be compared to the life cycle of people and plants, from youth to old age. While an organizational life cycle is not as predictable as a human's, it does have renewal capability.

John Gardner, former Secretary of Health, Education, and Welfare, is credited with saying that "people who are made to feel like cogs in a machine will behave like cogs in a machine. They will not produce ideas for change. Rather, they will resist such ideas when produced by others."

The effective department manager or supervisor is one who can manipulate people without letting them know they are being manipulated. In fact, an effective manager can make people enjoy this manipulation and can instill confidence and loyalty in subordinates by making them feel a part of the team.

There have been many attempts to define the qualities of an effective manager. Koontz and O'Donnell conclude that it is impossible to establish a specific set of qualities that an effective manager should possess.[2] However, Gwen compiled the following list of qualities of an effective executive:[3]

- wisdom
- integrity
- courage
- interest in people
- loyalty
- imagination
- depth of interest

CHARACTERISTICS OF AN EFFECTIVE ORGANIZATION

An effective organization may be defined as a group of individuals who are cooperating successfully to achieve a common objective. In building such a management team, one must weigh three factors:

- the organization structure—a proper grouping of functions to promote cooperation most effectively and determine the proper relationship among all such groups

- the proper delegation of responsibility and authority to all managers and supervisors
- the selection of the right people for the right job

The final test of the effectiveness of this organization will depend upon its ability to:

- provide the required services
- provide such services at minimum cost without sacrificing quality
- develop competent personnel[4]

Any successful organization has to achieve a wide assortment of complex tasks and objectives through the combined efforts of many participants. H. Fayson was quite correct when he stated that:

> The managerial function finds its only outlet through the members of the organization (corporate body). Whilst the other functions bring into play material and machines, the managerial function operates only on the personnel. [5]

Dale, in his discussion of management and the organization, concludes that "management is getting things done through other people."[6]

Whereas the organization may have specific objectives, activities, and work flows which need to be achieved, it relies on human beings who differ in their aspirations, perceptions, personalities, and capabilities to achieve them. Indeed, we need to understand why individuals join a particular organization, why they stay or leave it, and the principal processes around which organizations revolve.[7]

March and Simon have shown that the individual's decision to join, stay with, or leave any organization depends on the interaction of a number of personal and situational variables. Basically, the individual seeks an organization which in his estimation will be instrumental to the achievement of his personal goals while he is furthering the organizational goals. It is, however, clear that this does not imply a consistency between the individual's goals and the organization's goals.[8] These conflicts, as Cyert and March point out, revolve around the organization resource allocation processes, and are reflected in its continuing problem-solving and decision-making activities.[9] Similarly, O.E. Williamson observed that managers are motivated to achieve two sets of goals: the organization's goals and their personal goals. Personal goals, according to Williamson, are directly related to income (salary plus bonuses), size of staff, and discretionary control over allocation of resources.[10] While we may accept this thesis, the effective department managers and supervisors must align their loyalties with the organization to ensure its preservation.

This discretionary control over allocated health care resources is at the heart of an effective organization.

MANAGEMENT'S TASK

According to economist Dr. Charles J. Stokes, "Management's task is to manage; the function of the (department) manager (or supervisor) is to provide through one strategies decision after another for the needs, requirements, and demands of his institution." Stokes continues, "Indeed not all problems are economic, for there are political problems that involve the proper form of organization to ensure adequate:

- communication
- satisfaction
- psychological reward

for those employed and the firm's adjustment to a changing outside environment. There are sound problems involving responsibility to the community and its needs. There are the ethical, the personal, and the interpersonal problems that affect the enterprise . . . ."[11]

Summarily, management's task is to create the kind of environment within which effective systems and techniques can be developed and implemented so that the health care institution's goals and objectives may be achieved.

There appears to be a need to reappraise the health care priorities in decision making. That is, to consider that the health of our health care institutions is equally important, if not more important, than the health of the patient. Only with a healthy health care delivery system can the patients and the community ever hope to receive the quality of health care they need and deserve. The basis for this kind of healthy health care institution is its organizational design.

CARDINAL RULES OF DESIGNING AN EFFECTIVE DEPARTMENTAL ORGANIZATION STRUCTURE

In designing the department's organization structure, the department manager must adhere to the following cardinal rules.

First, identify primary responsibility centers of functional sections, such as administrative, clerical, secretarial, and technical, and assign one individual to each. This individual's responsibility and standard of performance must be well-defined, in writing, and the appropriate degree of authority must be allowed so that he or she can operate effectively. Exhibit 2–1 is an example of the job description of a follow-

---

Exhibit 2–1 Job Description

<u>Memorial Hospital</u>
Anytown, U.S.A.

POSITION: Follow-up Collection

SUPERVISOR: Patient Account Manager

PRIMARY RESPONSIBILITY:
Shall have the responsibility of billing, screening, collecting and evaluating the Hospital's self-pay patient (inpatient, outpatient, client services) accounts receivable.

PRIMARY RESPONSIBILITIES	STANDARD OF PERFORMANCE
1. To develop, implement, and operate a follow-up billing system for all the Hospital's self-pay private accounts receivable	1. All accounts must be billed and/or processed no less than once every thirty (30) days, average daily revenue uncollected not to exceed sixty (60) days.
2. To screen and evaluate all accounts routinely as to collectibility	2. A complete review evaluation of every account must be completed once every month.
3. To recommend and list accounts entitled to charity and courtesy allowances	3. A recommended list of charity and courtesy accounts must be generated once a month.
4. To recommend and list accounts to be written off as bad debts	4. A recommended list of bad debt accounts must be generated once a month.
5. To refer and manage all accounts referred to outside collection agencies	5. All outside collection agency accounts must be evaluated at a minimum of every three (3) months.
6. To perform any other relevant activities as delegated by the supervisor	6. Always perform relevant functions assigned by supervisor cheerfully, accurately, and in a timely manner.

up collection clerk, while Figures 2–1 and 2–2 illustrate the functions of a Patient Business Services Office and a Laboratory, respectively, divided into separate responsibility centers.

Second, determine a span of control with a realistic number of subordinates reporting to any one supervisor. When supervisors have an excessive number of subordinates reporting to them, there is a danger of creating a bottleneck of indecision. The exact number of subordinates reporting to any one supervisor depends upon:

Figure 2–1 Organization Structure—Patient Business Services

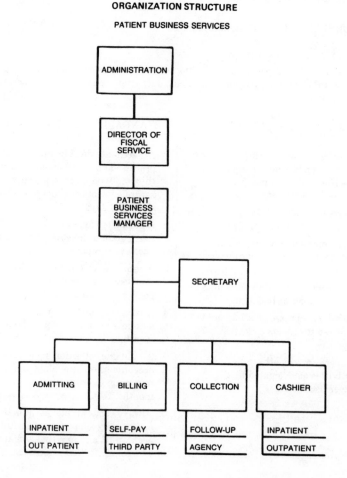

Figure 2–2 Organization Structure—Laboratory

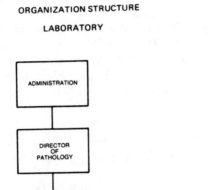

- the supervisor's ability to manage effectively
- the impact of the supervisor's decisions upon the entire institution or department
- the intensity or number of decisions the supervisor must make
- the ability of the subordinates to govern themselves and allocate their time effectively

Quantifiably, five to eight subordinates are generally accepted as a reasonable number for top level managers and section supervisors to supervise directly. As we progress down the organization's hierarchy, the manager is required to directly supervise more individuals, perhaps as many as twenty-five. Obviously, the overall capacity of the individual supervisor influences the assignment of subordinates for whom he is responsible.

Figure 2–3 illustrates an unreasonable span of control, while Figure 2–4 presents a realistic structure for a department.

Third, unity of command requires that a subordinate be responsible to only one supervisor. A subordinate should never be placed in the awkward position of determining which supervisor he should report to, for example:

- report to Supervisor I if the issue requires a medical decision
- report to Supervisor II if the issue requires a nonmedical decision

This condition is illustrated in Figure 2–5. Further, reporting to more than one supervisor may cause a split or conflict in loyalty to one

Figure 2–3 Unreasonable Span of Control for a Department Manager

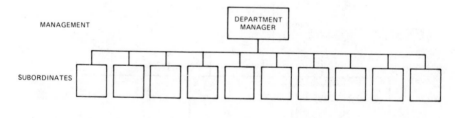

Figure 2–4 Realistic Span of Control for a Department Manager

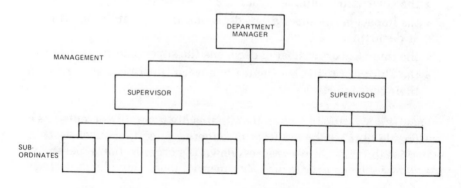

Figure 2–5 Unfavorable Reporting Condition for Subordinate X

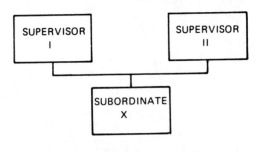

supervisor or the other. Frequently, staff nurses are placed in this awkward position with the Head Nurse, the Director of Nursing, and the physicians.

The primary value of organizational design is to establish a framework within which current operations can function with minimal direction from above (with a maximum utilization of health care resources). The scope and interrelationship of the responsibilities of each individual and group are specified.[12]

TYPES OF ORGANIZATION STRUCTURES

Two types of organization structures are most commonly used in health care facilities: the traditional, or military, configuration; and the matrix, or grid, structure. Interestingly, both structures can augment each other and can be used simultaneously.

The traditional organizational design can take the form of a pyramid with five levels of management hierarchy, as illustrated in Figure 2–6. The top three levels of the organization's hierarchy set policies and goals and plan strategy to effect the policies, obtain the goals, and assume the responsibility for implementing the plans. The department manager level serves as the middle line manager who is responsible to the division manager for a specific function or responsibility center, such as Housekeeping, Radiology, Dietary, or Engineering. The fifth level of the management hierarchy is the line manager, section head or supervisor, who is responsible to the department manager for a specialized or well-defined section within a department, such as the Hematology section in a Laboratory or the Diet Kitchen in the Dietary department. Figure 2–7 illustrates an Engineering department with its various sections.

Figure 2–6 The Pyramid of the Traditional Organization of Management Hierarchy

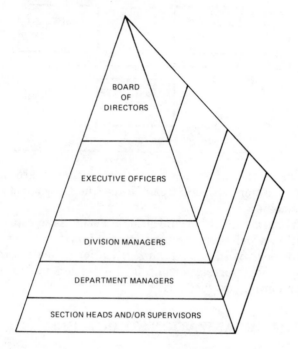

Traditionally, the strategic and long-range planning processes take place at the apex of the pyramid and are formalized by the division and department managers, while the day-to-day responsibility for operations is assumed by the line managers. Recently, the bottom-up top-down concept of management has been emerging as a viable management tool, as illustrated in Figure 2–8. This management decision-making process requires total involvement at all levels of the management hierarchy to communicate needs, ideas and solutions before arriving at a mutually acceptable decision.

The management information system assumes the pyramid configuration of the organization structure, whereas the managers at or near the apex of the pyramid require sharp, precise and abbreviated reports as illustrated in the highlight report in Exhibit 1–1. At the higher levels of the management hierarchy, exceptions, trends, and extreme variations in the profit plan or budget are of critical importance and usually sufficient to identify problem areas. The requirement for more detailed

Figure 2–7 Organization Structure of Engineering Department

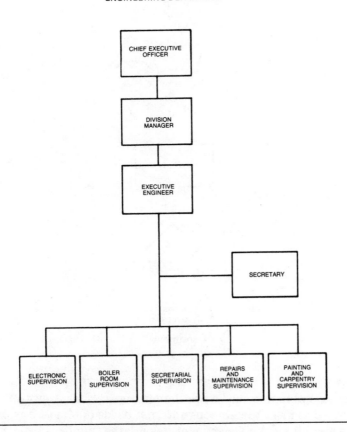

MEMORIAL HOSPITAL
ANYTOWN, U.S.A.

ENGINEERING DEPARTMENT

reports, as illustrated in Exhibit 2–2 and Exhibit 2–3, increases at the lower level of the management hierarchy to enable the department manager or supervisor to pinpoint specific problem areas. (Note: Exhibit 2–3 separates fixed and variable costs and hours.) Figure 2–9 illustrates the hourglass of management decision making and reporting.

The second type of organization structure, which can serve as a supportive management tool for the department manager, is the matrix, or grid, organization structure. The matrix organization requires extensive communication. If it becomes too big, the task of

Figure 2–8 Bottom-Up Top-Down Management Decision Process

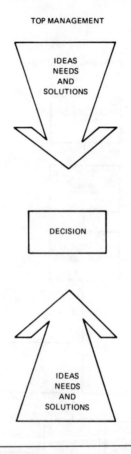

keeping everyone informed might hamper operations. However, it can be designed to meet the growing internal needs of almost any department, especially if the department has a large number of supervisors and supportive personnel.

Some advantages of the matrix organization structure are that it requires all managerial levels to be involved in the:

- shaping of the department's goals and objectives
- awareness of how each section and its supervisor fit into the total departmental operations
- training of section heads and supervisors to develop their skills and knowledge of the total operation

Exhibit 2–2 Comparative Analysis of Actual and Budget for Laundry Department

MEMORIAL HOSPITAL
ANYTOWN, U.S.A.

LAUNDRY DEPARTMENT

YEAR, 19x1

ACCOUNT DESCRIPTION	BUDGET 19x1		ACTUAL 19x1	
UNITS OF SERVICE (DEFINE) clean pounds processed	449,770	Pd. Hrs.	432,800	Pd. Hrs.
SALARIES				
Supervisors, Ass'ts. & Foreman	12,000	2,080	12,025	2,080
Washmen, Extractor Oper., etc.	9,080	3,328	9,120	3,330
Press, Flat Workers, etc.	12,020	4,576	11,995	4,570
Sorters	10,610	4,576	10,550	4,570
Collectors	2,890	1,144	2,900	1,150
Linen Service Salaries	20,800	8,112	20,750	8,100
Secretarial, Clerical	2,450	936	2,400	925
TOTAL SALARIES	69,850	24,752	69,740	24,725
NON-SALARIES				
Purchased Services & Fees				
Commercial Laundry				
Printed Forms and Stationery				
Soaps, Bleach, etc.	2,375		2,293	
Bags, Mangle Aprons, etc.	175		170	
Purchased Steam	10,830		10,550	
Uniforms	100		100	
Dues and Subscriptions				
Rental of Equipment				
Repairs and Maintenance	250		300	
Travel				
Miscellaneous	400		500	
TOTAL NONSALARIES	14,130		13,913	
DEPRECIATION	3,250		3,000	
GRAND TOTAL	87,230	24,752	86,653	24,725
FULL-TIME EQUIVALENT		11.90		11.887

Note: Linen service included in this report.

- communication with each other in order to combine efforts toward the approved objectives
- overall management of the department's operations

The first step in designing a departmental matrix organization is to select the department's general administrative functions, such as:

- objectives and planning
- budgetary control

Exhibit 2–3 Comparative Analysis of Laundry and Linen Department Budget and Actual

MEMORIAL HOSPITAL
ANYTOWN, U.S.A.

Laundry and Linen Department
Year, 19x1

A. UNITS OF SERVICE	BUDGET Fixed Costs (1)	Variable Costs (2)	Fixed Hours (3)	Variable Hours (4)	ACTUAL Fixed Costs (5)	Variable Costs (6)	Fixed Hours (7)	Variable Hours (8)
1. Lbs/clean laundry processed	449,770				432,800			
B. SALARIES								
2. Suprvs., Asst's, Foremen	12,000	9,080	2,080	3,328		9,120	2,080	3,330
3. Washmen, Extractors, Operators, etc.		12,020		4,576		11,995		4,570
4. Press, Flat Workers, etc.		10,610		4,576		10,550		4,570
5. Sorters		2,890		1,144		2,900		1,150
6. Collectors								
7. Maintenance								
8. Linen Service Salaries*		20,800		8,112		20,750		8,100
9. Secretarial, Clerical	2,450		936		2,400		925	
10.								
11. Total Salary	14,450	55,400	3,016	21,736	14,425	55,315	3,005	21,720
12. Units per Man-Hour (Line 1 ÷ Line 6)				20.69239				19.92633
13. Variable Hourly Wage Rate (Line II)		2.54876				2.54673		
C. SUPPLIES								
14. Commercial Laundry								
15. Supplies & Other Expenses								
16. Printed Forms & Stationery		2,375				2,293		
17. Soaps, Bleach, etc.		175				170		
18. Bags, Mangle Aprons, etc.								
19. Linen Replacement Purchases*		10,830				10,550		
20. Purchased Steam		100				100		
21. Uniforms								
22. Dues & Subscriptions								
23. Rental of equipment		250				300		
24. Repairs & Maintenance								
25. Travel								
26. Miscellaneous		400				500		
27.								
28. Total Supplies & Other	None	14,130			None	13,913		
29. Variable Unit Cost Line 28 ÷ Line 1		.03141				.03214		
D. DEPRECIATION	3,250				3,000			

*To be used when Linen Service is not separated

Figure 2–9 The Hourglass of Management Decision Making
and Reporting

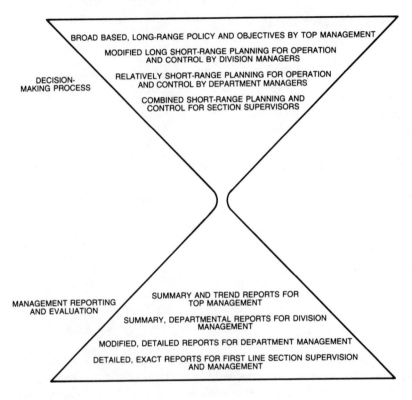

- personnel relations
- development and training
- performance standards and quality control

Each of the programs must be defined and formulated to serve as a guideline for the council membership. For example, the responsibility of the budgetary control council might be the preparation of the departmental budget, determining the types of budgetary control and reports, the types of feedback information required, the coordination of forecast work volumes, the explanation of actual variances to budget, and any other relevant activities.

The second step is to identify the primary functional sections in the department, such as, in the laboratory,

- clerical and secretarial
- hematology
- chemistry
- histology
- bacteriology
- autopsy
- microbiology

or, as in plant operation and maintenance,

- plant maintenance
- carpentry
- plumbing
- painting
- automotive services
- boiler room
- security
- parking

The functional sections serve as the horizontal committees, while the major administrative functions are the vertical councils. Once again, the areas of responsibility must be well defined for each of these committees and councils. An example of a matrix organization for a laboratory is illustrated in Exhibit 2–4.

Individuals are assigned positions on the matrix as their areas of responsibility. For example, Mary Jones is assigned to the Budgetary Control Council and represents the Hematology section.

In this manner, all administrative functions are represented when the Hematology committee meets and all functional committees are represented when the Budgetary Council meets.

Chairpersons are assigned the responsibility for the functions of each council and each committee. This sometimes presents problems when the chairpersons think that the others will take care of some matter when, in reality, no one is acting. Therefore, lines of authority and responsibility must be absolutely clear. Those lines will be crisscrossing, and any fuzziness will result in ambiguous and counterproductive conflict and perhaps ultimate chaos.

Exhibit 2–4 Matrix Organization for the Laboratory

LABORATORY MATRIX
ORGANIZATION

AS OF _____ 19 ___

MEMORIAL HOSPITAL
ANYTOWN, U.S.A.

FUNCTIONAL COMMITTEES	ADMINISTRATIVE COUNCILS				
	OBJECTIVES AND PLANNING	BUDGETARY CONTROL	PERSONNEL RELATIONS	DEVELOPMENT AND TRAINING	PERFORMANCE AND QUALITY CONTROL
CLERICAL AND SECRETARIAL					
HEMATOLOGY		MARY JONES			
CHEMISTRY					
HISTOLOGY					
BACTERIOLOGY					
AUTOPSY					
MISCELLANEOUS BIOLOGY					

ORGANIZATIONAL DEVELOPMENT OF HOSPITALS

The hospital organization can also be illustrated in an hourglass model (Figure 2–10).

A community, nontaxable hospital usually starts with a group of interested community individuals. Some of the community's citizens join forces as incorporators to form a hospital corporation. They elect a Board of Trustees to serve as the governing body. To expedite the decision-making process, the officers are appointed as the Executive Committee to act on behalf of the entire board. The chairperson serves

Figure 2–10 Hourglass Organizational Model of a Community, Nontaxable Hospital

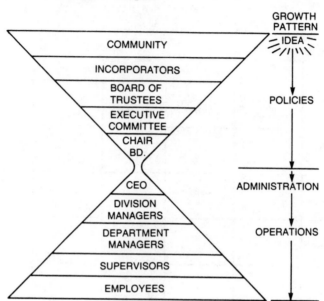

as the leader of the board and serves as the main liaison between the board and the hospital's CEO, who is appointed by the board.

A typical investor-owned, taxable hospital frequently starts with the idea of one individual, who may also interest a few close associates in the project. These individuals may become the corporation's executive committee, and the original catalyst becomes the chairperson of the board. In order to assemble the required financial resources, shares of stock are sold. The transfer of administrative responsibility from the board remains basically the same as the community, nontaxable model. The growth pattern, as illustrated in Figure 2–11, starts at the apex of the top half of the organizational hourglass, instead of starting at the top, as in the community, nontaxable model in Figure 2–10.

ORGANIZATION STRUCTURE AND ITS TIE-IN TO THE CHART OF ACCOUNTS

The American Hospital Association's (AHA) *Chart of Accounts for Hospitals* states that the effectiveness of managerial functions depends largely upon:

Figure 2–11 Hourglass Organizational Model of an Investor-Owned, Taxable Hospital

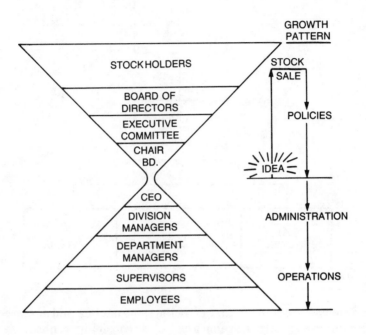

1. The existence of a sound organization structure.
2. The accumulation of relevant and reliable financial and statistical data, which reflect planned objectives and actual results and which relate actual results to the plans for each responsibility area.
3. The ability of management to make full use of such information.[13]

The responsibility centers and the responsible individual should be identified on the department organization structure. The chart of accounts used by accounting should be coded to the organization chart to enable it to accumulate and communicate financial and statistical data about the operations of the various departmental units to which managerial responsibility and accountability have been assigned. Figure 2–12 illustrates the coding of the Dietary department's organization structure, using the AHA Chart of Accounts coding system.

The responsibility centers should coincide with the assignment of responsibilities within the department as identified in the department's organization chart. Perhaps an extensive listing of responsibility centers or sections may be required; however, it should be remembered that no two

Figure 2–12 Organization Structure—Dietary Services

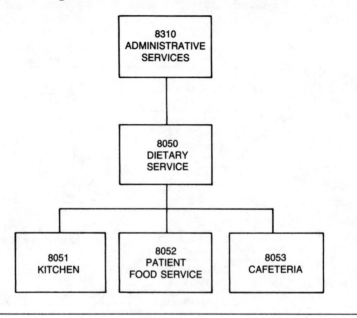

departments are organized in exactly the same manner and no two departments will use exactly the same array of responsibility centers.

THE ROLE OF THE DEPARTMENT MANAGERS AND SUPERVISORS

The role of department managers in a health care facility is the most critical in the financial planning, management, and control process because managers are the link between the plans of management and the accomplishments of the facility's personnel. If they fail to understand their responsibilities or in some way present a negative attitude, the negativism filters down to each departmental employee.

Without the complete and active cooperation and commitment of the department managers, the financial plans and budgets of the health care facility will not succeed. Top management must be totally committed to the financial plan and must convey its support to the department managers. They, in turn, must relate this support to their supervisors and employees. There can be no credibility gap between top administration and department managers; between department managers and supervisors; or between supervisors and employees.

Supervisors must openly support their department managers. If there is a disagreement between them, the problem must be resolved behind closed doors. Only with a united front between the department manager and his or her supervisors will the department function productively and with harmony among employees.

Effective department managers do encourage discussions or selection of alternative methods of completing a task. Effective department managers and supervisors will discuss their differences reasonably, not by argument. As long as the employees uphold and perform their assigned responsibilities, everyone will be able to work in a harmonious environment which produces quality health care services.

REFERENCES

1. Roger H. Davidson, "Those Carter Reforms-Reorganization a Long-Term Task," *Los Angeles Times,* January 16, 1977, Part V, p. 3.
2. Harold Koontz and Cyril O'Donnell, *Principles of Management* (New York: McGraw-Hill Book Co., 1964), pp. 401–402.
3. William B. Gwen, "Must Managers Specialize? The Case for Executive Versatility," *Management Review,* November 1956.
4. J. Brooks Heckert and James D. Willson, *Controllership* (New York: Ronald Press Co., 1963), 2nd edition.
5. H. Fayson, *General and Industrial Management* (New York: Putnam, 1949), p. 19.
6. E. Dale, *Management: Theory and Practice* (New York: McGraw-Hill, 1965), p. 4.
7. Michael Schiff and Arce Lewin, "The Impact of People on Budget," *The Accounting Review,* April 1970.
8. J.G. March and H.A. Simon, *Organization* (New York: Wiley, 1958), pp. 84–110.
9. R.M. Cyert and J.G. March, *The Behavioral Theory of the Firm* (Englewood Cliffs, N.J.: Prentice-Hall, Inc., 1963), pp. 26–127.
10. O.E. Williamson, *The Economics of Discretionary Behavior: Managerial Objectives in a Theory of the Firm* (Englewood Cliffs, N.J.: Prentice-Hall, 1964).
11. Charles J. Stokes, *Managerial Economics—A Textbook in the Economics of Management* (New York: Random House, 1969).
12. Glenn Welsch Co., *Budgeting, Profit Planning and Control* (Englewood Cliffs, N.J.: Prentice-Hall, 1964).
13. American Hospital Association, *Chart of Accounts for Hospitals* (Chicago, Ill.: American Hospital Association, 1976), pp. 2–17.

Chapter 3

Cost Characteristics and Behavior

In order to control health care costs, one must first understand how costs act, react, interact and intraact under various environmental situations. For example: What if patient service volume were to decline eight percent, and labor costs were to rise twelve percent? What would be the percentage effect on costs? Another example: Can a capital investment costing $150,000, projecting a fifty percent utilization factor, break even the first year?

These are only two examples of problems that routinely confront department managers and their supervisors. Under specific institutional conditions, the answers to these financial management questions can be forecast and applied to the appropriate financial and statistical formulae or models. This type of financial forecasting and planning is an application of management accounting principles to assist in making enlightened management decisions.

Exercising one's knowledge of cost behavior and applying it to management decision are integral parts of management accounting and health care financial management. Management accounting was discussed in Chapter 1. In this chapter, cost characteristics and their related behavior will be reviewed to demonstrate their impact upon a department or an institution's total operating costs.

MAJOR COST CLASSIFICATIONS

Health care departmental costs can be divided into the following three major classifications:

- operating
- opportunity
- social

Operating costs are the actual costs incurred by a department to generate patient services and other functions required by the department. Operating costs in the broad perspective include salaries, supplies, equipment depreciation, and other related costs. Under a financial planning and control system, these costs would be further subdivided into routine operating costs and capital expenditures. This text is primarily concerned with operating costs.

Opportunity costs are defined as the maximum contribution that is foregone by using limited resources for a particular purpose, or the maximum alternative earning that might have been obtained if the productive good, service or capacity had been applied to some alternative use.[1]

To illustrate opportunity costs, suppose that the total alternatives under formal consideration are described as choices A-1, A-2, A-3, and A-4, and related costs and revenues are as illustrated:

Alternatives

(Omit 000)

	A-1	A-2	A-3	A-4
Revenue	320	280	410	360
Relevant Costs:				
Inventory	90	90	90	90
Labor and Overhead	260	190	275	200
Net Advantage (Disadvantage)	(30)	00	45	70

According to this analysis, alternative A-4 offers the most rewarding opportunity, a *profit advantage of $70,000*. However, if management chose alternative A-3, there would be an opportunity cost of $25,000, as developed below:

OC—Opportunity Costs
A-4—Best Alternative
A-3—Selected Alternative
$$OC = A\text{-}4 - A\text{-}3$$
$$OC = \$70,000 - \$45,000$$
$$OC = \$25,000$$

Theoretically, health care department managers should accept only projects yielding more than their real operating and capital costs. By so doing, managers increase the department's contribution to the institution's net profit. However, all enlightened and appropriate decisions need more than financial and statistical information. General accounting systems usually confine their reporting to those facts that ultimately involve the actual exchanges of assets. Opportunity costs are not customarily included in the general accounting systems, since such costs represent foregone revenues and costs.

Social costs are those costs which management knowingly or unknowingly imposes upon the general or specific segment of society as a result of its decisions. For example, suppose that a health care facility's management installs a new sewage system which drains directly into a river. This new system would ultimately cause a health and environmental hazard which would eventually require a clean-up campaign. The related costs of this campaign would be classified as social costs. Occasionally, the best alternative from an opportunity or operating cost standpoint such as alternative A-4 in the above illustration may result in a substantial social cost. Perhaps this was the reason alternative A-3 was selected. In short, management decisions that impose costs, present or eventual, upon the general public are classified as social costs.

PRIMARY COST CLASSIFICATIONS

Primary operating costs may be classified into the following categories:

- historical
- current
- budget

Historical costs are either actual or budget costs for past accounting periods. Historical *actual* costs are frequently used as the basis for establishing future trends. Historical *budget* costs are usually compared to historical actual costs to evaluate the assumptions and projections made.

Current costs represent the real or actual costs spent for the present or immediate accounting period. Customarily, current costs are compared to the present accounting period's budgeted costs to evaluate a department's actual performance and its planned performance.

Budgeted costs are projected for the future. These are based upon historical costs—*known facts* and/or assumptions of present or future events. In summary, budgeted costs represent management's best judgment of costs in future accounting periods.

For all three of these primary cost classification systems, the accrual method of accounting is used. This method recognizes revenues and expenses as they are incurred, regardless of when the cash is received or disbursed.

SECONDARY COST CLASSIFICATIONS

Secondary cost classifications may be applied to historical, current, or budgeted costs. The identification of the secondary cost classifications is especially important in variable or flexible budgeting, which will be discussed in Chapter 7, and in the use of the break-even analysis, which will be reviewed later in this chapter. The following are the three secondary cost classifications:

- fixed
- variable
- step-variable

Departmental fixed costs tend to remain relatively constant regardless of volume of work output, as illustrated in Figure 3–1. Insurance, depreciation, and rent are excellent examples of a department's fixed nonlabor costs. The salary of the department manager is a fixed labor cost.

Departmental variable costs tend to change directly in relation to the volume of work output, as illustrated in Figure 3–2. Food, x-ray films, and drugs are variable costs which vary directly in proportion to volume changes. Nurse staffing and the resultant costs tend to require adjustment according to the patient census.

Probably the most confusing classification to project is the step-variable cost. This cost behavior is a combination of fixed and variable. A step-variable cost will change abruptly at intervals, according to periods of activity which can be measured in discrete segments.[2] Technicians, clerks, maids, and most other nonadministrative personnel costs tend to be classified as step-variable, because a staffing level will stay consistent for a relevant range of activity. This staffing level has a certain amount of elasticity. It can adequately serve a sudden lower volume of activity (negative elasticity) and, due to this staffing pattern's elasticity, it can adequately serve a slightly higher demand (positive elasticity). For example, suppose it was predetermined that a staff of

Figure 3–1 Departmental Fixed Costs

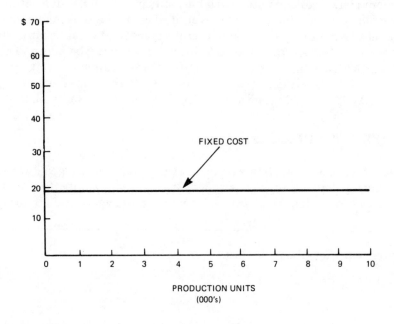

Figure 3–2 Departmental Variable Costs

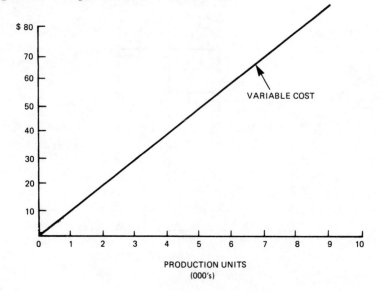

four billing clerks could adequately process from 6,000 to 10,000 bills. The four clerks' costs are step-variable because once the billing volume consistently maintains a 12,000 level, it exceeds the reasonable elasticity of this staffing pattern and, therefore, the staff must be abruptly increased a step—in this case, one billing clerk must be added. This automatically establishes a different relevant range of activity of 10,000 to 14,000, as illustrated in Figure 3–3. This remains fixed as long as the 10,000 to 14,000 relevant range of activity is maintained.

OTHER COST CLASSIFICATIONS

Direct costs, or controllable costs, are those that are charged directly to the using department's general ledger accounts. Usually these costs are expenditures requisitioned by department managers or their desig-

---

Figure 3–3 Step-Variable Costs

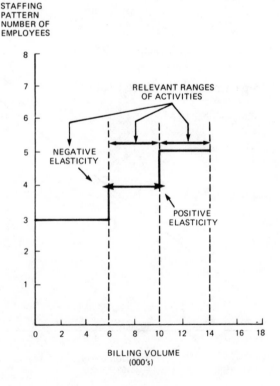

nates. Since the department manager has considerable control over these costs in most budget programs, the direct costs are frequently used to evaluate the effectiveness of the department.

Indirect, or noncontrollable costs, include those allocated or overhead expenditures over which the department managers and their supervisors have little or no control. These are not usually included in the department's budgets. It is, however, useful to know how these costs occur, since some depend upon the expected or actual occupancy of the health care institution. The same costs may be direct for one department and indirect for another department. For example, housekeeping supplies are direct costs to the Housekeeping Department, but indirect costs to the Physical Therapy Department.

Salary, or labor costs, include all labor-related costs such as direct salaries, wages, and fringe benefits. It is important to separate these costs into fixed, step-variable, and variable in order to properly forecast break-even points and establish staffing patterns. Labor costs for professional fees, i.e., physician, audit, and legal, are usually handled as purchased services and classified with nonlabor costs. They may also be isolated under the labor classification. One of the purposes of the breakdown is not to allow distortion in computing average labor rates, prospective labor costs, and employee benefits.

Nonsalary, or labor costs, are all costs not included in the above classification, such as supplies, depreciation, rent, utilities, purchased services, and insurance. However, it is advisable to separate nonlabor costs into categories such as direct supplies, purchased services, and depreciation. The degree of segmentation will depend upon management's requirements. Usually, capital related costs, such as depreciation, rent, and interest, are separated.

Committed costs consist largely of fixed costs which arise from the possession of plant, of equipment, and of a basic organization. Examples are depreciation, property taxes, rent, insurance, and salaries of key personnel.[3]

Programmed costs (sometimes called managed costs) are fixed costs that arise from periodic (usually annual) appropriation decisions directly reflecting top management policies, such as public relations, training programs, and consulting fees. Programmed costs have no relationship to volume.[4]

Capacity costs is an alternate term for fixed costs, emphasizing the fact that fixed costs are needed to provide operating facilities and an organization ready to produce and sell at a planned volume of activity.[5]

Replacement costs are the real or estimated costs required to replace a facility's present assets. Usually, the term is used in relation to the replacement cost of a piece of equipment, i.e., computer, trash compactor, laundry washer-dryer-extractor, or x-ray machine. However, replacement costs can be computed to determine the costs required to replace a supply inventory, i.e., fuel oil, medical and surgical supplies, and food.

Inflation costs are not routinely accounted for and because of economic conditions are highly unpredictable. However, they must be considered in any inflationary time—which, in most countries, means the present. Drucker tells us that inflation should be considered a genuine budget cost. He states that there is good reason to adopt, at least for internal purposes, a method of accounting in "constant dollars. . . ." At least, Drucker concludes, such a method will force management to realize that information, rather than its own performance, underlies a good profile showing.[6]

In summary, there is no end of the various types of costs. The degree of cost segmentation depends upon management and its needs to isolate and control specific costs. Major cost items, such as drugs in Pharmacy, sutures in the Operating Suite, films in Radiology, food in Dietary, and energy in Plant operations, are frequently isolated in order to maintain closer surveillance and control. Figure 3–4 illustrates the Cost Classification Tree of some of the cost behaviors discussed in this chapter.

CONTRIBUTION AND CONTRIBUTION MARGIN

Contribution is the dollar difference between the total net charges to patients and the related variable expenses. The contribution margin is expressed in the percent of the contribution to the total charges. Table 3–1 illustrates the use of contribution margin for the Emergency Department, while Table 3–2 is an analysis of three laboratory sections related to the combined Laboratory Department total. The contribution concept identifies the amount (sales-minus-variable expenses) contributed toward covering the total fixed costs of a department.

The contribution concept is utilized to compute the break-even point of a health care department or section.

BREAK-EVEN ANALYSIS

The break-even point determines the point at which total departmental revenue equals total departmental expense. The use of the break-even concept requires that all costs be classified as either fixed or variable. Step-variable costs should be included if they can be deter-

Figure 3–4 Cost Classification Tree

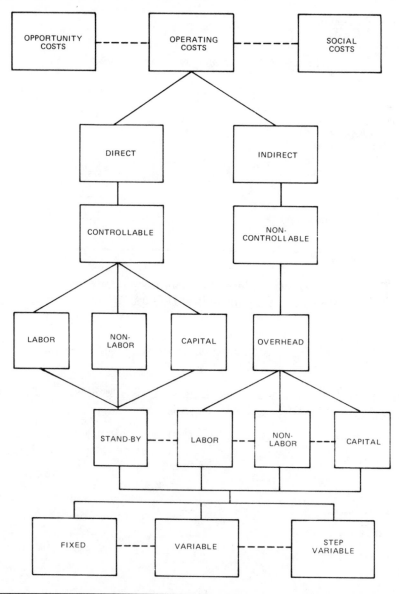

mined. Comparatively speaking, the higher the fixed costs, the higher the break-even point. Conversely, the lower the fixed costs, the lower the break-even point will be, as illustrated in Figures 3–5 and 3–6. Fig-

Table 3–1 Contribution Analysis of an Emergency Room Visit

Memorial Hospital
Anytown, U.S.A.

Emergency Department as of September 30, 19x1

		Total	Percent
Net charge per visit		$200	100%
Variable costs per visit:			
Labor	$100		
Nonlabor	20		
Total variable costs		120	60
Contribution		$ 80	N.A.
Contribution margin		N.A.	40%

Table 3–2 Contribution Method—Laboratory Departmental
Analysis (in Thousands of Dollars)

MEMORIAL HOSPITAL
ANYTOWN, U.S.A.   LABORATORY DEPARTMENT

Description	Total	Clinical Lab	Hematology	Histology
Net Charges	$3,800	$2,000	$1,600	$200
Variable Costs	2,840	1,600	1,120	120
Contribution	$ 960	$ 400	$ 480	$ 80
Contribution Margin	(25%) (a)	(20%)	(3%)	(40%)
Fixed Expenses				
Direct	$ 530	$ 300	$ 200	$ 30
Allocated	360	120	200	40
Total Fixed Expenses	$ 890	$ 420	$ 400	$ 70
Net Income	$ 70	$ 20	$ 80	$ 10

(a)   Includes salaries, depreciation, insurance, property taxes, etc.
       Also includes department salaries and other separable costs which could
       be avoided by not operating the specific department.

Figure 3–5 High Fixed-Cost Break-Even Point (Excluding Variable Costs)

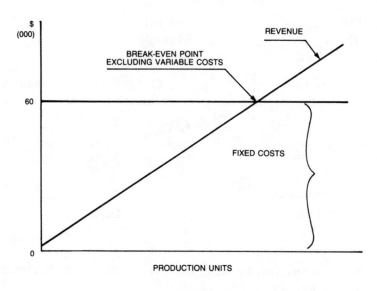

Figure 3–6 Low Fixed-Cost Break-Even Point (Excluding Variable Costs)

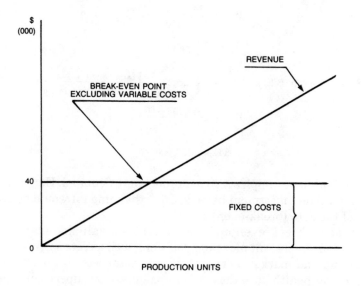

ure 3–7 illustrates the graphic determination of a department's break-even point, using the following data:

Variable Costs	$60,000
Fixed Costs	$40,000
Charge Per Unit	$ 100

Note that the break-even charges are $100,000 or 1,000 production units. This can be computed using the arithmetic method as follows:

	Per Unit	Total	Percent
1. Net charge(s)	$100	$100,000	100%
2. Variable cost(s)	60	60,000	60
3. Contribution	40	40,000	
4. Contribution margin	N.A.	N.A.	40
5. Total fixed costs		40,000	
6. Net profit (loss)		-0-	

A common approach in computing the break-even point is the formula technique that follows:

$$A\text{—Break-even (B/E) in units of service} = \frac{\text{Fixed Costs} + \text{Net Profit}}{\text{Contribution per unit}}$$

$$B/E = \frac{\$40,000 + 0}{\$40}$$

$$B/E = 1,000 \text{ Units}$$

$$B\text{—Break-even (B/E) in dollars of charges} = \frac{\text{Fixed Costs} + \text{Net Profit}}{\text{Contribution Margin}}$$

$$B/E = \frac{\$40,000 + 0}{.40}$$

$$B/E = \$100,000$$

Note that in these samples zero net profit was calculated. Had a profit or some return on investment been desired, that amount would be used in place of the zero (break-even).

In summary, break-even analysis provides a valuable statistical background for important planning decisions such as rate setting (pricing), staffing, and market methods. "Know your costs" is an essential theme for any health care department manager or supervisor. Also,

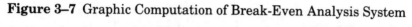

Figure 3–7 Graphic Computation of Break-Even Analysis System

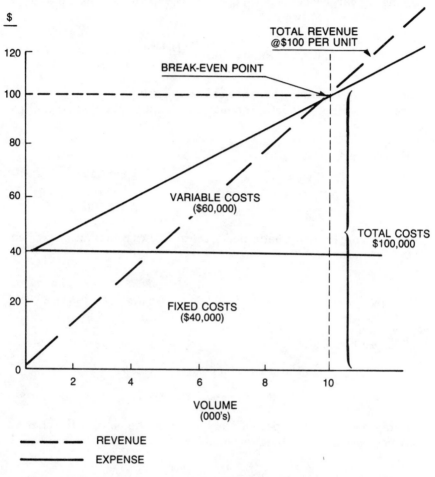

break-even analysis can direct managerial attention to potential problems (what may be called "cost hazards") and pave the way for their solution before they become major headaches.

MARGIN OF SAFETY

The margin of safety is an application of the break-even concept that develops a percentage (margin of safety) drop in charges (sales) that can occur before a loss starts in the department. This percentage is a dramatic way of calling to management's attention how close their pricing or charge level is to their break-even point. The formula can be expressed in one of two ways [7]

$$\text{Margin of Safety (MS)} = \frac{\text{Desired Profit}}{\text{Contribution}}$$

Note: Margin of Safety is always expressed as a percent.

Using the following data, the margin of safety is computed as illustrated below:

Known Facts:

Total Charges	$300,000
Contribution Margin	40%
Desired Profit	$ 30,000

By applying the arithmetic model, the unknown contribution is calculated as follows:

	Total	Percent
1. Charges	$300,000	100%
2. Variable costs	———	—
3. Contribution		
4. Contribution margin		40%

Contribution Margin × Charges = Contribution

.40 × $300,000 = $120,000

Using the above Margin of Safety formula, the percent the charges may decrease and still break even is

$$\text{MS} = \frac{\text{Desired Profit}}{\text{Contribution}}$$

$$\text{MS} = \frac{\$\,30,000}{\$120,000}$$

$$\text{MS} = \underline{25\%}$$

The 25 percent margin of safety is proved as follows:

	Desired Results	Percent	25% Decreased Volume
1. Charges	$300,000	100%	$225,000
2. Variable Costs	180,000	60	135,000

3. Contribution	$120,000	N.A.	$ 90,000
4. Contribution margin	N.A.	<u>40</u>	N.A.
5. Fixed Costs	<u>90,000</u>		<u>90,000</u>
6. Desired Profit	<u>$ 30,000</u>		<u>$ -0- </u>

Using this example, the department's charges could decrease 25 percent before losses develop. This means the department's break-even point is 75 percent of current pricing method. If the department is at the break-even volume, the margin of safety is zero.

DEPARTMENT AND UNIT COST ANALYSIS

In analyzing departmental costs, total departmental fixed costs stay constant over a relevant range of activity whereas the total variable departmental costs increase as volume increases. This is illustrated in Figure 3–8, using the Medical Records departmental totals in Table 3–3.

Figure 3–8 Total Medical Records Department Costs

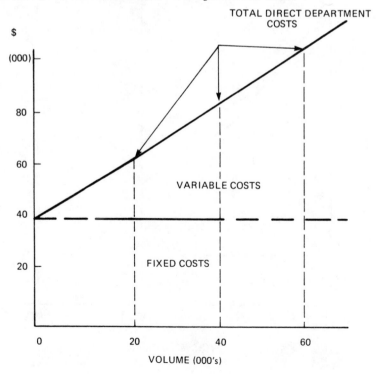

Table 3–3 Analysis of Medical Records Department and Units of Service Costs for Year Ending December 31, 19x1

Memorial Hospital
Anytown, U.S.A.

| | Units of Services Produced | | | | | |
| | 20,000 | | 40,000 | | 60,000 | |
	Total Costs	Unit Cost	Total Costs	Unit Cost	Total Costs	Unit Cost
Variable Costs	$20,000	$1.00	$40,000	$1.00	$ 60,000	$1.00
Fixed Costs	40,000	2.00	40,000	1.00	40,000	.67
Total Costs	$60,000	$3.00	$80,000	$2.00	$100,000	$1.67

Figure 3–9 Medical Records Department—Total Unit Costs

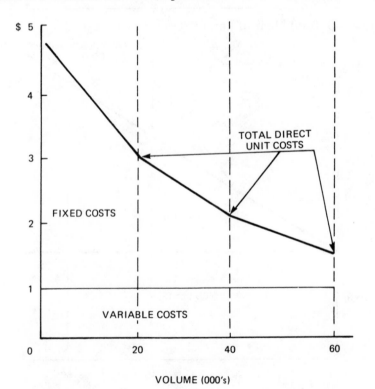

VOLUME (000's)

Conversely, total production unit costs decline as volume increases and total variable costs per production unit remain constant over a relevant range of activity, as illustrated in Figure 3–9, using the financial and statistical unit data for Anytown Memorial Hospital's Records Department.

The knowledge of costs and their behavior will help guide department managers, their supervisors and staff in controlling the costs of the department. The challenge to the department manager and supervisor is to develop methods of changing cost behavioral characteristics, especially fixed costs, to either variable or step-variable in any cost containment program. The *key* is to control the fixed costs before they are committed and to concentrate on controlling the variable costs on a day-to-day operational basis.

REFERENCES

1. Charles T. Horngren, *Cost Accounting—A Managerial Emphasis* (Englewood Cliffs, N.J.: Prentice-Hall, 1973), 3rd edition, pp. 364–365 and 944–948.
3. Ibid.
4. Ibid.
5. Horngren, *Accounting for Management Control.*
6. Peter F. Drucker, *Management: Tools, Responsibilities & Practices* (New York: Harper & Row, 1973), p. 210.
7. Spencer W. Tucker, *The Break-Even System: A Tool for Profit Planning* (Englewood Cliffs, N.J.: Prentice-Hall, 1963), p. 51.

Chapter 4

Management, Planning, and Control

We can automate the mechanics of financial planning and control, but we cannot automate the *humantology* of the process.

According to Harold Leavett, the problem of good human relations is a critical one in modern history. Many of the shortcomings attributed to budgets (financial planning and control) are due to poor human relations and insensitive attitudes on the part of management.[1] Welsch states that the human element is the dominant feature of effective management.[2]

In weak management, techniques such as financial planning and control are invariably used as the "whipping boys." Obviously, a technique by itself can do nothing; the individuals using it determine its good or bad administration. Successful financial planning and control must be based upon such fundamentals as recognition of accomplishment, consideration for the rights of individuals, and fair play—in other words, enlightened relationships among people.[3]

The most essential element in the health care department's financial planning and control system is *humantology*.[4]

Financial planning and control refer to the organization, techniques, and procedures whereby long- and short-range plans are formulated, considered, and approved; responsibility is provided to meet changing conditions; progress is reported in working the plan; deviations in operation are analyzed; and required corrective action is taken.[5]

But the *human* factor in financial planning and control is elusive.

As a department grows, it becomes increasingly difficult for the department manager to keep in close personal touch with each of the department's activities. Certain duties and responsibilities must be delegated to supervisors, section heads, and other levels of management, even though the department manager continues to retain final responsibility for the overall operations of the department.

Experience in observing many well-managed departments will usually lead to the conclusion that it is the organized efforts of a group of individuals, not individual genius, that achieve good operation. Through organization, the tasks are divided so that the work can be done properly, the performance supervised, and the results controlled.[6] It might be said also that no department managers can know the true capabilities of their departments until they are properly organized.

Financial planning and control result in a coordinated, documented, 24-hours a day, 7-days a week system that requires the involvement of people to

- set objectives and goals
- establish strategy and standards
- implement and produce
- review and evaluate

The financial planning and control system is an expanded development of the conventional budgetary process. When properly implemented and managed, the financial planning and control system, in conjunction with

- management by involvement
- management by objectives
- management for results
- management by exception
- zero-base budgeting
- theory Z

will help to develop a more efficient, more profitable working team. And critical to the successful implementation of a financial planning and control system is the element of humantology.

THE HUMANTOLOGY OF MANAGEMENT, PLANNING, AND CONTROL

Humantology of health care departmental financial planning and control may be defined as a responsive management application of structured and individual assignments of functional responsibilities.

Within a relevant range of authority, it comprises the basic principles of:

- faith in people
- knowledgeable participation of people

in the effort to achieve the planned goals of the health care facility.[7]

Faith in another's ability is based on hypothesis and will be substantiated by fact.[8] Faith in the department's staff is the first element of *humantology* for department managers and their supervisors.

MANAGEMENT BY INVOLVEMENT

All too frequently, health care department managers state that they cannot involve their supervisors or other staff members in the financial planning and control system because "*they* just don't have it." Is this the real problem? Or could it be that some department managers do not want to take the time required to assist in the development of their supervisors and staff? If either of these statements is true, then department managers should employ reliable people whom they can trust. The department managers must have faith in their supervisors and staff or they will suddenly find themselves so involved with routine operations that they will have little or no time for financial planning and control.

Department managers should not attempt, nor appear to be attempting, to usurp the line of authority of their supervisors and section heads. This can frequently cause friction, frustration, and subsequent lowering of morale. In the final analysis, department managers are responsible for the total operations of their departments, but they are only as good as their subordinates. Therefore, it is essential that managers train and develop strong, potential leaders through management by involvement. Aside from the fact that strong subordinates will be developed, and better financial planning and control will result, management by involvement also is conducive to better morale and greater initiative.[9]

However, as Chris Argyris discovered, there is such a thing as "pseudoparticipation"—that is, participation (involvement) that looks like, but is not, real participation.[10] When this happens, the first element of humantology, faith, will be jeopardized. If the supervisors and staff suspect that they are being overlooked or ignored, if they start wondering whether someone is trying to pull the wool over their eyes, then the credibility of the department manager is at stake. Faith is a two-way street and depends upon the depth of trust that exists between all levels of authority and responsibility.

Management by involvement may be defined as the process of decision making by the two or more individuals whom the decision will affect. Management by involvement is a more complex and difficult method than the unilateral management approach, which requires only the department manager (one individual) to make all the decisions. However, the involvement approach draws from the diffuse knowledge of all levels of responsibility. It requires much more selling and evaluating to implement the financial planning and control system than does the unilateral management style. Management by involvement enables the department's participants to know one another, to share, to communicate, and to interact—conditions which can easily lead to increased cohesiveness—a team approach to management. The ultimate synergetic benefits of this approach are immeasurable.

One word of caution: management by involvement is not a panacea. Whatever style of management is selected, it must be the style with which the department manager feels most comfortable.

MANAGEMENT STYLES

There is a wide variety of management styles with which department managers and their supervisors can experiment or adopt. A management style which has proved successful is the "bottom-up top-down" method. As briefly described in Chapter 2, this method utilizes the hands-on experience of each level of departmental employee, i.e., clerk, technician, skilled worker, and nonskilled worker, to help decide how work quality and performance can be improved, productivity increased, and how to adjust certain costs to enhance revenue. The "bottom-up top-down" management style never underestimates the contributions generated from all employee levels.

However, this system does require a considerable amount of screening and evaluation before viable information can be filtered to top management for consideration and possible future implementation. The collection and screening of information from the various bottom sources are critical steps in the management style. This system must be especially sensitive to feedback from each source as to the reasons for acceptance or rejection of any ideas. This feedback will encourage continued participation in the system. Figure 4–1 helps to illustrate the flow of information.

Figure 4–1 Development of Bottom-Up Top-Down Management Style

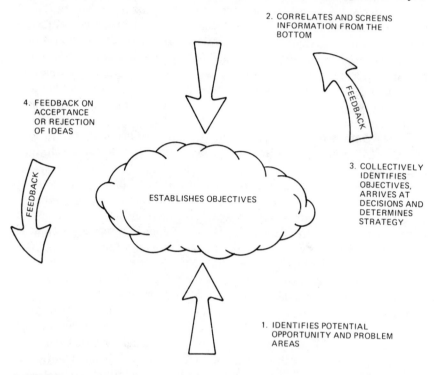

2. CORRELATES AND SCREENS INFORMATION FROM THE BOTTOM

FEEDBACK

4. FEEDBACK ON ACCEPTANCE OR REJECTION OF IDEAS

FEEDBACK

ESTABLISHES OBJECTIVES

3. COLLECTIVELY IDENTIFIES OBJECTIVES, ARRIVES AT DECISIONS AND DETERMINES STRATEGY

1. IDENTIFIES POTENTIAL OPPORTUNITY AND PROBLEM AREAS

THEORY Z*

Historically, healthcare management styles have been based on Douglas McGregor's "Theory X" and "Theory Y" or on some combination of the two. According to McGregor, a Theory X supervisor assumes that people are fundamentally lazy, irresponsible, and need constant supervising. This is an authoritarian management style. A Theory Y manager, however, assumes that people are fundamentally hard working, responsible, and need only to be supported and encouraged. This style is referred to as participative management.

In the traditional healthcare institution, the supervisor, department manager, and administrator typically behave as though they believe

*Excerpted with permission from the July 1984 issue of *Healthcare Financial Management.* Copyright 1984, Healthcare Financial Management Association.

"the buck stops here" and that they alone should take responsibility for making decisions. Recently, however, some organizations have adopted explicitly participative modes of decision making in which all of the members of a department develop consensus on what decision to adopt.

Decision making by consensus has been the subject of a great deal of research in Europe and the United States during the past 20 years, and the evidence strongly suggests that a consensus approach yields more creative decisions and more effective implementation than does individual decision making.

Theory Z offers a practical alternative to the traditional management styles. This approach helps healthcare supervisors build efficient departments.

Under Theory Z, management style is embodied in an arrangement that relies on trust and subtlety developed through intimacy. The net result is that fairness and equity are achieved over an extended period of time. Another key feature of the Theory Z decision-making process is the intentional ambiguity of who is responsible for what decisions. The Theory Z approach gives the decision-making process to a group or team of employees which assumed the responsibility for a given set of tasks.

When an important decision needs to be made under the Theory Z approach, everyone who will feel its effect is involved in making the decision. Making a decision this way usually takes longer, but once a decision is reached everyone affected by it will likely support it.

What is so unique in the Theory Z approach is not the decision itself but rather the extent to which people are committed and informed. The "best" decision can be bungled just as the "worst" decision can work just fine. The "control" has been dropped from almost all uses.

Quality Control Circles

Quality control circles, or simply quality circles, are designed in the spirit of Theory Z. Quality circles are small groups of volunteer employees usually from the same work area, led by a first-line supervisor, who meet for about an hour one or more times per month to identify, analyze, and solve specific quality and production problems.

Groups can range from three to 15 members, with seven to 10 being recognized as the optimum size. In the short run, quality circles can reduce waste, downtime and rework, and correct other inefficiencies. In the long run they can cause fundamental changes in the way employees relate to their jobs and their employer. But quality circles cost money, and they have drawbacks that suggest they may not be right for every employer.

The fundamental purposes of quality circles are to:

- Contribute to the improvement and development of the healthcare institution
- Respect humanity and build a happy, bright workshop which is meaningful to work in
- Display human capabilities fully, and eventually draw out infinite possibilities.

Quality Circle Methodology

Preimplementation planning and training are critical to a successful program. Not all quality circles programs are successful, but because success breeds success, the ideal department or section to start with is an area with a people-oriented and enthusiastic supervisor. It should also be a department not burdened with an excessive amount of problems. For beginners, it is best to implement only one or two circles. The need for more will grow when success is demonstrated.

The typical quality circle methodology is illustrated as a six-step process (Exhibit 4–1).

1. **Problem or identification** Members of the quality circles are assigned the responsibility of identifying problems. In one hospital, problems were identified as "opportunities." (Exhibit 4–2).
2. **Problem selection** Problems or opportunities are ranked in relationship to the group's criteria, and a specific problem is selected for concentration.

Exhibit 4–1 Quality Control Circle Methodology

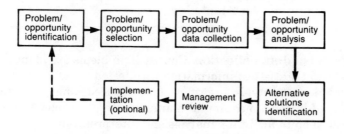

Source: Reprinted from *Healthcare Financial Management*, p. 36, with permission of Healthcare Financial Management Association, © July 1984.

Exhibit 4–2 Problem/Opportunity Identification Report

Department _____ Date _____19___ Submitted By _____ Reviewed By _____

Problem/Opportunity: (Describe)   Negative Impact
                                         Upon Departmental:
                                         ____ Efficiency
                                         ____ Quality
                                         ____ Productivity
                                         ____ Profitability
                                         ____ Other _____

Causes of Problem:
Alternative Solutions to Present System:

Action Decision:
 	
                              Approved By _____
                              Title _____
                              Date Approved _____19___

3. **Problem data collection** Causes of problems are identified and relevant statistical information is collected.
4. **Problem analysis** Information is reduced, analyzed, and displayed in some meaningful manner, such as graphs, time-series, and so on to facilitate analysis and interpretation.
5. **Alternate solutions identification** Group members brainstorm for alternate methods and solutions to eliminate the problems and

take advantage of the opportunity to improve quality of service and productivity. (Exhibit 4–3 is an example of a project work plan that can be used.) Alternate solutions are absolutely necessary; three or four solutions are optimal. This does not limit management to accepting or rejecting a single solution.

6. **Management review** The group makes a formal presentation of its findings and recommendations to management. The group members making the actual presentation are recognized for being creative individuals who are concerned with the healthcare institution's quality, productivity and growth.

This step in the process is extremely important, as this contributes to the employees' professional development. Implementation of the circle's recommendations is usually management's decision. Management must formally recognize and communicate these improvements throughout the entire organization. Top management must be totally committed to the program and its support must be constantly visible.

The National Productivity Report identifies five reasons for quality circle failure. They are:

1. inadequate management support,
2. restricting voluntary features by goading people into joining or enforcing joining by edict,
3. emphasizing a people-using theme instead of the people-building theme,
4. inadequate training of members in problem-solving methods,
5. emphasis on individual effort rather than on team effort.[11]

There are no shortcut methods or no one perfect program. Adequate time and money must be allowed for a quality circle program to mature and flower.

Finally, it is imperative to recognize the need for constant monitoring of the quality circles program. The concept of quality circles can change from one of concern primarily for quality to a strict focus on productivity and cost avoidance. Too often, quality plays a handmaiden's role when in reality quality improvement was the prime reason for the founding of circles in Japan. Productivity improvement cannot result unless quality is acceptable. The two concepts should be inseparable. Solve the quality problem and the road to productivity improvement will be open. Quality circles can help support enlightened people-oriented management.[12]

Exhibit 4-3 Project Work Plan

Project Work Plan

Page _____ Of _____

Project No. _____
Project Name _____

Starting date _____ 19 ___
Completion date _____ 19 ___

Progress report

Date _____ 19 ___

Work Plan Tasks

No.	Description	Objective	Responsible coordinator	Team members	Start date	Completion date	Status review

Prepared by _____ Date _____ 19 ___
Approved by _____ Date _____ 19 ___

Comments:

Reviewed by _____

Date _____ 19 ___

Source: Adapted from *Healthcare Financial Management*, p. 38, with permission of Healthcare Financial Management Association, © July 1984.

MANAGEMENT BY OBJECTIVES

Management by objectives (MBO) is a widely used management technique in a variety of enterprises. It is a method of management that emphasizes the purpose of a department, the goals to be reached, and the specific objectives to be established. This approach can be applied to an individual, a section, or a department. It has found exceptional success in health care facilities.

Two common attributes of the MBO concept are:

1. The more clearly the purpose and goals are defined, the better the chance of its accomplishment.
2. progress measurement is relevant only in terms of the accomplishment of objectives and goals.

Deegan gives us two distinct definitions of MBO. First, as the basic definition: "Management by objectives is a system of personal responsibility in which outputs (results) are the only claim on the resources of the organization, and outputs are the justification for approving, modifying, or abandoning programs of action."

> *Then the operational definition:* "Management by objectives is a continual process whereby superior and subordinate managers periodically identify their common goals, define each individual's major areas of responsibility in terms of results expected, and use these agreed-upon measures as guides for operating each department and for assessing contributions of each manager to the work of the entire organization."[13]

Management by objectives can provide significant benefits in the coordination of department purpose, goals and objectives with the total health care facility's purpose, goals and objectives. When properly implemented, MBO is especially helpful to department managers and their supervisors to assure "on-track" performance, coordination and evaluation. Specifically, MBO provides:

- more comprehensive planning tied to the achievement and evaluation of results
- more improved identification and diagnosis of problems
- better human relations through management by involvement

At the heart of the MBO process is a goal-setting session where the department managers, their supervisors and assistant supervisors, when deemed appropriate, clarify and agree upon specific purpose, target goals and timetables. The participants describe the direction in which they want to grow and how they plan to get there. The department manager receives the various sets of goals and reviews them to be sure that they are consistent with the broader objective of the department, which, in turn, must be consistent with that of the total health care facility. Exhibits 4–4 and 4–5 are illustrations of department objectives worksheets. Such objectives, when reasonable and attainable, have the great advantage of providing known and accepted criteria for performance evaluation and growth.

Precisely what is accomplished in managing by objectives and appraising results varies with each type of department and the manner in which the system is implemented and maintained. Experience has shown that there are some constant action points. Basically, these action points can be aligned in four clockwise and counter clockwise stages:

- identification of department's specific mission or purpose
- identification of goals and objectives that complement the purpose
- selection of strategy, resources, establishment of predetermined performance standards required to obtain identified goals and objectives, and operating assumptions
- implementation and execution of a selected strategic plan, and application of required resources
- comparative analysis and evaluation of actual performance standards and goals (feedback)
- corrective measures

As noted, these action points can be applied either clockwise before the performance process, or counter clockwise after the performance process, to assist during subsequent planning or evaluating periods. Figure 4–2 illustrates the key action points and how they relate to each other in the MBO management technique. It is interesting to note that only one of the action points, Performance and Production, is directly involved in the actual operating process, while the remaining three action points are related to the planning process. In short, one could assume that approximately seventy-five percent of a department manager's time should be spent in planning, rather than on day-to-day operational activities and firefighting.

Exhibit 4–4 Hospital Goals and Annual Operating Objectives

(1) GOALS	(2) OBJECTIVES	DATE (3) YEAR	APPROVED BY Governing Board 9/8/x3 (4) REFERENCE NO.
Provide outpatient services needed by community	Begin implementing long range plan for outpatient services for 19x0–19x5	19x4	1
	Close first-west and remodel for outpatient service needs.	19x5	2
	Build $1.5 million physicians' office complex	19x6	3
Increase person-hour productivity in nursing and ancillary service units by 15%	Reevaluate work flow, facility layout, organization and staffing in nursing and ancillary areas	19x4	4
	Modify facility layout and work flow	19x4	5
	Revise staffing standards	19x4	6
	Make organization and staffing changes	19x5	7
Reduce laundry/linen costs by 15%	Review linen usage and alternatives	19x4	8
Reduce working capital borrowings by 20%	Reduce patient receivables oustanding from 75 days to 55 days	19x4	9
	Reduce general stores inventory 15%	19x4	10
Improve management depth	Assess present management capabilities and needs	19x4	11
	Implement a management development program	19x5	12
	Establish an administrative residency position	19x6	13

Exhibit 4–4 continued

(1) GOALS	(2) OBJECTIVES	(3) DATE YEAR	APPROVED BY Governing Board 9/8/x3 (4) REFERENCE NO.
Improve communications & relations with Chicano community	Make available patient information booklets and forms in Spanish	19x4	14
	Participate in school careers programs	19x4	15
	Increase number of Spanish speaking personnel in admitting & emergency room	19x4	16
Improve quality of patients' medical care	Participate in Institute on Improving Medical Audit.	19x4	17
	Implement changes in medical audit procedures	19x4	18
	Implement patient care plan program in nursing units.	19x5	19
	Expand medical records program for outpatients	19x6	20
	Reduce incident reports 25% by 7/1/x4	19x4	21
Redirect medical education program to emphasize family practice	Discontinue surgery intern and residency program	19x5	22
	Begin family practice intern and residency program	19x6	23

Source: California Hospital Association/Hospital Financial Management Association Budget Manual (Sacramento, Calif.: 1974).

Exhibit 4–5 Corrective Action Plan

Memorial Hospital
Anytown, U.S.A.
Problem/Opportunity: Mail Returns in Emergency Room
P/O No. 005

Date: _____ 19____

Stopgap Day 1–Day 7	Immediate Day 8–Day 11	Intermediate Day 15–Day 30	Long Range After Day 30
1. Inform staff of problem	1. Sort and tabulate mail according to reasons for return in an attempt to identify source of problem	1. Review form for completeness or ambiguity	1. Redesign and modify admitting form, as necessary
2. Implement procedure to request two (2) pieces of identification from each patient or responsible party	2. Check admitting form for clerical errors or omissions	2. Observe department operations for workload and productivity	2. Train staff in use of new forms
3. Obtain name, address, and telephone number of nearest relative or friend of patient	3. Design and/or modify and order new admitting form, if necessary	3. Interview clerical staff for problem and/or opportunity identification	3. Reinforce and document departmental admitting policy and procedures for completing admitting form
4. Install cash payment policy at the time of admission	4. Install a credit card payment system	4. Review, refine, and document job descriptions	4. Conduct periodic audit of mail returns and admitting forms for effectiveness of systems
			5. Continue to audit and make appropriate corrective measures

Source: Lorna Small, California State University, Northridge, Department of Health Science, 1985.

Figure 4–2 Management by Objectives Cycle of Action Points

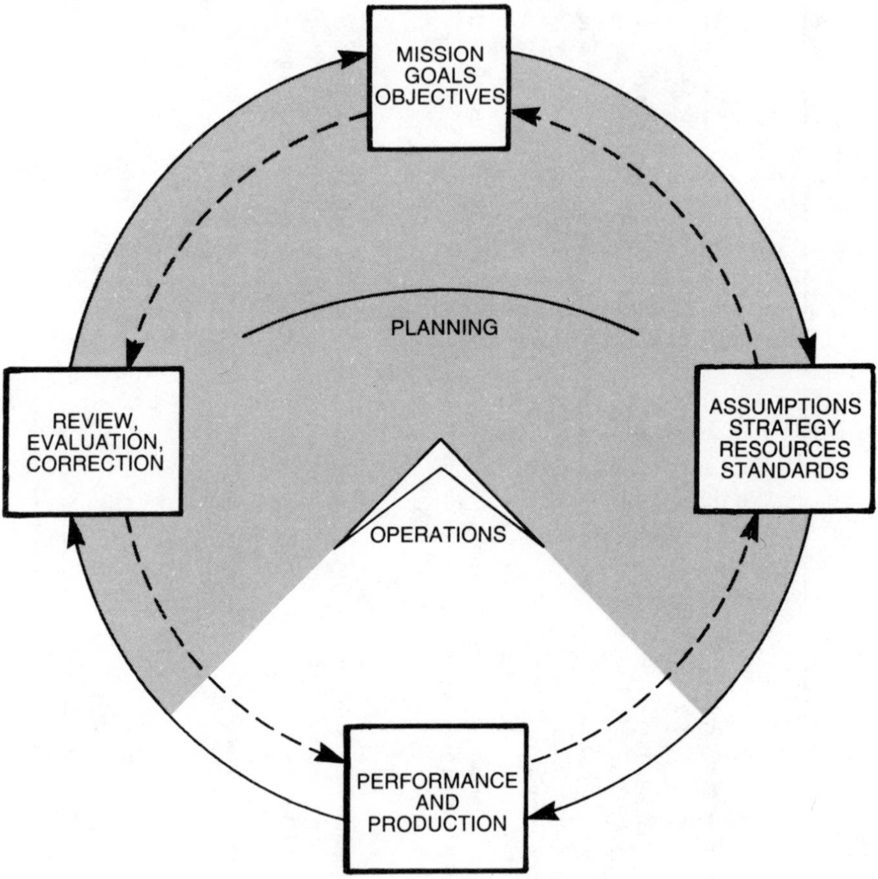

Shaded Area—Planning
White Area—Operating

MANAGEMENT FOR RESULTS

The management for results concept begins with the analysis of the result areas or the definition of the department output or service to be generated. The quality of the service and any other characteristics must be identified at the start of the management process.

During the management analysis process, which is required to identify the desired results, the department managers and their supervisors, before they start on tentative conclusions, must encourage the
total examination of any uncertainties, ambiguities, or disagreements
among themselves.

Drucker tells us that *concentration* is the key to economic results. He
states that economic results require that managers concentrate their
efforts on the smallest number of products or services that will produce
the largest amount of revenue. He further states that managers must
minimize the amount of attention devoted to services which are not cost
effective because their volume is too small or too splintered.[14] Even
Drucker places the emphasis upon revenue, and this small management principle can be applied to the health care facility and the entire
health care industry. Management must concentrate its efforts upon
the departmental services which represent the largest volume of work
in the department. The effective management of these services or
results will assure departmental efficiency. The word "concentration" is
key in the management for results concept. But, before this concentration process begins, the identification of the desired results, i.e., 10 percent return on investment, is a prerequisite to the entire management
concept.

MANAGEMENT BY EXCEPTION

Management by exception is a management performance reporting
system that concentrates on unplanned performance variations while
eventually ignoring items which are within accepted predetermined
performance standards. This reporting system allows department managers and their supervisors to concentrate their analytical and managerial talents only on the out-of-line items.

The exception principle of reporting holds that it is the out-of-line
items that need managerial attention; the items that are not out-of-line
don't require extreme managerial time.[15] It is essential to stress that
favorable variances, as well as unfavorable variances, need investigation. This variety of knowledge is vital for future planning. The
approach complements the key to cost control in the closing sentence of
Chapter 3. " . . . concentrate on controlling variable costs on a day-to-
day basis."

Performance reports as illustrated in Figure 4–3, whether the management by exception concept is applied or not, are designed for either
external or internal purposes. Regardless, the report content generally
falls into the following categories:

Figure 4–3 Example of a Management by Exception Report

Memorial Hospital
Anytown, U.S.A.

Comparative Analysis of Emergency Services Operations
for one-month period ending September 30, 19x3

| Description | Amount | | Quartile |
	Your Hospital	Group Average	Your Hospital
1. Number of paid hours	1,652	1,600	3
2. Number of outpatient admissions processed	1,865	1,973	2
3. Gross charges to patients	$139,875	$111,380	4
4. Salary and fringe expenses, excluding physicians	$28,910	$27,680	3
5. Nonsalary expenses	$18,556	$20,184	2
6. Paid hours per admission	1.13	0.81	4
7. Gross charges per admission	$75.00	$56.45	H
8. Salary and fringe expense per admission	$15.50	$14.03	3
9. Nonsalary expense per admission	$ 9.95	$10.23	L

Quartile Classification

L	=	Low compared with data base peer group
H	=	High compared with data base peer group
1	=	Questionably low
4	=	Questionably high
2 & 3	=	Borders around peer group average, acceptable

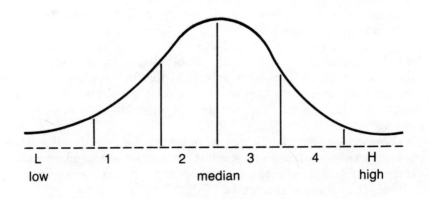

L   1   2   3   4   H
low   median   high

- statistical reports that record the basic quantitative data or key indices in regard to the operations of the health care facility
- special managerial reports that are devoted to nonrecurring and special problems

Included in all performance reports are the minimal operational requirements of:

- actual results
- planned or budgeted results
- variances or differences between the two

The hierarchy of performance reports forms a pyramid configuration as illustrated in Figure 1–4, with top management requiring condensed information while department managers and other line managers require more elaborate information. As stated in Chapter 1, graphs are very effective in performance reporting, with out-of-line items easily recognized when actual performance is below the charted planned performance standards.[16]

ZERO-BASE BUDGETING

The zero-base budget method starts on the premise that no department, program or cost center is forever, unless the unit can justify its existence. There are two basic steps in zero-base budgeting. These are:

- developing decision packages
- prioritizing decision packages

Decision packages identify a discrete activity, function or operation in a definite manner for management evaluation and comparison with other activities. This identification includes:

- purpose (or goals and objectives)
- consequences of not performing the activity (opportunity) costs
- measures of performance
- alternative courses of action
- cost and benefits

Once decision packages are developed and ranked, management can allocate resources accordingly. The most important activities or decision packages are funded, whether they are current or newly proposed. The final zero-base budget is produced by taking decision packages that are approved for funding, sorting them into their appropriate budget units, and adding up the costs identified on each package to produce the budget for each unit or department.[17]

ESTABLISHING AND PRIORITIZING ACTION PLANS

In this chapter, we have stated that concentration is the key to managing for results. During the analysis process, the various systems, procedures, and departmental needs will be recognized. However, additional needs must not be confused with the need to evaluate the present system. The system design evaluation and analysis process should be a never-ending cycle. The system design can be classified as either strong or weak.

Management's responsibility is to build upon a strong system design and improve upon a weak system design. The need for improvement calls for an action plan or a corrective measure. These action plans are classified in order of priority as:

- urgent or stopgap
- immediate
- intermediate
- long-range

The time frames for each of these action plans can vary depending upon the amount of authority and support the department manager has, and the complexity of the condition. However, the stopgap measure can be implemented with minimal expense and time and usually is implemented the same day the weakness is recognized. An immediate action plan ranges from one day to thirty days; an intermediate action plan ranges from thirty days to ninety days; and a long-range corrective action plan ranges from ninety days to one year.

To illustrate the use of the action plan approach, assume that Memorial Hospital of Anytown, U.S.A. is experiencing a substantial increase in the number of "mail returns," billings returned by the Post Office as "not deliverable," from its Emergency Room.

Some potential problem areas which have been identified include:

- circumstances surrounding hospitalization that make it difficult to obtain complete information
- communication barrier—patient does not understand what is asked
- patient who speaks a foreign language
- inadequate staffing
- illegible handwriting
- inadequate postage on envelopes
- incomplete addresses, zip codes, etc.
- delay between time of visit and the time of mailing the initial bills

Imagine that a hospital's system analyst has been assigned to analyze the situation, recommend tactical corrective measurements, and design a system that ensures proper and effective billing. Action time frames may be assigned as follows:

Stopgap	Day 1–Day 7
Immediate	Day 8–Day 14
Intermediate	Day 15–Day 30
Long-Range	Day 31–Open

and have identified the preliminary tasks in respective time frames, as illustrated in Exhibit 4–5. After these tasks have been randomly recorded in their respective timeframes on the action plan, they are displayed on a Gantt chart (Exhibit 4–6) to schedule and present the tasks more systematically as to

- number
- description
- assignment of responsibility
- time line

The following are some examples of potential problem areas and corrective actions that impact the volume of mail returns:

1. circumstances surrounding hospitalization that make it difficult to obtain complete information
2. communication barrier: patient did not understand what was being asked, patient speaks foreign language

Exhibit 4–6 Gantt Chart of Corrective Action Plan

Memorial Hospital
Anytown, U.S.A.
Problem Opportunity: Mail Returns in Emergency Room
P/O No. 005

Date: _____ 19___

Task No.	Task Description	Task Responsibility	Week 1	Week 2	Week 3	Week 4	Week 5	Week 6
1.0	Stopgap action							
1.1	Inform staff of problem	Department manager and systems analyst	▓					
1.2	Implement interim two (2) piece identification procedure	Department manager and systems analyst	▓					
2.0	Identify reasons for mail returns							
2.1	Sort and separate mail returns according to reasons	Sue Allen, clerk	▓	▓				
2.2	Analyze and tabulate reasons and other relevant sources	Sue Allen		▓				
3.0	Identify sources of problem							
3.1	Check admitting form for completeness	John Harris, clerk	▓					
3.2	Interview clerks	Systems analyst	▓	▓				
3.3	Observe mailroom operations	Systems analyst	▓	▓				
3.4	Review, refine admitting form	Systems analyst		▓				

Exhibit 4-6 continued

		Responsible party
3.5	Order new admitting form	Department manager
4.0	Implement corrective action	
4.1	Review present admitting procedures and job description	Department manager and systems analyst
4.2	Document refined procedures and job descriptions	Systems analyst
5.0	Develop refined admitting procedures	
5.1	Receive new refined admitting form	Purchasing and receiving department
5.2	Develop and document procedure for new admitting form	Systems analyst and department manager
6.0	Train staff	
6.1	Orient staff to new job descriptions	Department manager
6.2	Review and train staff how to use new admitting form	Systems analyst
6.3	Review and orient staff to the refined admitting procedures	Department manager
7.0	Implement new system and procedures	Department manager
8.0	Perform periodic and random audits and appropriate corrective actions	Department manager

Source: Lorna Small, California State University, Northridge, Department of Health, 1984.

3. staffing inadequate
4. illegible handwriting
5. inadequate postage on envelopes
6. incomplete addresses, zip codes
7. delay between time of visit and the time of sending out bills

Corrective action:

1. Staff training
2. Redesign new form—must be typed
3. Verification of identification
4. Periodic spot checks

The key to successful prioritizing of action plans is to build on the strengths of the present system while trying to correct its weaknesses, and involving those who are, and will be, working with the new system.

REFERENCES

1. Harold Leavett, *Managerial Psychology* (Chicago, Ill.: The University of Chicago Press, 1958), p. 459.
2. Glenn A. Welsch, *Budgeting: Profit Planning and Control* (Englewood Cliffs, N.J.: Prentice-Hall, 1964), p. 32.
3. James L. Pierce, "The Budget Comes of Age," *Harvard Business Review,* May–June, 1954, p. 58.
4. Allen G. Herkimer, Jr., *Concepts in Hospital Financial Management* (Paradise Valley, Ariz.: Alfa Associates, Inc., 1970), p. 91.
5. *Management Planning and Control: The Heinz Approach* (New York: Controllership Foundation, Inc., 1957) p. VIII.
6. J. Brooks Heckert and James D. Willson, *Controllership* (New York: Ronald Press Co., 1963), 2nd edition.
7. Herkimer, *Concepts in Hospital Financial Management.*
8. *The Random House Dictionary of the English Language* (New York: Random House, 1967), pp. 511, 750, 1051.
9. B.H. Lord and G.A. Welsch, *Business Budgeting* (New York: Controllership Foundation, Inc., 1958), p. 97.
10. Chris Argyris, *The Impact of Budgets on People* (New York: Controllership Foundation, Inc., 1958), p. 97.
11. Allen G. Herkimer, "Quality Control Circles: A Participative Team Approach," *National Productivity Report* (Wheaton, Ill.: William F. Schleicher and Associates, Inc.) vol. 10, no. 18, September 30, 1981.
12. Ibid.
13. Arthur Deegan, XII, *Management by Objectives for Hospitals* (Rockville, Md.: Aspen Publishers, Inc., 1977), pp. 18 and 94.
14. Peter F. Drucker, *Managing for Results* (New York: Harper & Row, 1964), p. 11.

15. Glenn A. Welsch, *Budgeting: Profit Planning and Control* (Englewood Cliffs, N.J.: Prentice-Hall, Inc., 1971), p. 25.

16. Allen G. Herkimer, Jr., *Concepts in Hospital Financial Management* (Paradise Valley, Ariz.: Alfa Associates, Inc., 1970), Chapters 13 & 14, pp. 113–128.

17. Peter A. Phyrr, *Zero-Base Budgeting* (New York: John Wiley & Sons, 1973), p. 5.

Chapter 5

Production Units and Performance Evaluation

The budgetary control process is developed from three key systems:

- the production measurement and evaluation system
- the volume (production) forecasting system
- the cost finding (allocation) system

These three systems serve as the basis for

- projecting revenues
- developing staffing requirements
- budgeting variable expenses
- establishing production (performance) standards
- allocating nonrevenue departmental costs to revenue-producing departments
- determining the total (direct and indirect) costs of a revenue-producing department
- establishing the total cost of a production unit
- determining the selling price (rate or charge) of a production unit

and other related budgetary requirements.

In this chapter, the identification, selection, and use of the production unit (unit of service) is described. Chapter 6 delineates how the production unit is used to forecast the volume of work to be performed during the budget year, Chapter 7 generally reviews the budgetary control process, and Chapter 8 describes the cost-finding and payment methods.

Unfortunately, many health care critics, especially from the governmental sector, have been comparing costs of health care facilities and health care departments. The emphasis has always been upon dollars. What does it cost per patient day, or what does a DRG cost? The dollar has been used primarily because there has been no other basis on which to evaluate performance.

What is so wrong about comparing costs? Basically, nothing, if each of the services are the same. But comparisons of costs of services usually do not consider such variables as:

- functional variations of the method used to perform the service
- technological differences—the type of equipment used to generate the service
- wage rate variances paid to personnel
- skill level differences used in the staffing patterns
- intensity of services rendered to the patient

Another important variable that distorts cost comparisons from one accounting period to another is the inflation factor.

If one were to depend solely upon the dollar cost to evaluate performance, adjustments for each of the above-mentioned variables would have to be made. In all probability, additional adjustments would be required to assure comparability. It is a time-consuming process to compute the desired results.

In another book, the author has stated that the present system of comparing health care institutions by dollar cost does not permit evaluation of the productive effectiveness of a department manager, nor does it stimulate greater productivity. Dollar comparisons yield only an unreliable gross figure, which raises many questions. Moreover, only pure rationalization can be used to answer the questions raised.[1] This is not to say that dollar cost comparisons are not necessary, rather, that cost comparisons must be supplemented with other quantitative measurements which will remain relatively constant over an extended period of time and will reasonably reflect the resources required to generate the service. Production units, or units of service, are the needed quantitative measurements. The selection of the exact production unit will be discussed later in this chapter.

Through effective use of production units, department managers and their supervisors can identify and determine

- productivity per employee
- costs per production unit
- charge (rate) per production unit

The use of production units will assist management in placing the responsibility of evaluating the performance of the dollars spent on those who spend them, as well as furnishing management the means to measure the production department's own effectiveness.

True, a dollar value will be assigned eventually to the proposed production unit. However, the dollar value should not be the only tool used to evaluate productive effectiveness.

Thus, the importance of production units is that they can enable the department managers and their supervisors to compare actual performance to a planned performance standard. In short, how much has been produced?

DEFINITION OF PRODUCTIVITY

Webster's Seventh New Collegiate Dictionary defines "productivity" as "the quality or state of being productive; the rate of production." "Production" is defined as "having the quality or power of producing in abundance; a yielding or furnishing of results, benefits or profits."

The National Commission on Productivity, in a bulletin entitled "Productivity and the Economy," stated that "Productivity is a concept that expresses the relationship between the *quantity* of goods and services produced (the outputs), and the *quantity* of labor, capital, land, energy and other resources that produced it (the inputs)."

The report continued, "The most commonly employed measure of productivity is using a single input-related output per man-hour. Labor time includes the man-hours of all persons employed in the production process. Man-hours are treated as homogeneous: no distinction is made between hours of employees at different levels of skills or pay."

Peter Drucker states, "Productivity is the *first test* of management's competence." He further states, "Productivity means the balance between all factors of production which will give the greatest output for the smallest effort."[2]

For the purposes of this discussion, we will define productivity as "the ratio of outputs per units of inputs over a specific period of time." Further, let the outputs be represented as the production units, i.e., tests, exams, cases, and meals, and the inputs be employee time, i.e., days, hours, and minutes.

PRODUCTION UNITS

A production unit is a non-dollar statistic which can be used to quantitatively measure the production of a health care department, such as: patients, operating room cases, laboratory relative values, pounds of laundry processed, and x-ray examinations.

It is most important, in the selection of a production unit, that the unit accurately identify and reflect the service or commodity produced and the amount of health care resources used to produce the individual unit. For the purpose of this discussion, the production units are separated into two major classifications:

- macro production unit
- micro production unit

MACRO PRODUCTION UNITS

Presently, macro production units are the most common measurements because they require no special studies to determine their weighted value. They are also relatively easy to identify, collect, and audit in the respective departments. Macro production units usually represent a collection or grouping of related tasks, which, when combined, can be identified as a service unit, such as an operating room surgical case. By collecting the number of surgical cases, there may have been some classification by type of surgical case. However, if there had been no identification of the time required to perform the cases, it would be impossible to project labor or facility costs, or to arrive at an equitable charge per surgical case.

Generally speaking, macro production units are better than no service units, but they do not accurately reflect the amount of work or health care resources required to perform the service.

MICRO PRODUCTION UNITS

In most cases, the key to micro or weighted production units is the amount of resources used to generate the service. Basically, each macro production unit has been computed into weighted values. Exhibit 5–1 displays a comparison of macro production units and micro production units. The objective is to reduce the macro production unit into a measurement which most accurately reflects the amount of health care resources; i.e., labor and/or material, capital, and overhead required to produce the service. Currently, relative value unit (RVU) is the term commonly used to describe a micro production unit.

Exhibit 5–1 Comparative Study of Health Care Departmental Macro Production Units and Micro Production Units

Department	Macro Production Unit	Micro Production Unit
Operating room	Surgical case	Person-Minutes
Anesthesiology	Anesthesia case	Person-Minutes
Postoperative rooms	Postoperative case	Person-Minutes
Radiology	Examinations	RVU's (A)
Laboratory	Tests	RVU's (A)
Physical therapy	Modalities	Person-Minutes
Isotopes	Treatments	RVU's (A)
Blood bank	Transfusions	RVU's (A)
Delivery room	Deliveries	Person-Minutes
Social service	Visits	Person-Hours
Emergency room	Visits	Person-Minutes
Housekeeping	Square footage	Weighted square footage
Nursing	Patient days	Hours of care
Nursery	Patient days	Hours of care

(A) See Appendix A for catalog of Laboratory Relative Value Units as established by the College of American Pathologists.

SELECTION OF PRODUCTION UNITS

Obviously, one of the most difficult and critical decisions is the selection of an appropriate statistical production unit which will meet the individual health institution's corporate objectives and will vary with the change in volume. The following are some criteria which should be recognized in the selection process:

1. The production unit must consider fixed *and* variable costs.

2. The production unit should be affected as little as possible by variable factors other than volume.

3. The production unit should be easily understood.

4. The production unit totals should be obtainable at minimal clerical expense, and easily audited.

When selecting production units for variable or flexible budgeting, one will frequently find that it is necessary to select more than one unit for one department. Perhaps one should even select a mixed group of gross and weighted service units such as:

Operating Room (OR) Production Units

Fixed Costs	Production Unit
Supervisory salaries	Number of calendar days
Clerical	Number of patients scheduled

Variable Costs	Production Unit
Supplies	Number of surgical cases
Technicians' salaries	Number of OR person-minutes
Transportation salaries	Number of patients transported

Basically, there are two primary purposes for production units, besides rate setting:

- production control
- cost allocation

One production unit for a department may not be appropriate to meet the health care institution's objectives; for example:

Purpose of Production Unit	Institution's Objective
Production control	To effectively evaluate productivity and to assist increased production
Cost allocation	To distribute indirect cost to revenue departments and to maximize cash flow

The production unit, also, must be sufficiently versatile in the use of historical and future costs or performance. It must lend itself to forecasting and be relatively simple to identify, to record for historical reference, and to audit. Figure 5–1 illustrates a production unit utility tree.

PRODUCTION CONTROL

Production control, under the health care financial management planning and control program, utilizes future projections for targets. These targets are set as follows:

Figure 5–1 Production Unit Utility Tree

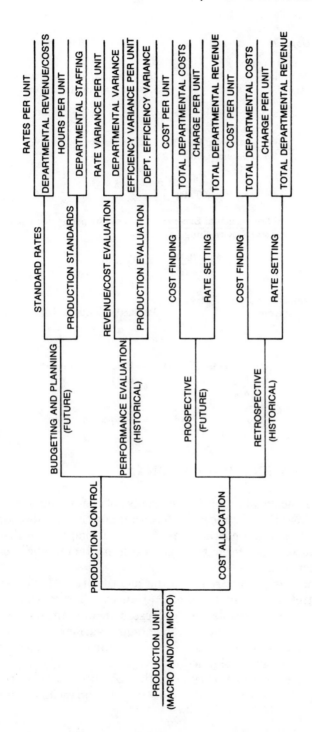

	Objective	*Standard*

1. Financial Control
   A. Revenue   Revenue rate per production unit
   B. Expense   Cost rate per production unit

Or

A. $\dfrac{\text{Total Departmental Revenue}}{\text{Total Service Units}}$ = Revenue rate per production unit

$$\frac{\$\ 500,000}{1,000,000} = \$.50 \text{ per unit}$$

B. $\dfrac{\text{Total Departmental Expense}}{\text{Total Service Units}}$ = Cost rate per production unit

$$\frac{\$\ 400,000}{1,000,000} = \$.40 \text{ per unit}$$

2. Production Control
   A. Production   Production units per hours worked

Or

B. $\dfrac{\text{Total Departmental Volume}}{\substack{\text{Total Departmental} \\ \text{Work Hours}}}$ = Production units per departmental work hours

$$\frac{1,000,000}{200,000} = 5 \text{ Production units per work hour}$$

PERFORMANCE EVALUATION

Performance evaluation is the process of comparing and analyzing actual or historical data to budgeted or planned standards to determine how well the actual operating performance compares to the planned performance. This information may result in either financial or production statistics.

The analysis process requires the identification of the variance to each control point. Usually, these variances can be classified as either favorable or unfavorable and expressed in quantitative terms, i.e., dollars, units of production, or percentage of variance to the plan or the predetermined standards. For example, assume that an operating room department manager planned or budgeted for 1,000,000 person-minutes of surgical production time for the accounting period and that the standard rates were as calculated above in the financial and production control process. Further, assume that the department produced only 900,000 person-minutes of surgical production time. A performance evaluation analysis report is illustrated in Table 5–1.

In this illustration, the standard rates were calculated based upon the target budget's revenue and expense. These standard rates were then applied to the actual volume to compute the revenue and expense of the control budget.

Graphs have been used most effectively in the performance evaluation process as illustrated in Figure 5–2 and Figure 5–3. The graph method is effective in communicating to nonaccounting-oriented individuals, because at one quick glance one can visualize what has happened. Graphs are also very effective in displaying and identifying established trends and projecting forecasts.

The thesis: control costs before they occur. Know where your department is headed, not where it has been. Don't wait until it is too late to take corrective action. This direction can be identified through the use of trend lines graphically illustrated as in Figure 5–4 using the data in Table 5–2.

COST ALLOCATION

Cost allocation is the result of the cost finding process to allocate nonrevenue-producing departmental costs to revenue-producing departments for the purpose of determining the total cost of a revenue department. Production units (i.e., meals served, hours of service) are used because they most accurately reflect the work performed for the revenue department. Some examples of gross production units used for cost allocation are:

Department	*Production Unit*
Housekeeping	Square feet serviced or hours of service
Laundry and Linen	Pounds of clean laundry processed
Pharmacy	Number of prescriptions processed
School of Nursing	Number of students or classroom hours
Dietary and/or cafeteria	Number of meals served
Medical records	Number of medical charts processed
Admitting office	Number of admissions processed

Table 5–1 Summary Performance Analysis of Operating Room for 12-Month Period Ending December 31, 19x1

MEMORIAL HOSPITAL
ANYTOWN, U.S.A.

SUMMARY PERFORMANCE ANALYSIS OF OPERATING ROOM
for 12 month period ending December 31, 19x1

Description	Standard Rate	Target Budget	Control Budget	Actual Performance	Variance $	Variance %
Volume	Person-minutes of Surgical Time	1,000,000	900,000	900,000	-0-	-0-
Revenue	$.50	$ 500,000	$ 450,000	$ 470,000	$ 20,000	4.4%
Expense	.40	400,000	360,000	405,000	45,000*	12.5%*
Net Profit (loss)	$.10	$ 100,000	$ 90,000	$ 65,000	$ 25,000*	27.8%*

Note: * Denotes unfavorable variance; favorable variances are not highlighted.

Figure 5–2 Graphic Summary of Patient Days for Obstetrics
Department as of July 31, 19x1

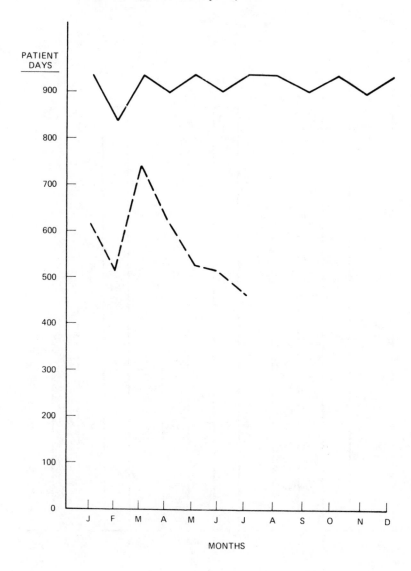

Figure 5–3 Graphic Summary of Performance Analysis of Operating Room for 12-Month Period Ending December 31, 19x1

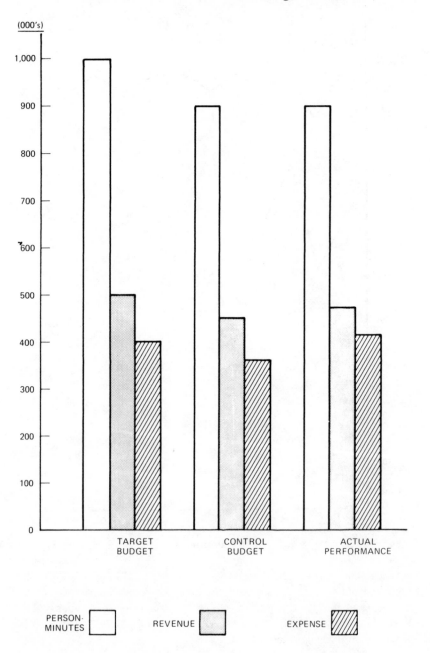

Figure 5–4 Graphic Summary of Average Daily Census in Obstetrics Department as of July 31, 19x1

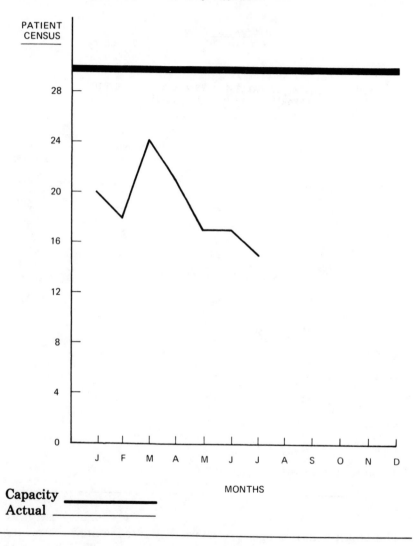

Capacity _____

Actual _____

In the selection of these production units, it is important to correlate the purpose of the unit. A unit such as the number of meals served in the cafeteria may be the appropriate statistic to allocate the cost of the cafeteria's operation, but it would be totally inappropriate to use for charging for meals served in the cafeteria.

Table 5–2 Monthly Summary of Patient Days for the Obstetrics Department as of July 31, 19x1

MEMORIAL HOSPITAL
ANYTOWN, U.S.A.

MONTHLY SUMMARY OF PATIENT DAYS FOR THE OBSTETRICS
DEPARTMENT AS OF JULY 31, 19x1

Month	Number of Days	Capacity (A)	Average Daily Census	Monthly Census
January	31	930	20	620
February	28	840	18	504
March	31	930	24	744
April	30	900	21	630
May	31	930	17	527
June	30	900	17	510
July	31	930	15	465
August	31	930		
September	30	900		
October	31	930		
November	30	900		
December	31	930		

(A) Capacity = 30 beds in department

The department manager's responsibility is to maximize reimbursement for services generated by the department. This means the department manager may have to test a variety of production units to evaluate their impact upon the department's cash flow. Cost allocation and the cost-finding process can be computed on either actual or budget data. Consideration should also be given to how often to test costs through the cost-finding process. A monthly basis or, preferably, a weekly or daily basis is recommended. (The cost-finding process will be discussed in greater detail in Chapter 8.)

DEVELOPMENT OF PRODUCTION STANDARDS

There are numerous methods used to develop production standards. For the purpose of this discussion, the following two methods will be reviewed:

- classical
- involvement

The classical industrial (management) engineering approach utilizes predetermined standard times for specific tasks. These times represent the average time to perform a task, based on hundreds of observations. Work sampling, which is testing and analyzing a segment of data from a total volume of data, will represent the total population within a reasonable degree of accuracy. This classical approach tends to build a considerable degree of dependency upon the industrial engineer to adjust the standard time requirements whenever there is the slightest change in task methodology or volume.

Further, it has been generally accepted that the predetermined standards developed in this manner tend to be rejected more frequently by department managers and their staff, simply because they weren't involved in the development process. To avoid such apathy, the classical industrial engineering methodology should be installed using production standards whose development is familiar to the employees.

The involvement or self-logging methodology requires that the employees in the department record all of their activities during the survey period. Whereas in the classical approach the individual employee is generally unaware that industrial engineering is being conducted, this self-logging process keeps the employee actively involved. True, the standards which are ultimately developed may not be as scientifically determined, but they are usually reasonably representative of the average time required by an average qualified employee to perform a specific task under actual working conditions. As with any production standards, the involvement method includes allowances for normal, unavoidable delays and human foibles, i.e., personal reasons, fatigue, and delay (PF&D).

There are seven basic steps required to develop production standards by the involvement method:

1. *Preliminary Orientation.* Department managers, supervisors, and section heads, by individual specialties, meet with management engineers to review the general purpose of the project and to explain the overall methodology. At this time, all employee fears, doubts, and reservations should be identified and resolved.

2. *Preliminary Department Review.* The management engineers perform an on-site survey of each of the department's activities, equipment and other facilities in order to acquaint themselves with the overall departmental operations.

3. *Departmental Workshop.* During a workshop session, the management engineer, with the assistance of department managers, their supervisors, and section heads, selects the tasks to be measured and the related production units or task units to be recorded. During the session, a self-logging task list (see Exhibit 5–2) is designed so that the employees in the department may record their activities on a daily task sheet (see Exhibit 5–3) for each test day.

4. *Self-Logging Test Run.* A preliminary self-logging test run of three or four days is conducted to identify any problem areas and to generally debug the recording system.

5. *Test Run Review.* During this review session, the management engineer reviews the preliminary self-logging test results with the department managers and their supervisors and they make any necessary adjustments to assure relatively accurate self-logging. Also, at this time, agreements are made for the specific calculations for personal, fatigue, and delay factors, as well as the general computation approach of the production standards and the number and frequency of the self-logging test periods.

6. *Self-Logging Test Periods.* All department employees record their activities with the self-logging schedules, as shown in Exhibit 5–4 for the specified test period. This test period will vary from four to six weeks, depending upon various factors. The management engineer will be continually monitoring the self-logging during the test period to assure consistency and integrity in the recording process.

7. *Calculation of Production Standards.* After the self-logging process is completed, the management engineer will calculate the production standards and meet with department managers and their supervisors to review the final production standards for reasonableness and attainability. (See Exhibit 5–5.)

Since the involvement methodology requires that standards be developed by and for the employees to which they apply, they most accurately reflect individual employee abilities and specific working conditions.

Exhibit 5–2 Self-Logging Task List for Radiology Department[3]

Task No.	Task	Task Unit
	X-RAY TECHNOLOGIST	
1	PREPARATION AND CLEAN-UP	
	1A. Prepare room (including supplies, material, solution, etc.)	Patient
	1B. Identify number of films, technician and additional data	Patient
	1C. Clean room	Patient
2	CONDUCT EXAM (specify procedure and if STAT or additional) (Includes patient into room, positioning and X-raying)	Patient
3	FLUOROSCOPY TIME (specify procedure)	Patient
4	PORTABLE EXAM (specify procedure)	Patient
5	OPERATING ROOM EXAM (specify procedure)	Patient
6	DARK ROOM PROCEDURE (only if performed by technologist) (Includes emptying cassettes, developing, reloading)	No. Films
7	REVIEW FILMS	Patient
8	STAT READINGS (specify procedure)	Patient
	DARK ROOM TECHNICIAN	
9	DEVELOPING AND LOADING CASSETTES	No. Films
	CLERICAL AND RECEPTION DUTIES	
10	FILE ROOM ACTIVITY	
	10A. Pull and assemble case	Patient
	10B. File case	Patient
	10C. File room "pruning"	Occ.
11	SCHEDULE EXAMS AND MAINTAIN APPOINTMENT BOOK	Occ.
12	TYPE AND DISTRIBUTE TRANSCRIBED REPORTS	Patient
13	REQUISITION, RECEIVE, STORE OR ISSUE DEPARTMENT SUPPLIES	Occ.
14	MAINTAIN DEPARTMENT LOG OR STATISTICS (specify)	Occ.
15	PERFORM SECRETARIAL, CLERICAL OR RECEPTIONIST DUTIES (specify) (Includes typing, general filing, etc.)	Occ.
16	BILLING OR PAYROLL ACTIVITY (specify)	Occ.
	TRANSPORTER	
17	TRANSPORTER OR MESSENGER DUTIES (specify)	Occ.
	GENERAL DUTIES	
18	DELAYS	
	18A. Equipment	Occ.
	18B. Patient	Occ.
	18C. Doctor	Occ.
	18D. Other (specify)	Occ.
19	PERSONAL	
	19A. Rest Periods	Occ.
	19B. Meals	Occ.
	19C. Others (specify)	Occ.
20	OTHER DUTIES (specify)	
	20A. On-Call	Occ.
	20B. Stand-By	Occ.
	20C. Preparation of material	Occ.
	20D. Cleaning	Occ.
	20E. Telephone (in excess of 3 minutes; if less, put into other task)	Occ.

Exhibit 5–2 continued

20F.	Help others (specify)	Occ.
20G.	Work for other departments (specify)	Occ.

21   TEACHING (specify)   Occ.

22   ADMINISTRATIVE AND SUPERVISORY ACTIVITY

22A.	Scheduling or staffing	Occ.
22B.	Supervision	Occ.
22C.	Attend meetings	Occ.

Exhibit 5–3 Self-Logging Daily Task Reporting Sheet[3]

DAILY TASK REPORTING SHEET

HOSPITAL _____

NAME _____

TITLE _____

DEPT. _____

SEC. _____

DATE _____

INSTRUCTIONS

1. INDICATE STARTING AND STOPPING TIME BY DRAWING A HORIZONTAL LINE AT THE APPROPRIATE TIME SCALES TO THE END OF THE END OF THE MINS. COLUMN.
2. FILL IN TASK NO., UNITS, AND TOTAL MINUTES.
3. USE THE STANDARD LIST OF TASK NUMBERS.
4. AT THE END OF EACH DAY TRANSFER THIS DATA ONTO THE WEEKLY TASK SHEET SUMMARY.

TASK NO.	DESCRIPTION/ EQUIPMENT	UNITS	MINS.	TIME	TASK NO.	DESCRIPTION/ EQUIPMENT	UNITS	MINS.	TIME	TASK NO.	DESCRIPTION/ EQUIPMENT	UNITS	MINS.
				—					—				
				05					05				
				10					10				
				15					15				
				20					20				
				25					25				
				30					30				
				35					35				
				40					40				
				45					45				
				50					50				
				55					55				
				—					—				
				05					05				
				10					10				
				15					15				
				20					20				
				25					25				
				30					30				
				35					35				
				40					40				
				45					45				
				50					50				
				55					55				
				—					—				
				05					05				
				10					10				
				15					15				
				20					20				
				25					25				
				30					30				
				35					35				
				40					40				
				45					45				
				50					50				
				55					55				

Exhibit 5–4 Self-Logging Completed Daily Task Reporting Sheet[3]

ITAL Hospital A	INSTRUCTIONS
Mary Smith	1. This form is to be used by employees who may perform more than one task simultaneously.
X-Ray Technologist "B"	2. Leave several blank lines following listing of tasks which may be interrupted during the day.
X-Ray	3. Log start and finish times whenever work is performed on task and record units produced. Total elapsed time (minutes) spent on task.
4/22/71	

Task Description and Equipment	Units	Start	Stop	Min-utes	Task No.	Task Description and Equipment	Units	Start	Stop	Min-utes
Personal Prep. &		8:00	8:10	10	35	Deliver Film &		9:10	9:15	5
Clean-up		4:10	4:30	20		Pick up Cassettes		9:40	9:45	5
Set up Films, etc.		8:10	8:25	15				10:25	10:35	10
								1:20	1:25	5
Process Req. &	4	8:25	8:40	15				3:30	3:35	5
I.D. Tape	3	11:10	11:25	15						
	1	2:05	2:15	10						
	1	3:10	3:20	10	40	Review Films		9:15	9:20	5
								9:45	9:50	5
Upper G.I.	1	8:50	9:10	20				10:35	10:45	10
	1	9:20	9:40	20				1:25	1:40	15
	1	10:00	10:25	25				3:35	3:55	20
Bone Exam	6	11:25	11:45	20	36	Reload Cassettes		11:00	11:10	10
Chest Exam	2	12:45	12:55	10						
	2	12:55	1:05	10						
	2	1:05	1:20	15	181	Rest & Personal		10:45	11:00	15
	2	3:20	3:30	10		Time		1:40	2:05	25
					182	Meals		11:45	12:15	30
Portable—Chest	1	2:15	2:55	40	161	Wait—Patient		12:15	12:45	30
Wet Reading—		2:55	3:10	15						
Repeat					162	Wait—Physician		8:40	9:50	10
								9:50	10:00	10
					116	Fill out CHREF		3:55	4:10	15
						Sheets				
								Sub-Total		230
	Sub-Total			280				Total		510

Production standards, regardless of quality, accuracy, or method of development, must be constantly monitored and updated. One unique feature of the involvement methodology is that, once it is understood, a relatively competent clerk or technician can maintain the production standards. This can be accomplished because the involvement approach establishes production standards based upon gross time measurement to accomplish a specific task, i.e., start I.V. in intravenous therapy,

Exhibit 5–5 Standard Time Development Sheet for X-Ray Transporter[3]

HOSPITAL_____Memorial_____   DEPT.__X-ray___ SECTION_____

EMPLOYEE
CLASSIFICATION____Transporter_____   REPORTING UNIT (R.U.)___Examinations charged___

TASK		NORMAL MINUTES PER TASK	FREQUENCY PER R.U.	REFER TO MATRIX	NORMAL MINUTES PER R.U.
NO.	DESCRIPTION				
17	Transport patient	10.92	.745	2A	8.139
17	Messenger duties (per exam. charged)		.345	1.00	3A	.345
20C, D	Make stretchers, clean up (per exam. charged)	.328	1.00	4A	.328
20F	Help others (per exam. charged)	.195	1.00	5A	.195

TOTAL NORMAL MINUTES PER REPORTING UNIT (R.U.)   9.007

STANDARD HOURS PER R.U. (INCLUDING 5.8% PERSONAL ALLOWANCE)   .159

whereas the classical approach dissects each task into minute subtasks, i.e., select I.V., approach patient, and identify patient.

The involvement methodology is not designed to be a management tool for external comparison and performance evaluation; rather, it is designed to be an internal management tool which will enable all levels of management to measure and evaluate production performance against itself, to set production goals, as in Exhibits 5–6 through 5–9, and to develop production standards for the departments.

USE OF PRODUCTION STANDARDS

There are two basic assumptions which must be used if the department manager is to effectively use production standards. First, regardless of the exactness of a production standard, it is only meaningful as long as it is used by those for whom it is intended. A standard is useless if not used. Second, standards must be accepted by the individual users. During the process of developing the standards, using the involvement approach, the user is unconsciously selling oneself the standards because he or she is understanding how the standards are being developed. This approach requires minimal "poststandard development" selling, which is frequently experienced when using the classical approach with predetermined time standards.

The key to the use of standards is that even loosely defined production standards accepted, used, and enhanced, are better than rejected scientific, accurate standards, or no standards at all. Production standards

---

Exhibit 5–6 Staffing Budget Worksheet Summary—Radiology Department[3]

STAFFING BUDGET WORKSHEET SUMMARY

HOSPITAL: __Memorial__ DEPARTMENT: __Diagnostic Radiology__

PERIOD FROM __Oct. 1, 19X1__ TO __Sept. 30, 19X2__

(PAGE 1 OF 4)

Employee Specification (Specify)	Page Reference	Forecast Hours	Salary Budget
Asst. Chief Technician, X-Ray Technologists, Working Students	(2 of 4)	44,286	$168,611
Transporter	(3 of 4)	10,429	28,680
Secretarial & Clerical	(4 of 4)	16,426	19,848
Subtotal		71,141	$217,139
Administrative Assistant			15,000
Physicians Fee for Service			-0-
Other (specify)			
Chief Technologist			12,500
Director of X-Ray Tech School			13,000
Total Department Staffing Budget Costs			$257,639

Exhibit 5-7 Staffing Budget—Assistant Chief Technician, etc.—Radiology Department[3]

STAFFING BUDGET
CALCULATION WORKSHEET

HOSPITAL __Memorial__ DEPARTMENT __Diagnostic Radiology__ SECTION __ALL__

EMPLOYEE CLASSIFICATION __Assistant Technician / X-ray Technologist / Working Students__

PERIOD FROM __Oct. 1, 19x1__ TO __Sept. 30, 19x2__

(PAGE 2 OF 4)

ITEM	Reporting Unit (Specify) (1)	Standard Hours Per Reporting Unit (2)	Forecast Performance Factor (3)	Adjusted Standard Hours Per Reporting Unit (4)=(2)÷(3)	Forecast Volume (5)	Forecast Hours (6)=(4)×(5)	Average Hourly Rate (7)	Salary Budget (8)=(6)×(7)
Measured Work	Exams Charged	.410	.673	.609	46,800	28,501	$4.20	$119,704
	Weeks	46.50	.673	69.09	52	3,593	4.20	15,091
Subtotal						32,094	4.20	134,795
Unmeasured Paid Work			Week		Year			
On-Call—Not Worked			161.00 hrs × 52 wks =	8,372	8,372	2.00	16,744
On-Call—Worked			19.77 hrs × 52 wks =	1,028	1,028	5.20	5,346
Special Shifts (total unmeasured hours)			180.77 hrs × 52 wks =	9,400			
Subtotal						9,400		22,090
Fringe Benefits								
Vacation								
Holiday			Estimated at 8.7% of measured work 32,094 hrs × .087 = 2,792		2,792	4.20	11,726
Illness, Absence								
Others (specify)								
Subtotal						2,792	4.20	11,726
Total Budget Hours and Salaries						44,286	—	$168,611

Exhibit 5–8 Staffing Budget—Transporter—Radiology Department[3]

STAFFING BUDGET
CALCULATION WORKSHEET

HOSPITAL __Memorial__   DEPARTMENT __Diagnostic Radiology__   SECTION __ALL__
EMPLOYEE CLASSIFICATION __Transporter__   PERIOD FROM __Oct. 1, 19x1__ TO __Sept. 30, 19x2__

(PAGE _3_ OF _4_)

ITEM	Reporting Unit (Specify) (1)	Standard Hours Per Reporting Unit (2)	Forecast Performance Factor (3)	Adjusted Standard Hours Per Reporting Unit (4)=(2)÷(3)	Forecast Volume (5)	Forecast Hours (6)=(4)×(5)	Average Hourly Rate (7)	Salary Budget (8)=(6)×(7)
Measured Work	Exams Charged	.159	.775	.205	46,800	9,594	$2.75	$26,384
Subtotal						9,594	2.75	26,384
Unmeasured Paid Work								
On-Call—Not Worked								
On-Call—Worked						NA	NA	NA
Special Shifts (specify)								
Subtotal						NA	NA	NA
Fringe Benefits (Estimated at 8.7% of Measured Work)								
Vacation								
Holiday						835	2.75	2,296
Illness, Absence								
Others (specify)								
Subtotal						835	2.75	2,296
Total Budget Hours and Salaries						10,429	NA	$28,680

Exhibit 5-9 Staffing Budget—Secretarial/Clerical—Radiology Department[3]

STAFFING BUDGET
CALCULATION WORKSHEET

HOSPITAL __Memorial__   DEPARTMENT __Diagnostic Radiology__   SECTION __ALL__
EMPLOYEE CLASSIFICATION __Secretarial/Clerical__   PERIOD FROM __Oct. 1, 19x1__ TO __Sept. 30, 19x2__

(PAGE 4 OF 4)

ITEM	Reporting Unit (Specify) (1)	Standard Hours Per Reporting Unit (2)	Forecast Performance Factor (3)	Adjusted Standard Hours Per Reporting Unit (4)=(2)÷(3)	Forecast Volume (5)	Forecast Hours (6)=(4)×(5)	Average Hourly Rate (7)	Salary Budget (8)=(6)×(7)
Measured Work	Exams Charged	.152	.894	.170	46,800	7,956	$3.40	$27,050
	Weeks	123.1	.894	137.6	52	7,155	3.40	24,327
Subtotal						15,111	3.40	51,377
Unmeasured Paid Work								
On-Call—Not Worked								
On-Call—Worked								
Special Shifts (specify)								
Subtotal						NA	NA	NA
Fringe Benefits (Estimated at 8.7% of Measured Work)								
Vacation								
Holiday						1,315	3.40	4,471
Illness, Absence								
Others (specify)								
Subtotal						1,315	3.40	4,471
Total Budget Hours and Salaries						16,426	NA	$19,948

are merely a means of measuring actual performance against what the department managers and their supervisors desire and expect from a certain work effort or dollar expenditure.

USE OF PRODUCTION STANDARDS IN STAFFING

Production standards are usually generated for personnel, but they may be established also for specific pieces or configurations of equipment. Regardless, neither personnel nor equipment can be worked at one hundred percent capacity, nor can either be divided into pieces. However, through the use of full- and part-time employees, work hours may be adjusted to meet fractions of a full-time equivalent (FTE = 2,080 hours per year) of one employee. Using production standards as the basis for determining staffing requirements, the department managers and their supervisors must consider total work hours required as they relate to FTEs and not to number of employees.

Since employees cannot be cut into pieces, the staffing requirements must be determined in a step-variable approach, or in range of production, rather than in direct variables or through a linear approach. Each production range assumes a new and higher plateau of production. When graphically illustrated, these production ranges assume a step-like characteristic, thus the classification of a step-variable. This step-like characteristic is highlighted in Figure 5–5.

To illustrate the computation of a step-variable production standard, assume that it has been determined that a laundry worker can, on an average, process 85,000 pounds of clean laundry during an average employee's normal working year. The normal annual work hours are determined as follows:

Line 1—Normal paid hours per week		40
Line 2—Normal weeks per year		52
Line 3—Normal annual paid hours (line 1 × line 2)		2,080
Line 4—Less: Benefit hours		
a. 9 holidays × 8 hours	72	
b. 15 vacation days × 8 hours	120	
c. 12 sick days × 8 hours	96	
d. Total benefit hours		288
Line 5—Normal annual work hours		
(line 3 minus line 4d)		1,792

Figure 5–5 Weekly Labor Staffing Chart for Laundry Department

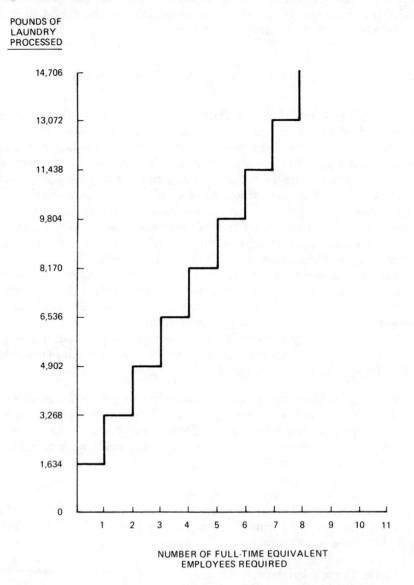

POUNDS OF
LAUNDRY
PROCESSED

NUMBER OF FULL-TIME EQUIVALENT
EMPLOYEES REQUIRED

The hourly production standard for the average laundry worker would be computed as follows:

$$\frac{\text{Total Annual Production Units per Employee}}{\text{Total Annual Normal Work Hours}} = \frac{\text{Production Standard}}{\text{per Work Hour}}$$
$$\text{per Employee}$$

Or

$$\frac{85,000 \text{ pounds}}{1,792 \text{ hours}} = 47.43 \text{ pounds per work hour}$$

To summarize, the annual and weekly standards are as follows:

Description	Annual Standards	Weekly Standards
Pounds of clean laundry processed	85,000	1,634
Number of weeks	52	1
Work hours	1,792	34.46
Benefit hours	288	5.54
Paid hours	2,080	40.00

Using the above data, the staffing requirement matrix is developed to convert work hours into paid hours and FTEs, and is illustrated in Table 5–3.

Table 5–3 Converting Work Hours into Paid Hours and FTEs

Laundry Weekly Staffing Requirement Matrix

Pounds of Laundry Processed	Work Hour Requirements	Paid Hour Requirements	Full-Time Employee Equivalent Requirements
1,634	34.46	40.00	1
3,268	68.92	80.00	2
4,902	103.38	120.00	3
6,536	137.84	160.00	4
8,170	172.30	200.00	5
9,804	206.76	240.00	6
11,438	241.22	280.00	7
13,072	275.68	320.00	8
14,706	310.14	360.00	9

In any step-variable staffing matrix, there is always a certain amount of elasticity at each staffing plateau. The key to the successful use of this staffing requirement approach is knowing the amount of elasticity at each level. It is important to know how much more or less volume a staffing level can accept before an additional employee must be added or reduced. This knowledge can only come through working experience and observations of employee stress, tension, "down time," morale, and productivity. This is the test of an effective department manager or supervisor.

REFERENCES

1. Allen G. Herkimer, Jr., *Concepts in Hospital Financial Management* (Paradise Valley, Ariz.: Alfa Associates, Inc., 1973), 2nd edition.

2. Peter Drucker, *Management Tasks, Responsibilities, Practices* (New York: Harper & Row, 1973).

3. Source for Exhibits 5–2 through 5–9:
   Allen G. Herkimer, Jr., *Developing Production Standards for Physician-Directed Hospital Departments*, an unpublished Master's Thesis, University of Bridgeport, Bridgeport, Connecticut, 1972, which used as its source the Department of Health, Education, and Welfare's Incentive Reimbursement Experiment, Contract No. 70-2520, conducted in the State of Connecticut under the direction of the Connecticut Hospital Research and Education Foundation. This experiment was cosponsored by the Department of Health, Education, and Welfare and the Connecticut Blue Cross, 1969–1972.

Chapter 6

Volume Forecasting

Volume forecasting is so vital to the success of any health care institution's financial plan, that it is frequently called the keystone step because it serves as the basis to project revenue and expenses especially variable expenses and literally ties the financial revenue and expense plans together (Figure 6–1).

Before any revenue or expense plan can be started, the statistical volume of work must be determined. This process is usually approached at two levels:

- macro
- micro

The macro level of units of service includes such measurements as number of

- inpatient days
- outpatient visits

These macro volumes are usually determined by top management, since departmental work volumes are directly related to these statistics. Once these macro statistical volumes have been determined for the entire health care facility, the department managers and their supervisors can apply their own department's volume requirements, or micro measurements, as illustrated in Tables 6–1 and 6–2. These tables illustrate the application of project annual budgets based upon patient days, patient visits, and standard rates. Traditionally, health care facilities have divided the annual financial plan into twelve equal parts, and used this as a means of allocating revenue and expenses. Obviously, this

Figure 6–1 Volume Forecasting—the Keystone to the Archway of Successful Health Care Financial Planning and Control

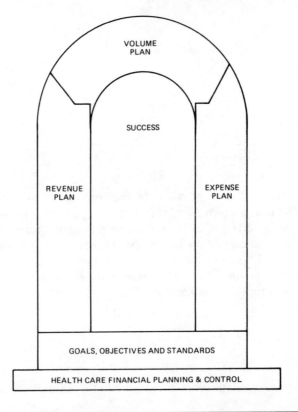

approach does not consider any seasonal or volume fluctuations which exist or may have been established by historical trends. This matter will be discussed later in this chapter.

As demonstrated in Tables 6–1 and 6–2, the only keystone statistics needed to project these two departmental financial plans are inpatient days and outpatient visits. Using these keystone macro units of service and related standard rates, the annual financial plan can be developed. These two examples help to illustrate the vital necessity for any health care financial planning and control program to be built around a realistic statistical volume forecast. The volume forecast should be neither overly optimistic nor extremely pessimistic. Since the statistical volume forecast is the keystone of the entire financial plan, it must reflect the most accurate and realistic opinions possible.

Table 6–1 Dietary Budget Projected Based upon Forecast Patient Days and Standard Rates

MEMORIAL HOSPITAL
ANYTOWN, U.S.A.

DESCRIPTION	STANDARD RATES	COMPUTATION	BUDGET
1) Inpatient Days	N.A.	N.A.	90,300
2) Patient Meals Served	3.15 patient meals served per patient day	Patient Days × Standard = Meals Served 90,300 × 3.15	284,445
3) Person-Hours Paid	1.68 patient meals served per person-hour paid	Patient Meals Served ÷ Standard = Person-Hour Paid 284,445 ÷ 1.68	169,313
4) Salary Expense	$2.85 average hour rate	Person-Hour Paid × Standard = Salary Expense 169,313 × $2.85	$482,539
5) Food Expense	$.96 per patient meals served	Patient Meals Served × Standard = Paid Expense 284,445 × $.96	$273,067
6) Other Nonsalary Expense	$.25 per patient meal served	Patient Meals Served × Standard = Other Nonsalary Expenses 284,445 × $.25	$ 71,111
7) Total Expense	$2.90 per patient meal served	Patient Meals Served × Standard = Total Expenses 284,445 × $2.90	$826,717

Table 6-2 Radiology Budget Projected Based upon Forecast Patient Days, Outpatient Visits, and Standard Rates

MEMORIAL HOSPITAL
ANYTOWN, U.S.A.

DESCRIPTION	STANDARD RATES	COMPUTATION	BUDGET
1) Inpatient Days	N.A.	N.A.	90,300
2) Outpatient Visits	N.A.	N.A.	270,000
3) X-Ray Exams - Inpatient	.75 X-ray exams per patient day	Patient Days × Standard = No. of Inpatient Exams 90,300 × .75	67,725
4) X-Ray Exams - Outpatient Visit	.50 X-ray per outpatient visit	Outpatient visits × Standard = No. of Outpatient Exams 270,000 × .50	135,000
5) Person-Hours Paid	2.12 X-ray exams per person-hour paid	Total Exams ÷ Standard = Person-Hours Paid (67,725 + 135,000) ÷ 2.12	95,625
6) Revenue Inpatient	$32.50 overcharge per inpatient exam	No. of Inpatient Exams × Standard = Revenue Inpatient 67,725 × $32.50	$2,201,062
7) Revenue Outpatient	$21.35 overcharge per outpatient exam	No. of Outpatient Exams × Standard = Revenue Outpatient 135,000 × $21.35	$2,882,250
8) Salary Expense	$4.15 average hour rate	Person-Hours Paid × Standard = Salary Expense 95,625 × $4.15	$ 396,843

Table 6-2 continued

DESCRIPTION	STANDARD RATES	COMPUTATION	BUDGET
9) Physician Fees	20% of revenue, gross	Total Revenue × 20% = Physician Fees (2,201,062 + 2,882,250) × 20%	$1,016,662
10) Other Nonsalary Expenses	$5.65 per exam	Number of Exams × Standard = Other Nonsalary Expenses (67,725 + 135,000) × $5.65	$1,145,396
11) Indirect Expenses	$10.87 per exam	Number of Exams × Standard = Indirect Expense 202,725 × $10.87	$2,203,620
12) Total Expense	$23.49 per exam	Number of Exams × Standard = Total Expense 202,725 × $23.49	$4,762,521
13) Net Profit or (Loss)	$1.58 per exam	Number of Exams × Standard = Net Profit (Loss) 202,725 × $1.58	$ 320,791

RESOURCES OF VOLUME FORECASTING

There is no magic formula that will accurately forecast the exact volume of work a department will produce during given times, nor is there any one variable, fixed statistic, or fact that will enable an individual to forecast each variable affecting a department's volume. The statistical volume forecast represents the most reasonable guesstimate the forecaster is able to develop using whatever tools and resources may be available. True, there are highly sophisticated formulas such as multiple regression analysis, exponential smoothing, and other quantitative models that require computers and computer programs to project a volume forecast. But even these models cannot forecast all the variables caused either by the human or natural elements. Perhaps the most reliable resource in volume forecasting is human intuition and just plain common sense.

The reader is encouraged to research and test various computer forecasting or simulation models, because they make excellent management tools for assisting in forecasting, but this chapter will address only the less sophisticated approaches.

The following are key resources, other than human intuition and common sense, which must be considered in the volume forecasting process:

- historical data and trends
- departmental goals and strategies
- governmental and third party decisions
- outside competition
- other known facts and rumors

Some of these resources will have a greater impact upon the final volume forecast than others. Some will only impact the short-range projection, while others will only impact the department's volume over a long-range period. But, if deemed appropriate, each component must be examined and others considered.

HISTORICAL DATA AND TRENDS

If there has been no significant change in either internal or external environment, the department's historical data and trends provide the most accurate and reliable source for starting the volume forecasting process. If the time series data were graphically illustrated, as in Figure 6–2, the reader could readily visualize a regressive trend during year 19x5.

Year	Patient Days
19x1	83,250
19x2	85,500
19x3	86,250
19x4	87,750
19x5	85,500

In forecasting year 19x6 and beyond, department managers would have to ascertain the answers to the following questions, among others, before they could identify the cause of the volume decrease:

- Were there fewer doctors?
- Did another health care facility open in the service area?
- Are the lengths of stays shorter?
- Are there fewer inpatient admissions?
- Are the patients using more outpatient services?
- Has there been a change in patient mix?
- Will this declining trend continue?
- What is the distribution of DRGs?

DEPARTMENTAL GOALS AND STRATEGIES

The department's short-range and long-range goals and strategies also play a major role in the volume forecasting process. If the manager is planning to convert some of the OR packs from washable cottons to disposable packs, then, obviously, the future year's volume of pounds of laundry processed will be reduced. The department manager will have to make appropriate adjustments to the volume forecast in order to reflect this system change. Usually, this type of system change does not come as any surprise during the management by involvement process. However, department managers and their supervisors must be tuned into the system change, because it will have an effect on their department.

Figure 6–2 Patient Days for the Five-Year Period from 19x1 through 19x5

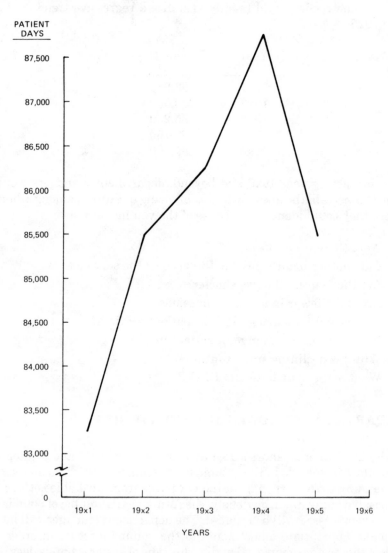

GOVERNMENTAL AND THIRD PARTY DECISIONS

The third resource to consider and examine in the volume forecasting process is the socio-economic impact of governmental and other third party purchasers, such as Blue Cross. Medicare, for example, is the result of a federal government socio-economic decision. Its related laws and regulations afforded those 65 or over the health care which many would not have received had the Act not been signed into law. Consequently, the inpatient day volume almost immediately increased; the mix of types of services changed; the method of reimbursement for service changed; new accounting and billing procedures were required; utilization review and professional standards review organizations (PSROs) were mandated; and many other systems and organizational changes were required. Just this one socio-economic decision—and its related laws and regulations—had a tremendous impact upon the 1965 volume forecasting process. National Health Insurance (NHI), if and when enacted, will have a similar impact upon the forecast.

The Social Security Amendments of 1983 (Public Law 98-21) contain provisions for the establishment of a Medicare prospective payment system (PPS) that bases payment for hospital inpatient services on preestablished rates per discharge. Under the PPS, the hospitals are no longer reimbursed for inpatient services on the basis of reasonable costs. Physicians who previously had utilized inpatient services extensively and kept their patients in the hospital longer than the "normal" length of stay were and are suddenly the "bad guys"; physicians who discharge their patients relatively promptly are the "good guys." The external environment created by the major health care purchasers usually helps to determine the internal health care delivery system the provider is going to use.

There is no question that health care is politics, and the public will get the type of health care services that the government is willing to pay for.

Finally, if any financial planning and control system is to be a meaningful management tool, the volume forecasting system must be sufficiently flexible to recognize, to cope with, and to respond to, similar types of socio-economic decisions. True, this singular impact may not be repeated frequently, but it may be amended and changed. For these changes, the department managers and their supervisors must keep themselves informed and prepared for pending changes due to socio-economic decisions from all levels of government and third party purchasers of health care services.

OUTSIDE COMPETITION

The outside competition to your health care institution and, more specifically, to your department, must be considered during the volume forecasting process. Quite possibly, there may be little or no competition for *your* department's services, but department managers and supervisors must keep an ear to the ground for rumors or plans that potential competitors may be developing, which will ultimately affect the department's volume. Outside competition may come from neighboring health care facilities such as hospitals, clinics, or independent businesses, i.e., outside laboratories or commercial laundries. The important point is that the department managers and their supervisors must continually keep abreast of potential outside competition. The short-range and long-range plans of your competitors must be known in order to relate the impact of their decisions and plans to your department's volume forecast, especially within this new, government-promoted, competitive market that is rapidly developing.

OTHER KNOWN FACTS AND RUMORS

Other known facts, such as the addition of two new doctors to the health care facility's staff, must be incorporated into the volume forecasting process. But rumors per se should not be included in the final volume forecast; rather, these tidbits of information should be documented for the next period volume review. Frequently, rumors are substantiated; but only when they are should the information be used to project the future of one's department and institution.

SHARED MANAGEMENT METHOD

In Chapter 4, the bottom-up top-down or shared management method was discussed. The volume forecasting process is an excellent application of this management style. However, we will discuss two other approaches to volume forecasting as well. They are:

- top-down
- bottom-up
- shared

The top-down approach can be best illustrated as an inverted pyramid shown in Figure 6–3. In this method, top management utilizes the above-mentioned five volume forecasting resources. Usually, these resources will be institutionally oriented, or on a macro-level basis, to the overall forecasting process. Using institutional or macro statistics

Figure 6–3 Top-Down Management Approach to Volume Forecasting

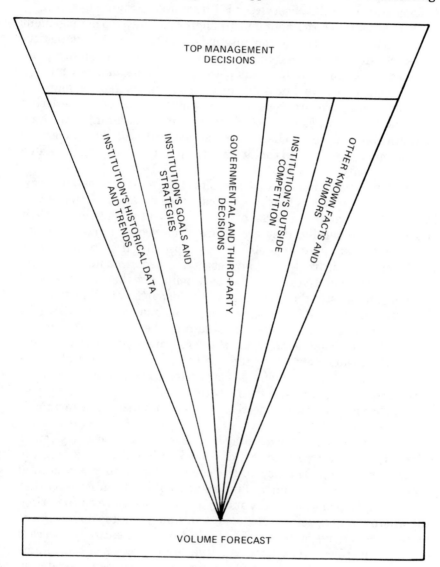

such as inpatient days and outpatient visits, they easily can be related to departmental units of services, as illustrated in Figure 6–4. There is a strong argument for this approach. Since top management is in a strategic position to control funds (and the health care institution's overall destiny), its own volume forecasting may be from a more knowledgeable and reliable standpoint than the department managers'. The one major weakness in this methodology is that top management does not necessarily have a feel for the mood of the ordering physicians; i.e., types of laboratory tests to be ordered, new pharmaceuticals being used, changes in radiological procedures, obsolete equipment, or the physical condition of the plant's facilities and related volume capacity.

The bottom-up approach is the opposite of the top-down methodology. This approach, which is best illustrated by the pyramid in Figure 6–5, starts with the volume forecast of the department managers and their supervisors. Generally, they are aware of most of top management's short-range and long-range objectives—especially if management by involvement is utilized—of their respective departments. They also have their own objectives for their departments, and these do not always coincide. Obviously, the objectives of the department managers and their supervisors must be the same as top management's or there will be not only a conflict in the strategy in obtaining these objectives, but also a doubt that the volume forecast of the department manager will assist top management in obtaining the health care facility's overall objectives. Certainly the disadvantages of the top-down method have been corrected by the bottom-up method. However, there is a strong possibility that neither set of objectives will be obtained if this method is the only one used.

The advantages and disadvantages of the above methodology can be relatively well incorporated and corrected with a *shared* approach to volume forecasting. The key to the success of this approach is total communication and exchange of information. It has been stated earlier that the department managers and their supervisors are on the firing-line where it all happens. It has also been stated that top management has the ultimate responsibility for the destiny of the entire health care facility. It is, therefore, vitally essential to the success of the volume forecasting process that the responsibility be shared, as illustrated in Figure 6–6. This hourglass illustrates how the shared method of volume forecasting utilizes the resources of the various levels of the institution's management hierarchy, and helps to share the knowledge and responsibility for a successful and reliable forecast.

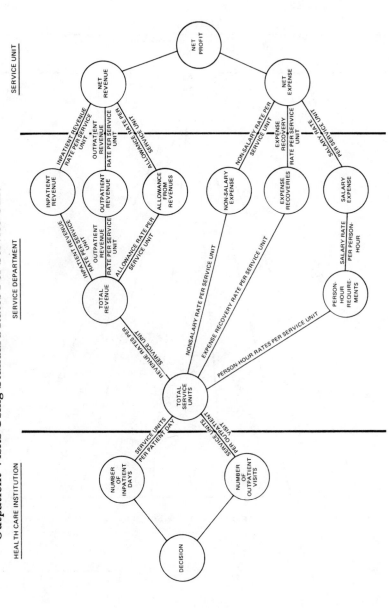

Figure 6-4 Departmental Service Unit Explosion of Statistical Volume Forecast of Inpatient Days and Outpatient Visits Using Standard Rates Per Service Unit

Figure 6–5 Bottom-Up Management Approach to Volume
Forecasting

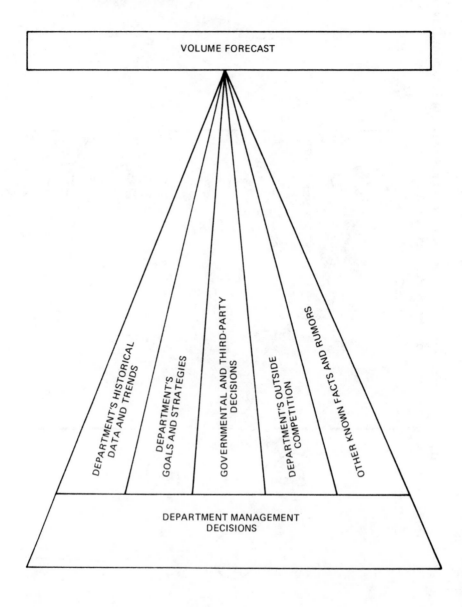

Figure 6–6 Shared Management Approach to Volume Forecasting

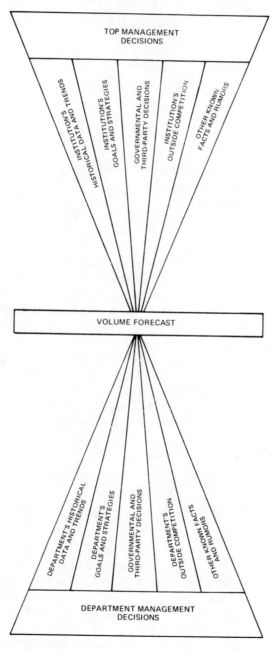

VOLUME FORECASTING METHODS

The methods currently used to forecast volume include the following categories:

- classical
- judgmental
- mathematical
- involved-combination

The *classical* forecasting method makes no effort to identify any specific direct or indirect variables which may affect the volume forecast. Rather, it utilizes only historical data, using time series charts and projecting the established trend for the ensuing years. Figure 6–2 is an example in historical data and, as plotted, a trend line would be very difficult to project because of the regressive trend during the last year 19x5. This fact points up one of the main weaknesses in this method: It does not consider known facts or variables which might have a tremendous influence upon the actual outcome for the ensuing years.

Judgmental forecasting requires the forecaster to use his knowledge and intuition to establish his volume forecast. Much of this subjective approach depends upon the experience, known facts, guessing skills, and logic of the forecaster. As crude as this approach may sound, the ingredients have been very helpful supplements to more conventional approaches to volume forecasting.

The *mathematical* forecasting method relies entirely upon historical data and mathematical formulas which consider such volume characteristics as:

- seasonal variations
- cyclical trends
- noncontrollable variables
- other known facts

Since this method of volume forecasting is based on mathematical formulas, there is little or no provision for judgmental or intuitional variables. Later in this chapter some of these approaches will be discussed in more detail. Most, but not all of these approaches require a computer to evaluate the vast number of equations which are necessary to arrive at the volume forecast. Since this method requires a considerable amount of historical data, the department manager must prepare the data collection process well in advance of the application of this method.

The *involved-combination* method of volume forecasting utilizes all three of the above approaches. The forecasters who use this approach recognize that there is no one approach to statistical volume forecasting. Consequently, they use all the forecasting tools available, taking their own skills, knowledge, and intuition and supplementing them with historical data and mathematical formulas. During this process, they will involve their peers and subordinates to test the overall logic and reasonableness of the forecast. This approach utilizes people's knowledge and skills, and makes them (the people) a part of the decision-making and planning process. The main weakness in this approach is that initially it requires much more time to finalize the forecast. However, the time required will shorten as the team members prepare themselves for the deliberations. This approach makes the volume forecast a shared product; therefore it has more support and credibility than forecasts generated using a more unilateral approach.

LEAST SQUARES METHOD

One of the most common mathematical formulas used to identify trend lines and to develop volume forecasts is the least squares, or the simple regression, method. This approach assumes that if a straight line is fitted to either graphic or time series data, it will serve as a reasonable trend line to project subsequent years' volume. The least squares method is a relatively simple mathematical formula, yet furnishes a reasonably accurate method of fitting a trend line to historical data to project the future, at least on a short-run basis.

Riggleman and Frisbee state that the method of least squares is a mathematical device which places a line through a series of plotted points in such a way that the sum of the squares of the deviations of the actual points above and below the trend line is at a minimum. This is as near as conveniently possible to get to a line of the least deviations, and is therefore accepted as the *"line of best fits."*[1] The least squares formula is shown in Table 6–3.

Figure 6–7 graphically plots the actual patient days with a solid line and displays the least squares trend line with a dotted line. Note that the trend line has been extended to year 19x7. The accuracy of the forecast tends to diminish as the projection extends from the middle year. Figure 6–7 is an illustration of a least squares fit on a regressive or

Table 6–3 Least Squares Formula

let: x = time deviation of each year from middle year
Y = number of historical volume (e.g., patient days)

The following time series data:

Year	Patient Days
19x1	83,250
19x2	85,500
19x3	86,250
19x4	87,750
19x5	88,000

have been scheduled on the worksheet below:

Year	Actual Patient Days	Time Deviation of Each Year from Middle Year	Square of x Deviation		Trend Ordinates
X	Y	x	x^2	xY	
19x1	83,250	-2	4	$-166,500$	83,800
19x2	85,500	-1	1	$-85,500$	84,975
19x3	86,250	0	0	0	86,150
19x4	87,750	$+1$	1	$+87,750$	87,325
19x5	88,000	$+2$	4	176,000	88,500
Total	430,750	0	10	$+11,750$	
Average	86,150				

$$\Sigma\, xY \div \Sigma\, x^2$$

Sum of xY divided by sum of x^2

Let: xY = $+11,750$

$x^2 = 10$

OR

$$\frac{+11,750}{10} = +1,175 \text{ annual increment}$$

In this illustration, the mid-point year, 19x3, equals 0 with the average value of 86,150 and annual increments of $(+)1,175$. To determine the trend ordinates, use the following formulas:

Table 6–3 continued

(1) YEAR	(2) MIDPOINT	(3) ± INCREMENT		(4) FORECAST
19x1	86,150 +	$(1,175\,x - 2)$	=	83,800
19x2	86,150 +	$(1,175\,x - 1)$	=	84,975
19x3	86,150 +	0	=	86,150
19x4	86,150 +	$(1,175\,x + 1)$	=	87,325
19x5	86,150 +	$(1,175\,x + 2)$	=	88,500
19x6	86,150 +	$(1,175\,x + 3)$	=	89,675
19x7	86,150 +	$(1,175\,x + 4)$	=	90,850

Figure 6–7 Fitting a Trend Line to a Regressive Trend Using the Least Squares Method

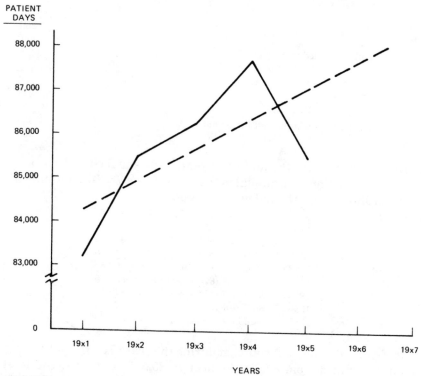

Actual ____
Trend ------

declining trend. Figure 6–8 is a graphic illustration of a least squares fit to a progressive or advancing trend, using the following data:

Year	Actual Patient Days	Time Deviation of Each Year from Middle Year	Squares of x Deviation		Trend Ordinates
X	Y	x	x^2	xY	
19x1	83,250	-2	4	-166,500	84,300
19x2	85,500	-1	1	-85,500	84,975
19x3	86,250	0	0	0	85,650
19x4	87,750	+1	1	+87,750	86,325
19x5	85,500	+2	4	+171,000	87,000
Total	428,250	0	10	+6,750	

Average 85,650

$$\Sigma\, xY \div \Sigma\, x^2$$

Sum of xY divided by sum of x^2

Let: xY = +6,750
     x^2 = 10

Or: $\dfrac{+6,750}{10}$ = +675 Annual Increment

In this illustration, the mid-point year, 19x3, equals 0 with the average value of 85,650 with annual increments of (+)675. To determine the trend ordinates, use the following formulas:

Year			
19x1	85,650 + (675 x -2)	=	84,300
19x2	85,650 + (675 x -1)	=	84,975
19x3	85,650 + (0)	=	85,650
19x4	85,650 + (675 x +1)	=	86,325
19x5	85,650 + (675 x +2)	=	87,000
19x6	85,650 + (675 x +3)	=	87,675
19x7	85,650 + (675 x +4)	=	88,350

In Figure 6–7, you will note that during the year 19x5, the patient day volume declined from 87,750 in 19x4 to 85,500. However, the least squares trend line does forecast a moderate annual increment of 675, as compared to 1,175 in Figure 6–8. Obviously, the least squares method is merely projecting trend lines based entirely upon historical data. This

Figure 6–8 Fitting a Trend Line to a Progressive Trend Using the
Least Squares Method

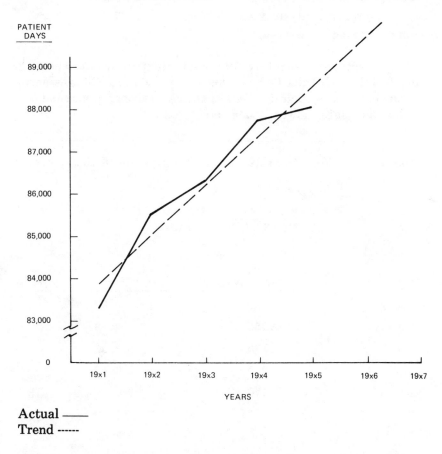

Actual ——
Trend ------

means that there has been no consideration given to other facts and variables, such as a possible decrease in number of admitting doctors, new competition, doctors' vacations, or changes in admitting and discharge procedures. This apparent weakness requires the forecasters to supplement the least squares forecast with their own and their staffs' judgmental values.

Once the annual volume forecast has been completed, there must be a method to distribute the annual total to reflect monthly variations and seasonal trends. There are a number of volume distribution approaches to use, such as:

- one-year monthly average
- two-year monthly average
- three-year monthly average
- moving monthly average

The percentages of monthly volume distribution are illustrated in Table 6–4 through Table 6–6. Whichever method is used, it is essential that the base years accurately reflect the general operations condition which will exist in the years to be forecasted.

Table 6–4 One-Year Monthly Volume Distribution Method for Year 19x5

MEMORIAL HOSPITAL
ANYTOWN, U.S.A.

MONTH	PATIENT DAYS	DISTRIBUTION PERCENTAGE
January	7,550	8.83
February	6,750	7.88
March	7,125	8.33
April	7,250	8.48
May	7,150	8.36
June	6,750	7.89
July	6,500	7.66
August	6,825	7.98
September	7,250	8.48
October	7,750	9.06
November	7,550	8.83
December	7,000	8.20
TOTAL	85,500	100.00
AVERAGE	7,125	

Table 6–5 Two-Year Monthly Average Volume Distribution for
Years 19x4 and 19x5

MEMORIAL HOSPITAL
ANYTOWN, U.S.A.

Patient Days

MONTH	19x4	19x5	Total	Percentage Distribution
January	7,750	7,750	15,300	8.83
February	6,950	6,750	13,700	7.91
March	7,250	7,125	14,375	8.30
April	7,500	7,250	14,750	8.51
May	7,250	7,150	14,400	8.31
June	6,800	6,750	13,550	7.82
July	6,375	6,550	12,925	7.47
August	7,000	6,825	13,825	7.98
September	7,500	7,250	14,750	8.51
October	8,125	7,750	15,875	9.16
November	7,750	7,550	15,300	8.83
December	7,500	7,000	14,500	8.37
Total	87,750	85,500	173,250	100.00
Average	7,312	7,125	7,219	

The moving monthly average approach is a method frequently used. This approach uses either a two- or three-year monthly average distribution method and adds the most recent year's data while deleting the oldest year's data such as:

	First Year		Second Year		Third Year	
	Actual	Average	Actual	Average	Actual	Average
19x1	83,250		-0-		-0-	
19x2	85,500		85,500		-0-	
19x3	86,250	85,000	86,250		86,250	
19x4			87,750	86,500	87,750	
19x5					85,500	86,500

In all probability, the moving monthly average approach more accurately reflects the volume distribution, as long as there has been no major operational change. The combination of least squares to determine the annual volume, and the moving monthly average distribution methods provides department managers and their supervisors with a

Table 6–6　Three-Year Monthly Average Volume Distribution for Years 19x3, 19x4, and 19x5

MEMORIAL HOSPITAL
ANYTOWN, U.S.A.

Patient Days

MONTH	19x3	19x4	19x5	Total	Percentage Distribution
January	7,590	7,750	7,550	22,890	8.82
February	6,750	6,950	6,750	20,450	7.88
March	7,150	7,250	7,125	21,525	8.29
April	7,350	7,500	7,250	22,100	8.52
May	7,150	7,250	7,150	21,550	8.30
June	7,450	6,800	6,750	21,000	8.09
July	5,860	6,375	6,550	18,785	7.24
August	6,900	7,000	6,825	20,725	7.99
September	7,250	7,500	7,250	22,000	8.48
October	7,950	8,125	7,750	23,825	9.18
November	7,500	7,750	7,550	22,800	8.79
December	7,350	7,500	7,000	21,850	8.42
Total	86,250	87,750	85,500	259,500	100.00
Average	7,188	7,312	7,125	7,208	

relatively simple, yet reasonably reliable, method of manually forecasting volumes. By applying standard utilization volumes, such as laundry pounds per patient day, nursing hours per patient day, x-ray exams per emergency room case, and laboratory tests per clinic visits, the micro statistical volumes can be projected for each department.

MULTIPLE REGRESSION ANALYSIS

One of the basic limitations of the simple least squares method is that it can utilize only one variable. A more sophisticated, comprehensive, and usually a more accurate method of statistical volume forecasting is the multiple regression analysis method. This approach allows the use of many or multiple variables which may or may not have some impact upon future volumes. For example, if the forecaster were to project patient days, he could input such time series data as:

- number of physicians on staff
- number of admissions per physician
- age of each physician
- number of patient days per physician
- population trend in service area
- unemployment rate in service area
- number of Medicare patients
- number of Medicare patient days
- number of other patients and patient days by insurance or noninsurance coverage
- share of service area health care market
- number of flu days
- air pollution trends
- patient by age, sex, etc.
- number of new doctors in service area
- number of snow, flood, or natural disaster days
- number of births per 1,000 population in service area
- new health care services expected in service area
- number and types of industrial accidents

These data, and many more variables, could have some relevance to the patient day forecast. Obviously, some data will have a greater impact than others. For example, the number of staff doctors might have a 99.25 percentage whereas the number of flu days may have only a 65.26 percentage relation factor. The fact is, multiple regression offers the department managers and their forecasting teams one of the most sophisticated management tools of forecasting. However, since the mathematical details of this complex procedure are beyond the scope of this book, the department managers and their supervisors are encouraged to investigate this approach with the health care facility's data processing manager or sales representative. There are a number of multiple regression programs available at most computer centers, making it relatively easy to utilize this volume management tool.

In summary, a successful health care financial management planning and control program depends upon the reasonableness and accuracy of the statistical volume forecast—the keystone of a successful plan. There is no one method (approach) to volume forecasting. The tools the department managers and their supervisors need are varied and include historical data, mathematical formulas, known future facts, and, most importantly, just plain good common sense and a skilled, knowledgeable individual's intuition.

REFERENCE

1. John R. Rigglemann and Ira N. Frisbee, *Business Statistics* (New York: McGraw-Hill Book Co., Inc., 1938), pp. 297–298.

Chapter 7

Budgetary Control Process

The budgetary control process is defined as a system that guides and assists all levels of the health care facility's management hierarchy in achieving its established financial and statistical goals, objectives, and performance standards. An effectively installed budgetary control process helps to assure management that it is on the planned course of action and that it is realizing the results from operations for which it had planned or budgeted.

The budgetary control process, management accounting in particular, assists in indicating to management where it is headed, as opposed to generally accepted accounting procedures and financial statements which serve as historical recordkeeping systems that tell management where it has been.

There are many methods of executing the budgetary control process. David F. Linowes tells us that the underlying problem, in his judgment, is the approach to the budgeting process. Linowes states,

> The present system of budgetary control ties next year's expenditures into how much was spent last year and then looks for the same kind of documentation for that year's expenditures as was established last year. Through this method, meaningless bases once adopted are used year-in and year-out to justify increased spending.[1]

Linowes concludes that this archaic tradition dominates our budgetary process, with little, if any, attention paid to whether the job is being done.

To assist the health care department managers and their supervisors in providing sufficient high quality patient care to the health care

143

facility's service area in an efficient, cost-effective manner, a plan of action and control is vital. The budgetary control process furnishes all management levels with just this sort of action plan and control. The basic plan, expressed in quantitative terms, is called a budget.

DEFINITIONS OF A BUDGET

An effective budget is the systematic documentation of one or more carefully developed plans for all individually supervised activities, programs, or sections. These individually supervised cost centers are frequently referred to as responsibility budgeting, which will be discussed later in this chapter. The plans of these responsibility centers are coordinated into a departmental budget, which is further consolidated with the health care facility's remaining departments into a master budget for the entire institution.

The budget is a tool that can aid decision makers in evaluating operating performance and projecting what future operations might produce. To be an effective instrument of planning, a budget must contain adequate, reasonable, attainable, and reliable information inputs on which appropriate decisions can be made. It should be emphasized that budgeting by itself is not a management tool but becomes this only through management use and action.

RESPONSIBILITY VS. FUNCTIONAL BUDGETING

Basically, there are two major budgetary systems. First, the responsibility budgeting approach focuses on one specific individual who is responsible for one specific cost center. Second, the functional budgeting approach focuses upon a specific function, i.e., housekeeping, nursing, and admitting, regardless of who is responsible for the supervision of the function.

Each of these two approaches has a specific purpose. First, responsibility budgeting gives responsible individuals information which relates specifically to their areas of responsibility. The hypothesis is that each manager should be held accountable for a specific responsibility center. The responsibility budgets should assist them so they can more effectively manage their responsibility centers. The responsibility budgetary system ties directly into a department's organization chart and its delegation of responsibility.

The primary purpose of the functional budgeting approach is to develop a system which can be used to compare one like department of one health care facility to another like department, i.e., Housekeeping, of another facility—outside surveillance. The purpose of this comparison capability is to enable the analyst to compare the revenue, cost, and production performance of one department to another. It assumes that the general accounting procedures are identical and that they are administered in like manners. If correctly administered, the functional budgeting approach could serve as a basis for comparing revenues, costs, and production, whereas the responsibility budgeting method does not lend itself to such comparison.

In short, if internal cost and production control is management's primary objective, then the responsibility budgeting approach should be used. If comparison to other departments is management's goal, then functional budgeting should be installed. Throughout this book references to budgeting or the budgetary control process refer only to responsibility budgeting. The term functional budgeting was presented only to acquaint the reader with the process. It is not advocated if one wants to *control* health care costs, especially from an internal management standpoint.

OBJECTIVES OF THE BUDGETARY CONTROL PROCESS

The basic objectives of the budgetary control process are to:

- provide a financial and statistical expression of the policies and plans of the department
- identify the allocation of resources, i.e., people, equipment, and finances, required
- provide a basis for measurement and evaluation of a department's actual performance to a plan
- provide periodic reports which serve as useful tools for the effective management of a department's resources, operations, and its profitability
- create cost awareness throughout the department
- assist management in program and rate or price evaluation, and determination

The budgetary control process tends to create a way of thinking which helps to develop:

- responsibility
- incentive
- leadership

- discipline
- cooperation

However, the following are some limitations of the budgetary control process:

- it does not work by itself
- it must have management's total support
- it needs constant review and attention
- it requires production standards

MANAGEMENT DEVELOPMENT

To be totally effective, all levels of the department's managers must actively participate in the budgetary control process. An effective program not only assists in management development and aids in stabilizing the financial and productivity position of the department, but also it brings into focus many fringe benefits—cooperation, mutual understanding, and the sharing of the decision-making process. This coordinating effort will enable the department to meet the constant demands for improved patient care through dynamic, imaginative, and concerned management.

ROLE OF DEPARTMENT MANAGER

The role of the department manager in the budgetary control process is clearly the most critical in a total health care facility's master budget plan. Accordingly, the supervisor's role is equally critical in a department's budgeting and goal-setting process. In each case, these individuals serve as the link between management plans and work force accomplishments. If either fails to understand or is not motivated, the budget plans will not filter down to the individual worker, and substandard performance may result.

There can be no credibility gap between top administration and the department managers, between the department managers and their supervisors, or between supervisors and the individual workers. Each management level must be totally committed to this program. This commitment will help to build confidence, faith, and trust in the program and consequently, motivate each sublevel team member.

The department managers and their supervisors must be able to recognize two classifications which can be applied to employees. Most employees approach their jobs from one of two viewpoints:

- goal oriented
- task oriented

When the department managers and their supervisors recognize these characteristics, they will be most effective in achieving the budgetary goals from the humantology level.[2] If department managers and supervisors can recognize which way each worker is inclined, they will be better equipped to set and obtain realistic goals.

Task oriented individuals just want to do their jobs and have little interest in overall results.

Goal oriented individuals do not like close supervision while they are working, but they are interested in finding out results. They are eager to accept challenges, want definite goals, and feel a need to reach these objectives with an above-average performance.[3]

More and more department managers and supervisors are recognizing their roles as leaders—managers—and not necessarily as skilled technicians. In a survey of health care department managers, the American Hospital Association's Hospital Research and Education Trust found that human relations ranked third overall in the general subjects considered as educational correspondence courses.[4] This interest in learning about the humantology of budgeting, of management, and general aspects of health care operations is a good indication that department managers and supervisors do want to, and need to, expand their knowledge.

TYPES OF BUDGETS

There are many approaches used in the budgetary control process. Before determining the type of budget approach to use, management must first identify:

- the overall objective of the budgetary control program
- how much time, personnel, equipment, and money is to be invested in the program
- the amount of accuracy and relevancy desired

The ranges of budgetary sophistication differ greatly. Accordingly, preparation and maintenance costs have a wide range. Frequently, a relatively simple budgetary approach is used to start the program and through use, constant review, and revision, a sophistication level is reached to fit the users' needs. However, it is probable that the budgetary control program will produce greater cost savings with a variable or flexible budget than with a fixed or static budget. In the end, the most important element in the budgetary control process is the effectiveness and the manner in which the budget is used, rather than the type of budget used. The budget is a management tool to be used frequently, and not a book to be placed on a shelf to collect dust.

The following are some types of budgets which are used in varying degrees in the health care industry (Figure 7–1).

Fixed or Target Budget

Currently, the fixed or target budget is probably the most common budgetary approach. This budget is based upon a fixed annual level of volume activity, i.e., number of patient days, tests performed, and pounds of laundry processed, to arrive at an annual budget total. Frequently, these totals are then divided into twelve equal parts for each month of the year. The primary weakness in this approach is that it does not allow for seasonal or monthly variations. To illustrate, assume a nursing station has 36 beds and the nursing supervisor and head nurse anticipate a 75 percent patient occupancy and a staffing requirement of 4.2 nursing hours per patient day. The nursing salary budget would be developed as follows:

- total capacity 36
- projected percent of occupancy .... 75 percent
- projected average daily census 27
- projected calendar days 365
- projected annual patient days 9,855
- average nursing hours per patient day 4.2
- annual nursing hours requirement 41,391
- average hourly rate $7.50
- annual nursing costs $310,433
- average monthly patient day census 822
- average monthly nursing hours requirement 3,449
- average monthly nursing costs $25,869

However, this approach is usually used to prepare a department's initial budget. This is especially true when there are relatively few

Figure 7–1 Budget Classification Tree

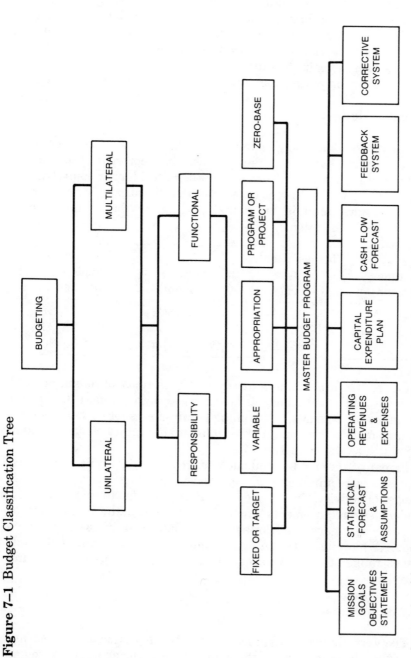

Source: Adapted from *Patient Account Management* by A.G. Herkimer, Jr., p. 126, Aspen Publishers, Inc., © 1983.

historical data upon which to project seasonal volume variations. Obviously, this is the simplest budget to prepare, but most managers feel it is too difficult to compare, evaluate, and relate to the department's actual performance since the fixed budget does not allow for volume variations in the initial plan. The target budget also serves as the basis for computing standard variable rates, as described below.

Flexible Budget

The flexible budgeting approach establishes relevant ranges of volume activity. A relevant range of activity represents the range of volume or production units from a low point to a higher point. Expanding upon the above illustration, assume that the nursing supervisor and the head nurse establish the following variations for patient census or occupancy level options:

Volume Options	Total Patient Pay Capacity	Volume Percent	Range of Activity Patient Days
1	36	60%–75%	22–27
2	36	76%–89%	28–32
3	36	90% & over	33–36

Figure 7–2 further illustrates this relevant range of volume activity. Revenue and expense budgets are then prepared to reflect the average revenue and expenses, i.e., staffing requirements for each of the three volume options. The monthly flexible nursing salary budget would be computed as shown in Table 7–1.

In reality, three individual budgets are prepared to reflect the hourly and salary requirements for the various volume levels or relevant ranges of activity. These ranges of activity will facilitate the fitting of budget level requirements to actual performance of the nursing station.

The two primary disadvantages of this budgeting approach are that it requires more preparation and maintenance time and that it establishes range of activity rather than pinpointing the actual volume activity.

Variable Budget

The variable budget approach allows the department manager and his supervisors to pinpoint the budget plan to the actual performance

Figure 7–2 Relevant Range of Patient Day Activity Options

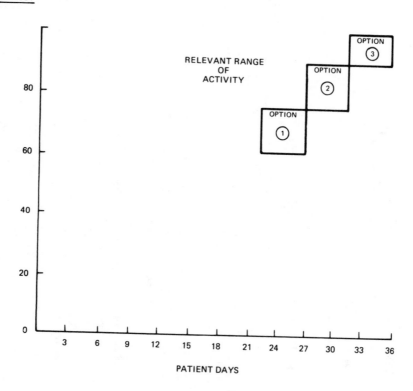

volume. In practice, the variable expense budget approach establishes a formula to enable the generation of a control budget that is directly related to volume activity. It is computed by using predetermined standards or budgeted rates and multiplying these rates by the actual volume. This eliminates variances that might occur due to volume differences.

To develop a variable expense budget, each cost item must be classified into one of three categories:

1. Fixed Costs—those which remain essentially constant in the short run, irrespective of changes in output volume.

Table 7–1 Computation of Monthly Flexible Nursing Salary Budget

MEMORIAL HOSPITAL
ANYTOWN, U.S.A.

COMPUTATION OF MONTHLY FLEXIBLE NURSING SALARY BUDGET

VOLUME OPTION	PERCENT OCCUPANCY	AVERAGE ANNUAL PATIENT DAYS	NURSING HOURS PER PATIENT DAY	AVG. ANNUAL NURSING HRS. REQUIREMENT	AVG. HOURLY RATE	AVERAGE ANNUAL NURSING SALARY BUDGET	AVERAGE FLEXIBLE NURSING BUDGET		
							PATIENT DAYS	NURSING HOURS	NURSING COSTS
1	60%–75%	8,943	4.2	37,560	$7.50	$281,700	745	3,130	$23,475
2	76%–89%	10,950	4.2	45,990	$7.50	$344,925	913	3,833	$28,744
3	90%–over	12,593	4.2	52,890	$7.50	$396,675	1,049	4,408	$33,056

Source: California Hospital Association/Hospital Financial Management Association Budgeting Manual, Sacramento, Calif., 1974.

2. Variable Costs—those that vary directly (in proportion) with changes in output volume.

3. Semi- or Step-Variable—those that are neither fixed nor variable (optional).[5]

To illustrate and to expand upon the above data, assume that the 4.2 nursing hours are divided into the following classifications:

Position	Hourly Standard	Hourly Rate
Head Nurse	0.2	$12.00
Registered Nurse	1.0	9.00
Licensed Practical Nurse	2.0	6.50
Nurse Aide	.5	6.50
Ward Clerk	.5	6.70
Total hours and average wage	4.2	$ 7.50

Using 173.3 paid hours per month, assume that the head nurse, one registered nurse, one licensed practical nurse, and the ward clerk have been classified as fixed costs and the remaining personnel are considered as variable costs as follows:

	Salary Costs	
	Fixed	Variable Standard Rate
Position		(Per Patient Day)
Head Nurse ($12.00 × 173.3 hrs.)	$2,080	
Registered Nurse ($9.00 × 173.3 hrs.)	1,560	
Licensed Practical Nurse ($6.50 × 173.3 hrs.)	1,127	
Ward Clerk ($6.70 × 173.3 hrs.)	1,161	
Total monthly fixed costs	$5,928	
VARIABLE COSTS		
Licensed Practical Nurse		1 hour @ $6.50 = $6.50
Nurse Aide		½ hour @ $6.50 = $3.25
Total variable cost per patient day		$9.75

Assume the actual patient days (P/D) for the month were 950. Applying the above standard variable costs, the month's variable control budget would be compared to the actual performance as follows:

Description	Control Budget	Actual	Variance
Patient Days	950	950	0
FIXED COSTS			
Head Nurse	$ 2,080	$ 2,080	0
Registered Nurse	1,560	1,560	0
Licensed Practical Nurse	1,127	1,369	[242]*
Ward Clerk	1,161	919	242
Total fixed costs	$ 5,928	$ 5,928	$ 0
VARIABLE COSTS			
Licensed Practical Nurse			
($6.50 × 950 P/D) =	$ 6,175	$ 6,276	$[101]
Nurse Aide			
($3.25 × 950 P/D) =	3,088	2,969	119
Total variable costs	$ 9,263	$ 9,245	$ 18
Total nursing salary costs	$15,191	$15,173	$ 18

*[ ] Brackets denote "unfavorable" variance.

The variable budget approach is occasionally referred to as dynamic cost control.[6] It is effective in departments where it is difficult to budget work load volume, such as nursing, laboratory, radiology, emergency service, medical records, and patient accounts, but is less effective in departments that have relatively fixed or routine output volume requirements such as housekeeping, and plant operations.

In summary, the variable budget can be a very effective management tool when used with discretion, but it requires a considerable amount of preparation, maintenance time, and cost.

Appropriations Budget

The appropriations budget approach is most commonly used by governments and municipalities. Usually, the amount of expenditures is fixed by some external body through appropriations of funds after review of an expense estimate on an almost line-by-line basis. After approval by the external body, the budget is not subject to implementation by the facility without a cumbersome and sometimes fruitless process of appending to the approving body on a line-by-line item-by-item appeal.

The appropriations budget is an archaic method of budgeting. It serves its purpose of estimating how much funding may be required to run an agency, and the basis from which the agency can calculate the tax rate required to generate sufficient funds to support the budget.

However, even though the appropriations budget is very rigid, it is an ineffective management tool for controlling costs because it tends to encourage spending to the appropriation limit in order to assure at least the same amount of funds for the subsequent year. The appropriations budget is not recommended.

Rolling or Moving Budget

The rolling or moving budget concept is basically an expansion upon any of the above-mentioned budgeting approaches. Under this method, the most recent month or quarter is deleted and a new projection is added for a corresponding month or quarter, so that the budget continually projects a fixed period of time, usually a minimum of a year.

The rolling or moving budget approach is especially effective in a department or facility which is exceptionally dynamic as far as costs and volume changes are concerned. Also, this concept ties very nicely into the belief that the budget is a management tool and must be continually monitored and updated.

This concept should be considered for eventual use in the budgetary control process in most departments and health care facilities.

Program or Project Budget

The meaning of program budget, sometimes referred to as project budget, has not become standardized through general use. To some it suggests no more than a restructuring of budget exhibits by accumulating costs in more meaningful categories.[7]

In many respects, the history of program budgeting started with President Lyndon Johnson's news conference of August 25, 1965, when he stated that cabinet members and heads of federal agencies were requested to "immediately begin to introduce a very new and very revolutionary system of planning and programming the budgeting throughout the vast Federal Government."[8] I will not comment on the effectiveness of the federal budgetary control system, since so frequently the budgetary approach used does not determine the effectiveness of a program. Rather, it is the people that are responsible for making the system work.

The program budget approach can be very effectively used in the health care industry. This is especially true when a department manager is interested in projecting estimated revenue and expense of a specific new program, such as a body scanner, a mental health program, or a new patient billing system, i.e., Patient Service Representative

System. The program budget is usually developed separately from the conventional budgetary process, and simply serves to supplement the overall department budget. Frequently, the time period for a program budget is over the anticipated life of a program or piece of equipment. The program budget concept is a very effective management tool to determine the cost/benefit of a specific project or program, but the concept should never be considered as the replacement of the responsibility budgetary control system.

Zero-Base Budgeting

Zero-base budgeting is a relatively recent innovation in the budgetary control process. It was first implemented by Texas Instruments, Inc., and most recently has been popularized by President Jimmy Carter, who, as governor, used it in the state of Georgia and planned to implement the process in the federal government.

The zero-base budgeting approach began on the premise that no department or program is forever, unless the unit can justify its existence. There are two basic steps required in the concept:

- development of decision packages
- ranking of decision packages

A decision package identifies the project, program, department, or unit and includes goals, objectives, revenue, expenses, and benefits to the overall organization.

Once decision packages are developed and ranked, management can allocate resources accordingly—funding the most important activities or decision packages, whether they are current or new. The final budget is produced by taking packages that are approved for funding, sorting them into their appropriate budget units, and adding the costs identified on each package to produce the budget for each unit or department.[9]

COMPONENTS OF A BUDGETARY CONTROL PROGRAM

Once the volume or statistical forecast and statement of purpose have been completed, the budgetary control program consists of three major budgets:

1. operating budget
2. cash flow forecast
3. capital expenditure plan

This program, as illustrated in Figure 7–3, is frequently supplemented with a projected balance sheet and statement of changes in financial position. The budget is concerned primarily with operational revenues and expenses, while the statements relate to the facility's assets, liabilities, and net worth.

Operating Budget

The term operating budget is used to designate the sum of three separate parts of the overall budgetary plan:

- estimates of the volume and mix of activities expressed in terms of statistical measures and other production units
- estimates of salary and nonsalary expenses
- estimates of patient and other revenues

Figure 7–3 Budgetary Control Process

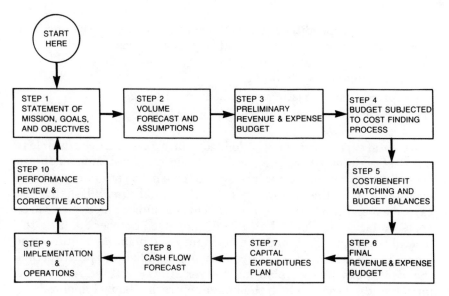

Frequently, the operating budget is synonymously referred to as the "revenue and expense budget."

Cash Flow Forecast

The cash flow forecast is an estimate of future cash receipts, disbursements, and other cash requirements, i.e., short- or long-term loans, and estimated ending balances for appropriate time intervals, usually on a month-end basis. The total cash flow forecast period should cover, at the minimum, the same period of the operating budget. Preferably, it should include the capital expenditures budgetary requirement and relate to the department or institution's long-range plan in order to provide adequate funding and to test its fiscal responsibility and/or profitability.

Since the cash flow is critical to any operation, the cash budget provides an excellent application of the rolling or moving budget approaches. In this application, cash is usually projected on a monthly basis for twelve months and then on a quarterly basis for the next two years and beyond the third year. The cash flow is projected on an annual basis over the desired period of time, i.e., two or three years. (See Tables 7–2, 7–3 and 7–4.)

Capital Expenditures Plan

The capital expenditures plan consists of estimates of the purchase and/or the carrying costs for capital acquisition, such as:

- new equipment or buildings
- replacement of existing equipment or buildings
- improvement of existing equipment or buildings

A capital expenditure may be defined as an expenditure chargeable to an asset account where the asset acquired has an estimated life in excess of one year and is not intended for sale in the ordinary course of operations. It is the opposite of revenue expenditure.[10] Usually, the capital expenditure budget is projected over a minimum period of three years. In fact, with Public Law 92-603, approved October 30, 1972, the federal government set forth the budgetary and planning requirement for all health care facilities as a condition in the Medicare program that the capital expenditure plan must cover *at least* a three-year period including the year to which the annual operating budget applies.[11]

Table 7-2 Memorial Hospital: Projected Statement of Operations

Memorial Hospital
Projected Statement of Operations
(Purchase Price $3,000,000; Downpayment Investment $500,000)

	1st Quarter (A)	2nd Quarter	3rd Quarter	4th Quarter	Total First Year	Second Year
Volume						
Total Bed Capacity	52	52	52	52	52	52
Total Calendar Days	92	92	90	91	365	365
Total Patient Day Capacity	4784	4784	4680	4732	18980	18980
Patient Days	2760	3220	3600	4095	13675	16425
% of Patient Day Capacity	58%	67%	77%	87%	72%	87%
Average Days Length of Stay	17	17	17	17	17	17
Admissions	162	189	212	241	804	966
Average Daily Census	30	35	40	45	37.5	45
Revenue						
Gross Patient Charges						
Routine Service @ $180.00 PPD	$496800	$579600	$648000	$737100	$2461500	$2956500
Ancillary Services @ $9.60 PPD	26496	30912	34560	39312	131280	157680
Total Gross Patient Charges	$523296	$610512	$682560	$776412	$2592780	$3114180
Less Deduction & Allowance @ 20% (B)	104659	122102	136512	155282	518555	622836
Net Patient Revenue	$418637	$448410	$546048	$621130	$2074225	$2491344
Expenses						
Operating Expenses (See Page 2 for Details)	$367459	$381995	$392623	$429777	$1571854	$1722636
Interest Expense-Mortgage (C)	62500	62500	62500	62500	250000	243000
Interest Expense-Working Capital (D)	7500	7500	8750	8750	32500	30000
Depreciation	15375	15375	15375	15375	61500	71500
Management Fees (F)	41864	48840	54605	62113	207422	249134
Total Expenses	$494698	$516210	$533853	$578515	$2123276	$2316270
Net Operating Margin	($ 76061)	($ 27800)	$ 12195	($ 42615)	($ 49051)	$ 175074
Return on Investment					(9.8%)	35.0%

(A) July, August and September.
(B) 30% Revenue from Medicare @ 45% Allowance & 10% Bad Debts on Other = Weighted Average – 20%.
(C) $2,500,000 @ 10%.
(D) $350,000 @ 10%.

(E) Depreciation:

Building	$1,500,000 @ 3.3%	=	$49500
Equipment	100,000 @ 12%	=	$12000
Land	100,000 NONE		NA
Goodwill	800,000 NONE		NA
Total	$2,500,000		$61500

(F) 8% of Gross Charges.

Table 7–3 Projected Statement of Operating, Administrative, and General Expenses

Memorial Hospital

	1st Quarter	2nd Quarter	3rd Quarter	4th Quarter	Total First Year	Second Year
Operating Expenses						
Nursing	$ 87000	$102000	$112000	$132000	$ 433000	$ 528000
Professional Services						
Medical Director & Program Director	15000	15000	15000	15000	60000	60000
Psychologists	4800	4800	4800	4800	19200	19200
Ancillaries	17664	21196	24192	27956	91008	91008
Rehabilitation Therapy	3300	3300	3300	3300	13200	13200
Central Service	1725	2070	2363	2730	8888	12319
Medical Records	11145	11215	11275	11345	44980	45663
Dietary Service	12300	12300	15500	15500	55600	62000
Food	12650	15180	17325	20020	65175	90338
Laundry & Linen	2070	2484	2835	3276	10665	14783
Social Services	5000	5000	5000	5000	20000	20000
Housekeeping Service	6000	6000	9000	9000	30000	36000
Plant Operations & Maintenance	12000	12000	12000	12000	48000	48000
Maintenance & Repairs	4500	4500	4500	4500	18000	18000
Utilities	6000	6000	6000	6000	24000	24000
Patient Business Services	16150	16380	19575	22820	74925	92213
Administrative & General						
Salaries & Wages	15000	15000	15000	15000	60000	60000
Telephone	10500	7500	7500	7500	33000	30000
Other	33000 (G)	18000	18000	18000	87000	72000
Public Relations	15000	15000	15000	15000	60000	60000
Advertising	30000 (H)	15000	15000	15000	75000	60000
Insurance	12075	14490	16638	19110	62213	86232
Employee Benefits	34580	37580	40920	44920	158000	179680
OPERATING EXPENSES	$367459	$381995	$392623	$429777	$1571854	$1722636

(G) Indicates $15,000 Costs in Training.
(H) Includes $15,000 Costs for Initial Advertising Campaign.

Table 7–4 Cash Flow Projection

Memorial Hospital
Cash Flow Projection

	1st Quarter	2nd Quarter	3rd Quarter	4th Quarter	Total First Year	Second Year
Beginning Cash Balance	$ -0-	$ 59050	$ 12181	$ 14063	$ -0-	$ 10148
Cash Inflow:						
Investment	$ 500000	$ -0-	$ -0-	$ -0-	$ 500000	$ -0-
Borrowings for Working Capital	300000	25000	50000	-0-	375000	(175000)
Accounts Receivable-Current (I)	145637	442870	500568	575590	1664665	2491344
Accounts Payable (J)	122486	4846	3542	12385	143259	294
Total Cash Inflows & Beginning Balance	$1068123	$531766	$566291	$602038	$2682924	$2326786
Cash Outflows:						
Downpayment on Investment	$ 500000	$ -0-	$ -0-	$ -0-	$ 500000	$ -0-
Fixed Assets Improvements	5000	5000	10000	10000	30000	30000
Operating Expenses	367459	381995	392623	429777	1571854	1722636
Prepaid Expenses & Inventory	16000	5000	15000	10000	46000	-0-
Interest Expense	70000	70000	71250	71250	282500	273000
Management Fees	41864	48840	54605	62113	207422	249134
Amortization of Mortgage (K)	8750	8750	8750	8750	35000	45000
Total Cash Outflows	1009073	519585	552228	591890	2672776	2319770
Ending Cash Balance:	$ 59050	$ 12181	$ 14063	$ 10148	$ 10148	$ 7016

(I) 60 Days Average Net Daily Revenue Uncollected.
(J) 30 Days Expenses Unpaid.
(K) 20 Year Mortgage at $24K Monthly Payment, Including Interest.

Finally, the law requires that the provider's (health care institution's) overall plan and budget has to be 1) reviewed and updated at least yearly, and 2) prepared under the direction of the provider's governing body by a committee consisting of representatives of that governing body, the administrative staff, and the medical staff.[12]

Balance Sheet and Statement of Change in Financial Position

The balance sheet is a statement of financial condition showing the health care facility's assets, liabilities, and net worth at a specific date. This represents a difference in time to the statement of operations, which reflects the results of operations over a period of time.

The statement of changes in financial position summarizes the application (users) and sources of funds within a health care institution for a given period of time. Tables 7–5 and 7–6 are illustrations of these two types of financial statements. These statements are usually prepared by the health care institution's accounting or finance department.

Budget Coordination

To assure an orderly and timely development of the departmental budget program, the coordinating team must be well defined. Usually, the department managers or their assistants will assume the role of departmental budget coordinator. This individual will work directly with the total health care facility's budget director, who may be the chief financial officer, controller or a special budget director, in the preparation of the technical aspects of the budget preparation, execution, and monitoring.

Budget Committee

Depending upon the size of the department, it may be advisable to form a departmental budget committee of top management and supervising personnel to assist the department's budget coordinator. The departmental budget committee can assist the department manager in the monitoring of the budget and in the budget preparation. Although the budget coordinator does have most of the work in the budget preparation, the critical part of the budgeting is performed by the line supervisors and section heads. Unless the parties to be controlled by the budget have a voice in developing the budget and agree with the reasonableness of the final departmental budget, control will be rela-

Table 7–5 Comparative Balance Sheet as of December 31, 19x1 and 19x2

MEMORIAL HOSPITAL
ANYTOWN, U.S.A.

Assets	19X1	19X2	Increase (Decrease)
Cash on Hand	$ 40,000	$ 40,000	$ -0-
Short-term Investments	30,000	30,000	-0-
Net Patient Accounts Receivable	700,000	820,000	120,000
Inventories	50,000	45,000	(5,000)
Prepaid Expenses	25,000	30,000	5,000
Total Current Assets	$ 845,000	$ 965,000	$ 120,000
Land, Plant, and Equipment	6,000,000	6,250,000	250,000
Less Accumulative Depreciation	1,250,000	1,350,000	100,000
Net Land, Plant, and Equipment	$4,750,000	$4,900,000	$ 150,000
Total Assets	$5,595,000	$5,865,000	$ 270,000
Liabilities			
Accounts Payable	$ 60,000	$ 70,000	$ 10,000
Payroll Taxes Payable	55,000	50,000	(5,000)
Short-term Notes Payable	75,000	165,000	90,000
Total Current Liabilities	$ 190,000	$ 285,000	$ 95,000
Mortgage Payable	3,510,000	3,445,000	(65,000)
Total Liabilities	$3,700,000	$3,730,000	$ 30,000
Net Worth	1,895,000	2,135,000	240,000[a]
Total Liabilities & Net Worth	$5,595,000	$5,865,000	$ 270,000

[a]Net operating profit for 19X2 = $240,000

tively ineffective. To assist in the budget coordination process, a budget planning worksheet as illustrated in Exhibit 7–1 can be used.[13]

Budget Time Period

The departmental budget time period should cover the same time period as the total health care facility's master budget. This time period

Table 7–6 Statement of Changes in Financial Position for Year Ending December 31, 19x2

MEMORIAL HOSPITAL
ANYTOWN, U.S.A.

Beginning Cash Balance 12-31-X1		$ 70,000[A]
plus:		
Operating Profit	$240,000	
Depreciation	100,000	
Net Cash Available from Operations		340,000
Increase in funds:		
Decrease in Inventories	$ 5,000	
Increase in Accounts Payable	10,000	
Increase in Short-Term Notes Payable	90,000	
Net Increase in Balance Sheet Funds		105,000
Total funds available		$515,000
Decrease in funds:		
Increase in Patient Accounts Receivable	$120,000	
Increase in Prepaid Expenses	5,000	
Increase in Land Plant, and Equipment	250,000	
Decrease in Payroll Taxes Payable	5,000	
Decrease in Mortgage Payable	65,000	
Net Decrease in Balance Sheet Funds		445,000
Ending Cash Balance 12-31-X2		$ 70,000[A]
[A]Includes Cash on Hand	$ 40,000	
and Short-Term Investments	30,000	
	$ 70,000	

Source: California Hospital Association/Hospital Financial Management Association Budget Manual, Sacramento, Calif., 1974.

will differ among health care facilities, since each facility has individual requirements. In some facilities, a one-year operating budget is adequate; in others, a three-year budget would be more appropriate.

Note, however, that the reliability of the budget decreases as the length of time increases. An institution or department can predict more accurately what will happen next year than it can predict what will

Exhibit 7–1 Budget Planning Worksheet

	BUDGET PLANNING WORKSHEET			Prepared by Zelda Date 7/1/x3
	Budget Year 19x4			Approved by J.M. Date 7/3/x3
WEEK ENDING	BUDGET COMMITTEE	BUDGET DIRECTOR	DEPARTMENT HEADS	CLERICAL HELP
Dec. 14	Final Approval of Budget			
Dec. 7	Approve operating budget and rates. Approve capital expenditure and cash budgets.	Complete capital expenditures and cash budgets. Identify rates and other financial alternatives.		Assist in preparation of cash budget.
Nov. 30		Complete operating budget, cost-finding, and contractual allowance calculations.		Summarize capital expenditures. Cost-finding.
Nov. 23	Review expense, capital expenditure and preliminary revenue budgets and recommend modifications.	Complete expense, capital and preliminary revenue budgets.	Revise expense and capital expenditure budgets if necessary.	Summarize expenses and capital expenditures and assist preparation of revenue budget.
Nov. 16		Complete nonsalary expense budget.	Complete nonsalary expense forms.	
Nov. 2		Complete departmental salary expense and capital expenditures budgets.	Complete departmental salary expense and capital expenditure worksheets.	
Oct. 16		Complete nonsalary expense support package and distribute.		
Oct. 9	Approve forecast of units of service and objectives.	Distribute salary and capital forms to department heads.	Discuss budget memo and begin preparation of additional department forms.	

Exhibit 7-1 continued

WEEK ENDING	BUDGET COMMITTEE	BUDGET DIRECTOR	DEPARTMENT HEADS	CLERICAL HELP
Oct. 5		Forecast units of service.	Review units of service forecast with budget director.	Assist in forecast preparation.
Sept. 28		Complete statistics and expense data, physician questionnaire summaries, and departmental objectives and review.		
Sept. 21		Receive physician questionnaires and departmental objective forms.	Formulate objectives and plans for their attainment.	Assist with physician questionnaires & accumulate units of service & expense data.
Sept. 10		Distribute department objective & capital asset justification forms & the board approved hospital objectives to department heads.	Discuss budget memo & begin preparation of department forms related to planning.	
Sept. 7	Approve budget plan, calendar.	Send physician questionnaires.		
Aug. 21		Complete budget plan & calendar.		Begin accumulating statistics & expense data.

happen two or three years hence. For this reason, the budget period must be based on timely and reliable data so the institution and department can base performance reporting and evaluation on the most current and reliable information.

Rolling or moving budgets, as described earlier, can be used to maintain budget visibility in as many of the coming twelve months as possible. Usually, this approach means updating the budget at least quarterly for the following twelve months. This principle would also apply to those department managers and supervisors who wished to maintain budgets for twenty-four or more months ahead.

Within the budget period, the incremental time units should agree with the units utilized for the total health care facility's accounting system. Generally, health care facility accounting is performed on a monthly cycle; in this case, the budget would also be prepared on a monthly basis. Should another accounting cycle be used (such as thirteen four-week periods per year), the budget would be prepared on that basis. An exception might be the case of an institution budgeting for a long period of time, in which case it is possible to budget some of the years by quarters. A budget of one year by months and the next three by quarters would reduce the amount of clerical effort over that required for a four-year monthly budget.

In summary, the departmental budget period must coincide with the total health care facility's budget time period. However, if the department managers and their supervisors believe other time periods, either shorter or longer in time ranges, could more appropriately assist in improved management, these time budget periods could be used to supplement the budget where time periods coincide with the institution's budget time period. An example of a shorter budget time period would be one which ties in with the payroll schedule, i.e., weekly, biweekly, or semimonthly.

Budgetary Tools

There are a number of budgetary tools required to achieve the desired quality budgetary control program. Some of the budgetary tools which the department managers and their budget teams should consider are:

Formal Budget Plan—the departmental budget developmental steps should conform to a prescribed plan that coordinates a series of interactions performed by many people. These interactions include:

- Planning—What are the goals and objectives of the department?
- Strategy—How can the department achieve these goals and objectives?

- Coordinating—Who is responsible for executing the budget strategy operations?
- Controlling—Who will monitor the actual department performance to the budget plan and how will it be done?

Budget Calendar—This budgetary tool establishes target dates for specific tasks to be completed and determines to whom these tasks have been assigned. It helps to maintain an orderly development of the various required steps in the budget preparation process. This timetable is frequently included in the budget manual. Exhibit 7–2 is an illustration of a budget calendar for a total health care facility budget program that also can be related to departmental activity.[14] The task and responsibility schedule, Gantt Chart, in Exhibit 7–3 is a budgetary tool to assist the budget coordinator in identifying tasks, assigning prime and support responsibilities, and establishing target dates for task completion and time lines for tasks.

Budget Manual—Generally, the health care facility will have a budget manual which serves as a guide to all the facility's department managers. This should be designed to assist the institution's and the departments' budget committees in the preparation of the budget. It should include the necessary budgetary tools, forms, and guidelines to assure proper and uniform development and coordination of the entire budget program, such as:

- organization chart
- chart of accounts
- position control
- production standards

Budget Feedback

Regardless of how professionally the budgetary control program was developed and how high the initial level of aspiration, the responsible departmental supervisors, section heads, and others will very soon lose their enthusiasm if there is no communication of comparative results of the actual budget performance.

Absence of feedback will not only adversely affect productivity, but also will undermine the entire department's morale.[15]

In their study to determine the effects of feedback on communication, Leavitt and Mueller found that task accuracy increased as feedback increased. They also found that "zero" feedback is accompanied by low

Exhibit 7–2 Budget Calendar for Year 19x4

BUDGET CALENDAR
Budget Year 19X4

WORK WEEKS REMAINING	USER'S GUIDE REFERENCE	DATE	PARTICIPANTS/ RESPONSIBILITY	ACTIVITY
15	3-5	Aug. 31	Budget Director	Budget plan and calendar completed.
14	4-3	Sept. 7	Governing Board	Formulate overall goals and objectives.
14	5-4	Sept. 7	Budget Director	Physician questionnaires sent. Begin accumulating statistics & expense data.
14	3-5	Sept. 7	Budget Committee & Governing Board	Approval of budget plan and calendar.
13	3-5, 4-3	Sept. 10	Budget Director, Department Heads & Administration	Planning meeting for conveying budget memo & discussion. Dept. objective & equipment justification forms distributed. Work begins on Dept. objectives & capital asset needs.
12	4-3	Sept. 21	Department Heads & Administration	Formulate objectives & plans for their attainment.
12	3-5, 4-3	Sept. 21	Budget Director	Receive physician questionnaires and department objectives.
11	4-3, 5-4	Sept. 28	Budget Director	Complete accumulation of statistics and expense data, summarize physician questionnaires, and complete department objective forms.
10	5-4	Oct. 5	Budget Director & Department Heads	Forecasts of units of service prepared and reviewed with appropriate department heads.
9	4-3, 5-4	Oct. 9	Budget Committee	Approval of forecasts and objectives.
9	3-5, 6-4, 7-2, 13-3	Oct. 9	Budget Director, Department Heads & Administration	Meeting on budgeting salary and capital expenditures forms distributed. Work begins on form preparation.
8	8-5	Oct. 16	Budget Director	Complete nonsalary expense support package and distribute.
6	7-2, 13-3	Nov. 2	Budget Director & Department Heads	Departmental salary expense and capital expenditure worksheets completed.
4	8-5	Nov. 16	Budget Director & Department Heads	Departmental nonsalary expense budget completed.
3	9-3, 13-3, 10-4	Nov. 23	Budget Director & Administration	Capital & expense budgets summarized and preliminary revenue budget completed.
3		Nov. 23	Budget Committee	Review capital, expense & preliminary revenue budgets and recommend modifications.
2	15-2, 11-2, 14-3	Nov. 30	Budget Director	Cost-finding & contractual allowance done, operating budget completed.
1	13-3, 16-3, 14-3	Dec. 7	Budget Director & Administration	Capital expenditures & cash budgets completed. Identify rates and other financial alternatives.
1		Dec. 7	Budget Committee	Capital expenditure & cash budgets approved.
0		Dec. 14	Budget Committee & Governing Board	Operating budget and rates approved. Final approval of budget and rates.

Exhibit 7-3 Finance Department Task and Responsibility Schedule

MEMORIAL HOSPITAL
ANYTOWN, U.S.A.

NO.	DESCRIPTION	PRIME	SUPPORT	Month Day								

confidence and hostility while "free" feedback is accompanied by high confidence and amity.[16]

A budget is not designed to reduce the managerial function to a formula. It is a managerial tool, one purpose of which is to measure subsequent performance against the budgetary plan.[17] The control function is a most important phase of the budgetary program. The disclosure of the need for remedial action (feedback) and the taking of remedial (corrective) steps are just as important as the original drafting of the budget. To be effective, the feedback and corrective action must be systematically organized.

PRELIMINARY BUDGET AND THE COST-FINDING CONNECTION

Generally, the desired results of the preliminary or initial budget are not totally achieved. For example, either the bottom line is a loss, or the profit does not meet management's goals and objectives. In this case, it is advisable to subject the preliminary budget to the cost-finding process. This process will assist management in identifying the department(s) or other cost/revenue center(s) that are producing insufficient profits. Once these cost centers are identified, the appropriate standard revenue rates per production units can be adjusted to generate the desired profit results. After unfavorable cost center revenue rates have been adjusted through *budget balancers,* the entire operating budget can be regenerated until the desired profit results and the budget are finalized.

SUMMARY OF BUDGETING FUNCTIONS

All of the department's personnel that share responsibility for the performance under the budgetary control program should be involved in the preparation of the budget. Who performs what functions depends on the particular department's needs and management organization. However, the budgetary control process should include the following functions:

- establishment of overall departmental goals and policies which relate directly to those of the total health care facility
- translation of these goals into management objectives for the various departmental sections
- development of a formal system of budget preparation and review that ties into the entire facility's budget manual, provides recommended forms and methods for each step in the process, and assures uniformity throughout the entire institution
- provision of historical, statistical, and financial data to the individuals preparing the budget
- actual budget preparation by those individuals responsible for the result of the budget, followed by the coordination of their various aspects
- review and revisions of the departmental budget, followed by the preparation of the final budget
- testing the financial feasibility of the final budget and demonstrating the results of other patient load or production volume possibilities and financial alternatives
- approval of the final budget, with final notification going down the line of command

- periodic performance reporting by responsibility centers of budget and actual revenues and expenses incurred, progress toward objectives, and capital asset acquisitions

Finally, the completed departmental budget should parallel the department's organizational structure, the institution's accounting system, and its formal budgetary reporting program. The projected financial and statistical data used to estimate revenues and expenses should acknowledge historical trends. However, the projection should incorporate both new and established policies and objectives approved for the department by the facility's management. In this way, the budget will flow from these data trends and policies and should most accurately forecast the results of future operations.

REFERENCES

1. David, F. Linowes, *Notable & Quotable* (New York: The Wall Street Journal, July 23, 1974).

2. Allen G. Herkimer, Jr., *Concepts in Hospital Financial Management* (Paradise Valley, Ariz.: Alfa Associates, Inc., 1970), p. 94.

3. *How to Set and Achieve Goals* (Waterford, Conn.: Bureau of Business Practices, 1969).

4. *Correspondence, Education and the Hospital* (Chicago, Ill.: Hospital Continuing Education Project of American Hospital Association's Hospital Research and Education Trust, 1969).

5. Glenn A. Welsch, *Budgeting, Profit Planning and Control* (Englewood Cliffs, N.J.: Prentice-Hall, Inc., 1957), pp. 68–69.

6. Ibid.

7. David Novick, *Program Budgeting* (Cambridge, Mass.: Harvard University Press, 1967), pp. 286 and XV.

8. Ibid.

9. Peter A. Phyrr, *Zero-Base Budgeting* (New York: John Wiley & Sons, 1973), p. 5.

10. L. Vann Seawell, *Hospital Financial Accounting Theory & Practice* (Chicago, Ill.: Hospital Financial Management Association, 1975), p. 549.

11. *1973 Social Security and Medicare Explained Including Medicaid* (New York: Commerce Clearinghouse, Inc., 1973), p. 199.

12. Ibid.

13. *Budgeting Manual* (Sacramento, Calif.: California Hospital Association, 1974).

14. Ibid.

15. Allen G. Herkimer, Jr., *Concepts in Hospital Financial Management* (Paradise Valley, Ariz.: Alfa Associates, Inc., 1970), pp. 99–100.

16. H.J. Leavitt and R.A.H. Mueller, *Some Effects of Feedback on Communication* (Human Relations, IV, 1951), pp. 401–410.

17. Herman C. Heiser, *Budgeting Principles and Practices* (New York: Ronald Press Company, 1959), p. 48.

Chapter 8

Cost Finding and Payment Methods

The budgetary control process incorporates several management tools. One of the most important is cost finding because it determines the total cost for producing a department's patient services. It also informs department managers of nonrevenue-producing departments of the cost of services their departments perform for other departments. Accordingly, this information should be used to establish the charge for patient services.

Traditionally, the health care industry has looked upon the cost-finding process as a means of determining how much an agency such as Blue Cross or Medicare owes the health care facility or how much the institution owes the agency. Only recently have health care financial managers effectively used the cost-finding process as an integral part of the budgetary control program.

DEFINITION OF COST FINDING

Cost finding is the allocation of the costs of the nonrevenue-producing departments in relation to each other, and to the revenue-producing centers in relation to the statistical data that measure the amount of service rendered by each department to other departments.[1]

PURPOSE AND OBJECTIVES OF COST FINDING

Basically, the purpose of cost finding is to determine the true or total costs of operating the revenue-producing departments of the health care industry by allocating nonrevenue-producing departmental expenses to the revenue-producing departments.

Some of the objectives of cost finding in a health care facility or a department are to provide information for:

- managerial decision making regarding the profitability of a specific revenue/cost center
- establishment of rates for departmental services
- use in negotiating
- payment systems with third party payers, i.e., Workmen's Compensation, Blue Cross, or Medicare
- public relations efforts to explain costs of health care services
- reports to external groups such as health facility associations, commissions, and other governmental agencies

THE COST-FINDING PROCESS

Generally, departments that provide the greatest number of services to other departments, and receive the least services from others, are apportioned in the first, or earlier, series of the cost allocation procedures, i.e., depreciation. Departments that provide less service to fewer departments are apportioned in the latter series of the process, i.e., medical education.

Realistically, the order of apportionment is not, and should not be, identical in all health care facilities. Nor should it necessarily be consistent from year to year in the same institution, because the use of services may vary from institution to institution and from department to department.

However, a word of caution is necessary. Consistency from period to period in order of apportionment and the basis of allocation should not be regarded lightly. When there is too much fluctuation from period to period, the results of a cost-finding procedure lose much of their usefulness. Changes in the order of apportionment and basis of allocation should be instituted only where such changes would produce a significant improvement in the quality of the results of the cost-finding procedure.

Cost finding, then, is the process of reclassifying the costs accumulated in the routine accounts maintained by the health care facility for responsibility reporting purposes. It is a procedure that is apart from, but supplemental to, the regular accounting and budgetary control system. The results produced by cost finding are not recorded in the accounts, nor are they presented in the health care facility's usual income or operating statement. Instead, the results of cost finding are incorporated in a special cost-finding report,[2] and used primarily as an internal management tool.

Under current federal reimbursement programs, there is a mandate that cost finding must be performed uniformly by all health care facilities. Method Two, or the step-down method, (as discussed later) is required to allocate overhead costs.

PREREQUISITES TO COST FINDING

The basic prerequisites to cost finding are:

- a sound organizational structure
- a related and appropriate accounting system
- relevant and adequate statistical data

Sound Organizational Structure

If cost finding is to produce meaningful and managerially relevant results, the health care facility and its various departments must first have sound organizational structure (Chapter 2). However, it is necessary to reiterate that clear lines of authority and detailed, relevant definitions of responsibilities are essential. It is vital to the cost-finding process that revenues and expenses be directly related to a responsibility center. Also, if a department or cost center generates revenue, it is important that the cost required to produce that revenue be charged to that particular cost center.

Related Accounting System

The second most important prerequisite to cost finding is an appropriate accounting system related directly to the organizational structure. This system should provide for the accumulation, on an accrual basis, of direct costs according to the organizational departments and subdivisions that are responsible for incurring them. The same is true of revenues. (With respect to supplies, best results are obtained when an inventory requisitioning system is employed.) In short, expenses, revenues, and their related statistics should be accumulated by responsibility centers defined by the health facility's organizational structure.

Adequate Statistical Data

In addition to the accumulation of revenues and expenses by responsibility centers, it is essential that adequate statistical data of relevant and meaningful statistics be developed to measure the performance of each center (Chapter 5). Information regarding total dollars of revenue and expense has little value unless nonmonetary measurements (pounds of laundry processed, patient bills typed, etc.) also are known. Each nonrevenue-producing center should have at least one parameter that measures its production or volume of service, and is clerically feasible to report and to audit.

Ordinarily, it is advisable to develop a written procedure for the collection of statistical data. The procedure should be developed in cooperation with department managers, their supervisors, and their various section heads. Each of these individuals should understand and accept the selected statistics as an equitable and meaningful basis for cost allocation.

Many of the normally reported statistics can be used in the cost-finding process. For example, if "number of meals served" is used as the basis for appropriating dietary costs, this figure should be broken down into the "number served to each cost center or department." Further, if "pounds of laundry processed" is used as the basis for distributing the laundry department's cost to other cost centers, the number of pounds of laundry should be broken down into "cost centers served."

Whatever statistical basis is used, the major factors in determining the most appropriate ones are:

- equitable allocation of costs
- economical means for gathering[3]
- ease of verification and audit

METHODS OF COST FINDING

Presently, whenever health care managers speak of cost finding, they automatically think of step-down. The step-down or the American Hospital Association's (AHA) Method Two, is the universally used cost-finding process, because variations of it are mandated by Medicare and other rate setting and/or review agencies. The cost-finding formulas as prescribed by Medicare should *not* be used for internal use in allocating costs and establishing rates because they are designed specifically for the purpose of reimbursement—more specifically, for reimbursement by the federal government. Therefore, they eliminate costs which should be included for an internal management tool. Usually, the order and statistical basis used to allocate departmental costs are not the most meaningful or appropriate ones for the facility's advantage. However, there are numerous other cost-finding systems, including the traditional step-down, designed specially for the health care industry.

For a number of years, three basic methods of cost finding were promoted by the American Hospital Association. They were often referred to simply as Method One, Method Two, and Method Three. The cost data found using these methods differ slightly in some respects, and significantly in other respects. These differences make it important that the most equitable and useful method be selected to meet the facility's objectives and be used consistently.

The three methods differ primarily in the manner in which the cost allocation is made.

Method One

Using Method One, the costs of the nonrevenue-producing centers are allocated only to the revenue-producing centers. Most nonrevenue-producing centers render services to each other as well as to the revenue-producing centers, but this fact is ignored in the mechanics of Method One. None of the costs of the nonrevenue-producing centers is allocated to other nonrevenue-producing centers.

Method One is the simplest of the traditional methods of cost finding, because it requires less clerical effort and fewer statistics. Under certain circumstances, the end results of Method One may not differ significantly from the end results of the more sophisticated methods. Method One, however, does not produce the full costs of the nonrevenue-producing centers. For this reason, and because the equity and accuracy of the end results may be subject to question, the managerial usefulness of Method One is limited.[4]

Method Two

Method Two, as mentioned above, is better known as the step-down method, and recognizes the important fact that the services rendered by certain nonrevenue-producing centers are utilized by certain other nonrevenue-producing centers, as well as by the revenue-producing centers or departments. The accumulated costs in a nonrevenue-producing center, therefore, are allocated to those nonrevenue-producing centers that utilize its services, as well as to the revenue-producing centers to which it renders service. The unique feature of the step-down method is that once the costs of a nonrevenue-producing center have been allocated, the cost center is considered closed. Being closed, it will not receive any portion of the costs of the other nonrevenue-producing centers, whose costs are yet to be allocated. The choice of sequence in which the nonrevenue-producing centers are to be closed, therefore, is very important. To reduce the amount of cost distortion that can occur because of this feature of Method Two, careful consideration should be given to the determination of:

- the number of nonrevenue-producing centers served by each center
- the amount of service rendered to other nonrevenue-producing centers by each center

The closing sequence should be based upon these determinations. In other words, the first center to be closed should be the center that renders the greatest amount of service to the largest number of centers and, in turn, receives the least amount of service from the fewest number of centers. An excellent example of this type of cost center is Interest and/or Depreciation Expense.

The last center to be closed should be the center that renders the least service to the fewest nonrevenue-producing centers and, in turn, receives the greatest amount of service from the largest number of centers, such as the School of Nursing.

Method Two is more difficult and time consuming than Method One, but, more importantly, it is likely to provide significantly more accurate cost information with respect to revenue-producing centers. While it recognizes that certain nonrevenue-producing centers render service to other nonrevenue-producing centers, Method Two (like Method One) does not produce the total nonrevenue-producing costs used by the revenue-producing departments. Since the primary emphasis of cost finding is on determining the true or full costs of revenue-producing centers, Method Two is acceptable for most purposes, including rate setting and reimbursement. (This statement is true with the condition mentioned in reference to the Medicare formula for the step-down process.)* If the total costs of the nonrevenue-producing centers need to be developed, the determination can be made through special cost studies.

The term step-down was adopted from Method Two's worksheet configuration, which looks like a series of steps (Exhibit 8–1).

---

*Parentheses Per Author.

Exhibit 8–1 Step-Down Cost Apportionment

BLANK HOSPITAL

Cost Apportionment – General Services

Oct. 1, 19 to Sept. 30, 19

Line No.	Cost Center	1 TOTAL DIRECT EXPENSES FOR APPORTIONMENT (from Worksheet A Col. 6, lines 1-32)	1(a) PROVISION FOR DEPRECIATION (See Schedule B-1 Part C)	2 EMPLOYEE HEALTH AND WELFARE (See Schedule B-2)	3 OPERATION OF PLANT (See Schedule B-3)	4 MAINTENANCE OF PLANT (See Schedule B-4)	5 LAUNDRY AND LINEN SERVICE (See Schedule B-5)	6 HOUSEKEEPING (See Schedule B-6)	7 DIETARY RAW FOOD (See Schedule B-7)
	GENERAL SERVICE COST CENTERS:	OMIT CENTS							
1	Provision for Depreciation	$ 88,994	$88,994						
2	Employee Health & Welfare	85,117	105	$85,222					
3	Operation of Plant	115,330	1,174	401	$116,905				
4	Maintenance of Plant	71,338	823	2,717	601	$75,479			
5	Laundry and Linen Service	61,262	1,680	2,322	2,748	1,784	$69,796		
6	Housekeeping	121,976	584	4,450	172	112	160	$127,454	
7	Dietary—Raw Food	91,288							$91,288
8	—Other	122,213	1,589	4,964	3,133	2,033	685		
9	Cafeteria	104,337	2,602	1,500	3,267	2,120	490		
10	Maintenance of Personnel	10,523	14,388	395	32,915	21,361	1,989	15,307	
11	Nursing Service	620,202	943	26,567	1,115	724	571		
12	Medical Supplies and Expense	168,964	1,593	2,516	641	416	114	586	
13	Pharmacy	96,596	949	697	475	308	24	586	
14	Medical Records	39,292	1,243	1,623	633	411		3,557	
15	Social Service	18,783	598	801	332	216	142	586	
16	Nursing School	52,956	4,988	1,898	2,812	1,825	938	6,600	
17	Intern-Resident Service	93,397	269	4,013			1,121		
18	Administration and General	325,582	4,893	8,262	6,966	4,521	82	10,680	
19	Cost of Meals Sold								
20	Cost of Rooms Rented								
	SPECIAL SERVICE COST CENTERS:								
21	Operating Rooms	149,701	8,582	5,179	4,775	3,099	14,792	586	
22	Delivery Rooms	42,735	2,169	1,730	2,058	1,335	4,687	3,124	
23	Anesthesia	20,608	740		27	17	488		
24	Radiology	118,860	3,535	3,717	2,27	1,474	1,089	3,557	
25	Laboratory	157 135	2,335	5,809	2,683	1,745	300	3,231	
26	Blood Bank	67,255	623	675	418	271	27	326	
27	BMR-EKG	14,594	460	277	322	209	53	1,784	
28	Oxygen Therapy	10,666	681	129					
29	Physical Therapy	49,341	1,668	2,080	1,291	840	1,707	3,557	
30	Cost of Medical Supplies Sold								
31	Cost of Drugs Sold								
	INPATIENT COST CENTERS:								
32	Inpatients		23,862		36,781	23,870	32,128	62,388	91,288
33	Nursery	2,706	1,518		2,977	1,934	4,706	2,092	
	OUTPATIENT COST CENTERS:								
34	Outpatients	24,542	2,993	936	6,242	4,051	1,043	7,123	
35	Emergency	38,134	1,407	1,564	1,237	803	2,460	1,784	
36	Private Ambulatory								
37	Total	$2,985,127	$88,994	$85,222	$116,905	$75,479	$69,796	$127,454	$91,288

Line No.	Cost Center	8 DIETARY OTHER (See Schedule B-8)	9 CAFETERIA (See Schedule B-9)	10 MAINTENANCE OF PERSONNEL (See Schedule B-10)	11 NURSING SERVICE (See Schedule B-11)	12 MEDICAL SUPPLIES & EXPENSE (See Schedule B-12)	13 PHARMACY (See Schedule B-13)	14 MEDICAL RECORDS (See Schedule B-14)	15 SOCIAL SERVICE (See Schedule B-15)
	GENERAL SERVICE COST CENTERS:								
1	Provision for Depreciation								
2	Employee Health & Welfare								
3	Operation of Plant								
4	Maintenance of Plant								
5	Laundry and Linen Service								
6	Housekeeping								
7	Dietary—Raw Food								
8	—Other	$134,617							
9	Cafeteria	22,672	$136,988						
10	Maintenance of Personnel			$96,878					
11	Nursing Service			510	$650,632				
12	Medical Supplies and Expense					$174,830			
13	Pharmacy						$99,635		
14	Medical Records							$46,759	
15	Social Service								$21,458
16	Nursing School		61,900	56,597					
17	Intern-Resident Service		28,644	26,004					
18	Administration and General			510					
19	Cost of Meals Sold		46,444						
20	Cost of Rooms Rented			13,257					
	SPECIAL SERVICE COST CENTERS:								
21	Operating Rooms					21,789	4,306		
22	Delivery Rooms					16,483	1,657		
23	Anesthesia						4,823		
24	Radiology						1,119		
25	Laboratory						725		
26	Blood Bank								
27	BMR-EKG						59		
28	Oxygen Therapy								
29	Physical Therapy						106		
30	Cost of Medical Supplies Sold					8,942			
31	Cost of Drugs Sold						66,848		
	INPATIENT COST CENTERS:								
32	Inpatients	111,945			570,898	112,139	16,111	38,342	12,772
33	Nursery				79,734	5,772	1,321		
	OUTPATIENT COST CENTERS:								
34	Outpatients					478	1,030	6,546	8,536
35	Emergency					9,227	1,530	1,871	150
36	Private Ambulatory								
37	Total	$134,617	$136,988	$96,878	$650,632	$174,830	$99,635	$46,759	$21,458

Line No.	Cost Center	16 SUBTOTAL (Columns 1 to 15, lines 16 to 37)	17 DEDUCT RECOVERY OF EXPENSES	18 NURSING SCHOOL (See Schedule B-16)	19 INTERN-RESIDENT SERVICE (See Schedule B-17)	20 SUBTOTAL AFTER DEDUCTIONS (Col. 16 minus Col. 17, plus cols. 18 and 19)	21 ADMINISTRATION AND GENERAL (See Schedule B-18)	22 TOTAL (Columns 18 through 21, lines 17 through 37)	Line No.
	GENERAL SERVICE COST CENTERS:								
1	Provision for Depreciation								1
2	Employee Health & Welfare								2
3	Operation of Plant								3
4	Maintenance of Plant								4
5	Laundry and Linen Service								5
6	Housekeeping								6
7	Dietary—Raw Food								7
8	—Other								8
9	Cafeteria								9
10	Maintenance of Personnel								10
11	Nursing Service								11
12	Medical Supplies and Expense								12
13	Pharmacy								13
14	Medical Records								14
15	Social Service								15
16	Nursing School	$ 190,514	$13,320	$177,194					16
17	Intern-Resident Service	153,448			$153,448				17
18	Administration and General	361,496				$ 361,496			18
19	Cost of Meals Sold	46,444	46,774			(330)			19
20	Cost of Rooms Rented	13,257	12,393			864	$362,030		20
	SPECIAL SERVICE COST CENTERS:								
21	Operating Rooms	212,809		17,950	21,048	251,807	36,836	$ 288,643	21
22	Delivery Rooms	75,978		15,717	15,000	106,695	15,608	122,303	22
23	Anesthesia	26,703			13,838	40,541	5,931	46,472	23
24	Radiology	135,622				135,622	19,840	155,462	24
25	Laboratory	174,668				174,668	25,550	200,218	25
26	Blood Bank	69,595				69,595	10,181	79,776	26
27	BMR-EKG	17,758				17,758	2,598	20,356	27
28	Oxygen Therapy	11,476				11,476	1,679	13,155	28
29	Physical Therapy	60,593				60,593	8,864	69,457	29
30	Cost of Medical Supplies Sold	8,942				8,942		8,942	30
31	Cost of Drugs Sold	66,848				66,848		66,848	31
	INPATIENT COST CENTERS:								
32	Inpatients	1,132,527		114,697	75,870	1,323,094	193,548	1,516,642	32
33	Nursery	102,762		12,882		115,644	16,917	132,561	33
	OUTPATIENT COST CENTERS:								
34	Outpatients	63,520		7,318		70,838	10,363	81,201	34
35	Emergency	60,167		8,630	27,692	96,489	14,115	110,604	35
36	Private Ambulatory								36
37	Total	$2,985,127	$72,487	$177,194	$153,448	$2,912,640	$362,030	$2,912,640	37

Source: Reprinted from *Cost Finding for Hospitals*, pp. 68–69, with permission of the American Hospital Association, © 1957.

In summary, many, if not most, health care facilities will find Method Two most suitable. It is recognized that Method Two does not give reliable approximations of costs of the intermediate, nonrevenue-producing centers. The degree of accuracy and equity achieved in the final revenue-producing centers, however, is reasonable, assuming a proper order of allocation.[5]

Method Three

The most complex of the three original AHA methods of cost finding is Method Three, which is frequently referred to as the "double distribution" or the "double apportionment" method. This method gives greater recognition to the fact that nonrevenue-producing centers render services to other nonrevenue-producing centers, as well as to the revenue-producing centers. Using Method Three, the nonrevenue-producing centers are *not* considered permanently closed after their costs have been initially allocated (as in Method Two). Instead, they are reopened in the second apportionment process, to receive cost allocations from other nonrevenue-producing centers from which services are received. After the costs of each nonrevenue-producing center have been allocated once, some costs will remain in some departments, representing services received from other departments.

For example, in this method, direct costs of the housekeeping department will be distributed to the other nonrevenue-producing centers it serves, and to the revenue-producing centers. The other nonrevenue-producing centers' direct costs are similarly distributed, while the housekeeping department receives cost allocations from the other departments during the first apportionment process. To close the housekeeping department, and the other nonrevenue-producing departments, it is necessary that a second or a "double apportionment" process be made to allocate and to close out the nonrevenue-producing department's total direct and accumulated costs.

OTHER COST-FINDING METHODS

Other methods of cost allocation involve the use of algebraic formulas to determine the costs to be transferred. These formulas are designed to identify the cost in the departments that serve each other by recognizing the existing relationships. This can be accomplished by using simultaneous equations. The number of departments that serve each other in health care facilities may be large, which necessitates the task of solving equations with many unknowns. It is also possible to approximate the amounts to be allocated by assigning costs back and forth until the major portion of the costs of the interrelationships is defined. This approximates the algebraic methods very closely. In the algebraic methods, as well as in Method Three, this allocation must be followed by a routine allocation to those departments with which there was no relationship.[6]

The Short-Formula 1 method of cost finding is a very simple, abbreviated approach to cost allocation, and is based upon the health care facility's most recent comprehensive cost-finding report. Percentages of a revenue-producing department's share of overhead or of a non-revenue-producing department's costs, overhead ratio, are established. These overhead percentages are applied to the facility's current actual or budgeted total nonrevenue-producing department costs and added to the respective revenue-producing departments to develop a total cost. These costs, in turn, can be matched to the department's actual or budgeted revenue to evaluate the department's profitability. The Short-Formula 1 procedure is described in the following steps and illustrations:

Short-Formula 1 Cost-Finding Method

(Refer to Table 8–1, and Exhibits 8–2 and 8–3)

Step One—List net (direct) expenses for all revenue-producing departments.

Step Two—List total expenses after the final apportionment process for all revenue-producing departments.

Step Three—Compute the amount of overhead or allocated expense by subtracting direct expense (column 1) from total expense, after final apportionment (column 2).

Step Four—Compute overhead percent for each revenue-producing department by dividing the department's share of overhead (column 3) (operating room, $205,451) by the *total* overhead or allocated costs ($2,605,582). The resulting percentage will serve as the basis for allocating total nonrevenue-producing or overhead costs during subsequent reporting periods.

The Short-Formula 1 method of cost finding is relatively accurate, and requires a minimal amount of time, when compared with a comprehensive cost-finding process. It is especially useful when approximations are required. However, if there is a major change in statistical or

Table 8-1 Analysis of Direct and Indirect Expenses

MEMORIAL HOSPITAL
ANYTOWN, U.S.A.

	(1) Direct Expense[A] Exhibit 8-2, Col 6	(2) Total Expense[B] Exhibit 8-3, Col 7	(3) Indirect Expense (Col 2 - Col 1 = Col 3)	(4) Percent of Overhead
Operating Room	237,665	443,116	205,451	8.0
Post Oper. Room	64,378	88,620	24,242	.9
Anesthesiology	167,259	205,017	37,758	1.4
Delivery Room	81,783	155,071	73,288	2.8
Radiology	379,921	500,922	121,001	4.6
Laboratory	504,405	845,294	340,889	13.0
EEG	13,361	20,641	7,280	.3
EKG	75,294	114,446	39,152	1.5
Physical Therapy	29,285	54,694	25,409	.9
Central Supply	81,942	59,660	(22,282)	(.8)
Respiratory Therapy	52,356	74,250	21,894	.8
IV Therapy	122,841	160,851	38,010	1.5
Pharmacy	185,238	175,178	(10,060)	(.4)
Emergency Room	83,659	146,660	63,001	2.4
Isotopes	90,286	106,626	16,340	.6
Mental Health	(6,924)	7,732	14,656	.6
Radiation Therapy	9,591	12,734	3,143	.1
Nonmaternity Nur.	1,095,663	2,514,349	1,418,686	54.4
Maternity	74,660	170,726	96,066	3.8
Newborn	67,032	119,305	52,273	2.0
Outpatient	16,655	56,040	39,385	1.6
Total	3,426,350	6,031,932	2,605,582	100.0

A   Source: Exhibit 8-2, lines 13 through 52.
B   Source: Exhibit 8-3, lines 12 through 43-B.

Exhibit 8-2 General Fund Expense Summary

Memorial Hospital
Anytown, U.S.A.

Form 3   Memorial   Hospital   (Omit Cents)

General Fund Expense Summary 12 Months Ended Sept. 30, 1968	1 Salary & Fee Expense	2 Non- salary Expense	3 Depre- ciation Expense (Form 5)	4 Debit & (Credit) Adjust- ments (Form 8)	5 Credits to Expense (Form 3)	6 Net Expense
General Service Departments						
1 *Administration & General	518,015	580,551	28,391	20,982	2,811	1,145,128
2 Dietary	213,980	221,310	9,944		141	445,093
3 Housekeeping	150,733	29,466	1,905			182,104
4 Laundry	80,957	8,984	6,571			96,512
4A Linen Service	9,258	12,956	1,634		4,770	19,078
5 Maintenance of Personnel	9,312	723	12,188		3,046	19,277
6 Operation of Plant	37,601	64,084	13,929			115,614
7 Repairs & Maintenance	158,431	79,509	4,391		13,456	228,879
Professional Service Departments						
8 Nursing Service Administration	101,111	5,023	2,093			108,227
9 Nursing Education						

10 Interns, Residents & Physicians	63,016	20,266	1,396	(11,274)		73,404
11 Medical Records & Library	91,018	16,460	4,810		8,449	103,839
12 Social Service	16,307	132	405			16,844
Special Service Departments						
13 Operating Rooms	142,392	85,266	10,007			237,665
14 Post Operative Room	62,269	598	1,511			64,378
15 Anesthesiology	146,430	19,872	957			167,259
16 Delivery Rooms	64,418	13,339	4,394		368	81,783
17 Radiology	262,152	121,038	15,364	(16,310)	2,323	379,921
18 Laboratory	463,361	123,035	16,988	(8,979)		504,405
19 Electroencephalography	11,959	513	889			13,361
20 Electrocardiology	67,244	6,013	1,392	645		75,294
21 Physical Therapy	26,352	572	2,413	(52)		29,285
22 Medical & Surgical Supplies			35,009			35,009
23 Central Sterile Supply	42,839	903	3,191			46,933
24 Inhalation Therapy	31,576	ʼ 16,561	2,908	1,311		52,366
25 Intravenous Therapy	59,214	63,488	139			122,841
26 Pharmacy	38,335	145,642	1,561	(127)	173	185,238
27 Emergency Service	59,818	19,415	4,432	(6)		83,659
28 Isotope Therapy	39,599	46,806	3,881			90,286
29 Cost of Drugs Sold						
30 Routine Special Services						
31 M. Health	46,492	562	1,022		55,000	(6,924)
32 R. Therapy	5,496	3,987	108			9,591
33						
34						
35 Radium Therapy						
36 Shock Therapy						
37 Occupational Therapy						
38 Non-CBC Special Services						
39						
40						
41						
42						
43						
Routine Service						
44 Non-Maternity	964,138	82,202	51,289	(1,966)		1,095,663
45						
46						
47						
48						
Total (Lines 44–48)						
49 Maternity	61,523	8,762	4,375			74,660
50 Newborn Infants	55,819	9,625	1,588			67,032
51 Outpatient Clinics	12,013	2,771	1,871			16,655
52 Private Referred Outpatients						
Other Expense						
53 Real Estate & Property Taxes						
54 Research						
55 Fund Raising Expense						
56 Ambulance Service			638			638
57 Special Nurses & Guest Meals						
58 Pay Cafeteria						
59 Coffee & Gift Shops	33,499	1,761	4,188	15,776	85,706	(30,482)
60 Blood & Blood Derivatives			1,375			1,375
61						
62						
63 Miscellaneous						
64 Total	4,146,677	1,847,204	224,138	-0-	176,243	6,041,776

*Interest expense in the amount of $ 36,831 included.

Post to
Form 3
Col. 1

Source: Connecticut Hospital Association, *Cost Analysis Manual*, Form 3, Wallingford, Conn., 1959.

Exhibit 8-3 Final Apportionment

Form 11

Final Apportionment
Memorial Hospital
Anytown, U.S.A.

(Omit Cents)

Final Apportionment — 12 Months Ended September 30, 1968

Line		Inpatient Services			Outpatient Services			
		1 Non-Maternity	2 Maternity	3 Newborn Infants	4 Clinics	5 Private Referred	6 Emergency Room (Note)	7 Total
12	Routine Services (Lines 44–52)	2,514,349	170,726	119,305	52,312	3,728		2,860,420
13	**Special Service Departments** Operating Rooms	88,620						443,116
14	Post Operative Room							83,620
15	Anesthesiology	196,474	8,279	254		10		205,017
16	Delivery Rooms		155,071					155,071
17	Radiology	375,501	2,069	1,733		121,619		500,922
18	Laboratory	660,969	26,382	888		157,055		845,294
19	Electroencephalography	11,626				9,015		20,641
20	Electrocardiology	108,741	246	117		5,342		114,446
21	Physical Therapy	40,819	63	13		13,799		54,694
22	Medical & Surgical Supplies	55,824	2,803	42		991		59,660
23	Central Sterile Supply	74,050	167			33		74,250
24	Inhalation Therapy	150,959	7,151	143		2,598		160,851
25	Intravenous Therapy							
26	Pharmacy	15,043	1,115				130,502	146,660
27	Emergency Service	90,289	398			15,939		106,626
28	Isotope Therapy	160,638	3,814	2,770		7,956		175,178
29	Cost of Drugs Sold							
30	Routine Special Services							
31	Mental H.	138	5			7,589		7,732
32	Rad. Ther.	1,432				11,302		12,734
33								
34								

35	Radium Therapy						
36	Shock Therapy						
37	Occupational Therapy						
38	Non-CBC Special Services						
39							
40							
41							
42							
43							
43A	Total Special Services	2,473,698	207,563	5,960		353,789	130,502	3,171,512
43B	Total Services to Patients	4,988,047	378,289	125,265	52,312	357,517	130,502	6,031,932
	Other Expense						
53	Real Estate & Property Taxes						
54	Research				4,635		
55	Fund Raising Expense						
56	Ambulance Service						
57	Special Nurses & Guest Meals						
58	Pay Cafeteria						
59	Coffee & Gift Shops				5,209		
60	Blood & Blood Derivatives						
61							
62							
63	Miscellaneous						
64	Total—Same as Form 3, Line 64, Column 6						6,041,776

NOTE: For convenience in allocating routine emergency room expense, distribution is made on Line 27 between patients treated and admitted and patients treated and discharged as reflected by the statistics shown on Form 7B and worksheet 21.

Source: Connecticut Hospital Association, *Cost Analysis Manual,* Form 11, Wallingford, Conn., 1959.

expense distribution, i.e., increased square footage of a department or a new department, the overhead percent must be adjusted to accommodate these changes.

In summary, the Short-Formula 1 method, as illustrated in Table 8–2, is a "quick and dirty," manual or mechanical approach to cost finding and departmental profitability testing when accuracy is not a major requirement.

FREQUENCY OF COST FINDING

Since departmental profitability is as essential as facility profitability, it is recommended that some form of cost finding be performed at a minimum of a quarterly basis. A monthly basis is preferable. The cost-finding process gives management the information necessary to assure a favorable charge/cost relationship.

Obviously, if the health care facility's cost-finding system is computerized, the cost-finding process can be, and should be, performed as frequently as desired. However, for those health care facilities that are not computerized, the Short-Formula 1 method of cost finding can be used on a monthly basis with a minimum of clerical effort.

In conclusion, cost finding should not be performed only at the time of establishing budgets and rates, or determining the liability to or from a third party agency. Rather, cost finding is an essential management tool which should be continually and routinely used to monitor profitability.

COMPONENTS OF TOTAL COSTS FOR RATE SETTING

The cost-finding process results are only some of the components of total costs to be considered in the rate-setting process in order to assure a viable health care facility and a profitable department.

The American Hospital Association's Statement on the "Financial Requirements of Health Care Institutions and Services" identifies the following components of financial requirements:

A. *Current Operating Needs Related to Patient Care*
   1. direct patient care expense
   2. interest
   3. educational programs
   4. research programs

Table 8-2 Short-Formula 1 Method of Cost Finding

MEMORIAL HOSPITAL
ANYTOWN, U.S.A.

Departmental Operating Statement for Three Months Ending March 31, 19x2

Department	% of Gross Charges(A)	Overhead Ratio	Gross Charges to Patients	Less: Deductions & Allowances(B)	Net Charges to Patients	Direct Expense	Indirect Expense(C)	Total Expense	Net Gain or (Loss)
Operating Room	7.4	8.0	$ 509,583	$ 48,444	$ 461,139	$ 261,143	$ 174,385	$ 435,528	$ 25,611
Postoperative Room	1.5	0.9	101,913	9,820	92,093	70,815	19,618	90,433	1,660
Anesthesiology	3.4	1.4	235,770	22,258	213,512	183,985	30,517	214,502	(990)
Delivery Room	1.9	2.8	132,332	12,438	119,894	89,960	61,035	150,995	(31,101)
Radiology	8.4	4.6	576,060	54,990	521,070	417,913	100,271	518,184	2,886
Laboratory	14.2	13.0	972,088	92,960	879,128	554,845	283,375	838,220	40,908
EEG	0.3	.3	23,737	1,964	21,773	14,697	6,539	21,236	537
EKG	1.9	1.5	131,613	12,438	119,175	82,823	32,697	115,520	3,655
Physical Therapy	0.9	.9	62,898	5,892	57,006	32,213	19,618	51,831	5,175
Central Supply	1.0	(.8)	68,909	6,546	62,363	90,136	(17,438)	72,698	(10,335)
Respiratory Therapy	1.2	.8	85,388	7,856	77,532	57,592	17,438	75,030	2,502
IV Therapy	2.7	1.5	184,979	17,675	167,304	135,125	32,697	167,822	(518)
Pharmacy	2.9	(.4)	201,455	18,985	182,470	203,760	(8,719)	195,041	(12,571)
Emergency Room	2.4	2.4	168,659	15,711	152,948	92,025	52,315	144,340	8,608
Isotopes	1.8	.6	122,620	11,784	110,836	99,315	13,079	112,394	(1,558)
Mental Health	0.1	.6	8,892	655	8,237	7,616	13,079	20,695	(12,458)
Radiation Therapy	0.2	.1	14,644	1,309	13,335	10,550	2,180	12,730	605
Nonmaternity Nursing	42.0	54.4	2,891,501	274,952	2,616,549	1,205,229	1,185,817	2,391,046	225,503
Maternity Nursing	2.8	3.8	196,335	18,330	178,005	82,126	82,833	164,959	13,046
Newborn Nursing	2.1	2.0	137,200	13,748	123,453	73,735	43,596	117,331	6,122
Outpatient	0.9	1.6	64,446	5,892	58,554	18,320	34,877	53,197	5,357
Total	100.0	100.0	$6,891,022	$654,647	$6,236,375	$3,783,923	$2,179,809	$5,963,732	$272,643

(A) Source: Percent of departmental charges to total gross charges to patients.
For example: operating room $\frac{\$509,583}{\$6,891,022} = .074$ or 7.4%.

(B) Source: Departmental percent of total gross charges to patients multiplied by total deductions and allowances.
For example: operating room .074 × $654,647 = $48,444.

(C) Source: Total indirect expense represents the balance of expenses after direct expenses have been deducted.
For example: $5,963,732 less $3,783,923 = $2,179,809.
Departmental indirect expenses are computed by multiplying overhead ratio by total indirect expenses.
For example: operating room .08 × $2,179,809 = $174,385.

    5. credit losses
    6. patient unable to pay
  B. *Capital Needs*
    1. plant capital
      a. preservation and replacement of plant and equipment
      b. improvement of plant
      c. expansion
      d. amortization of plant capital indebtedness
    2. operating cash needed
    3. return on investment

The one element which is not mentioned by the AHA statement is *profit*. Without profit, no business can survive. In true tradition of capitalistic economy, there is nothing wrong with profit in the health care industry, as well as in other industries. It is the abuse of profit that must be avoided.

PAYMENT FOR SERVICES

Even though the above components of financial requirements have been identified as vital to the perpetual growth and continuity of health care facilities, there is no assurance that all these components will be accepted by all purchasers of health care services. This is especially true when government is one of the major purchasers, i.e., Medicare and Medicaid, or when a major insurance company or any other organization is a dominant purchaser. In any case, through either a monopolistic position or by federal mandate, the health care facility is approached to enter a third party agreement to accept payment for services at less than published charges. In these cases, the difference between published charges and third party payment is written off the patients' accounts and the facility's assets (accounts receivable) as a contractual allowance.

The department's net income is thereby reduced, decreasing the facility's cash flow and eliminating assets. For example, assume that a patient's total published charges were $5,000 and the third party agreement was to pay eighty-five percent of published charges. Further, assume that the total cost for the service was $4,000. The following is a comparative analysis of the net profit from the third party patient as compared to a non-third party patient, i.e., self-pay, or commercial insurance.

Description	Third Party	Non-Third Party
Total published charges	$5,000	$5,000
Less: contractual allowances	750	-0-
Net charges	$4,250	$5,000
Less: cost of service	$4,000	$4,000
Net profit	$ 250	$1,000

To summarize, the non-third party patient is helping to support the third party patient. The basic premise behind such agreements originally was the savings the health facility would realize due to the economies of scale, steady cash flow, and fewer bad debts. Since Medicare, the third parties have become more demanding and literally dictate what costs are reimbursable and what costs are not. In short, these third parties set the rates they will pay the health care facility. Again, in rate setting, these contractual allowances must be considered a vital component in setting the published charges or rates.

Therefore, it becomes increasingly important to *make a clear distinction between published charges and reimbursement rates or payments.* (See Appendix C, The Impact of Third Party Payers on Hospital Rates and the Bottom Line.)

Published charges are the rates established which include all of the above-mentioned components of total financial requirements. They are the charges which are posted to the patient's account receivable, regardless of type of paying agent, and they are the charges that are credited to the respective revenue-producing department's revenue account. Finally, published charges are the gross rates established by the health care facility and its departments in order to pay for the services rendered. These charges are set prospectively.

PROSPECTIVE VS. RETROSPECTIVE PAYMENTS

Traditionally, most industries use the prospective method of setting payment rates. For example, the automobile industry sets the price of new cars before the customer purchases the car. Similarly, food, drugs, and freight rates are established prospectively before the purchase. Currently, most published charges for health services are established prior to the rendering of service. Prospectively, setting rates for payments requires:

- knowledge of the true cost of the service

- knowledge of the competition's price
- knowledge of the amount of the profit required to satisfy management

There is one element in prospective rate setting that is always prevalent and on which one cannot place a tangible cost: the risk factor. There is always the risk that costs will rise and the charges will not cover costs. But, that risk is the prime ingredient that has so greatly contributed to the success of our nation's capitalistic economy.

Not to be outmaneuvered, the third party purchasers devised a scheme to eliminate this risk factor. The scheme was called *retrospective reimbursement*. Very simply, it means "spend the money, render service to the patients, and we will pay you after the fact." The health care managers fell for the scheme because it eliminated risk, and the facilities had virtually a blank check to spend. But, in time, the third parties became selective in what costs they would reimburse, and, consequently, there is now a regenerated interest in prospective payment plans. Under the retrospective payment system, the health care provider calculates its allowable costs and compares them to the amount of interim payments received from the financial intermediary, i.e., Blue Cross or Medicare, and compares these totals to determine whether the hospital owes monies or is due monies from the intermediary. Because of the lack of incentives to control costs, the retrospective payment system is losing favor with third party payers.

Prospective payment systems (PPSs) may be computed in various methods. The following are three methods commonly used:

1. per unit of service
2. per patient day
3. per case

A prospective payment system based on unit of service can be established at a fixed rate for a specific service, such as

Complete blood count (CBC)	$37.00
Chest x-ray	$74.00,

or the prospective payment agreement may be determined at a fixed rate per relative value unit (RVU):

Complete blood count	
50 RVUs @ $0.74 =	$37.00

Chest x-ray
100 RVUs @ $0.74 = $74.00

A prospective payment system based upon a per patient day or per diem rate agrees to pay the health care provider a fixed amount per patient day regardless of the type or amount of service rendered to the patient. If a patient is in the intensive care unit (ICU) for three days and in the medical and surgical routine nursing unit for seven days, the provider would be paid the same flat rate for ten days. For example, if the PPS per diem rate is $450, the provider (hospital) would receive $4,500, computed as follows:

3 ICU days @ $450. =	$ 1,350.00
7 M&S days @ $450. =	3,150.00
10 total days @ $450. =	$ 4,500.00

In 1984, the Health Care Financing Administration (HCFA) published regulations implementing the Medicare version of a PPS that pays the provider on a per case or admission basis. Under Medicare's PPS, prospective payments are made to the hospital based upon the type of case or DRG for which the patient is admitted to the hospital. The DRG system was developed by Yale University for classifying patient admissions into clinically coherent and homogeneous groups with respect to resources used. There are 467 such DRGs, separated into 23 major diagnostic categories (MDC), broad clinical categories differentiated from all others based on body system involvement and disease etiology. Each DRG is assigned a classification. For example, a cardiac arrest has the following identification:

DRG-129:	Cardiac arrest
MDC-15:	Diseases and disorders of the circulatory system
1.5506:	Relative weighting factor
4.6:	Mean length of stay

A hospital operating under the DRG prospective payment system is informed of the dollar value of one DRG, and the respective relative weighting factor is multiplied by this amount to arrive at the payment the hospital will receive for that specific patient. If Memorial Hospital's DRG rate is $3,515.00, the prospective payment for a cardiac arrest would be computed as follows:

$$\begin{array}{ll}
\text{DRG value (1.000)} = & \$3,515.00 \\
\text{DRG-129 relative weighting factor} & 1.5506 \\
\text{Prospective payment} & \\
\quad (\$3,515.00 \times 1.5506) = & \$5,450.36
\end{array}$$

Prospective payment systems are designed to accomplish two purposes:

1. to serve as an incentive to the health care provider to utilize cost-effective procedures and keep operating costs below the prospective rate in order to generate a profit
2. to provide the purchasing agent a "hard" amount of health care costs that can be utilized in the budgetary process

Generally speaking, prospective payment systems allow the provider to keep the difference (profit) between the rate and the provider's cost of rendering the service. Conversely, if the provider's operating cost exceeds the prospective payment rate, the provider must absorb the loss.

Another prospective payment system that appears to be attracting considerable attention, not only from the Medicare and Medicaid programs, but also from the major health insurance companies, is the capitation method. The capitation method has been universally used by health maintenance organizations (HMOs) since their inception.

Capitation payment systems pay the health care provider a fixed amount per month, or other specific period of time, or per individual subscriber, regardless of whether the person is treated by the provider or not. The provider agrees to give the subscriber (member) whatever type of care is required, as long as it is included on the payer's menu (contract) of services. The key to controlling costs under a capitation environment is to have an efficient primary or "gatekeeper" physician screen and/or treat subscribers before they are admitted to the hospital.

Since capitation payments are usually paid to the provider on a monthly basis, the capitation payment system provides a relatively steady and predictable cash flow to the hospital. However, the hospital must be constantly aware of the relationship between the cash inflows (revenues) and the cash outflows (costs). For example, if Memorial Hospital's HMO has 10,000 subscribers, and their monthly per capitation rate is $192, the monthly cash inflows would be computed as follows:

10,000 subscribers @ $192 = $1,920,000.

These cash inflows must be constantly monitored to ensure that they are not exceeded by cash outflows.

Another capitation payment system promoted by the Department of Health and Human Services (HHS) is the Competitive Medical Plan (CMP). A CMP may be defined as an entity that

1. provides a minimum of the following:

   - physician services
   - inpatient hospital services
   - laboratory, x-ray, emergency, and preventive services
   - out of area coverage

2. receives compensation on a periodic prepaid capitated basis
3. provides physician services through physicians who are employees or partners of the entity or are under contract to the entity
4. assumes full financial risk
5. adequately insures against the risk of insolvency

In summary, it appears that the trend is toward some form of prospective payment system, especially capitation, and negotiated contracts, and that the retrospective payment systems are obsolete.

METHODS OF RATE SETTING

One of the most frequent errors in rate setting is the exclusive use of historical costs and statistics. Only budgeted or planned costs and statistics should be used to establish a published charge. Although historical data, and even competitors' charges, can serve as reference points, they should only be used as benchmarks. Published charges or prospective rates are for future services. Therefore, it is logical to base these rates on future costs and statistics.

There are four generally used methods of establishing rates for individual departmental services:

1. *Relative Values*

   Each departmental service or output procedure is assigned a relative value unit (RVU) as discussed in Chapter 5. This is based on the relative time and/or resources required to perform it. Each is multiplied by the number of services or outputs in the cost period to determine a weighted value. The total amount (financial requirements) to be recovered from rates, divided by total weighted values, produces the unit value. The unit value is then multiplied by the relative units for each service to provide the weighted rate per service. For example:

Service	RVU	Number Performed	Weighted Value	Rate per RVU	Rate per Service
Complete Blood Count	50	2,000	100,000	$.25	$12.50
Pap Smear	30	1,000	30,000	$.25	$ 7.50
Micor Tissue	150	250	37,500	$.25	$37.50
Total Weighted Values				167,550	
Total Financial Requirements				$ 41,875	
Average Financial Requirements Per RVU				$.25	

2. *Cost Plus a Percentage*
This method of rate setting is used in merchandising-type departments, such as pharmacy and central supply.

For example:

Central Supply	Direct Supply Costs	%	Mark-Up on Cost $	Rate
Disposable syringe	$ 1.00	100%	$ 1.00	$ 2.00
Disposable OR packs	$15.00	100%	$15.00	$30.00

It is important to determine a method of mark-up. The percentage of mark-up can be based either on cost or on selling price, illustrated as follows:

Mark-Up on Cost		%
Cost	$10.00	100
Plus mark-up	10.00	100
Selling price	$20.00	

Mark-Up on Selling Price		%
Selling price	$20.00	100
Less: mark-up	10.00	50
Cost	$10.00	

3. *Hourly or Time Rates*

The hourly rate method is used in such departments as operating and recovery rooms, anesthesiology, physiotherapy, and emergency services. There are two basic approaches: straight hourly (partial hour) or person-minute rates, and a base or set-up charge plus time. Table 8–3 illustrates four variations upon the hourly or time rate method of rate setting, to illustrate the versatility of this approach.

Table 8–3 Four Variations upon the Hourly or Time Rate Method of Rate Setting

Straight Hourly Rate

Number of OR Minutes	90	
Rate per Hour	$150	
Total Charge per Case		$225

Ranges of Time

30–60 minutes	$150	
61–90 minutes	$225	
Total Charge per case 90 minutes		$225

Set-up Base Plus Hourly Rate

Fixed Set-up Charge	$150	
Rate per OR Hour	$ 50	

Charge for 90 Minute Case

Set-up Charge	$150	
90 OR Minutes	75	
Total Charge per Case		$225

Set-up Base Plus Person-Minute Rate

Number of OR Minutes	90	
Number of Paid OR Personnel	3	
Number of OR Person-Minutes	270	
Charge per Person-Minutes	$ .50	
Set-up Base Charge	$ 90	

Charge for 90 Minute Case

Set-up Charge	$ 90	
270 Person-Minutes @ $.50	$135	
Total Charge per Case		$225

4. *Routine Services*
   The routine service method is directly related to the type or desirability of accommodation. To calculate rates, computations are based on fixed and variable costs related to a specific type of routine service.[7] Table 8–4 is an illustration for developing room rates for routine medical and surgical nursing service, using a weighted method in which a ward patient equals 1, a semiprivate patient equals 1.5 and a private patient equals 3.

Potential Cash Method

The potential cash method evaluates the health care facility's current charge structure in order to alternate the charge structure and identify the source of cash in-flows by departments.[8] To accomplish this objective, each revenue-producing department is individually analyzed. The potential cash method's basic goals are:

- to program each department to recover, through net revenue or charges, its own direct and allocated costs, plus a profit margin
- to maintain a direct relationship between the
  - unit of service
  - cost per unit of service
  - charge per unit of service

Table 8–4 Developing Room Rates for Routine Medical and Surgical Nursing Service

Description	Total	Private	Semiprivate	Ward
Patient Days	40,940	8,188	21,290	11,462
% Patient Days	100%	20%	52%	28%
Weighted Value	-0-	3	1.5	1
Weighted Patient Days	67,961	24,564	31,935	11,462
% Weighted Patient Days	100%	36%	47%	17%
Total Costs	$5,117,500	$1,842,300	$2,405,225	$869,975
Computer Average Cost Per Patient Day	$125.00	$225.00	$112.97	$75.90
Rounded Published Charge Per Room	$125.00	$225.00	$115.00	$80.00
Projected Gross Charge	$5,207,610	$1,842,300	$2,448,350	$916,960
Favorable Charge/Cost Variance	$90,110	none	$43,125	$46,985

- to reduce contractual allowances
- to assist in adjusting to an equitable charge structure
- to maximize cash in-flow

Table 8–5 illustrates the worksheet used to analyze the actual charges, costs, and respective potential cash in-flows by paying agents of the laboratory department. It is important that the percentage of the total units and the percentage of total charges are basically the same. This implies that the department is charging in direct proportion to the volume produced. In this case, the laboratory is charging by the RVU system.

The potential cash was determined on the basis of the reimbursement method. In this case, the following primary paying agents paid on the basis of gross charges:

- other
- self
- commercial insurance

while the remaining paid the hospital on the basis of costs.

The proposed change in rates is from an above of 14.3¢ to a charge of 12¢ per RVU, thus reducing net cash flow from $221,571 to $208,145 or $13,426, while reducing contractual allowances $34,680 as follows:

	Before	*After*
Gross charges	$294,705	$246,599
Potential cash	221,571	208,145
Contractual allowances	$ 73,134	$ 38,454

In the operating room illustration, Table 8–6, potential cash was increased $6,585 from $116,215 to $122,800, while the comparative gross operating margins were improved as follows:

	Before	*After*
Gross charge	$ 95,732	$122,932
Cost	$122,758	122,758
Gross margin (loss)	⟨$ 27,026⟩	$ 174

In summary, the potential cash method of analyzing charges, cost and cash in-flow is a necessary management tool to assure that charges for

Table 8-5 Analysis of Actual Charges and Cost and Potential Cash Flow by Primary Paying Agents

DEPT. NO. 552   DEPARTMENT: LABORATORY   PERIOD FROM OCTOBER 1, 19x8   TO DECEMBER 31, 19x8

MEMORIAL HOSPITAL
ANYTOWN, U.S.A.

[X] INPATIENT   [ ] OUTPATIENT   [ ] NEWBORN

| | CURRENT STATISTICS, CHARGES & COST AS OF DECEMBER 31, 19x8 | | | | | | | | PROPOSED CHARGE ADJUSTMENT | | |
PRIMARY PAYING AGENT	UNITS OF SERVICE	GROSS CHARGES	% OF TOTAL UNITS	% OF TOTAL CHARGES	CHARGE PER UNIT	DISTRIB. OF TOTAL COST	COST PER UNIT	POTENTIAL CASH	ADJUSTED GROSS CHARGES	ADJUSTED COST DISTRIB.	ADJUSTED POTENTIAL CASH
OTHER	6,340	840	0.3	0.3	13.3	615	9.7	840	761	596	761
SELF	85,172	12,327	4.1	4.2	14.5	8,603	10.1	12,327	10,221	8,341	10,221
CONN. B.C.	687,111	97,287	33.4	33.0	14.2	67,598	9.8	67,598	82,453	65,534	65,534
AHS OF N.Y.	93,445	13,340	4.5	4.5	14.3	9,218	9.9	9,218	11,213	8,936	8,936
COM. INSUR.	298,893	42,074	14.5	14.3	14.1	29,292	9.8	42,074	35,867	28,398	35,867
WORK. COMP.	14,380	2,046	0.7	0.7	14.2	1,434	10.0	1,434	1,726	1,390	1,434
CITY/TOWN											
STATE	78,185	11,369	3.8	3.9	14.5	7,989	10.2	7,989	9,382	7,745	7,745
MEDICARE	790,871	115,335	38.6	39.0	14.6	79,887	10.1	79,887	94,905	77,449	77,449
M.A. TITLE 19	590	88	0.1	0.1	14.9	204	-0-	204	71	198	198
TOTAL	2,054,987	294,705	100.0	100.0	14.3	204,841	10.0	221,571	246,599	198,587	208,145

RATIO –

	PRESENT	PROPOSED		
POTENTIAL CASH: GROSS CHGS.	75.2	84.4	INPAT. CHGS.	294,705
POTENTIAL CASH: TOTAL COST	108.2	104.8	TOTAL CHGS.	$\frac{294,705}{343,434}$ = 85.8% X TOTAL COST 238,742 = COST PER PERIOD 204,841
TOTAL COST: GROSS CHGS.	69.5	80.5	COMMENTS:	

Source: Reprinted from *Concepts in Hospital Financial Management* by A.G. Herkimer, Jr., pp. 61–72, with permission of Alfa Associates, Inc., © 1970.

Table 8–6 Analysis of Actual Charges and Cost and Potential Cash Flow by Primary Paying Agents

MEMORIAL HOSPITAL
ANYTOWN, U.S.A.

DEPT. NO. 547   DEPARTMENT OPERATING ROOM   PERIOD FROM OCTOBER 1, 19x8 TO DECEMBER 31, 19x8

X INPATIENT   OUTPATIENT   NEWBORN

CURRENT STATISTICS, CHARGES & COST AS OF DECEMBER 31, 19x8 — PROPOSED CHARGE ADJUSTMENT

PRIMARY PAYING AGENT	UNITS OF SERVICE	GROSS CHARGES	% OF TOTAL UNITS	% OF TOTAL CHARGES	CHARGE PER UNIT	DISTRIB. OF TOTAL COST	COST PER UNIT	POTENTIAL CASH	ADJUSTED GROSS CHARGES	ADJUSTED COST DISTRIB.	ADJUSTED POTENTIAL CASH
OTHER	1,891	475	0.8	0.5	.25	614	.33	475	615	614	615
SELF	8,545	2,946	3.4	3.1	.35	3,805	.45	2,946	3,811	3,805	3,811
CONN. B.C.	111,287	43,201	44.3	45.1	.39	55,364	.50	55,364	55,442	55,364	55,364
AHS OF N.Y.	12,180	4,983	4.8	5.2	.41	6,383	.52	6,383	6,392	6,383	6,383
COM. INSUR.	49,862	19,498	19.9	20.4	.39	25,043	.50	19,498	25,078	25,043	25,078
WORK. COMP.	6,368	2,390	2.5	2.5	.38	3,069	.48	3,069	3,073	3,069	3,069
CITY/TOWN											
STATE	5,085	2,128	2.0	2.2	.42	2,701	.53	2,701	2,705	2,701	2,701
MEDICARE	55,693	19,931	22.1	20.8	.36	25,534	.46	25,534	25,570	25,534	25,534
M.A. TITLE 19	590	180	0.2	0.2	.31	245	.42	245	246	245	245
TOTAL	251,501	95,732	100.0	100.0	.38	122,758	.49	116,215	122,932	122,758	122,800

PRESENT/PROPOSED

RATIO –

POTENTIAL CASH: GROSS CHGS.	121.4	99.9 INPAT. CHGS.
POTENTIAL CASH: TOTAL COST	94.7	100.0 TOTAL CHGS.
TOTAL COST: GROSS CHGS.	128.2	99.9 COMMENTS:

$$\frac{95,732}{95,732} = 100\% \times \text{TOTAL COST} \quad 122,758 = \frac{\text{COST}}{\text{PER PERIOD}}$$

Source: Reprinted from *Hospital Financial Management* by A.G. Herkimer, Jr., pp. 61–72, with permission of Alfa Associates, Inc., © 1970.

services are equal to or above the cost of generating the services and that charges are adjusted to maximize cash in-flow.

MEDICARE OVERVIEW

Hospitals will be paid prospectively toward operating costs for inpatient hospital services on a per discharge (DRG) or principal admission basis. The principal admission diagnosis is defined as "the condition established after study to be chiefly responsible for causing the patient's admission to the hospital." Inpatient operating costs subject to PPS include routine operating costs, ancillary costs, special care unit costs, and malpractice insurance costs.[9]

Excluded from the prospective rate and still paid on a reasonable cost basis (e.g., "pass-through" costs) are capital-related expenses, direct medical education costs, outpatient costs, costs for direct medical and surgical services of physicians in teaching hospitals, and kidney acquisition costs. Surely coverage of other extraordinary inpatient costs, such as artificial hearts and transplants of various sorts will be questionable under the PPS.

Additional payments will be made for atypical cases (i.e., outliers), bad debts associated with beneficiary deductibles and coinsurance, and indirect medical education costs.

Medicare considers the prospective rate payment in full for designated inpatient operating costs and will make payment if the beneficiary is eligible for at least one day of inpatient care upon admission.

Finally, PPS places hospitals at risk for providing services to Medicare patients. Hospitals with per case costs in excess of the prospective rates will have to absorb the difference between the rates and their cases; those hospitals keeping their case costs below the rates will keep the difference.

While the hospitals are busily adjusting their operating and accounting systems to the DRG case payment system, Medicare is conducting a series of experimental projects using the capitation (per person) payment system. Very possibly capitation will be Medicare's payment system in the near future, and then hospitals will again have to reconstruct their operations and accounting systems.

In the meantime, the marketplace is changing from a highly protective, retrospective payment system to a very competitive marketplace with no holds barred. Price-driven and consumer-driven purchase and sales discounts, discounting receivables to financing institutions, and other most-favored purchaser pricing and marketing strategies will all be utilized in future hospital financial management.

REFERENCES

1. American Hospital Association, *Cost Finding and Rate Setting* (Chicago, Ill.: 1968), pp. 1–2.
2. Ibid.
3. American Hospital Association, *Cost Finding and Rate Setting* (Chicago, Ill.: 1968), pp. 20–24.
4. Ibid.
5. Ibid.
6. Ibid.
7. American Hospital Association, *Cost Finding and Rate Setting* (Chicago, Ill.: 1968), pp. 94–96.
8. Allen G. Herkimer, Jr., *Concepts in Hospital Financial Management* (Paradise Valley, Ariz.: Alfa Associates, Inc., 1970), pp. 61–72.
9. "Description and Analysis of Medicare Prospective Price Setting Including Changes for Year Two" (Oakbrook, Ill.: Healthcare Financial Management Association, 1983), pp. 1–3.

Chapter 9

Revenue Budgeting

The Social Security Amendments of 1983 (Public Law 98-21) contain provisions that have caused the most drastic changes in hospital financial management since the implementation of Medicare in 1966 by paying hospitals according to a prospective payment system. As discussed in Chapter 8, the establishment of a Medicare PPS that bases its payments for hospital inpatient services on a preestablished per discharge (DRG) rate has forced hospital financial managers to incorporate case-mix management and the traditional method of departmental revenue budgeting.

The first part of this chapter discusses the traditional departmental revenue budgeting approach. This method of revenue budgeting can be used to budget general outpatient services and nonreimbursed inpatient services. Later in the chapter, the case-mix management concept is presented to familiarize the reader with revenue budgeting based on types of discharges rather than on departmental services.

DEPARTMENTAL REVENUE BUDGETING

The revenue budget predicts the amount of revenue the institution can expect from each department. The accuracy of the departmental revenue budget is critical, since it determines how much departmental reimbursement can be expected for services rendered.

Traditionally, many health care financial managers would develop an expense budget first and then develop a revenue budget that would either allow the department to break even or generate a modest profit. This approach emphasized the expenses rather than volume of revenue that should be ultimately fitted to meet the expense budget.

The approach presented here places the emphasis first on the volume of service. Second is the anticipated revenue that can be expected with the volume forecasted at the existing rate structure. Third is developing the expense budget, which is based upon the same projected volume. After the preliminary revenue and expense matching process, and the inclusion of cost containment, the final revenue budget can be established.

Departmental revenue budgeting is divided into the following three primary components:

- inpatient revenue
- outpatient revenue
- deduction from gross charges

The components are completely dependent upon:

- volume forecast
- service utilization factor
- patient mix

In Chapter 6, the volume forecast was identified as the keystone to a successful budgetary control program, since it identifies the amount of units of service generated for a certain period of time. In the initial volume forecasting process, the following macro statistical units of service are generated:

- patient days of forecast inpatient service
- visits of forecasted outpatient, clinic, and/or emergency services

The service utilization factor is the average number of departmental units of service used during the macro statistical units. For example:

- 200 radiology micro (relative value) units of service per one inpatient day

or

- 150 radiology micro (relative value) units of service per one outpatient visit

The macro statistical units multiplied by the service utilization factor establish the total number of micro departmental units of service.

These, in turn, can be multiplied by the average current charge per service to determine the gross charges for the department.

In most businesses, the revenue budget would stop right here. But, since the health care industry has numerous third party purchasers, departmental revenue budgets must incorporate provisions for:

- third party contractual allowances
- free and charitable work
- bad debts

in order to ultimately determine the net amount the facility can expect to receive for its services. The key to this determination is the patient mix, or paying agent mix. A typical inpatient patient day mix might be as follows:

• Medicare	50.6%
• Medicaid	1.5%
• Blue Cross	12.0%
• Private pay & commercial insurance	35.9%
• Total	100%

Patient mix will vary greatly between health care facilities and between departments within each facility. Such factors as geographic location of the facility, insurance carriers for local major employers, population age, area physicians, competition, and other demographic components help to determine the patient mix for each health care facility and its respective departments. Once the patient mix has been determined, factors can be developed to allow for contractual allowances, either by each department or by an overall average for the institution. Only experience and good common sense can assist in the determination of courtesy and bad debt factors.

In this chapter, we will develop a total health care facility's patient revenue budget in order to illustrate how each department's revenue budget fits into the facility's total revenue plan.

SHARED RESPONSIBILITY

Although the chief executive and the chief financial officers of the health care facility have the ultimate responsibility for the development of the budgetary control program, those individuals who are held accountable for controlling each department must be directly involved. The attainability of the financial plan, especially the revenue budget, should be the result of a series of meetings between the department managers, their supervisors, and the budget director. The budgetary accountants, management engineers, and other related individuals from budget and/or accounting departments should offer their technical guidance, but the reasonableness of the statistical and revenue budgets should have considerable input from the department managers and their supervisors. These individuals are the ones on the firing line and the only ones who can exercise any degree of control over the activities of the department. Their involvement and acceptance are critical to a successful program.

IMPORTANCE OF HISTORICAL DATA

In Chapter 6, the use of historical data and how they could be utilized to establish the volume forecast was discussed. These data contribute greatly to one's knowledge of the department's activities, but they should be used only as a point of reference from which to start the revenue budget. Frequently, historical data, especially statistics, are used as the only source in projecting the future. In this case, past inefficiencies are built in, while changes in technology and methodology are not considered along with other facts. In reality, there is not a mathematical model, at this time, which incorporates all variables needed to project volume and/or revenue. But it can be programmed and projected with a reasonable degree of accuracy. The key is the risk-judgment decision-making process of the department managers and their supervisors. Their knowledge and experience, coupled with mathematical projection, should develop a logical and accurate revenue budget. Historical data are especially important in the development of monthly or seasonal trends projection.

MONTHLY VOLUME DISTRIBUTION

Initially, the inpatient revenue budget should be developed. First, establish a monthly distribution of the total forecasted patient days. This process requires the following analysis:

- month
- paying agent
- type of service
- type of accommodation

For the purpose of illustration, the previous year's monthly patient distribution was used in Table 9–1 to distribute the forecasted patient days, excluding newborn, of 85,500. However, it is generally believed that a three-year moving average would smooth out most peaks and valleys in the volume distribution and therefore more accurately forecast the budget year's activity.

The initial monthly distribution has been further refined in Table 9–2 to distribute the patient days according to paying agents. This classification of patient days was based upon the historical monthly percentage distribution by paying agent as developed in Table 9–3.

Table 9–1 Monthly Distribution of Total Adult and Pediatric Patient Day Forecast Based upon the Previous Year's Actual Patient Days

MEMORIAL HOSPITAL
ANYTOWN, U.S.A.

PATIENT DAYS

MONTH	ADULT & PEDIATRIC	NEWBORN	PERCENTAGE OF TOTAL PATIENT DAYS
January	7,550	322	8.82
February	6,750	287	7.88
March	7,125	303	8.29
April	7,250	311	8.52
May	7,150	303	8.30
June	6,750	295	8.09
July	6,550	264	7.24
August	6,825	292	7.99
September	7,250	310	8.48
October	7,750	335	9.18
November	7,550	321	8.79
December	7,000	307	8.42
TOTAL	85,500	3,650	100.00

Table 9–2 Monthly Distribution of Total Adult and Pediatric Patient Day Forecast by Paying Agent, Using Monthly Distribution Percentage Factor Developed in Table 9–3

MEMORIAL HOSPITAL
ANYTOWN, U.S.A.

PATIENT DAY FORECAST

MONTH	TOTAL	MEDICARE	MEDICAID	BLUE CROSS	PRIVATE
January	7,550	3,616	136	838	2,960
February	6,750	3,726	94	770	2,160
March	7,125	3,655	86	762	2,622
April	7,250	3,611	87	761	2,791
May	7,150	3,675	114	744	2,617
June	6,750	3,705	68	797	2,180
July	6,550	3,360	33	825	2,332
August	6,825	3,856	89	812	2,068
September	7,250	3,647	180	943	2,480
October	7,750	3,735	124	1,085	2,806
November	7,550	3,239	136	1,019	3,156
December	7,000	3,332	112	980	2,576
TOTAL	85,500	43,157	1,259	10,336	30,748

Through further analysis of the historical data, it has been determined that the following distribution most accurately represents the patient day percentage utilization by types of services:

- Medical-Surgical (including Pediatrics)   88.78%
- Intensive Care Units/Coronary Care Units (ICU/CCU)   3.28%
- Maternity   3.85%
- Newborn   4.09%
   Total   100.00%

Table 9-3 Monthly Distribution Percentage of Total Adult and Pediatric Patient Days by Paying Agent Based upon Previous Year's Actual Patient Days

MEMORIAL HOSPITAL
ANYTOWN, U.S.A.

MONTHLY DISTRIBUTION PERCENTAGE

MONTH	TOTAL	MEDICARE	MEDICAID	BLUE CROSS	PRIVATE
January	100.0	47.9	1.8	11.1	39.2
February	100.0	55.2	1.4	11.4	32.0
March	100.0	51.3	1.2	10.7	36.8
April	100.0	49.8	1.2	10.5	38.5
May	100.0	51.4	1.6	10.4	36.6
June	100.0	54.9	1.0	11.8	32.3
July	100.0	51.3	0.5	12.6	35.6
August	100.0	56.3	1.3	11.9	30.3
September	100.0	50.3	2.5	13.0	34.2
October	100.0	48.2	1.6	14.0	36.2
November	100.0	42.9	1.8	13.5	41.8
December	100.0	47.6	1.6	14.0	36.8
TOTAL	100.0	50.6	1.5	12.0	35.9

Using the above analysis, the total patient day forecast including newborn, would be as follows:

	Number	Percent
• Medical-Surgical (including Pediatrics)	79,150	88.78
• ICU/CCU	2,920	3.28
• Maternity	3,430	3.85
Total Adult and Pediatrics	85,500	95.91
• Newborn	3,650	4.09
Grand Total Patient Days	89,150	100.00

Incorporating this annual analysis of patient days with the monthly patient day distribution in Table 9–1, a monthly distribution of total patient days can be developed as illustrated in Table 9–4.

Table 9–4 Distribution of Total Patient Days by Type of Service

MEMORIAL HOSPITAL
ANYTOWN, U.S.A.

		TYPE OF SERVICE			
DESCRIPTION	TOTAL	MEDICAL SURGICAL	ICU/CCU	MATERNITY	NEWBORN
Number of Beds	295	245	10	20	20
Annual Patient Day Capacity	107,675	89,425	3,650	7,300	7,300

DISTRIBUTION OF PATIENT DAYS

MONTH					
January	7,872	6,982	258	303	322
February	7,037	6,237	230	270	287
March	7,428	6,562	242	284	303
April	7,561	6,744	249	292	311
May	7,453	6,569	242	284	303
June	7,045	6,403	236	277	295
July	6,814	5,730	211	248	264
August	7,117	6,324	233	274	292
September	7,560	6,712	248	292	310
October	8,065	7,266	268	315	335
November	7,871	6,957	257	302	321
December	7,307	6,664	246	289	307
TOTAL	89,150	79,150	2,920	3,430	3,650
Percent of Distribution	100.00	88.78	3.28	3.85	4.09
Percent of Occupancy	82.80	88.51	80.00	46.99	50.00

The next step in manipulating the patient day statistics is to distribute each type of service by the various types of room accommodations. The following is a summary of the annual patient day distribution forecast by types of accommodations.

Type of Service	Total	One Bed	Two Beds	Four Beds	Ward
Medical/Surgical	79,150	6,570	43,289	23,360	5,931
Maternity	3,430	367	1,626	—	1,437
ICU/CCU	2,920	2,920	—	—	—
Total Adult and Pediatric	85,500	9,857	44,915	23,360	7,368
Newborn	3,650	3,650	—	—	—
Grand Total Patient Days	89,150	13,507	44,915	23,360	7,368

The distribution of patient days by room is essential. In this illustration, the health care facility had four separate charges, based upon the number of beds in a room. The extent of the distribution of patient days by type of room accommodations is determined by the number of different charge levels for rooms. No extended distribution was made for ICU/CCU and newborn patient days, since each type of service had only one charge level or one type of service. Tables 9–5 and 9–6 illustrate a monthly distribution of the medical and surgical and maternity patient days by room accommodation.

The next step in analyzing statistical data for the revenue budget is to analyze each department's revenue by paying agent. This is accomplished by analyzing the previous year's actual distribution. Table 9–7 is an illustration of a percentage distribution of inpatient departmental services by paying agent. This schedule highlights the variations in utilization of departmental services by the various paying agents.

Table 9–7 can also be used to assist in establishing charges for services in order to maximize reimbursement. For example, a department, such as respiratory therapy, which has relatively high third party reimbursements at cost, and low private pay, should keep its charges close to cost in order to minimize the amount of contractual allowance. A department such as radiology, which has a relatively high percentage of private purchasers, such as commercial insurance and self-pay, should set its charges substantially over cost in order to improve the cash flow.

Table 9–5 Monthly Distribution of Medical and Surgical Patient
Day Forecast by Type of Room Accommodation

MEMORIAL HOSPITAL
ANYTOWN, U.S.A.

		TYPE OF ROOM ACCOMMODATION			
DESCRIPTION	TOTAL	ONE BED	TWO BED	FOUR BED	WARD
Number of Beds	245	20	120	80	25
Annual Patient Day Capacity	89,425	7,300	43,800	29,200	9,125

DISTRIBUTION OF PATIENT DAYS

MONTH					
January	6,982	579	3,818	2,060	525
February	6,237	518	3,411	1,841	467
March	6,562	545	3,589	1,937	492
April	6,744	560	3,688	1,990	505
May	6,569	545	3,593	1,939	492
June	6,403	532	3,502	1,890	480
July	5,730	475	3,134	1,691	429
August	6,324	525	3,459	1,866	474
September	6,712	557	3,671	1,981	503
October	7,266	603	3,974	2,144	544
November	6,957	578	3,805	2,053	521
December	6,664	553	3,645	1,968	499
TOTAL	79,150	6,570	43,289	23,360	5,931
Percent of Distribution	100.00	8.30	54.69	29.52	7.49
Percent of Occupancy	88.51	90.00	98.83	80.00	64.99

Table 9–6 Monthly Distribution of Maternity Patient Day Forecast by Type of Room Accommodation

MEMORIAL HOSPITAL
ANYTOWN, U.S.A.

DESCRIPTION	TOTAL	TYPE OF ROOM ACCOMMODATION		
		ONE BED	TWO BED	WARD
Number of Beds	20	3	12	5
Annual Patient Day Capacity	7,300	1,095	4,380	1,825

DISTRIBUTION OF PATIENT DAYS

MONTH				
January	303	32	143	128
February	270	29	128	113
March	284	30	135	119
April	292	31	139	122
May	284	30	135	119
June	277	30	132	116
July	248	27	118	104
August	274	29	130	115
September	292	31	138	122
October	315	34	149	132
November	302	32	143	126
December	289	32	136	121
TOTAL	3,430	367	1,626	1,437
Percent of Distribution	100.00	10.70	47.40	41.90
Percent of Occupancy	46.99	33.52	37.12	78.74

Table 9–7 Percentage Analysis of Inpatient Departmental Service Utilization by Paying Agent

MEMORIAL HOSPITAL
ANYTOWN, U.S.A.

| DEPARTMENT | TOTAL | TYPE OF PAYING AGENTS (PERCENT) | | | |
		MEDICARE	MEDICAID	BLUE CROSS	PRIVATE
Routine Services					
Medical & Surgical	100.00	52.79	1.19	12.49	33.53
ICU/CCU	100.00	55.31	2.07	12.56	30.06
Maternity	100.00	--	5.72	30.64	63.64
Newborn	100.00	--	6.03	29.96	64.01
Total Routine Service	100.00	52.79	1.22	12.60	33.39
Special Services					
Operating Room	100.00	45.83	2.17	27.05	24.95
Postoperative Room	100.00	46.07	2.03	27.14	24.76
Anesthesiology	100.00	45.92	2.12	27.09	24.87
Delivery Room	100.00	--	5.40	31.16	68.84
Cardiology	100.00	54.42	0.06	8.27	37.25
Radiology	100.00	33.38	1.08	11.09	54.45
Laboratory	100.00	48.54	1.25	12.95	37.26
Respiratory Therapy	100.00	65.81	1.59	6.59	26.01
Physical Therapy	100.00	52.99	0.03	4.76	42.22
Central Sterile Supply	100.00	43.04	0.07	11.03	45.86
Pharmacy	100.00	53.81	1.74	11.68	32.77
Emergency Room	100.00	5.24	2.30	2.21	90.25
TOTAL SPECIAL SERVICES	100.00	36.12	1.36	12.40	39.88

This schedule will also be used to calculate the deductions from gross charges, such as:

- contractual allowances
- provision for bad debts
- provision for free services

This will be discussed in greater detail later in this chapter. Up to this point, we have been examining inpatient statistical data to gather information regarding:

- monthly distribution of patient days
- annual utilization of patient days by types of services
- annual utilization of patient days by paying agent
- annual utilization of departmental routine and special services by paying agents
- annual utilization of routine service by room accommodations

These statistical analyses have been essential to project an annual revenue budget on a monthly basis. However, for the purpose of the remainder of this text, only an annual revenue budget will be illustrated.

Tables 9–8, 9–9, and 9–10 are examples of worksheets which have been used to develop a preliminary revenue budget. The empty columns at the extreme right will be used to develop the final target revenue budget after the preliminary revenue budget has been matched with the final expense budgets. This developmental phase of the revenue budget allows for rate changes to the present charge structure to enable the final target revenue budget to meet the expense and profit needs of the health care facility.

OUTPATIENT REVENUE BUDGET

The development of the outpatient revenue budget starts from the distribution of the second prime statistical volume indicator: visits. As stated earlier, a multi-year average distribution, i.e., two or three years, is usually more representative of what can be expected for the budget year than a one-year average.

Table 9–11 presents a monthly distribution of outpatient visits based upon a two-year average. This can be used to develop a monthly

Table 9–8 Summary of Annual Projection of Routine Service Revenue by Room Classification for Fiscal Year 19x2

Memorial Hospital
Anytown, U.S.A.

(1) Description	(2) Projected Patient Days	(3) Present Daily Room Rate	(4) Preliminary Revenue 2 × 3 = 4	(5) Revised Daily Room Rate	(6) Revised Target Revenue Budget 2 × 5 = 6
Medical & Surgical—One Bed	6,570	$ 75.00	$ 492,750		
" " —Two Bed	43,289	60.00	2,597,340		
" " —Four Bed	23,360	53.00	1,238,080		
" —Ward	5,931	49.00	290,619		
Total Medical & Surgical	79,150	-0-	$4,618,789		
Maternity—One Bed	367	$ 75.00	$ 27,525		
" —Two Bed	1,626	60.00	97,560		
" —Ward	1,437	49.00	70,413		
Total Maternity	3,430	-0-	$ 195,498		
ICU/CCU	2,920	$125.00	$ 365,000		
Newborn Nursery	3,650	35.00	127,750		
Total	89,150	-0-	$5,307,037		

Table 9–9 Summary of Annual Projection of Inpatient Special Service Revenue (Excluding Newborn) for Fiscal Year 19x2

(1)	(2)	(3)	(4)	(5)	(6)	(7)	(8)	(9)
Department	Production Unit	Average Production Units Per Patient Day (Excluding N.B.)	Projected Patient Days (Excluding N.B.)	Projected Annual Production Units (3 × 4 = 5)	Present Charge Per Production Unit	Preliminary Annual Revenue (5 × 6 = 7)	Revised Charge Per Production Unit	Revised Target Revenue Budget (5 × 8 = 9)
Operating Room	Person—Minutes	30.00	85,500	2,565,000	$ 1.15	$ 2,949,750		$
Recovery Room	Person—Minutes	10.00	85,500	855,000	0.75	641,250		
Anesthesiology	Person—Minutes	30.00	85,500	2,565,000	0.90	2,308,500		
Delivery Suite	Deliveries	0.90 (Maternity Pat.) (Day Only)	3,430	3,087	125.00	385,875		
Cardiology	Relative Value Unit	0.75	85,500	64,125	2.50	160,313		
Radiology	Relative Value Unit	80.00	85,500	6,840,000	0.15	1,026,000		
Laboratory	Relative Value Unit	90.00	85,500	7,695,000	0.12	923,400		
Respiratory Therapy	Relative Value Unit	15.00	85,500	128,250	1.00	128,250		
Physical Therapy	Relative Value Unit	20.00	85,500	1,710,000	0.50	855,000		
Central Sterile Supply	Requisitions	1.50	85,500	128,250	2.50	320,625		
Pharmacy	Prescriptions	2.00	85,500	171,000	1.75	299,250		
Emergency Service	Person—Minutes	5.00	85,500	427,500	0.50	213,750		
Total						$10,211,963		$

Table 9–10 Summary of Annual Projection of Newborn Revenue for Fiscal Year 19x2

(1)	(2)	(3)	(4)	(5)	(6)	(7)	(8)	(9)
Department	Production Unit	Average Production Units Per Newborn Patient Day	Projected Newborn Patient Days	Projected Annual Production Units (3 × 4 = 5)	Present Charge Per Production Unit	Preliminary Annual Revenue (5 × 6 = 7)	Revised Charge Per Production Unit	Revised Target Revenue Budget (5 × 8 = 9)
Operating Room	Person—Minute	3.00	3,650	10,950	$1.15	$12,593		
Recovery Room	Person—Minute	1.50	3,650	5,475	0.75	$ 4,106		
Anesthesiology	Person—Minute	3.50	3,650	12,775	0.90	11,498		
Cardiology	Relative Value Unit	0.15	3,650	548	2.50	1,370		
Radiology	Relative Value Unit	11.00	3,650	40,150	0.15	6,023		
Laboratory	Relative Value Unit	15.00	3,650	54,750	0.12	6,570		
Respiratory Therapy	Relative Value Unit	0.75	3,650	2,738	1.00	2,738		
Physical Therapy	Relative Value Unit	0.10	3,650	365	0.50	183		
Central Sterile Supply	Requisitions	0.35	3,650	1,278	2.50	3,195		
Pharmacy	Prescriptions	0.25	3,650	913	1.75	1,598		
Total						$49,874		$

Table 9–11 Monthly Forecast Distribution of Outpatient Visits
Based on a Two-Year Actual Average

MEMORIAL HOSPITAL
ANYTOWN, U.S.A.

MONTHLY FORECAST DISTRIBUTION OF

OUTPATIENT VISITS

MONTH	NUMBER OF VISITS	PERCENT OF VISITS
January	5,364	7.53
February	5,377	7.55
March	5,489	7.71
April	5,472	7.68
May	5,566	7.81
June	6,341	8.90
July	7,136	10.02
August	6,937	9.74
September	6,211	8.72
October	5,935	8.33
November	5,765	8.09
December	5,632	7.92
TOTAL	71,225	100.00

distribution of total annual budget revenue as developed in Table 9–12.
Table 9–13 is the preliminary annual departmental budget of inpatient,
outpatient, newborn, and total special service revenue budgets based
upon present charge systems. The annual departmental outpatient
revenue can then be distributed on a monthly basis as illustrated in
Table 9–14 for the emergency service department.

Table 9–12 Annual Budget of Outpatient Special Service Revenue

MEMORIAL HOSPITAL
ANYTOWN, U.S.A.

1 DEPARTMENT	2 DESCRIPTION OF SERVICE AMOUNT	3 AVERAGE SERVICE UNIT PER OUTPATIENT VISIT	4 PROJECTED OUTPATIENT VISITS	5 PROJECTED SERVICE UNITS 3x4=5	6 PRESENT CHARGE PER SERVICE UNIT	7 PROJECTED REVENUE 5x6=7	8 REVISED CHARGE ON SERVICE UNIT	9 TARGET REVENUE 5x8=9
Cardiology	Relative Values	0.80	71,225	56,980	$2.50	$142.450		$
X-Ray	Relative Values	60.00	71,225	4,273,500	0.15	641,025		
Laboratory	Relative Values	55.00	71,225	3,917,375	0.12	470,085		
Respiratory Therapy	Relative Values	2.50	71,225	178,063	1.00	178,063		
Physical Therapy	Relative Values	25.00	71,225	1,780,625	0.50	890,313		
Pharmacy	Requisition	0.80	71,225	56,980	1.75	99,715		
Emergency Service	Person-Minutes	60.00	71,225	4,273,500	0.50	2,136,750		
TOTAL						$4,558,401		$

Table 9-13 Departmental Summary of Preliminary Annual Budget of Special Service Revenue

MEMORIAL HOSPITAL
ANYTOWN, U.S.A.

| DEPARTMENT | Present Charge Structure | | | | Revised Charge Structure | | |
	Inpatient	Outpatient	Newborn	Total	Inpatient	Outpatient	Newborn	Total
Routine Nursing Service	$ 5,179,287	$ --	$127,750	$5,307,037	*	*	*	*
Operating Room	2,949,750	--	12,593	2,962,343				
Recovery Room	641,250	--	4,106	645,356				
Anesthesiology	2,308,500	--	11,498	2,319,998				
Delivery Room	385,875	--	-0-	385,875				
Cardiology	160,313	142,450	1,370	304,133				
X-Ray	1,026,000	641,025	6,023	1,673,048				
Laboratory	923,400	470,085	6,570	1,400,055				
Inhalation Therapy	128,250	178,063	2,738	309,051				
Physical Therapy	855,000	890,313	183	1,745,496				
Central Sterile Supply	320,625	-0-	3,195	323,820				
Pharmacy	299,250	99,715	1,598	400,563				
Emergency Service	213,750	2,136,750	-0-	2,350,500				
TOTAL PATIENT REVENUE	$15,391,250	$4,558,401	$177,624	$20,127,275				

Table 9–14 Monthly Forecast Distribution of Outpatient and
Emergency Service Revenue

MEMORIAL HOSPITAL
ANYTOWN, U.S.A.

MONTH	PERCENT OF VISITS	OUTPATIENT REVENUE
January	7.53	$ 160,897
February	7.55	161,325
March	7.71	164,743
April	7.68	164,102
May	7.81	166,880
June	8.90	190,171
July	10.02	214,102
August	9.74	208,119
September	8.72	186,325
October	8.33	177,991
November	8.09	172,863
December	7.92	169,232
TOTAL	100.00	$2,136,750

ROUTINE SERVICE REVENUE BUDGET

In projecting a routine service revenue budget, the following are key
statistical and financial requirements:

- type of service
- type of room accommodation
- number of patient days by category
- average charge for room accommodation

Table 9–15 is an illustration of the monthly distribution of a routine
nursing service revenue budget using the projected monthly distribution of patient days and the current daily room rate.

Table 9–15 Monthly Distribution of Routine Service Revenue and Patient by Room Classification for Fiscal Year 19x2

Memorial Hospital
Anytown, U.S.A.

(1)	(2)	(3)	(4)	(5)	(6)	(7)	(8)	(9)	(10)	(11)	(12)	(13)	(14)
Description	Daily Rate	Pat. Days / Rev.	January	February	March	April	July	August	September	October	November	December	Total
Medical & Surgical—One Bed	$ 75	*days*	*579*	*518*	*545*	*560*	*475*	*525*	*557*	*603*	*578*	*553*	*6,570*
		rev.	$ 43,425	$ 38,850	$ 40,875	$ 42,000	$ 35,625	$ 39,375	$ 41,775	$ 45,225	$ 43,350	$ 41,475	$ 492,750
—Two Bed	60	*days*	*3,818*	*3,411*	*3,589*	*3,688*	*3,134*	*3,459*	*3,671*	*3,974*	*3,805*	*3,645*	*43,289*
		rev.	229,080	204,660	215,340	221,280	188,040	207,540	220,260	238,440	228,300	218,700	2,597,340
—Four Bed	53	*days*	*2,060*	*1,841*	*1,937*	*1,990*	*1,691*	*1,866*	*1,981*	*2,144*	*2,053*	*1,968*	*23,360*
		rev.	109,180	97,573	102,661	105,470	89,623	98,898	104,993	113,632	108,809	104,304	1,238,080
—Ward	49	*days*	*525*	*467*	*492*	*505*	*429*	*474*	*503*	*544*	*521*	*499*	*5,931*
		rev.	25,725	22,883	24,108	24,745	21,021	23,226	24,647	26,656	25,529	24,451	290,619
Total Medical & Surgical		*days*	*6,982*	*6,237*	*6,563*	*6,743*	*5,729*	*6,324*	*6,712*	*7,265*	*6,967*	*6,665*	*79,150*
		rev.	$407,410	$363,966	$382,984	$393,495	$334,309	$369,039	$391,675	$423,953	$405,988	$388,930	$4,618,789
Maternity—One Bed	$ 75	*days*	*32*	*29*	*30*	*31*	*27*	*29*	*31*	*34*	*32*	*32*	*367*
		rev.	$ 2,400	$ 2,175	$ 2,250	$ 2,325	$ 2,025	$ 2,175	$ 2,325	$ 2,550	$ 2,400	$ 2,400	$ 27,525
—Two Bed	60	*days*	*143*	*128*	*135*	*139*	*118*	*130*	*138*	*149*	*143*	*136*	*1,626*
		rev.	8,580	7,680	8,100	8,340	7,080	7,800	8,280	8,940	8,580	8,160	97,560
—Ward	49	*days*	*128*	*113*	*119*	*122*	*104*	*115*	*122*	*132*	*126*	*122*	*1,437*
		rev.	6,272	5,537	5,831	5,978	5,096	5,635	5,978	6,468	6,174	5,929	70,413
Total Maternity		*days*	*303*	*270*	*284*	*292*	*249*	*274*	*291*	*315*	*301*	*290*	*3,430*
		rev.	$ 17,252	$ 15,392	$ 16,181	$ 16,643	$ 14,201	$ 15,610	$ 16,583	$ 17,958	$ 17,154	$ 16,489	$ 195,498
ICU/CCU	$125	*days*	*258*	*230*	*242*	*249*	*211*	*233*	*248*	*268*	*257*	*246*	*2,920*
		rev.	32,250	28,750	30,250	31,125	26,375	29,125	31,000	33,500	32,125	30,750	365,000
Newborn Nursery	$ 35	*days*	*322*	*287*	*303*	*311*	*292*	*292*	*310*	*335*	*321*	*307*	*3,650*
		rev.	11,270	10,045	10,605	10,885	9,240	10,220	10,850	11,725	11,235	10,745	127,750
Total Routine—Service Revenue		rev.	$468,182	$418,153	$440,020	$452,148	$384,125	$423,994	$450,108	$487,136	$466,502	$446,914	$5,307,037
Average Routine Services Charge Per Patient Day			$ 62.01	$ 61.95	$ 61.76	$ 62.37	$ 58.65	$ 62.12	$ 62.08	$ 62.86	$ 61.79	$ 63.84	$ 62.07
Number of Patient Days (Excluding Newborn)			7,550	6,750	7,125	7,250	6,550	6,825	7,250	7,750	7,550	7,000	85,500

ANNUAL DEPARTMENTAL REVENUE BUDGETS

In summarizing an annual departmental revenue budget there are various methods used (see Table 9–16). Similarly, the calculation and reporting of monthly revenue budgets can be variously displayed. Tables 9–17 and 9–18 are two methods for consideration.

Table 9–16 Summary of Annual Projection of Total Routine and Special Service Revenue

MEMORIAL HOSPITAL
ANYTOWN, U.S.A.

SUMMARY OF ANNUAL PROJECTION OF TOTAL ROUTINE & SPECIAL
SERVICE REVENUE
FOR BUDGET YEAR ENDING DECEMBER 31, 19x2

REVENUE CLASSIFICATION	REVENUE PROJECTED AT PRESENT CHARGE STRUCTURE	REVENUE PROJECTED AT REVISED CHARGE STRUCTURE	ADDITIONAL REVENUE
Routine Nursing Service			
(Source: Table 9–15)			
Medical & Surgical	$ 4,618,789		
Maternity	195,498		
ICU/CCU	365,000		
Newborn Nursery	127,750		
TOTAL ROUTINE			
NURSING SERVICE	5,307,037		
Special Services			
Inpatient			
(Source: Table 9–17)	10,211,963		
Outpatient			
(Source: Table 9–18)	4,558,401		
Newborn	49,874		
TOTAL SPECIAL SERVICE	14,820,238		
TOTAL REVENUE	$20,127,275		

Table 9–17 Summary Monthly Distribution of Target Inpatient Special Service Revenue

MEMORIAL HOSPITAL
ANYTOWN, U.S.A.

For Budget Year Ending December 31, 19x2

DESCRIPTION	JANUARY	FEBRUARY	MARCH	APRIL	MAY	JUNE	JULY	AUGUST	SEPTEMBER	OCTOBER	NOVEMBER	DECEMBER	TOTAL
Average Special Service Charge per Patient Day (dollars)	119.43816	119.43816	119.43816	←			same					→	119.43816
Number of Patient Days	7,550	6,750	7,125	7,250	7,150	6,750	6,550	6,825	7,250	7,750	7,550	7,000	85,500
Inpatient Special Service Revenue (dollars)	901,758	806,208	850,997	865,927	853,983	806,207	782,320	815,165	865,927	925,646	901,758	836,067	10,211,963

Table 9–18 Summary Monthly Distribution of Target Outpatient Special Service Revenue

MEMORIAL HOSPITAL
ANYTOWN, U.S.A.

For Budget Year Ending December 31, 19x2

DESCRIPTION	JANUARY	FEBRUARY	MARCH	APRIL	MAY	JUNE	JULY	AUGUST	SEPTEMBER	OCTOBER	NOVEMBER	DECEMBER	TOTAL
Average Special Service Charge per Outpatient Visit (dollars)	64.00	64.00	64.00	←			same					→	64.00
Number of Outpatient Visits	5,364	5,377	5,489	5,472	5,566	6,341	7,136	6,937	6,211	5,935	5,765	5,362	71,225
Outpatient Special Service Revenue (dollars)	343,296	344,128	351,296	350,208	356,224	405,824	456,706	443,968	397,504	379,840	368,960	360,447	4,558,401

Deductions from Gross Charges

Deductions from gross patient charges are probably the most critical items in revenue budgeting. These deductions represent the difference between the published or gross patient charges for services rendered and the amount of cash the institution actually receives. Deductions are placed in three major classifications:

- contractual allowances
- courtesy and charity allowances
- bad debts

Contractual allowances represent the amount of deductions or discounts resulting from agreements the health care facility has made with major third party purchasers. This amount usually represents either a formula arrangement or a prospective rate determined by the third party before the service is rendered. In short, it represents the difference between the total published charges and the total actual cash received. Contractual allowances will increase as the number of HMO contracts hospitals are negotiating increases.

Courtesy and charity allowances are amounts which are written off the patient's bill because of some administrative policy that has been established by the institution.

Bad debts are a unique deduction from gross patient charges, since they can be expressed as either gross or net.

Gross bad debts represent the exact amount of patient accounts receivable that have been written off. Net bad debts are the resulting amount after bad debts cash recoveries have been subtracted from the gross bad debts total.

The health care industry's accounting policies for bad debts are entirely different from what the Internal Revenue Service (IRS) allows. In the health care industry, bad debts are considered a deduction from gross patient charges, thus reducing the revenue. The IRS considers bad debts a business expense. The net result may be the same, but the health care industry is penalized, especially on a cost reimbursement basis, since expenses are less than what the IRS would allow.

There are numerous formulae to calculate distributions from gross patient charges. Below is a summary of these allowances as they relate to inpatient and outpatient charges. It is interesting to note in this illustration that deductions are greater for outpatient services than for inpatient services. This can be attributed to such factors as poor patient credit information, poor admitting procedures, poor billing and collection procedures, and poor insurance coverage.

Service	Gross Charges	Deductions	Net Charges	Net Gross Percentage
Inpatient & newborn	$15,568,874	$ 584,973	$14,983,901	96.3%
Outpatient	4,558,401	434,314	4,124,087	90.5%
Total	$20,127,275	$1,019,287	$19,107,988	94.9%

When gross charges to patients are consolidated with deductions from gross patient charges on a statement of operations, they are presented in a format similar to the one in Table 9–19.

MATCHING PRELIMINARY REVENUE BUDGETS WITH EXPENSE BUDGETS

We have been discussing the development of the preliminary revenue budget based upon the present charge structure. This revenue budget must be matched to the final expense budget, and rate and expense adjustments must be made to net the desired operating results. The preliminary budget should be subjected to cost finding to identify "loser" departments if the initial profit margin is not sufficient, and then corrective actions or "budget balancers" should be incorporated into the preliminary budget to achieve the desired profit.

Comparing Revenue Budget to Actual Results

In comparing a revenue budget to actual operating results, there are two key considerations. First, compare the percentage variance, as well as the dollar variance. Second, compare the impact that volume changes have upon the analysis. Table 9–20 is a comparative analysis of the revenue budget as presented in Table 9–16 to actual results of a control budget which has been adjusted to the actual volume using the standard revenue rates.

The analysis in Table 9–20 can be further used to develop such variances as volume and rate.

Volume variance determines the financial impact of the difference between the actual volume and the budget volume, while *rate* variance determines the financial impact of the actual rate charged to the budget rate. Figure 9–1 illustrates the computation of these two variances using outpatient visits and outpatient revenue.

Table 9–19 Statement of Patient Revenue Budget

MEMORIAL HOSPITAL
ANYTOWN, U.S.A.

STATEMENT OF PATIENT REVENUE BUDGET
For Budget Year Ending December 31, 19x1

Patient Revenue

    Routine Services

Inpatient	$ 5,179,287	
Newborn	127,750	
Total Routine Services		$ 5,307,037

    Special Services

Inpatient	10,211,963	
Newborn	49,874	
Outpatient	4,558,401	
Total Special Services		$14,820,238

Total Gross Charges to Patients	$20,127,275

Less: Deductions from Gross Charges

Contractual Allowances	$838,125	
Courtesy Allowances	87,500	
Net Bad Debts	93,662	
Total Deduction from Gross Charges		$ 1,019,287

NET PATIENT REVENUE	$19,107,988

The rate of variance of $147,300 is identical to the variance identified in the control budget in Table 9–20 while the total volume variance of $302,499 is the same as the variance of the actual to the target budget. In this illustration, both variances were favorable, consequently, they were added together. However, had the rate variance been unfavorable, the total budget variance would be calculated as follows:

Volume variance	$155,499	Favorable
Rate variance	147,300	Unfavorable
Total budget variance	$ 8,199	Favorable

In summary, the revenue budget is a dynamic management tool to be monitored at least monthly for variance differences and adjusted as the financial requirements, patient mix, and volume change. The use of standard budget rates and control budgets that utilize the actual volume of service will assist management in evaluating performances while eliminating the need to rationalize for volume variances.

CASE-MIX REVENUE BUDGETING

The case-mix or DRG prospective payment system requires the hospital information system to collect considerable additional details regarding each admission and/or discharge, such as charges for services rendered, cash received, attending physician, paying agent, and other relevant data. It is imperative to develop at least the following profitability matrix profiles:

• diagnosis
• department
• physician
• paying agent

in order to identify unprofitable or marginal profiles; these will need to be evaluated and corrected. The zero-based budgeting approach is an excellent approach to evaluating the costs and benefits of each of the above categories.

To begin the evaluation process, the hospital must identify its case or DRG mix. Generally, most hospitals will not, to any meaningful degree, be rendering service in all 468 DRG categories (see Appendix B, Listing of DRGs Weighting Factor and Related Data). The case-mix distribu-

Table 9-20 Comparative Analysis of Patient Revenue Budget to Actual Operations for 12-Month Period Ending December 31, 19x2

MEMORIAL HOSPITAL
ANYTOWN, U.S.A.
For 12-Month Period Ending December 31, 19x2

DESCRIPTION	ACTUAL	TARGET BUDGET	CONTROL BUDGET	ACTUAL TO CONTROL VARIANCE Favorable (Unfavorable) $	%	ACTUAL TO TARGET VARIANCE Favorable (Unfavorable)	%
Patient Volume							
Inpatient Days	84,900	85,500	84,900	-0-	-0-	(600)	(0.70%)
Newborn Days	3,460	3,650	3,460	-0-	-0-	(190)	(5.21%)
Outpatient Visits	73,650	71,225	73,650	-0-	-0-	2,425	3.40%
Patient Revenue							
Routine Service							
Inpatient	$ 5,142,393	$ 5,179,287	$ 5,269,743	$(127,350)	(2.36%)	$(36,894)	0.71%
Newborn	121,100	127,750	121,100	-0-	-0-	(6,650)	5.21%
Total Routine Service	$ 5,263,493	$ 5,307,037	$ 5,390,843	$(127,350)	(2.36%)	$(43,544)	0.82%
Special Service							
Inpatient	$ 9,933,300	$10,211,963	$ 9,772,839	$ 160,461	1.64%	$(278,663)	2.73%
Newborn	44,980	49,874*	39,479	5,501	13.93%	(4,894)	9.81%
Outpatient	4,860,900	4,558,401	4,713,600	147,300	3.13%	302,499	6.64%
Total Special Service	$14,839,180	$14,820,238	$14,525,918	$ 313,262	2.16%	$ 19,942	0.13%

Total Gross Charges to Patients	$20,102,673	$20,127,275	$19,916,761	$ 185,912	0.93%	$(24,602)	0.12%
Less: Deduction from Gross Charges	$ 1,018,800	$ 1,019,287	$ 1,010,310	$(8,490)	(0.84%)	487	0.05%
Net Patient Revenue	$19,083,873	$19,107,988	$18,906,451	$ 177,422	0.93%	$(24,115)	(0.13%)

*Newborn Special Service Standard Rate $\frac{\$49,874}{3,650} = \$13.664$

Figure 9–1 Computation of Actual Outpatient Special Services
Variances to Target Budget

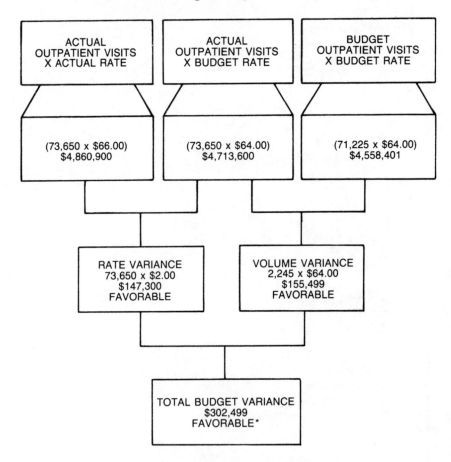

*REFER TO TABLE 9-20 FOR OUTPATIENT SPECIAL SERVICES
ACTUAL VARIANCE TO TARGET (BUDGET) VARIANCE.

tion chart in Table 9–21 displays the cumulative frequencies of DRGs.
These data will be used in this book as the basis of a case-mix revenue
budget. For example, assume that the data in Table 9–22 represent
Memorial Hospital's case mix. The resulting DRG revenue is computed
by using a national rate of $3,874.21 per 1.0000 DRG. The potential cash
flow of $16,956,045 represents the maximum net revenue the hospital
can expect to receive for its inpatient services if payment for all of its

Table 9–21 Cumulative Frequencies of DRGs

Rank	DRG #	Description	Percentage of Occurrence Each	Cumulative
1	132	Atherosclerosis age >69 and/or C.C.	5.29%	
2	182	Esophagitis, Gastrcent. + Misc. Digest. Dis age >69 +/or C.C.	4.20	
3	127	Heart Failure + Shock	3.52	
4	039	Lens Procedures	3.08	
5	014	Specific Cerebrovascular Disorders Except TIA	2.93	19.02%
6	088	Chronic Obstructive Pulmonary Disease	2.47	
7	089	Simple Pneumonia + Pleurisy age >69 and/or C.C.	2.24	
8	294	Diabetes age =>36	2.21	
9	122	Circulatory Disorders with AMI W/O C.V. Comp. Disch. Alive	2.13	
10	243	Medical Back Problems	1.92	30.00
11	467	Other Factors Influencing Health Status	1.72	
12	140	Angina Pectoris	1.67	
13	134	Hypertension	1.45	
14	130	Peripheral Vascular Disorders age >69 and/or C.C.	1.38	
15	096	Bronchitis + Asthma >69 and/or C.C.	1.35	37.57
16	138	Cardiac Arrhythmia + Conduction Disorders age >69 and/or C.C.	1.31	
17	015	Transient Ischemic Attacks	1.27	
18	320	Kidney + Urinary Tract Infections age >69 and/or C.C.	1.18	
19	082	Respiratory Neoplasms	1.15	
20	336	Transurethral Prostatectomy age >69 and/or C.C.	0.99	43.48
21	395	Red Blood Cell Disorders age >17	0.97	
22	174	G.I. Hemorrhage age >69 and/or C.C.	0.93	
23	183	Esophagitis, Gastrcent. + Misc. Digest. Dis age 18-69 W/O C.C.	0.88	
24	133	Atherosclerosis age <70 W/O C.C.	0.87	
25	188	Other Digestive System Diagnoses age >69 and/or C.C.	0.85	
26	172	Digestive Malignancy age >69 and/or C.C.	0.85	47.98
27	197	Total Cholecystectomy W/O C.D.E. age >69 and/or C.C.	0.84	

Table 9–21 continued

Rank	#	DRG Description	Percentage of Occurrence Each	Cumulative
28	296	Nutritional + Misc. Metabolic Disorders age >69 and/or C.C.	0.84	
29	244	Bone Diseases + Septic Arthropathy age >69 and/or C.C.	0.76	
30	207	Disorders of the Biliary Tract age >69 and/or C.C.	0.75	52.02
31	210	Hip + Femur Procedures Except Major Joint age >69 and/or C.C.	0.73	
32	209	Major Joint Procedures	0.70	
33	161	Inguinal + Femoral Hernia Procedures age >69 and/or C.C.	0.68	
34	430	Psychoses	0.68	
35	413	Other Myeloprolif Disord or Poorly Diff Neopl Dx age >69 +/or C.C.	0.66	55.47
36	235	Fractures of Femur	0.62	
37	101	Other Respiratory Diagnoses age >69 and/or C.C.	0.60	
38	331	Other Kidney + Urinary Tract Diagnoses age >69 and/or C.C.	0.59	
39	429	Organic Disturbances + Mental Retardation	0.59	
40	403	Lymphoma or Leukemia age >69 and/or C.C.	0.57	58.44
41	148	Major Small & Large Bowel Procedures age >69 and/or C.C.	0.55	
42	233	Other Musculoskelet Sys + Conn Tiss. O.R. Proc age >69 +/or C.C.	0.55	
43	012	Degenerative Nervous System Disorders	0.54	
44	177	Uncomplicated Peptic Ulcer age >69 and/or C.C.	0.53	
45	253	Fx,Sprns,Strns + Disl of Uparm,Lowleg Ex Foot age >69 +/or C.C.	0.53	61.14
46	348	Benign Prostatic Hypertrophy age >69 and/or C.C.	0.53	
47	280	Trauma to the Skin, Subcut Tiss + Breast age >69 +/or C.C.	0.52	
48	123	Circulatory Disorders with AMI, Expired	0.51	
49	316	Renal Failure W/O Dialysis	0.50	63.20%
		All others—less than ½% each	36.80	
			100.00%	100.00%

Note: Accumulated by Laventhol & Horwath from HCFA Bureau of Data Management and Strategy, Report dated June 21, 1982, of 20 percent sample discharges by diagnosis (1,766,107 discharges).

Source: Reprinted with permission of Laventhol & Horwath from *A Desk Reference Guide for Defensive Revenue Gambits,* September 1, 1983.

Table 9–22 Case-Mix Revenue Budgeting

MEMORIAL HOSPITAL
ANYTOWN, U.S.A.

CASE-MIX REVENUE BUDGETING
For Year Ending December 31, 19x2

No.	DRG No.	No. of Cases	Case Percent	Accum. Percent	Cost Weight	DRG* Value	DRG Revenue
1	182	189	5.29	5.29	0.6185	$ 2,396.14	$ 452,870
2	88	150	4.20	9.49	1.0412	4,033.73	605,060
3	127	126	3.52	13.01	1.0408	4,032.18	508,055
4	39	110	3.08	16.09	0.5010	1,940.93	213,502
5	14	105	2.93	19.02	1.3527	5,240.52	550,254
6	209	88	2.47	21.49	2.2912	8,876.38	781,121
7	89	80	2.24	23.73	1.1029	4,272.77	341,822
8	243	79	2.21	25.94	0.7551	2,925.35	231,103
9	140	76	2.13	28.07	0.7548	2,924.19	222,238
10	96	68	1.92	29.99	0.7996	3,097.75	210,647
11	336	61	1.72	31.71	1.0079	3,904.73	238,188
12	467	60	1.67	33.38	0.9799	3,796.25	227,775
13	82	52	1.45	34.83	1.1400	4,416.50	229,658
14	210	49	1.38	36.21	2.0833	8,070.95	395,477
15	15	48	1.35	37.56	0.6673	2,585.20	124,090
16	122	47	1.31	38.87	1.3651	5,288.56	248,562
17	138	45	1.27	40.14	0.9297	3,601.77	162,080
18	197	42	1.18	41.32	1.4868	5,760.04	241,922
19	430	41	1.15	42.47	1.0934	4,235.96	173,674
20	320	35	0.99	43.46	0.8123	3,146.95	110,143
21	294	35	0.99	44.45	0.8087	3,131.84	109,614
22	403	33	0.93	45.38	1.1715	4,538.53	149,771
23	132	31	0.88	46.26	0.9182	3,557.22	110,274
24	5	31	0.88	47.14	1.6780	6,500.77	201,524
25	12	30	0.85	47.99	1.1136	4,314.22	129,427
26	125	30	0.85	48.84	1.6455	6,374.86	191,246
27	183	30	0.85	49.69	0.5652	2,189.65	65,690
28	106	30	0.85	50.54	5.2624	20,387.17	611,615
29	110	27	0.76	51.30	2.9328	11,362.02	306,775
30	468	26	0.75	52.05	2.1037	8,149.99	211,900
31	130	25	0.73	52.78	0.9645	3,736.59	93,415
32	134	24	0.70	53.48	0.7049	2,730.87	65,541
		(1,903)					$8515,039
All others		1,671					
Average					1.3039	5,051.47	8,441,006
Total		3,574					$16,956,045

*DRG dollar value @ $3,874.12 per DRG weighted value of 1.0000.

patients is based on the DRGs. The DRG prospective payment system recognizes the following key data (see Appendix B):

1. relative weights
2. geometric mean length of stay (LOS)
3. LOS outlier cutoffs (days)

For example, DRG-004, spinal procedures, has the following assigned criteria:

1. relative weight = 2.2452
2. geometric mean LOS = 16.0
3. LOS outlier cutoff = 36

Since not all patients can be treated within the assigned criteria, the DRG system recognizes the following types of outliers or exceptions:

1. Day Outlier: a per diem payment adjustment is allowed for each covered day of care beyond the outlier threshold.
2. Cost Outlier: a case not eligible as a day outlier may qualify as a cost outlier when extraordinary costs are incurred in a short period of time.

In conclusion, the DRG prospective payment system presents new operational problems that are not insurmountable if management and medical staffs cooperate closely. This cooperation is absolutely essential if the institution is to achieve any semblance of financial viability for the future. Since case-mix revenue budgeting is such a substantial departure from the traditional department budgeting approach, financial managers from all levels of the institution's hierarchy must constantly monitor regulation changes, diagnosis trends, physician/LOS relationships, and other relevant trends in order to identify unprofitable services. Most importantly, the hospital must be managed with a risk-oriented team that is willing to innovate in pricing, marketing, and management strategies to assure the hospital's financial viability and its share of the marketplace.

Chapter 10

Wage and Salary Budgeting

For most health care departments, the wage and salary budget represents approximately 50 to 70 percent of the department's total operating costs. With this in mind, there is an increasing need to develop a more effective wage and salary budgetary control system. In this chapter, the duo-wage and salary budget plan is presented as a method to achieve this need.

DUO-WAGE AND SALARY BUDGET SYSTEM

The duo-wage and salary budget system places the emphasis upon the time an employee spends on the job, rather than on the total amount of an employee's paid time. This approach allows department managers and their supervisors to place similar emphasis upon controlling work hours (controllable on-the-job hours) and not paid hours. This system requires the separation of work hours and benefit hours to arrive at the total wage and salary time. Hence, the duo-wage and salary budgetary system requires two separate budgetary plans:

- Work-Hour Budget—The work-hour plan accounts for all the hours the employee spends on the job. (This budget provides time for personal needs, fatigue, and delay.) It is directly related to production volume and/or the production standards that have been developed for forecasting staffing requirements and evaluating actual performance.
- Benefit-Hour Budget—The benefit-hour plan incorporates all the benefit hours to which each employee is entitled on an off-the-job basis. Since benefit hours do not relate directly to work volume, an

alternative method of budgeting is required to account for this expenditure as compared to the method required for work hours.

THE WORK-HOUR BUDGET

With the growing emphasis upon the need to staff cost centers in as direct proportion to production volume as possible, department managers and supervisors will find that the work-hour budget is an excellent management tool since it identifies both fixed and variable salary positions.

Once the components are identified, each position is assigned a specific production standard. For example:

Fixed Salary Position	Service Unit	Production Standard
Department manager	Weeks	40 hours per week
Cashier	Calendar days	8 hours per calendar day

Variable Salary Positions		
Billing clerk, inpatient	Inpatient Discharge	60 per week 8 hours per day
Billing clerk, outpatient	Outpatient Discharge	75 per week 8 hours per day

The third component of the work-hour plan requires assigning each position an average hourly wage rate as follows:

Position	Name	Average Hourly Wage Rate
Department manager		$10.00
Cashier		$ 3.50
Billing clerk, inpatient		$ 3.75
Billing clerk, outpatient		$ 3.65
General clerical relief		$ 3.25

After these components of the work-hour plan have been identified, they are related to the statistical volume forecast for the respective department.

To continue the example, assume that the above data relate to the business office, and that the statistical volume forecast given to the department manager is as follows:

Service Unit	Number of Service Units
Weeks	52
Calendar days	365
Inpatient discharges	16,500
Outpatient discharges	24,500

The salary and statistical volume data are then plotted on a worksheet similar to the chart in Table 10–1.

Note that the fixed and variable identifications have been retained. The forecasted annual work-hour expense is, in fact, the control plan, based upon the original statistical volume forecast. Using these data, the control plan can be adjusted to the actual volume and then ultimately compared to the actual performance as illustrated in Table 10–2.

The work-hour budget makes no effort to relate to any specific individual in the department. It recognizes only the work position, its related hourly wage, and its production standard. The primary purpose of the work-hour budget is to furnish department managers and their supervisors with a global budget within which they can operate based upon accepted production levels at a certain statistical work volume.

With these as benchmarks, there is little need to relate the work-hour expense to an individual. If a marked deviation in the work-hour budget appears, the departmental position will be identified and the department manager can take corrective action.

On initial observation of the comparative summary or work-hour control plan to actual performance (Table 10–2), there seems to be a relatively good relationship—$3,969.00 to the control plan of $3,973.00, or a $4.00 favorable variance (see Table 10–3). However, when we compare the actual work hours at standard wage rates to the target plan, we find that there is a $143.00 unfavorable variance in the total variable salary expense (see Table 10–4). Here we see that there were 277 outpatient billing clerk work hours actually used as compared to a plan of 221 hours, thus creating a $204.00 unfavorable variance.

These data can be further analyzed in the following manner:

Outpatient Billing Clerk

	Actual	Budget	Variance
1. Work hours	277	221	(56)U
2. Wage rate	$2.95	$3.65	$.70F
3. Total salary expense	$817	$807	($10)U

Table 10–1 Departmental Worksheet for the Development of the Work-Hour Plan and Related Social Security Expenses for the Year Ending December 31, 19x1

MEMORIAL HOSPITAL
ANYTOWN, U.S.A.

Business Office

Position	Serviced Unit	Production Standard	Statistical Forecast	Work Hours Required	Average Hourly Wage Rate	Forecasted Annual Work = Hour Expense	(B) Social Security Expense
Fixed							
Dept. Mgr.	week	40-hours	52	2,080	$ 10.00	$ 20,800	$ 624.4
	calendar day	8-hours	365	2,920	3.50	10,220	593
Total Fixed				5,000	$ 13.50	$ 31,020	$1,217
Variable							
Billing Clk. Inpatient	(A) Inpatient Admissions	60 per work-day	16,500	2,200	$ 3.75	$ 8,250	$ 479
Billing Clk. Outpatient	(A) Outpatient Discharge	75 per work-day	24,500	2,416	$ 3.65	$ 8,818	$ 511
Total Variable				4,616	$ 7.40	$ 17,068	$ 990
GRAND TOTAL				9,616		$ 48,088	$2,207

(A) Work-day is a conventional 8 hour, 5 day week, and includes provision for personal, fatigue, delays and time.
(B) Include unemployment taxes, if applicable, Social Security, calculated @ 5.8% up to first $10,800 with $624 limit.

Table 10–2 Departmental Comparative Summary of Work-Hour Control Plan to Actual Performance for the Period from January 1, 19x1 to January 31, 19x1

Memorial Hospital
Anytown, U.S.A.
Business Office

Position	Serviced Unit	Production Standard	Adjusted Control Plan (A)				Actual					Variance					
												Rate		Hours		Expense	
			Volume	Standard Hours	Standard Rate	Total Expense	Production	Volume	Work Hours	Rate	Total Expense	Amount	Percent	Amount	Percent	Amount	Percent
Fixed																	
Dept. manager	Week	40-hours	4	160	$10.00	$1,600	40-hours	4	160	$10.00	$1,600	-0-	-0-	-0-	-0-	-0-	-0-
Cashier	Calendar Day	8-hours	31	248	$ 3.50	$ 868	8-hours	31	248	3.50	$ 868	-0-	-0-	-0-	-0-	-0-	-0-
Total fixed				408		$2,468			408		$2,468	-0-		-0-		-0-	
Variable																	
Billing clerk in-patient	In-patient admission	60 per work-day	1,395	186	$ 3.75	$ 698	65 per work-day	1,395	171	$ 4.00	$ 684	$(.25)	(6.67)%	15	8.06%	$14	2.01%
Billing clerk out-patient	Out-patient discharge	75 per work-day	2,075	221	3.65	807	60 per work-day	2,075	277	2.95	$ 817	.70	19.18	(56)	25.34%	(10)	(1.24)
Total variable				407		$1,505			448		$1,501			(41)	(10.07)%	$ 4	0.27%
Grand total				815		$3,973			856		$3,969						

(A) Volume has been adjusted to actual.

Table 10–3 Comparative Analysis of Variable Salary Expense to Adjusted Control Plan

	Position		
Variable Salary Expense Variance	In-Patient Clerk	Out-Patient Clerk	Total
1. Actual Work Hours	171	277	448
2. Actual Wage Rate	$ 4.00	$ 2.95	N/A
3. Actual Work Hour Expense (line 1 times line 2)	$ 684	$ 817	$ 1,501
4. Standard Wage Rate	$ 3.75	$ 3.65	N/A
5. Control Standard Work Hr. Expense (line 1 times line 4)	$ 698	$ 807	$ 1,505
6. Wage Rate Variance (line 5 minus line 3)	$ 14 (F)	$ 10 (U)	$ 4 (F)

(F) Favorable
(U) Unfavorable

Table 10–4 Comparative Analysis of Variable Salary Expense to Target Plan

	Position		
Variable Production Variance	In-Patient Clerk	Out-Patient Clerk	Total
7. Actual Work Hours	171	277	448
8. Standard Wage Rate	$ 3.75	$ 3.65	N/A
9. Adjusted Actual Work Hr. Exp.	$ 641	$ 1,011	$ 1,652
10. Standard Work Hours	186	221	407
11. Standard Work Hr. Exp. (line 8 times line 10)	$ 698	$ 807	$ 1,505
12. Production Variance (line 11 minus line 9)	$ 57	$ 204 (U)	$ 147 (U)
13. Total Variable Salary Expense (line 6 + line 12)	$ 71 (F)	$ 214 (U)	$ 143 (U)

(F) Favorable
(U) Unfavorable

The inpatient billing clerk hours actually used were 171, as compared to a budgeted total of 186. However, this favorable efficiency variance was offset by an unfavorable wage rate variance of $ .25 per hour, as illustrated in Table 10–4.

Inpatient Billing Clerk

	Actual	Budget	Variance
1. Work hours	171	186	15F
2. Wage rate	$4.00	$3.75	($.25)U
3. Total salary expense	$648	$698	$14F

To summarize, the work-hour budget method provides department managers and their supervisors with a system that enables them to isolate and compare actual work hours to budgeted work hours and to relate these data to established production standards.

These comparisons of the actual statistical work volume to the plan can be made as frequently as desired. For example, since the production standard has been reduced to a micro service unit, a department's staffing level can be evaluated on a daily basis, if desired, or as infrequently as weekly, monthly, or quarterly. Obviously, the more frequently the actual performance is compared to the standard, the more aware and sensitive the department manager will be to any variances that might directly be related to work volume. One of the primary advantages of the work-hour budget system is that it can and should be related to accepted production standards and actual performance, thus enabling a unique system for performance evaluation.

THE BENEFIT-HOUR BUDGET

A big difference between the work-hour budget and the benefit-hour budget is that the benefit-hour budget relates directly to a specific individual's time and wage while the work-hour budget concerns itself only with work positions and related average hourly rates. The one important feature both plans share is that each system attempts to forecast the related payroll taxes and other applicable expenses, i.e., social security, unemployment taxes, pension retirement, or health and life insurance. The purpose of the benefit-hour budget is to forecast the anticipated benefit hours and related expenses of each department so that these hours and expenses can be accrued on a monthly, or within an accepted, accounting period basis. Here are some of the advantages and disadvantages of the benefit-hour budget methodology:

Advantages

- offers a method with which to accrue and allocate benefits on an equal distribution basis, so as not to distort the comparative analysis to actual work volume
- isolates nonproductive or nonwork hours and expenses so that they can be identified as separate expense items
- helps management to prepare its financial reserves to meet the benefit-hour demands, rather than having them lumped into two or three months
- helps management to prepare staffing requirements and to recruit replacement help if necessary
- offers the personnel department an opportunity to keep benefit-hour records for each employee, to pinpoint any violations, and to appraise the overall personnel benefit package
- offers all levels of management a better opportunity to plan, to finance, and to control the benefit-hours of an institution's employees

Disadvantages

- requires a considerable amount of additional planning and clerical work to compile and to monitor the individual employee benefit-hour plan
- assumes that the present roster of employees will be the same for the entire plan's period
- may assume that everyone will utilize, and be reimbursed for, all of their benefit hours earned
- will require at least a year-end reconciliation to the actual expenditures

To examine how the plan works, remember that, as stated earlier, the benefit-hour budget identifies the department and the employee.

For illustration, we will refer again to the business office and examine some of the data available from the personnel files of each employee.

Name	*Position*	*Date of Hire*	*Wage Rate*
Brown, Mildred	Department manager	06–01–x1	$10.00
Jones, Margaret	Cashier	06–10–x3	3.50
Smith, Mary	Billing clerk—inpatient	10–01–x2	3.75
White, Josephine	Billing clerk— outpatient	09–01–x4	3.65

Levy, John   Billing clerk—
                 outpatient   07–01–x1   3.75

Other information required from the personnel department may include:

1. Holidays—recognized holidays are:
   New Year's Day
   Memorial Day
   Independence Day
   Labor Day
   Thanksgiving Day
   Christmas
   Plus: three personal holidays up to a maximum of nine paid holidays (8 hours each)
2. Vacations
   2 weeks (80 hours) after one year of employment
   3 weeks (120 hours) after five years of employment
   4 weeks for each department manager after one year of employment (160 hours)
3. Sick Days
   Each employee is entitled to one day for each month of employment; after six months employment, an accumulation to a total of 12 days. Note: the average employee takes 4 sick days or 32 hours per year.

Assuming that the benefit-hour plan is for the fiscal year 19x5, the above data are plotted on a worksheet (see Table 10–5) to develop the forecast expense.

After the benefit-hour has been completed and the total salary and related payroll tax expenses have been determined, the following series of journal entries is made to establish the benefit-hour budget as a liability on the health care facility's books of record and to prorate the liability on a monthly basis.

Initial Entry
1. debit ...... Deferred planned employee
               benefit-hour expense $5,644
   credit ...... Planned employee
               benefit-hour expense payable $5,644
   (To establish the planned employee benefit-hour expense
   as a payable.)

Table 10–5 Departmental Worksheet for the Development of the Benefit-Hour Budget and Related Social Security Expenses

MEMORIAL HOSPITAL
ANYTOWN, U.S.A.

Business Office

Name	Position	Date of Hire	Wage Rate	Benefit Hours Earned				Total Salary Expense	Social Security Expense, etc.
				Holiday	Vacation	Sick(A)	Total		
Brown, Mildred	Department Manager	06-01-X1	$10.00	72	160	32	264	$2,640	$ None
Jones, Margaret	Cashier	05-10-X3	3.50	72	80	32	184	644	31
Smith, Mary	Billing Clerk, Inpatient	10-01-X2	3.75	72	80	32	184	690	40
White, Josephine	Billing Clerk, Inpatient	09-01-X4	3.65	72	80	32	184	671	39
Levy, John	Billing Clerk, Outpatient	07-01-X1	3.75	72	120	32	224	840	49
Summary Total				360	520	160	1,040	$5,485	$159
Grand Total								$5,644	

(A) Estimated at average of 4 days (32 hours) per employee, per personnel department.

Monthly Entries

   2. debit ...... Employee benefit-hour expense .... $ 464
      credit ...... Deferred planned employee benefit-hour
           expense .... $ 464
   (To accrue the planned employee benefit-hour expense
   for the month ($5,644 − 365) × 30 days = $464.)
   3. debit ...... Planned employer benefit-hour expense
           payable .... $ 500
      credit ...... Cash .... $ 500
   (To record the actual amount paid for employee
   benefit-hour expense.)

OTHER SALARY-RELATED EXPENSE ITEMS

So far we have discussed only the primary salary expenditures:

- fixed work-hour expenses
- the variable work-hour expenses
- the benefit-hour expenses

There are, however, other salary expense items, such as

- premium or shift pay
- on-call pay

Since premium pay is earned only during certain work shifts and does not affect the total scheduled work hours, the control will be in total dollars spent. Therefore, a provision is made in the work-hour budget for premium pay or shift differential. For example:

	Hourly Average Rate	*Shift Differential*	*Total Average Rate*
RN—day shift	$4.20	$ None	$4.24
RN—evening shift	$4.20	$ .42	$4.62
RN—night shift	$4.20	$ .50	$4.70

Again, on-call pay does not reflect productive hours but only reimbursement for employees to stand by and to be available for service if the need arises. Under the duo-salary plan concept, on-call hours and related expenses are considered a fixed salary expense so not to distort the expected production standards of the variable salary positions. The wage rate used shall be the most common on-call time for the related position.

PHYSICIAN SALARIES AND FEES

Occasionally, the salaries and fees paid to physicians may be included with the salaries and wages paid to the nonphysician staff of a health care facility. This is not advisable. The inclusion of this portion of the salary expense tends to distort the salary plan and the related production standards. It overstates the average hourly wage and understates the production levels. Since reimbursement to the physician represents a substantial portion of the salary expense budget, it is recommended that it be listed as a separate item as "physician salaries and fees" in the summary of the plan. For example:

Wage and Salary Expense Budget
Work hours	$ xxx,xxx
Benefit hours	xxx,xxx
Total salary—expense staff	$x,xxx,xxx
Plus:	
Physicians—salary and fees	xxx,xxx
Grand total salary expense plan	$x,xxx,xxx

SUMMARY SALARY PLAN

After the work-hour and benefit-hour budgets have been completed, they are summarized on a departmental duo-salary plan summary worksheet (see Table 10–6). These departmental summary worksheets are summarized to develop the:

• total standard hours
• total salary expense
• total payroll tax expense

There are possible variations to the duo-salary plan concept:

1. Eliminate the separation of fixed and variable salary components, and establish a standard production rate for the entire department based on hours worked.

Table 10–6 Departmental Duo-Salary Plan Summary Worksheet for the year 19_____ through _____ 19_____

MEMORIAL HOSPITAL
ANYTOWN, U.S.A.

Business Office

Work-Hour Plan	Standard Hours	Salary Expense	Payroll Tax Expense		Production Standard
			Work Hours	Benefit Hours	
Fixed Positions					
Department Manager	2,080	$ 20,800	$ 624	$	40 hours per week
Cashier	2,920	10,220	593		8 hours per calendar day
On-Call	None	None	None	$ None	None
Total Fixed	5,000	$ 31,020	$ 1,217	$ None	
Variable Positions					
Billing Clerk Inpatient	2,200	$ 8,250	$ 479		60 inpatient admissions per 8-hr. work day
Billing Clerk Outpatient	2,416	8,818	511		75 outpatient discharge per 8 hr. work day
Total Variable	4,616	$ 17,068	$ 990	$ None	
Total Work Hour Budget	9,616	$ 48,088	$ 2,207	$ None	
Benefit Hour Budget					
Holiday	360				
Vacation	520				
Sick	160				
Total Benefit Hour Budget	1,040	$ 55,485	$ None	$ 159	$15.46 per calendar day
GRAND TOTAL	10,656	$ 53,573	$ 2,207	$ 159	$15.46 per calendar day

2. Use only one statistical service unit; for example, hours per patient day (nursing), hours per full time equivalent (administration), or hours per square feet (housekeeping).
3. Use a position control system with the maximum staffing level for an established level of occupancy and assume that all salary positions and related expenses are fixed.

The duo-wage and salary budget system is a somewhat radical change from the method traditionally used by many salary and human resources planners. It is offered here for the purpose of giving the reader a conceptual idea of alternate methods with which to control the health care institution's most costly item, and to provoke thought about a more flexible budgeting approach to the overall financial management planning and control process. In this chapter, fixed and variable wages and salaries were discussed with full awareness that much of the variable wage and salary expenses are handled as semi- or step-variable expenses. The reason step-variables were not incorporated into this discussion is that it is intended to encourage department managers and their supervisors to manage the variable expenses more effectively by eliminating the step-variable expenses. Department managers must concentrate on managing the variable wage and salary expenses.

Chapter 11

Non-Wage and Salary Budgeting

There are three components of the development of the non-wage and salary budget:

- volume forecast
- cost behavior classification
- standard variable costs

Just as in the wage and salary budget, the volume forecast is the key component in projecting expenses. In this case, unit cost and/or unit utilization per patient day or outpatient visit determines the cost of variable expenses, while fixed cost projections are based upon a fixed amount for a period of time.

The second component is the separation of the expense items into either a fixed or variable cost behavior classification. In fact, these costs could be further refined to step-variable or semifixed. For the purpose of this discussion, costs will be classified only as fixed or variable.

The third component, standard variable cost, per production unit, which stays constant within a relevant range of volume activity, is used to project the total departmental variable expense based upon a fixed volume forecast where the total departmental fixed costs remain relatively the same, regardless of the change.

COST BEHAVIOR CLASSIFICATION

The cost behavior classification process begins by identifying each fixed cost for each department. As stated earlier, a fixed cost is an expense item that will not change within a relevant range of activity or

251

volume. For example, assume that the rental cost of the dietary department's equipment at $8,400.00 per year will not change until the number of meals served exceeds 400,000 meals. (The relevant range of activity being 0 to 400,000 meals.) When the 400,000 meal count volume is reached, the dietary department's equipment must be expanded with one additional range and oven unit, a steam table, and a steam kettle at an annual rental of $3,600.00. With this additional equipment, the dietary department reaches another volume plateau or relevant range of activity of 400,001 to 600,000 meals served, as illustrated in Figure 11–1.

Further, each relevant range of activity establishes fixed equipment rental costs as follows:

Range	Activity	Fixed Costs
1	0–400,000 meals served	$ 8,400
2	400,001–600,000 meals served	$12,000

A third volume range of activity could occur, if necessary, after examining the equipment needs.

Once the relevant range of activity has been determined, expenses must be classified as either fixed or variable. One of the most common methods used to achieve this is as follows:

Figure 11–1 Costs for Rental of Dietary Equipment

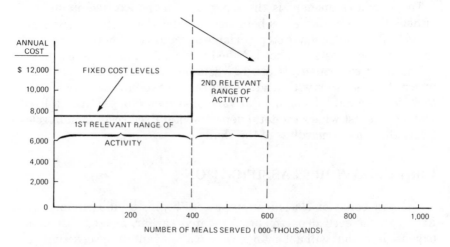

- First, identify each fixed cost item in the department's chart of accounts.
- Second, make the basic assumption that all remaining cost items are variable in nature.

This last assumption may sound somewhat erroneous, but this methodology has been used with considerable success. As one gathers more working experience, these cost items can be further refined as required. Exhibit 11–1 is an example of a worksheet format that can be used for cost behavior classification.

Once the cost behavior classification has been determined, these behavior characteristics are applied to the actual budget total as illustrated in Table 11–1, and total costs are determined and summarized as follows for a 375,000 meal served volume:

Expense description	Amount
Fixed	$73,500
Non-Food variable	57,300
Food variable	339,000
Total	$469,800

Earlier, we had established two relevant ranges of activity. Below is a comparative direct cost analysis for each volume range:

Description	First Range: 0–400,000 meals served Total Department Expense	First Range: 0–400,000 meals served Average Cost Per Meal Served	Second Range: 400,001–600,000 meals served Total Department Expense	Second Range: 400,001–600,000 meals served Average Cost Per Meal
Number of meals served	375,000	1	450,000	1
Non-Food variable expense	$ 57,300	$ .15	$ 67,500	$ .15
Food variable expense	339,000	.90	405,000	.90
Total variable expense	$396,300	$1.05	$472,500	$1.05
Fixed expense	73,500	.20	77,100	.17
Total expense	$469,800	$1.25	$549,600	$1.22

As illustrated, the variable net expense per meal served remains constant within an established range of activity, while the fixed cost per

Exhibit 11–1 Cost Behavior Classification Guide of Expense Items per Chart of Accounts—Dietary Department

MEMORIAL HOSPITAL
ANYTOWN, U.S.A.

DEPARTMENT - Dietary

Account Number	Expense Description	Fixed Costs	Variable Cost
650.25	Depreciation		
.26	Plant and Building	X	
.27	Fixed Equipment	X	
.28	Major Moveable Equipment	X	
.29	Minor Equipment	X	
650.30	Purchased Services and Fees		
.31	Food Service		X (1)
.32	Refuse Collection	X	
.33	Employees Laundry		X
650.40	Supplies and Other Expenses		
.41	Office Supplies	X	
.42	Selective Menus & Printed Forms		X
.43	Dishes, Glassware, Silverware		X
.44	Kitchen Utensils		X
.45	Paper Goods		X
.46	Soaps, Detergents		X
.47	Disposable Dishes & Flatware		X
.50	Public Relations - Meal Costs	X (2)	
.54	Uniforms & Aprons (Employees)		X
.55	Dues and Subscriptions	X	
.56	Rental of Equipment	X	
.57	Repairs and Maintenance	X	
.58	Travel	X	
.59	Miscellaneous	X	
650.60	Food, General		
.61	Meat, Fish, Poultry		X
.62	Dairy Products (Milk, Butter, Ice Cream)		X
.63	Eggs		X
.64	Fresh Produce		X
.65	Breads and Pastries		X
.66	Groceries & Canned Goods		X
.67	Frozen Foods - Fruits ¢ Vegetables		X
.68	Frozen Foods - Meats		X
.69	Frozen Foods - Convenience Meals		X

COMMENTS and ASSUMPTIONS:
(1) Purchased food service expense is based upon standard cost per patient day and number of employee meals served.
(2) Public Relations-Meal Costs - fixed amount established by Public Relations Department and Administration.

Table 11-1 Detailed Listing of Total Annual Non-Wage and Salary Budget with Cost Behavior Classification, Based upon a Projected Volume of 375,000 Meals Served—Dietary Department

MEMORIAL HOSPITAL
ANYTOWN, U.S.A.

DEPARTMENT—Dietary

Account Number	Description	Total Annual Budget	Fixed Costs	Variable Costs
650.25	Depreciation	$ 50,000	$ 50,000	
650.31	Outside Purchased Food Service	5,000		$ 5,000*
650.32	Refuse Collection	1,200	1,200	
650.33	Laundry (employees)	3,600		3,600*
650.40	Supplies and other Expenses	4,000		4,000*
650.41	Office Supplies	3,000	3,000	
650.42	Selective Menus	3,200		3,200*
650.43	Dishes, Glassware, Silverware	12,000		12,000*
650.44	Kitchen Utensils	18,000		18,000*
650.45	Paper Goods	2,000		2,000*
650.46	Soaps, Detergents	3,500		3,500*
650.47	Disposable Dishes and Flatware	4,000		4,000*
650.50	Public Relations—Meal Costs	6,000	6,000	
650.54	Uniforms and Aprons (employees)	2,000		2,000*
650.55	Dues and Subscriptions	500	500	
650.56	Rental of Equipment	8,400	8,400	
650.57	Repairs and Maintenance	3,000	3,000	
650.58	Travel	1,200	1,200	
650.59	Miscellaneous	200	200	
650.60	Food, General	20,000		20,000
650.61	Meat, Fish, Poultry	80,000		80,000

Table 11-1 continued

DEPARTMENT—Dietary

Account Number	Description	Total Annual Budget	Fixed Costs	Variable Costs
650.62	Dairy Products—Milk & Butter, Ice Cream, etc.	30,000		30,000
650.63	Eggs	10,000		10,000
650.64	Fresh Produce	50,000		50,000
650.65	Breads and Pastries	35,000		35,000
650.66	Groceries, Canned Goods	60,000		60,000
650.67	Frozen Foods—Fruit & Vegetables	12,000		12,000
650.68	Frozen Foods—Meats	24,000		24,000
650.69	Frozen Foods—Convenience Meals	18,000		18,000
	TOTAL NON-SALARY EXPENSES	$469,800	$ 73,500	$396,300

*Non-Food Variable Costs.

unit of service decreases with the increase in volume activity. The variable and fixed cost behavior can best be illustrated using the same relevant range of volume activity, but different actual volumes, as illustrated below:

First Range of Activity: 0–400,000

Description	Total Department Expense	Average Cost Per Meal Served	Total Department Expense	Average Cost Per Meal Served
Number of meals served	250,000	1	375,000	1
Non-Food variable expense	$ 37,500	$ .15	$ 57,300	$ .15
Food variable expense	225,000	.90	339,000	.90
Total variable expense	$262,500	$1.05	$396,300	$1.05
Fixed expense	73,500	.29	73,500	.20
Total expense	$346,000	$1.34	$469,800	$1.25

The average cost per meal decreases from $1.34 for a volume of $250,000 to $1.25 for a volume of 375,000 meals served. This is because the total fixed expense component was spread over a larger volume thus reducing the fixed cost component of $.09 per meal served.

NEED TO RECOGNIZE COST BEHAVIOR

Frequently, financial analysts, whether they are the department managers, their supervisors, or the chief financial officers of their health care facilities, may be misled by a financial report if the budget is not adjusted to actual volume. For example, assume that the dietary department's fixed budget and actual costs were as follows:

Dietary Department—Comparative Analysis of Fixed Budget to Actual

Description	Budget	Actual	Variance (Unfavorable) $	%
Fixed expense	$ 73,500	$ 73,500	$ -0-	-0-
Variable expense	396,300	373,750	22,550	5.69
Total expense	$469,800	$447,250	$22,550	4.80

The one component which is missing is the volume comparison. Assume that the actual number of meals served was 325,000 or 50,000 less than budgeted for or a 4.25 percent unfavorable variance. Such analysis is dangerously misleading because the expenses were not adjusted to the actual volume. Below is an example of a comparative analysis of the same budget totals adjusted to the actual volume of a control budget based upon standard variable unit costs:

Dietary Department—Comparative Analysis of Control Budget to Actual

Description	Standard Unit Variable Cost	Control Budget	Actual	Variance (Unfavorable) $	%
Actual volume of meals served		325,000	325,000	-0-	-0-
Fixed expense		$ 73,500	$ 73,500	$-0-	$ -0-
Variable expense	$1.05	341,250	373,750	(32,500)	(9.52)
Total expense		$414,750	$447,250	$(32,500)	(7.84%)
Average cost per meal served		$1.28	$1.38	$(.10)	(7.81%)

These possible misinterpretations of financial analysis dramatize the need to incorporate volume and cost behavior adjustments when comparing budget to actual total. In this case, the total variance switch is $55,050 from a $22,550 favorable variance to an unfavorable variance of $32,500. Not only did the variable expense component increase $.10 per meal served due to increased spending, but also the fixed cost per unit increased from $.20 to $.23 due to the decrease in volume.

STANDARD VARIABLE COST

The key component to developing a control budget is a standard variable cost. The standard variable cost can be developed in at least four different methods:

- aggregate
- grouping
- item
- combination

The aggregate method collects the total variable expenses and develops one standard variable cost for the department, as illustrated below.

$$\frac{\text{Total Departmental Variable Expenses}}{\text{Total Department Budget Volume}} = \begin{array}{c}\text{Standard Variable Cost Per}\\ \text{Unit of Service}\end{array}$$

or

$$\frac{\$\ 396,300}{375,000} = \$\ 1.05$$

The grouping method collects and separates the department's total variable expenses, for example:

Non-Food variable expense	$ 57,300
Food variable expense	$339,000
Total variable expense	$396,300

The formula is basically the same as above. The calculations are as follows:

	Non-Food	Food	Total
Total departmental variable expense	$ 57,300	$339,000	$396,300
Total departmental volume	375,000	375,000	375,000
Standard cost per grouping	$ .15	$ .90	$ 1.05

In Table 11–2, the standard cost for the grouping is first carried out to the nearest cent. It is advisable to carry the standard cost either to the nearest tenth or hundredth of a cent. The variance amount becomes increasingly significant, as illustrated, when high volumes are concerned, while the percent of variance remains the same.

The item method of establishing variable standard costs identifies each subaccount item within a department's chart of accounts and computes a standard cost for each of these as illustrated in Table 11–2.

The combination method of computing standard costs recognizes that one unit of production, i.e., meals served, does not utilize all items, as in the case of all food items, but does rationalize that most of the non-food items are utilized per meal served. In this case, the non-food item would be separated out per item while the food costs were combined to establish one standard food cost per meal served. The selection of method used depends primarily on the degree of accuracy and detail with which

Table 11–2 Item Method of Establishing Variable Standard Costs

Description	Nearest Cent	Nearest Tenth	Nearest Hundredth
Non-Food Cost Per Meal Served	$ .15	$ .153	$ .1528
Food Cost Per Meal Served	.90	.904	.9040
Total Cost Per Meal Served	$ 1.05	$ 1.057	$ 1.0568
Volume (medium)	375,000	375,000	375,000
Total Departmental Expense	$393,750	$396,375	$396,300
Amount Variance	-0-	$ 2,625	$ 2,550
Percent Variance	-0-	0.67%	0.65%
Volume (high)	750,000	750,000	750,000
Total Departmental Expense	$787,500	$792,750	$792,600
Amount Variance	-0-	$ 5,250	$ 5,100
Percent Variance	-0-	0.67%	0.65%

the department managers wish to effectively control the variable costs within their departments. Table 11–3 shows how to establish a standard variable cost using the combination method, as well as the item method.

SELECTION OF PRODUCTION UNIT

Once the variable expense items have been identified, the next step is to select the most appropriate statistical unit of production. This unit will most accurately reflect the behavior of the cost item, especially as it relates to the way it reacts within the department to which it is charged. It is highly conceivable that one cost item will be measured by one production unit in one department, and another in a different department. For example, food cost per meal served in the dietary department and cost per patient day in nursing.

Another example of a production unit which neither reflects what the actual circumstances are, nor fairly evaluates performance is square

Table 11–3 Establishing a Standard Variable Cost Using the Item and the Combination Methods

Description	Total Variable Cost	Standard Variable Cost
VOLUME—MEALS SERVED	375,000	1
Non-Food		
Outside Purchased Food Service	$ 5,000	$ .013
Laundry (employees)	3,600	.010
Supplies and Other Expenses	4,000	.011
Selective Menus	3,200	.009
Dishes, Glassware, Silverware	12,000	.032
Kitchen Utensils	18,000	.048
Paper Goods	2,000	.005
Soaps, Detergents	3,500	.009
Disposable Dishes and Flatware	4,000	.011
Uniforms and Aprons (employees)	2,000	.005
SUBTOTAL NON-FOOD	$ 57,300	$ .153
Food		
Food, General	$ 20,000	$ .053
Meat, Fish, Poultry	80,000	.213
Dairy Products—Milk, Butter, etc.	30,000	.080
Eggs	10,000	.027
Fresh Produce	50,000	.134
Breads and Pastries	35,000	.093
Groceries, Canned Goods	60,000	.160
Frozen Foods—Fruits & Vegetables	12,000	.032
Frozen Foods—Meats	24,000	.064
Frozen Foods—Convenient Meals	18,000	.048
SUBTOTAL FOOD	$339,000	$ .904
TOTAL DEPARTMENTAL EXPENSES	$396,300	$1.057

footage serviced. This unit is commonly accepted as a service unit measurement for the housekeeping department. The problem is that all square footage is not the same—some being very congested as in a business office or auditorium, and some being open space as in hallways and corridors. Some may even be carpeted while others may be tiled. With these variables recognized, separate standard costs and performance standards can be developed for employees who actually work at maintaining these areas.

But not all housekeeping employees perform the same kind of work. Discharge maids make up beds and clean rooms of discharged patients, so their standards of cost and performance must be developed using a different production unit from square footage. The important factor here is to emphasize the need to examine the cost behavior of *each* cost item, *each* type of work performed, and select a production unit which most accurately reflects the behavior of each, and assists the department managers in more effectively managing their departments.

There are innumerable varieties of production units to select, such as a treatment degree,[1] the hospital resource unit,[2] relative value units, and others as discussed in Chapter 5. The important factors in the selection of production units must be easily identified, counted, and audited, and they must quantifiably reflect the activity's behavior.

REFERENCES

1. Allen G. Herkimer, Jr., *Treatment Degree: A Standard Unit of Measure for all Components of the Health Care Industry* (Chicago, Ill.: Hospital Financial Management, March, 1972), pp. 7–13.
2. M. Eberhard, A. Herkimer, Jr., and K. Uhl, *The HRU—Measuring Input to Find Productivity* (Chicago, Ill.: Hospital Financial Management, February, 1976), pp. 44–48.

Chapter 12

Capital Expenditure Planning

Customarily, capital expenditure planning is a long-term program for identifying, evaluating, and financing proposed alternative capital investments. This process is frequently called fixed asset management.

FIXED ASSET MANAGEMENT VS. WORKING CAPITAL MANAGEMENT

Fixed asset management is substantially different from working capital management in that once the decision is made and the contract is signed, the health care facility is committed to a pattern or route of financial demands, managerial styles, production techniques, service selection—even geographical location—over an *extended period of time.* Working capital management can affect an economic change or management policy *almost immediately,* i.e., increase or decrease departmental charges for services.

The similarity in these two areas of health care financial management is that both affect cash flow.

PURPOSE OF CAPITAL EXPENDITURE PLANNING

The capital expenditure plan is one of the most important management tools included in the budgetary control system, because it does impact future operation and cash flow over an extended period of time regardless of volume fluctuations. Its primary function is to assure that cash outlays for fixed assets are based upon a carefully planned and systematic program of development. Well-planned capital decisions, coordinated with area-wide health care planning, will lead to the organized growth necessary to meet long-range goals. Unless there is a systematic and formal approach to project selection, including replacement of existing fixed assets, with reasonable acceptance and rejection criteria, capital decisions will be made on a crisis or squeaky-wheel basis. However, these decisions may not provide the resources and fixed assets needed to meet future challenges.

The preparation of the capital expenditure plan normally involves the allocation of scarce and/or limited dollars to a wide variety of projects. Consequently, capital rationing or prioritizing is involved in the selection of capital projects.

CURRENT GOVERNMENT REGULATIONS

Current government regulations require each health care facility to have a three-year plan for capital expenditures. Since the capital expenditure plan is a management tool of long-range planning, it is advisable that it span the same time period as the long-range plan, and at least the three years required by the government. Specific capital expenditures should be projected on a monthly basis for the first year, while quarterly expenditure projects are adequate for subsequent years.

Many health care experts believe that some hospitals will survive neither the current revolution in third party payment systems nor the increasing competition in the health care industry. One key determinant of a hospital's success is its ability to generate sufficient capital to make necessary renovations within its facilities and to acquire new technologies that improve medical outcomes and increase cost efficiency.[1] The hospital must raise funds for new services and facilities as well.

The Medicare PPS mandated by the Social Security Amendments of 1983 and implemented on October 1, 1983, excluded capital costs from PPS for cost reporting periods beginning before October 1, 1986, because there is no generally accepted method of including them in the Medicare prospective payment system. However, Congress mandated that the Secretary of HHS develop an equitable system of including capital-related costs in the prospective payment system. During the transition period, capital costs are to be computed on the same basis as during the base period.[2] Capital-related costs include

1. net depreciation expense, adjusted by gains and losses realized from the disposal of depreciable assets

2. leases and rentals for the use of assets that would be depreciable if the provider owned them outright
3. improvements that extend the estimated useful life of an asset at least two years beyond its original estimated useful life
4. minor equipment that is capitalized rather than charged off to expense
5. interest expense incurred in acquiring land or depreciable assets
6. insurance on depreciable assets used for patient care, or insurance that provides for the payment of capital-related costs during business interruption
7. taxes on land or depreciable assets used for patient care
8. return on equity for proprietary providers
9. capital-related costs of a supplying organization if it is related to the provider and furnishes the provider with services, facilities, or supplies[3]

With capital expenditures as a cost pass-through item, some health care experts believe that capital markets would perceive less risk. While they may perceive less risk in the short run, in the long run rating agencies are likely to realize that Medicare operating payments are a much more significant concern because they affect the hospital's operating margin and introduce substantial added risk, thus limiting a hospital's access to capital funds.

Because both the prospective payment system and the incorporation of capital into the prospective rates are based on industry averages, it is inevitable that some hospitals will be winners and others losers. Consequently, capital expenditures will require extensive evaluation and planning to reduce risk and to improve access to capital financing.

DEFINITION OF CAPITAL EXPENDITURE

A capital expenditure for purposes of Medicare provisions is an expenditure that, under generally accepted accounting principles, is not properly chargeable as an expense of operation and maintenance. For the purpose of most health care facilities, a capital expenditure is an expenditure that has an estimated life of more than one year and is not intended for sales in the ordinary course of operation.[4]

Usually, the costs of purchased capital expenditures are recovered on the basis of net depreciation provision; leased and/or rented capital expenditures are regained at the actual leased or rental expense.

IDENTIFICATION OF CAPITAL EXPENDITURE NEEDS

Since the capital expenditures budget supports the health care facility's overall growth plan, the institution and the departmental objectives (Exhibits 12–1 and 12–2) will identify many of the budget year's primary needs for capital outlay.

The importance of the department managers' and their supervisors' involvement in identifying capital asset needs cannot be overemphasized. The departmental objectives stem primarily from programs and plans prepared by and approved by the department manager. The department manager is in the most strategic position to identify the department's particular capital asset needs and the priority ranking of these needs.

Once these capital asset needs have been identified, the assistance of the purchasing agent or the materials manager is needed to identify and

Exhibit 12–1 Hospital Goals and Annual Operating Objectives

(1) GOALS	(2) OBJECTIVES	(3) YEAR	(4) REFERENCE NO.
Provide outpatient services needed by community	Begin implementing long range plan for outpatient services for 1975–1980	19x4	1
	Close first-west and remodel for outpatient service needs	19x5	2
	Build $1.5 million physicians' office complex	19x6	3
Increase person hour productivity in nursing and ancillary service units by 15%	Reevaluate work flow, facility layout, organization and staffing in nursing and ancillary areas	19x4	4
	Modify facility layout and work flow	19x4	5
	Revise staffing standards	19x4	6
	Make organization and staffing changes	19x5	7
Reduce laundry/ linen costs by 15%	Review linen usage and alternatives	19x4	8
Reduce working capital borrowing by 20%	Reduce patient receivables outstanding from 75 days to 55 days	19x4	9
	Reduce general stores inventory 15%	19x4	10

Improve management depth	Assess present management capabilities and needs	19x4	11
	Implement a management development program	19x5	12
	Establish an administrative residency position	19x6	13
Improve communications & relations with Chicano community	Make available patient information booklets and forms in Spanish	19x4	14
	Participate in school careers programs	19x4	15
	Increase number of Spanish speaking personnel in admitting & emergency room	19x4	16
Improve quality of patients' medical care	Participate in Institute on Improving Medical Audit	19x4	17
	Implement changes in medical audit procedures	19x4	18
	Implement patient care plan program in nursing units	19x5	19
	Expand medical records program for outpatients	19x6	20
	Reduce incident reports 35% by 7/1/x4	19x4	21
Redirect medical education program to emphasize family practice	Discontinue surgery intern and residency program	19x5	22
	Begin family practice intern and residency program	19x6	23

Source: California Hospital Association/Hospital Financial Management Association Budget Manual, Sacramento, California, 1974, Exhibit 4–1.

select equipment alternatives and estimated relative costs. Frequently, the chief engineer can assist in assessing the need for site preparation and/or facility modifications, in estimating related costs, and in estimating equipment installation costs. Early knowledge of facility modification and equipment costs helps to assure a more appropriate selection in capital assets. It is important to have alternative bids, since they can be studied and evaluated to arrive at the most favorable terms from suppliers and contractors. An important rule of thumb is always to obtain at least three alternatives to the capital asset need, whether it seems initially appropriate or not.

Exhibit 12–2 Departmental Objectives for Year 19x4

DEPARTMENT OBJECTIVES
For Year _____

Radiology ___ Department or Unit

Cost Center Number ___7140___

(1) OBJECTIVE	(2) ACTION PLAN	(3) Obj. Ref. No.	(4) Cost Classification Nat'l	(5) Cost Classification F/V	(6) Impact on Productive Hours	(7) Cost Impact Due to Change in: Practice	(8) Cost Impact Due to Change in: Volume	(9) Impact on Units of Service Volume	(10) Period over Which Impact Is Spread
Improve out-patient access to radiology area	Relocate entryway and reception area by 6/1/x4	1	7	F		40,000			May
Expand radiation treatment services	Install new linear accelerator by 11/30/x4	1	7	F			350,000		Nov
	Hire one radiology technician by 8/31/x4		1	V			2,400		Sep-Dec
			2	V			500		Sept-Dec
	Begin service 1/4/x4		4	V			1,000	800	Dec

Reduce spoiled X-ray films by 25%	Institute inservice training class on X-ray procedures and patient preparation	—	4	V	(600)	Apr-Dec
Encourage professional growth of staff	Send radiologist and technicians to radiologic and nuclear medicine meetings	—	6	F	600	May

Natural Cost Classifications are: 1—(Salaries & Wages); 2—(Employee Benefits); 3—(Professional Fees); 4—(Supplies); 5—(Purchased Services); 6—(Other Direct Expenses); and 7—(Capital Expenditures).

F/V Cost Classifications are: F—(Fixed); and V—(Variable).

Source: California Hospital Association/Hospital Financial Management Association Budget Manual, Sacramento, California, 1974, Exhibit 4-2.

CAPITAL EXPENDITURE WORKSHEET AND CAPITAL ASSET JUSTIFICATION

Each department manager should prepare a Capital Expenditure Worksheet (see Exhibit 12–3) for equipment requests and one worksheet for facility or plant remodeling requests. The worksheet should identify the years covered, and include at least three fiscal years. If the department has no additional needs for capital assets during the budget period covered, it should be so noted. The forms explaining why should be returned to the budget director.

Each health facility's departmental capital expenditures worksheets are summarized by the budget director in a capital expenditure summary. This process is performed for two basic reasons. First, it allows summation of capital asset acquisitions by major classifications:

- land
- plant (buildings)
- fixed equipment
- major movable equipment
- leasehold improvements

Second, it allows scheduling of actual cash disbursements for capital assets on a month-by-month basis and identifies the balances requiring financing. Exhibit 12–4 illustrates a departmental (radiology) capital expenditures summary and a health care facility's capital expenditures summary.

REVIEW OF CAPITAL EXPENDITURE REQUESTS

The capital expenditure requests of each department manager should be reviewed with a designated administration representative before being sent to the budget committee. The budget committee can select from the following three basic recommendations regarding capital expenditure requests:

Approve . . . . finance project immediately due to health care desirability and favorable cost benefit analysis; implement as soon as possible

Reject . . . . project appears to be unsuitable for the institution in the foreseeable future because its value is unclear, because some other community agency

Exhibit 12–3 Capital Expenditure Worksheet

CAPITAL EXPENDITURE WORKSHEET—EQUIPMENT ☒ FACILITIES ☐

(Individual items over $200—Year(s) 19x4–x8

Radiology Department

Prepared by A. Bauer   Date 10/20/x3
Approved by R.H.   Date 11/3/x3

Item	*Description of Item	New Service	Addition	Replacement	Priority**	Disposal***	Quantity	Estimated Cost (Salvage) Each	Total	Acquisition Year****	Recommended Supplier or Construction	Objective	Reference No.	Administrative Use Approved/Remarks
1	Linear Accelerator	x			B		1	350,000	350,000	11	Besting	1		
2	Overhead Lamp-Surgery	x			B		1	2,500	2,500	10	Besting	1		
3	Desk & Chair	x			B		1	400	400	12	Capital Office	1		
4	Rectilinear Scanner	x			B		1	10,000	10,000	11	Besting	1		
5	Wall Detector w/Scales	x			B		1	3,000	3,000	11	Besting	1		
6	Relocate Entryway			x	C		1	40,000	40,000	5	J&D Const.	1		
7														
8														
9														
10														

*List in order of year and within that year, priority, disposals last

**Priority:
A. Required for continued licensure or certification
B. Required to implement approved objective
C. Construction
D. Desirable for other reasons

***Disposal:
T. Trade In   D. Donation
S. Sale   J. Junk
R. Retire & Store

****Acquisition Year: Indicate month desired in column

REMARKS:
_____
_____
_____
_____
_____

Source: California Hospital Association/Hospital Financial Management Association Budget Manual, Sacramento, California, 1974, Exhibit 13–1, Example B.

Exhibit 12–4 Capital Expenditures Summary—Radiology

Year 19x4

Prepared by A.I. Date 10/4/x3
Approved by B.C. Date 10/10/x3

Department/ Item (1)	Land (2)	Plant & Fixed Equipment (3)	Major Equipment (4)	Minor Equipment (5)	Lease-hold Improve. (6)	TOTAL (7)	MONTHLY SCHEDULE OF EXPENDITURES (000 omitted)												Balance Financed
							Jan	Feb	Mar	Apr	May	Jun	Jul	Aug	Sep	Oct	Nov	Dec	
Linear Accelerator		*50,000	**350,000			400,000								35	50		70		245
Relocate Entryway		40,000				40,000					20	20							
Total		90,000	350,000			440,000					20	20		35	50		70		245

NOTES:
*Installation Costs:
**10% del. 8/x4, 20% additional down 11/x4, after installation and test, balance financed—$245,000 with 60 payments of $4,083 plus 8% interest on unpaid balance beginning 12/x4.

Source: California Hospital Association/Hospital Financial Management Association Budget Manual, Sacramento, California, 1974, Exhibit 13–3, Example A.

can implement it with better results, or because its implementation is inconsistent with institutional goals

Defer . . . . project appears to have considerable value; however, it cannot be undertaken because of human shortages, special situations inflating the capital requirement, or because the project requires preliminary action on some other proposal

Usually, final approval rests upon either the chief executive officer or the board of directors, and, of course, on the availability of funds.

At this juncture of the capital asset acquisition process, a catalog of available funds is provided to the primary decision maker, such as:

- unrestricted funds
- endowment income
- donations
- bequests
- profits from operations
- borrowings
- leasing

The catalog of funds and the departmental priority ranking of acquisitions provide part of the basis for capital expenditure selection decision making. At the same time, policies relating to the funding of depreciation and portfolio maintenance are reviewed. All anticipated changes are included in the various statements to support this portion of the budgetary control process.

In the final analysis, the techniques used in establishing capital spending priorities probably are not as important as the formalized procedures that require the administrative group to consider the capital needs of the health care facility. They must determine the most economical and practical method to satisfy capital needs and remain consistent with the desired level of quality health care in a systematic, orderly method, rather than by the crisis identification approach.

MARKETING OPPORTUNITY PACKAGE

The marketing opportunity package is an application of program budgeting that can be used in planning an evaluation process for selecting a capital expenditure. This process forces the department manager to separate all related costs, direct and indirect, which are required to support a specific capital investment. The program, or capital expenditure project budget, can either cover a period of three to five years, or, preferably, it can cover the estimated life of a capital investment. This latter process is referred to as life cycle costing, which will be discussed later in this chapter.

The meaning of the term program budget has not become standardized through general use. To some it suggests a restructuring of budget exhibits, accumulating costs in more meaningful categories, which, as we see them in the current budget array, are generally inputs with some mixture of ill-related outputs, all heavily influenced by administrative and organization history.[5]

To many, a program budget implies one that employs a longer term horizon than is found in the present budgeting systems with forward projection limited to one year. To others, the concept of program budgeting includes, in addition, the use of cost-utility analysis, a logical and measuring relation of inputs to outputs.

Basically, program budgeting concentrates its detailed information on a specific program, project, capital equipment, or investment, i.e., body scanner or mental health clinic, measuring the relationship of its programmed and actual life revenues to the related expenditures. In summary, the program budget process has been found to be an effective planning tool for selecting capital expenditures and for evaluating and monitoring its performance after implementation. The marketing opportunity package (MOP) illustrated in Exhibit 12–5 is an application of program or project budgeting to assemble and evaluate data on a capital expenditure.

KEY FACTORS IN EVALUATING CAPITAL EXPENDITURES

The following are the key factors, in order of importance, in evaluating capital expenditures:

- the merits of each capital expenditure request
- future net increases in cash inflows or net savings in cash outflows
- required total or life-time investment

Generally speaking, the best quantitative approach to capital commitments is to estimate the effect of the alternatives on cash flow in relation to the required investments. Thus, all projects whose rate of

Exhibit 12-5 Marketing Opportunity Package

Hospital name: _____

Hospital address: _____

Marketing opportunity package no. _____

Name of package: _____

Name of sponsoring department: _____

Name of sponsor: _____ Title: _____

Date submitted: _____ 19 ___ Date of ranking: _____ 19 ___

Priority Rating:

Priority Ranking:

Administrative decision

Immediate	Defer	Reject
Finance		

Administrative decision approved by: _____ Title: _____

Date of decision _____ 19 ___

1. Purpose of Opportunity Package

2. Patient or Community Need Served

3. Description of Patient Market Segment Need Meets

Exhibit 12–5 continued

Marketing opportunity package no. _____ Prepared by _____ Date _____
Marketing opportunity package name _____

4. Description of Competition That Furnishes Same Service

5. Alternative Services That Can Satisfy Same Need

Alternative 1 (A-1)	Alternative 2 (A-2)	Alternative 3 (A-3)

6. Technological Status and Cost of Capital Equipment Required

A-1	A-2	A-3

7. Personnel Staff Required

A-1

A-2

A-3

7a. Personnel Training Required

A-1

A-2

A-3

Marketing opportunity package no. _____ Prepared by _____ Date _____

Marketing opportunity package name _____

8. Advantages To Providing New Services

A-1	A-2	A-3

9. Consequences If Organization Does Not Furnish Service

A-1	A-2	A-3

10. Description of Unit of Service To Quantitatively Measure Volume and Productivity

11. Rationale for Alternative Selected

Exhibit 12–5 continued

Marketing opportunity package no. _____ Prepared by _____ Date _____

Marketing opportunity package name _____

12. Price and Breakeven (A) Forecast

Description	Alternative	Price	
1. Volume of Units Sold (Patient Days)			
2. Price Per Unit	$	$	$
3. Variable Cost Per Unit	$	$	$
4. Contribution to Overhead	$	$	$
5. Contribution Margin	%	%	%
6. Total Fixed Costs			
7. Break-even Units 6 ÷ 4 = 7			
8. Breakeven Revenue 6 ÷ 5 = 8			

Productivity and Staffing Requirements

1. Units Produced Per Person-Hour			
2. Full-Time Equivalent Employees Required			

13. Total Projected Direct Operating Summary

Description	Fiscal Year 19__	Fiscal Year 19__	Fiscal Year 19__
Gross Revenue	$	$	$
Deductions From Gross Revenue			
Net Revenue			
Salary Expense			
Fringe Benefit Expense			
Non-Salary Expense			
Depreciation			
Total Expense			
Profit (Loss)			

Comments:

(A) Items 12, 13, 14, and 15 should be developed for each alternative.

Marketing opportunity package no. _____ Prepared by _____ Date _____
Marketing opportunity package name _____

14. Development and Start-up Investment
    and Source of Funds

Description	Fiscal Year 19__	Fiscal Year 19__	Fiscal Year 19__
Operations (Accounts Receivable Working Capital)			
Bank Loans			
Grants			
Lease			
Other: (Describe Capital Equipment)			
Total Investment Required			

Comments:

Exhibit 12–5 continued

Marketing opportunity package no. _____ Prepared by _____ Date _____
Marketing opportunity package name _____

15. <u>Return on Investment</u>

A—Original Investment $ _____

B—Useful Life   _____

C—Annual Cash In-Flow From Operation $ _____

D—Desired Rate of Return   _____ %

E—Salvage Value $ _____

Simple Payback: $ _____ (A) = _____ Years
                 $ _____ (C)

<u>Bail-Out Payback:</u>

Year	Accumulated Cash In-Flow (C)	Plus	Salvage Value	Accumulated Cash Flow and Value
1	$ _____	+	$ _____	$ _____
2	$ _____	+	$ _____	$ _____
3	$ _____	+	$ _____	$ _____
4	$ _____	+	$ _____	$ _____
5	$ _____	+	$ _____	$ _____

Comments:

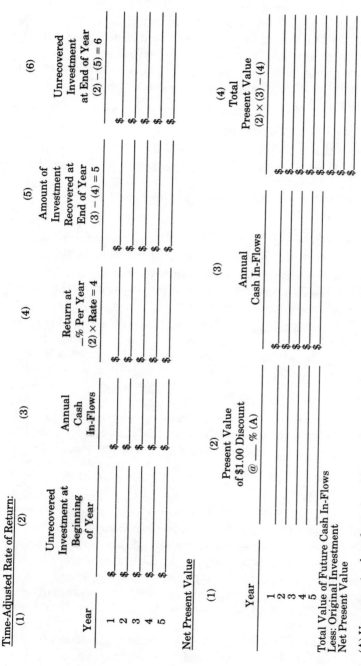

Time-Adjusted Rate of Return:

(1) Year	(2) Unrecovered Investment at Beginning of Year	(3) Annual Cash In-Flows	(4) Return at __% Per Year (2) × Rate = 4	(5) Amount of Investment Recovered at End of Year (3) − (4) = 5	(6) Unrecovered Investment at End of Year (2) − (5) = 6
1	$	$	$	$	$
2		$	$	$	$
3	$	$	$	$	$
4	$	$	$	$	$
5	$	$	$	$	$

Net Present Value

(1) Year	(2) Present Value of $1.00 Discount @ __% (A)	(3) Annual Cash In-Flows	(4) Total Present Value (2) × (3) − (4)
1		$	$
2		$	$
3		$	$
4		$	$
5		$	$
			$
			$

Total Value of Future Cash In-Flows
Less: Original Investment
Net Present Value

(A) Use present value of annuity of $1.00 in arrears table.

return exceeds the minimum acceptable rate of return could be the alternative to select and vice versa. The minimum acceptable rate of return is usually determined by top management and it represents the rate that can be earned by alternative uses of investment capital.

Economic or cost-benefit ratios are not the only quantitative considerations to be used in evaluating capital expenditures. The following are other criteria for consideration:

• number of patients who benefit
• degree to which the patients will benefit
• demographic characteristics of the patients who will benefit

These criteria can be further refined, as follows, assuming that everything else is equal:

• If two proposals could prevent a fatal illness, the one serving the larger number of patients at the same cost would be better.
• If two proposals served the same number of patients at the same cost, but one could prevent a disease while the other could simply make the disease nonfatal, the first condition would be preferred.
• If two proposals could prevent fatal illness for the same number of patients at the same cost, but one could prevent a disease in children and young adults while the other could prevent a disease occurring only among the aged, the first condition would be preferred.

Cost-benefit estimates can be computed using these criteria to assist in objective decision making. However, the final project selection decision must be made on the basis of the merits of each individual project, and its long-range impact upon the department and the health care facility.

In estimating the demand for the services of a specific capital project, the number of patients who are likely to receive benefits seems the most appropriate criterion. However, the number of patients must be further segmented to evaluate the benefits furnished. Most people agree that extreme efforts are desirable to preserve the life of the president of the United States, but few would support more general distinctions in this direction. Only age seems an acceptable variable to assess benefits, but this must be qualified within very broad humanitarian limits and supported with common sense.

For example, the young adult could have the highest economic value, reflecting substantial investments that have been made in his rearing, and, hopefully, greater length of productive years. Most societies also place high values on the life of the young children. Senior citizens' economic value could be set lower due to fewer remaining productive years. Using these basic observations, the health care benefits could be crudely characterized according to the following weighted scale of benefit values:

- 2.0—preventive care, partial recovery to normal health
- 4.0—complete recovery to normal health
- 6.0—prevents near fatal diseases
- 8.0—saves lives with partial disability
- 10.0—saves lives with complete recovery
- 12.0—prevents fatal diseases

The above evaluation scale is based upon the following controversial assumptions:

- Continuing a life is always better than providing preventive measures or health restoration.
- Preventing illness is always better than using therapy to treat it.

The following factors, after considerable investigation of alternative variables used to evaluate capital proposals, have been identified as key elements to analyze cost-benefits:

- anticipated time span (years) of project
- original capital investment
- annual operating expenses
- present value of all expenditures
- average annual savings or net earnings
- number of patients served
- age of patients served
- average cost per patient served
- intangible health care benefits, both from a short and long (building-block) range approach

For illustrative purposes, assume the four proposals in Table 12–1 are being considered by the budget committee for possible capital investment.

Table 12–1 Proposal for Capital Investments for Fiscal Year 19x2

Memorial Hospital
Anytown, U.S.A.

Proposal A—preventive medicine facility
Construction cost	$1,150,000—30 year life
Equipment cost	$ 200,000—over two years
Outpatient capacity	65,000 visits
Present outpatient volume	15,500 visits
Office space for 16 physicians	
Estimated operating costs	$ 230,000 per year
Equipment maintenance and replacement	$ 15 on fifth year
	10% thereafter
Building maintenance and renovation	10% every 10 years

Discounted present value of these costs is $5,297,000 at 4% (See Table 12–2)

Proposal B—community home care
Original investment for office and minor equipment	$ 10,000—10 year life
Annual operating costs	$ 48,000
Estimated number of patients	275 per year
Savings to hospital from beds not used due to	
community home care—10 beds × 275 admissions	
× $600 cost	$ 165,000
Discounted present value at 4%	$ 398,000 (See Table 12–3)

Proposal C—store front dental clinic
Original investment for building	$ 40,000—30 year life
Equipment	$ 110,000—10 year life
Estimated patients	7,500 per year
Annual operating costs	$ 175,000
Discounted present value at 4%	$1,565,000 (See Table 12–3)

Proposal D—open heart surgical unit
Original investment for space and equipment	$ 275,000—10 year life
Annual operating expenses	$ 125,000
Estimated cases	300
Discounted present value at 4%	$1,280,000 (See Table 12–3)

Tables 12–2 and 12–3 are computations of the discounted values of expenses for Preventive Medicine Facility (Proposal A) and Proposals B, C, and D, respectively. The table used to compute the discounted cash flows is Table 12–4.

The four proposals and their respective cost-benefit data have been arranged in a comparative analysis worksheet in Table 12–5.

Table 12–2 Discounted Values of Expenses for Preventive Medicine Facility in Thousands of Dollars—Proposal A

Year	Building	Equipment	Operating	Total Expenses	4% Present Value	Discounted Cash Flow*
1	$1,150	$1,150		$1,300	.962	$1,250
2		50	$ 100	150	.925	139
3			230	230	.889	204
4			230	230	.855	197
5			230	230	.822	189
6			230	230	.790	182
7		15	230	245	.760	186
8		20	230	250	.731	183
9		20	230	250	.703	176
10		20	230	250	.676	169
11	115	20	230	365	.650	237
12		20	230	250	.625	156
13		20	230	250	.601	150
14		20	230	250	.577	144
15		20	230	250	.555	139
16		20	230	250	.534	134
17		20	230	250	.513	128
18		20	230	250	.494	124
19		20	230	250	.475	119
20		20	230	250	.456	114
21	115	20	230	365	.439	160
22		20	230	250	.422	106
23		20	230	250	.406	102
24		20	230	250	.390	98
25		20	230	250	.375	94
26		20	230	250	.361	90
27		20	230	250	.347	87
28		20	230	250	.333	83
29		20	230	250	.321	80
30		20	230	250	.308	77
	$1,380	$ 675	$6,540	$8,595		$5,297

*Total Expenses times 4% Present Value

This study illustrates a method that could assist the department manager in assembling pertinent data on capital expenditure proposals.

Table 12–3 Discounted Values of Expenses for Proposals B, C, and D in Thousands of Dollars

Year	Building	Equipment	Operating	Total Expenses	4% Present Value	Discounted Cash Flow
			Proposal B			
1	$ 8	$ 2	$ 48	$ 58	.962	$ 56
2			48	48	.925	44
3			48	48	.889	43
4			48	48	.855	41
5			48	48	.822	39
6			48	48	.790	38
7			48	48	.760	36
8			48	48	.731	35
9			48	48	.703	34
10			48	48	.676	32
Total	$ 8	$ 2	$ 480	$ 490		$ 398
			Proposal C			
1	$ 40	$110	$ 175	$ 325	.962	$ 313
2			175	175	.925	162
3			175	175	.889	156
4			175	175	.855	150
5			175	175	.822	144
6			175	175	.790	138
7			175	175	.760	133
8			175	175	.731	128
9			175	175	.703	123
10			175	175	.676	118
Total	$ 40	$110	$1,750	$1,900		$1,565
			Proposal D			
1	$125	$150	$ 125	$ 400	.962	$ 385
2			125	125	.925	116
3			125	125	.889	111
4			125	125	.855	107
5			125	125	.822	103
6			125	125	.790	99
7			125	125	.760	95
8			125	125	.731	91
9			125	125	.703	88
10			125	125	.676	85
Total	$125	$150	$1,250	$1,525		$1,280

Table 12-4   Present Value of $1.00

$$P = \frac{S}{(1 + r)^n}$$

Periods	4%	6%	8%	10%	12%	14%	16%	18%	20%	22%	24%	26%	28%	30%	40%
1	0.962	0.943	0.926	0.909	0.893	0.877	0.862	0.847	0.833	0.820	0.806	0.794	0.781	0.769	0.714
2	0.925	0.890	0.857	0.826	0.797	0.769	0.743	0.718	0.694	0.672	0.650	0.630	0.610	0.592	0.510
3	0.889	0.840	0.794	0.751	0.712	0.675	0.641	0.609	0.579	0.551	0.524	0.500	0.477	0.455	0.364
4	0.855	0.792	0.735	0.683	0.636	0.592	0.552	0.516	0.482	0.451	0.423	0.397	0.373	0.350	0.260
5	0.822	0.747	0.681	0.621	0.567	0.519	0.476	0.437	0.402	0.370	0.341	0.315	0.291	0.269	0.186
6	0.790	0.705	0.630	0.564	0.507	0.456	0.410	0.370	0.335	0.303	0.275	0.250	0.227	0.207	0.133
7	0.760	0.665	0.583	0.513	0.452	0.400	0.354	0.314	0.279	0.249	0.222	0.198	0.178	0.159	0.095
8	0.731	0.627	0.540	0.467	0.404	0.351	0.305	0.266	0.233	0.204	0.179	0.157	0.139	0.123	0.068
9	0.703	0.592	0.500	0.424	0.361	0.308	0.263	0.225	0.194	0.167	0.144	0.125	0.108	0.094	0.048
10	0.676	0.558	0.463	0.386	0.322	0.270	0.227	0.191	0.162	0.137	0.116	0.099	0.085	0.073	0.035
11	0.650	0.527	0.429	0.350	0.287	0.237	0.195	0.162	0.135	0.112	0.094	0.079	0.066	0.056	0.025
12	0.625	0.497	0.397	0.319	0.257	0.208	0.168	0.137	0.112	0.092	0.076	0.062	0.052	0.043	0.018
13	0.601	0.469	0.368	0.290	0.229	0.182	0.145	0.116	0.093	0.075	0.061	0.050	0.040	0.033	0.013
14	0.577	0.442	0.340	0.263	0.205	0.160	0.125	0.099	0.078	0.062	0.049	0.039	0.032	0.025	0.009
15	0.555	0.417	0.315	0.239	0.183	0.140	0.108	0.084	0.065	0.051	0.040	0.031	0.025	0.020	0.006
16	0.534	0.394	0.292	0.218	0.163	0.123	0.093	0.071	0.054	0.042	0.032	0.025	0.019	0.015	0.005
17	0.513	0.371	0.270	0.198	0.146	0.108	0.080	0.060	0.045	0.034	0.026	0.020	0.015	0.012	0.003
18	0.494	0.350	0.250	0.180	0.130	0.095	0.069	0.051	0.038	0.028	0.021	0.016	0.012	0.009	0.002
19	0.475	0.331	0.232	0.164	0.116	0.083	0.060	0.043	0.031	0.023	0.017	0.012	0.009	0.007	0.002
20	0.456	0.312	0.215	0.149	0.104	0.073	0.051	0.037	0.026	0.019	0.014	0.010	0.007	0.005	0.001
21	0.439	0.294	0.199	0.135	0.093	0.064	0.044	0.031	0.022	0.015	0.011	0.008	0.006	0.004	0.001
22	0.422	0.278	0.184	0.123	0.083	0.056	0.038	0.026	0.018	0.013	0.009	0.006	0.004	0.003	0.001
23	0.406	0.262	0.170	0.112	0.074	0.049	0.033	0.022	0.015	0.010	0.007	0.005	0.003	0.002	
24	0.390	0.247	0.158	0.102	0.066	0.043	0.028	0.019	0.013	0.008	0.006	0.004	0.003	0.002	
25	0.375	0.233	0.146	0.092	0.059	0.038	0.024	0.016	0.010	0.007	0.005	0.003	0.002	0.001	
26	0.361	0.220	0.135	0.084	0.053	0.033	0.021	0.014	0.009	0.006	0.004	0.002	0.002	0.001	
27	0.347	0.207	0.125	0.076	0.047	0.029	0.018	0.011	0.007	0.005	0.003	0.002	0.001	0.001	
28	0.333	0.196	0.116	0.069	0.042	0.026	0.016	0.010	0.006	0.004	0.002	0.002	0.001	0.001	
29	0.321	0.185	0.107	0.063	0.037	0.022	0.014	0.008	0.005	0.003	0.002	0.001	0.001		
30	0.308	0.174	0.099	0.057	0.033	0.020	0.012	0.007	0.004	0.003	0.002	0.001	0.001		
40	0.208	0.097	0.046	0.022	0.011	0.005	0.003	0.001	0.001						

Source: Charles T. Horngren, *Cost Accounting: A Managerial Emphasis*, 5th ed., © 1982, p. 960. Adapted by permission of Prentice-Hall, Englewood Cliffs, N.J.

Table 12–5 Comparative Analysis of Proposed Projects

(1) Proposal Name	(2) Life	(3) Original Capital Investment	(4) Annual Operating Expenses	(5) Present Value I=4% (A)	(6) Average Annual Savings	(7) Annual Patient Served	(8) Cost Per Patient Serviced(B)	(9) Comments	(10) Health Care Benefit Value
Proposal A									
Preventive Medicine Facility	30	$1,350,000	$230,000	$5,297,000	–	15,500	$ 11.39	Wide range of age limits of patients facility will, as a part of Hospital Health Care Training Program open 24-hours every day to serve all patients.	2.0
Proposal B									
Community Home Care Program	10	10,000	43,000	398,000	$165,000	275	$144.73	Should relieve hospital beds and save $165,000 per year in costs. With new patients, should net about 45% – convalescent and supportive service to middle to elderly patients.	4.0
Proposal C									
Store-Front Dental Clinic	10	150,000	175,000	1,565,000	–	7,500	$ 20.87	Heavy emphasis on Preventive Dental Care for Young Welfare Recipients – location should encourage more concern to one's dental care – possibly reduce hospital costs of these youths in future years.	2.0
Proposal D									
Open Heart Surgical Unit	10	275,000	125,000	1,280,000	–	300	$426.67	Life savings benefits with nearly 85% total recovery – patients primarily middle aged to elderly – no open heart surgical unit in service area.	10.0

(A) Calculated on capital investments plus operating costs.

(B) Col. (5) $\div$ (Col. (2) X Col. (7)).

IDENTIFYING CAPITAL EXPENDITURE PROJECTS

There are several key factors to consider in identifying capital expenditure projects, such as:

- community needs
- marketability
  internal
  external
- urgency
  replacement
  new technology
- competition
  internal
  external

Community need requirements probably lead this list. The health care needs of the community must be identified and then the capital investments selected which will best serve this need. There is no use in internally selecting a capital project which management *thinks* the community needs, then trying to convince the citizenry that they need it. They key is to know the health care needs of the service area and design the health care facility and its department's long-range plan on serving this need.

Hand in hand with recognizing the community's needs is the potential marketability of the service to the medical staff and to the people of the community in that order. There is no better way to assure an unsuccessful project than to select one which cannot be sold to the medical staff and to the community. Let's face it—any new project requires selling, whether it's health care or widgets.

The degree of urgency of the need is another factor in identifying the capital expenditure. Replacement, either with the same model or a newer one, can usually be fairly easily justified, but a change in technology or a new technology may require more preparation in appropriate selection of the capital investment.

Competition is the most overlooked factor used in selecting capital expenditure. Some prefer to look at the health care industry as though they were Florence Nightingale, ignoring the competitive nature of the business. Health care is competitive—competitive for the services of the physicians (the salesmen and the purchasers of health care), and for the patients they can generate for the health care facility. Competition does not necessarily require that each facility or department has the latest equipment or program, but that the institution's management must be acutely aware of the buyers' and sellers' market needs, and constantly reviewing these needs with the medical staff to assure understanding and support in the identification of appropriate capital expenditures.

Underlying all of the above considerations, perhaps the most dominant one is that of governmental permission through its certificate of need (CON) and other regulations. But government regulations should not prohibit an investment that generates a substantial benefit to the consumer and the investor.

MATHEMATICAL METHODS TO EVALUATE CAPITAL EXPENDITURES

Conceptually, the discounted cash flow analysis is superior to most mathematical methods, but this method must be used with a reasonable portion of common sense in evaluating capital expenditures.

Before examining this method, however, we will review the more traditional methods such as payback and bail-out payback.

Assume that the original capital expenditure (I) is $37,900 and that it is anticipated that the net annual cash operating profit (O) is $10,000 and (P) is the payback period of time. Using the following formula:

$$\frac{I}{O} = P$$

Let: I = Investment
       O = Operating profit
       P = Payback (time)

Or

$$\frac{\$37,900}{\$10,000} = 3.79$$

The payback period would be 3.79 years. It should be noted that in calculating payback, time is the key factor in mathematically evaluating a capital expenditure.

The bail-out payback system considers the salvage value of a capital investment. Using the above information, assume that the salvage value is $25,000 at the end of the first year and that this amount declines at the rate of $5,000 per year thereafter. The bail-out payback system would be calculated as follows:

At End of Year	Cumulative Cash Operating Profits	Plus:	Salvage Value	Cumulative Total
1	$10,000	+	$25,000	$35,000
2	20,000	+	20,000	40,000
3	30,000	+	15,000	45,000
4	40,000	+	10,000	50,000
5	50,000	+	5,000	55,000
6	60,000	+	None	60,000

The cumulative total at the end of the second year is $40,000, or more than the original investment of $37,900, therefore, the bail-out payback time is two years. Anytime after this period, the capital investment may be totally scrapped, and the investors have made the expenditure pay for itself.

Discounted Cash Flow

The discounted cash flow (DCF) method of mathematically analyzing capital expenditures recognizes that the use of money has a cost (interest), just as the use of an x-ray may have a cost (rent). Further, it assumes that, especially in an inflationary economy such as ours, a dollar today is worth more than a dollar four or five years from now. For example, cash can be invested in a savings account; the original amount will grow during the investment because of the interest it would earn. The discounted cash flow analysis is one of the best methods for long-range capital decisions because it explicitly and routinely weighs the time value of money.

Another major aspect of the DCF method is that it focuses on cash inflows and outflows, rather than on net income as computed according to generally accepted accounting principles. In short, cash is invested in the present with the hope of receiving cash in a greater amount in the future. To compute this future worth of cash, the DCF method has two variations:

- time-adjusted rate of return
- net present value

Time-Adjusted Rate of Return Method

The National Association of Accountants (NAA) in its research report on "Return on Capital as a Guide to Managerial Decisions" defines the time-adjusted rate of return as "the maximum rate of interest that could be paid for the capital employed over the life of an investment without loss on the project." Alternatively, rate of return may be defined as the discounting rate that makes the present value of a capital expenditure equal to the cost of the initial expenditure. Further, this rate corresponds to the effective rate of interest currently and widely computed for bonds purchased or sold at discounts or premiums.

For example, assume a pathologist has told the chief executive officer that he would like to purchase a $37,900 piece of laboratory equipment, which is expected to have a five-year useful life, have zero salvage value, result in cash operating savings of $10,000 annually, and have a required rate of return of 10 percent which was computed by the trial and error method, and is summarized as follows:

Original investment	$37,900
Useful life	5 years
Annual cash inflow from operations	$10,000
Rate of return	10%

Simply, the capital expenditure is the present value. The 10 percent is the rate of interest that equates the amount invested ($37,900) with the present value of the cash inflow of $10,000 per year for five years. Specifically, if money were borrowed at an effective interest rate of 10 percent, the cash inflow produced by the capital investment would exactly repay a hypothetical loan plus interest over five years. If the minimum desired rate of return is less than 10 percent, the capital expenditure will be profitable. If the cost of the capital investment exceeds 10 percent, the cash inflow will be insufficient to pay interest and repay the principal of the hypothetical loan. Therefore, 10 percent is the appropriate time-adjusted rate of return for this capital expenditure.

The minimum desired rate of return or cost of capital is usually a long-run weighted average based on both debt and equity. Cost of capital is not a piecemeal computation based on the market rate of interest; that is, cost of capital is not interest expense on borrowed money as the accountant usually conceives it to be. For example, a mortgage-free building still has a cost of capital—the amount that could be earned with the proceeds if the building were sold. The economist would call this opportunity cost.

The time-adjusted rate of return is computed on the basis of the funds in use from period to period instead of the original investment. The rate of return in this example is 10 percent of the capital investment during each year. The cash inflows in excess of the 10 percent rent on the capital are regarded as recoveries of the original investment. In this example, the five-year cash inflow recovers the original investment plus interest at a rate of 10 percent on the as yet unrecovered capital. This is illustrated in Table 12–6.

Net Present Value Method

Computing the exact time-adjusted rate of return entails trial and error and sometimes cumbersome hand calculations and interpolations within a compound-interest table. In contrast, the net present value method initially assumes some minimum desired rate of return. Basically, all expected cash inflows are discounted to the present, using this minimum desired rate. If the result is positive (greater returns over the life of the project than the initial investment), the proposed capital proposal is desirable because its return exceeds the desired minimum. If the result is negative, the proposal is mathematically undesirable.

Table 12–6 Evaluation of Capital Investment Using the Time-Adjusted Rate of Return Method

MEMORIAL HOSPITAL
ANYTOWN, U.S.A.

YEAR	Unrecovered Investment at Beginning of Year	Annual Cash Inflows	Return at 10% Per Year (2) x 10% = ($)	Amount of Investment Recovered at End of Year (3)-(4) = 5	Unrecovered Investment at End of Year (2)-(5) = 6
19x1	$ 37,900	$10,000	$ 3,791	$ 6,209	$ 31,691
19x2	31,691	10,000	3,170	6,830	24,861
19x3	24,861	10,000	2,487	7,513	17,348
19x4	17,345	10,000	1,736	8,264	9,084
19x5	9,084	10,000	909	9,091	(7)
TOTAL		$50,000	$12,093	$37,907	N.A.

Exhibit 12–6 illustrates the net present value approach. The new capital equipment purchase price is $37,900 and the minimum desired rate of return is eight percent. The example indicates a net present value of $2,030, therefore, the investment is desirable. Summarily, management would be able to invest $2,030 more, or a total of $39,930, and still break even at eight percent on the project.

Tables 12–7 and 12–8 are illustrations of the present value of steady and variable cash inflows and present value with various cash inflows with salvage value, respectively. Table 12–9 is used to calculate these values.

Life Cycle Costing

Life cycle costing is the process by which a capital expenditure is evaluated to alternatives by computing the total costs over the anticipated life span of the asset or program. Operating costs included are:

- personnel by skill level
- materials and supplies
- maintenance and operations
- allocated overhead

Investment and equipment costs are determined for each individual capital investment, plus factors for inflation and a discounted rate of return.

A comparative analysis of two alternative capital expenditures, using the life-cycle method, is illustrated in Table 12–10.

FINAL DECISION-MAKING PROCESS AND ALTERNATIVE SELECTION

In the final analysis, department managers and their supervisors must make a decision to present the most appropriate capital expenditures to the budget committee. They must be discriminating in their selection; their rationale for each expenditure must be logical and practical, or their credibility will be damaged with the committee. This selection process presents, at least, these four alternatives:

1. Do nothing—either do not furnish the new service or allow the present capital equipment to deteriorate gradually and ultimately break down.

Exhibit 12–6 Net Present Value Techniques

MEMORIAL HOSPITAL
ANYTOWN, U.S.A.

Method – One

Discounting Each Year's Cash Inflow Separately (Using Table 12-4 - Present Value of $1.00)

Original Investment	$ 37,900
Useful Life	5 Years
Annual Cash Inflow	$ 10,000
Minimum Desired Rate of Return	8%

Year	Present Value of $1.00 Discounted @ 8%	Total Present Value	0	19 x 1	19 x 2	19 x 3	19 x 4	19 x 5
			1	1	1	1	1	1
End of Year Cash Flows:			$ (37,900)					
Annual Cash Savings								
19 x 1	.926	$ 9,260		$ 10,000				
19 x 2	.857	8,570			$ 10,000			
19 x 3	.794	7,940				$ 10,000		
19 x 4	.735	7,350					$ 10,000	
19 x 5	.681	6,810						$ 10,000
Present Value of Future Cash Inflows		$ 39,930						
Original Investment	1,000	37,900	$ (37,900)					
Net Present Value		$ 2,030						

Method – Two

Discounting Using Present Value of $1.00 in Arrears (Table 12-9)

			19 x 1	19 x 2	19 x 3	19 x 4	19 x 5
Annual Cash Savings	3,993	$ 39,930	$ 10,000	$ 10,000	$ 10,000	$ 10,000	$ 10,000
Original Investment	1,000	37,900	$ (37,900)				
Net Present Value		2,030					

Table 12–7 Present Value of Steady and Variable Cash Flows

MEMORIAL HOSPITAL
ANYTOWN, U.S.A.

Steady Cash Flows

Year	Est. Cash Flow	Discount* @ 6%	Present Value @ 6%	Present Value @ 4%	Present Value @ 8%
1	$ 3,000	.943	$ 2,829	$ 2,886	$ 2,778
2	3,000	.890	2,670	2,775	2,571
3	3,000	.840	2,520	2,667	2,382
4	3,000	.792	2,376	2,565	2,205
5	3,000	.747	2,241	2,466	2,043
Total	$ 15,000		$ 12,636	$ 13,359	$ 11,979

Decreasing Cash Flows

1	$ 5,000	.943	$ 4,715	$ 4,810	$ 4,630
2	4,000	.890	3,560	3,700	3,428
3	3,000	.840	2,520	2,667	2,382
4	2,000	.792	1,584	1,710	1,470
5	1,000	.747	747	822	681
Total	$ 15,000		$ 13,126	$ 13,709	$ 12,591

Increasing Cash Flows

1	$ 1,000	.943	$ 943	$ 962	$ 926
2	2,000	.890	1,780	1,850	1,714
3	3,000	.840	2,520	2,667	2,382
4	4,000	.792	3,168	3,420	2,940
5	5,000	.747	3,745	4,110	3,405
Total	$ 15,000		$ 12,156	$ 13,009	$ 11,367

*Source: Table 12–4.

2. Replace the present capital equipment with comparable equipment.

3. Replace the present capital equipment with lower capacity equipment.

4. Replace the present capital equipment with higher capacity equipment.

Each of these alternatives will have a direct impact upon the department's productivity and profits. For example, if the decision is to do nothing, the events and results could be:

Table 12–8 Present Value with Various Cash Flows and Salvage Value

MEMORIAL HOSPITAL
ANYTOWN, U.S.A.

Steady Cash Flows

Year	Est. Cash Flow	Discount* @ 6%	Present Value @ 6%
1	$ 3,000	.943	$ 2,829
2	3,000	.890	2,670
3	3,000	.840	2,520
4	3,000	.792	2,376
5	3,000	.747	2,241
Salvage	1,500	.747	1,120
Total	$ 16,500		$ 13,756

Decreasing Cash Flows

1	$ 5,000	.943	$ 4,715
2	4,000	.890	3,560
3	3,000	.840	2,520
4	2,000	.792	1,584
5	1,000	.747	747
Salvage	1,500	.747	1,120
Total	$ 16,500		$ 14,246

Increasing Cash Flows

1	$ 1,000	.943	$ 943
2	2,000	.890	1,780
3	3,000	.840	2,520
4	4,000	.792	3,168
5	5,000	.747	3,745
Salvage	1,500	.747	1,120
Total	$ 16,500		$ 13,276

*Source: Table 12–4.

Events
• gradual increase in equipment repairs
• eventual total equipment breakdown
Results
• decreased productivity
• eventual total loss in productivity

Table 12–9 Present Value of Annuity of $1.00 in Arrears

$$P_n = \frac{1}{r}\left[1 - \frac{1}{(1+r)^n}\right]$$

Periods	4%	6%	8%	10%	12%	14%	16%	18%	20%	22%	24%	25%	26%	28%	30%	40%
1	0.902	0.943	0.928	0.909	0.893	0.877	0.862	0.847	0.833	0.820	0.806	0.800	0.794	0.781	0.769	0.714
2	1.886	1.833	1.783	1.736	1.690	1.647	1.605	1.566	1.528	1.492	1.457	1.440	1.424	1.302	1.361	1.224
3	2.775	2.673	2.577	2.487	2.402	2.322	2.246	2.174	2.106	2.042	1.981	1.923	1.868	1.816	1.816	1.589
4	3.630	3.465	3.312	3.170	3.037	2.914	2.798	2.690	2.589	2.494	2.404	2.362	2.320	2.241	2.166	1.879
5	4.452	4.212	3.993	3.791	3.605	3.433	3.274	3.127	2.991	2.864	2.745	2.689	2.635	2.532	2.436	2.035
6	5.242	4.917	4.623	4.355	4.111	3.889	3.685	3.498	3.326	3.167	3.020	2.951	2.855	2.769	2.643	2.168
7	6.002	5.582	5.206	4.868	4.584	4.288	4.039	3.812	3.605	3.416	3.242	3.181	3.083	2.937	2.802	2.203
8	6.733	6.210	5.747	5.335	4.968	4.639	4.344	4.078	3.837	3.619	3.421	3.329	3.241	3.076	2.925	2.331
9	7.435	6.802	6.247	5.759	5.328	4.946	4.607	4.303	4.031	3.786	3.566	3.463	3.366	3.184	3.019	2.379
10	8.111	7.300	6.710	6.145	5.650	5.216	4.833	4.494	4.192	3.923	3.682	3.571	3.465	3.269	3.092	2.414
11	8.700	7.887	7.139	6.405	5.988	5.453	5.029	4.656	4.327	4.035	3.776	3.658	3.544	3.335	3.147	2.438
12	9.385	8.384	7.536	6.814	6.194	5.000	5.197	4.793	4.439	4.127	3.851	3.725	3.606	3.387	3.190	2.456
13	9.986	8.853	7.904	7.103	6.424	5.842	5.342	4.910	4.533	4.203	3.912	3.780	3.656	3.427	3.223	2.468
14	10.563	9.295	8.244	7.387	6.628	6.002	5.468	5.008	4.611	4.265	3.962	3.824	3.695	3.459	3.249	2.477
15	11.118	9.712	8.559	7.606	6.811	6.142	5.575	5.092	4.675	4.316	4.001	3.859	3.726	3.483	3.268	2.484
16	11.652	10.106	8.851	7.824	6.974	6.285	5.669	5.162	4.730	4.357	4.033	3.887	3.751	3.503	3.263	2.489
17	12.166	10.477	9.122	8.022	7.120	6.373	5.749	5.222	4.775	4.391	4.059	3.910	3.771	3.518	3.295	2.492
18	12.659	10.028	9.372	8.201	7.250	6.467	5.818	5.273	4.812	4.419	4.080	3.928	3.786	3.529	3.304	2.494
19	13.134	11.158	9.604	8.365	7.366	6.550	5.877	5.316	4.844	4.442	4.097	3.942	3.799	3.539	3.311	2.496
20	13.590	11.470	9.818	8.514	7.469	6.623	5.929	5.353	4.870	4.460	4.110	3.954	3.808	3.546	3.316	2.497
21	14.029	11.764	10.017	8.649	7.562	6.687	5.973	5.384	4.891	4.476	4.121	3.963	3.818	3.551	3.320	2.498
22	14.451	12.042	10.201	8.772	7.645	6.743	6.011	5.410	4.909	4.488	4.130	3.970	3.822	3.556	3.323	2.498
23	14.857	12.303	10.371	8.883	7.718	6.792	6.044	5.432	4.925	4.490	4.137	3.976	3.827	3.559	3.325	2.499
24	15.247	12.550	10.529	8.985	7.784	6.835	6.073	5.451	4.937	4.507	4.143	3.981	3.831	3.562	3.327	2.499
25	15.622	12.703	10.675	9.077	7.843	6.873	6.097	5.467	4.948	4.514	4.147	3.985	3.834	3.564	3.329	2.499
26	15.003	13.003	10.810	9.161	7.896	6.900	6.118	5.480	4.956	4.520	4.151	3.988	3.837	3.566	3.330	2.500
27	16.330	13.211	10.935	9.237	7.943	6.935	6.136	5.492	4.964	4.525	4.154	3.990	3.839	3.567	3.331	2.500
28	16.003	13.406	11.051	9.307	7.984	6.901	6.152	5.502	4.970	4.528	4.157	3.992	3.840	3.568	3.331	2.500
29	16.904	13.991	11.153	9.370	8.022	6.080	6.166	5.510	4.975	4.531	4.159	3.994	3.841	3.569	3.332	2.500
30	17.292	13.765	11.250	9.427	8.055	7.003	6.177	5.517	4.979	4.534	4.160	3.995	3.842	3.569	3.333	2.500
40	19.793	19.040	11.925	9.779	8.244	7.106	8.234	5.545	4.997	4.544	4.166	3.509	3.848	3.571	3.333	2.500

Source: Charles T. Horngren, Cost Accounting: A Managerial Emphasis, 5th ed., © 1982, p. 962. Adapted by permission of Prentice-Hall, Englewood Cliffs, N.J.

Table 12–10 Comparative Analysis of Life Cycle Costs of
Alternatives A and B

<u>MEMORIAL HOSPITAL</u>
<u>ANYTOWN, U.S.A.</u>

(1)	(2)	(3)	(4)	(5)	(6)	(7)
ALTERNATIVE	Initial Facility Cost	Initial Equipment Cost	Total Investment Initially (2+3 = 4)	Initial Investment Savings 4A-4B = 4	25-Year Life Cycle Cost	Life Cycle Savings 6A-6B = 7
				$223,400		$5,540,000
A	$736,200	$209,200	$945,400		$23,130,000	
B	$529,600	$192,400	$722,000		$17,590,000	

NOTE: Alternative B appears to be the more favorable capital expenditure, and its accumulated or life cycle savings is $5,540,000 more than Alternative A.

SOURCE: "Study of Health Facilities Construction Costs Report to the Congress," prepared for the GAO by Westinghouse Electric Corporation Health Systems B - 164031 (3), November 20, 1972.

If the decision is to replace the equipment with comparable equipment, the events and results could be as follows:

Events
- productivity remains basically the same
- under capacity to meet the demand for services

Results
- no increase in profit margin
- no increase, perhaps a loss in productivity

If the decision was to replace the equipment by a smaller capacity machine, the events and results could include:

Events
- processing system about the same
- under capacity to meet demand

Results
- possible decrease in profits
- lower productivity

If the selection decision was to purchase a piece of equipment with a greater capacity than the current machine, the events and results could be as follows:

Events
- increased productivity
- greater capacity than needed to meet demand

Results
- potential higher profits
- underutilization of equipment

To summarize, a capital expenditure should never be made with only one alternative. The ultimate decision maker needs alternatives to compare to the initial alternative. Without the opportunity to compare alternatives, the decision maker will have no basis for evaluating options. Appropriate decisions require, and are made by, enlightened managers.

REFERENCES

1. Ernst & Whinney, *Medicare Prospective Payments for Capital: The Issues and the Alternatives* (Cleveland, Ohio: Ernst & Whinney, No. J58522, 1984), pp. 1–31.
2. Ernst & Whinney, *The Medicare Prospective Payment System* (Cleveland, Ohio: Ernst & Whinney, No. J58475, 1984), p. 45.
3. Ibid, pp. 100–101.
4. L. Vann Seawell, *Hospital Financial Accounting Theory In Practice* (Chicago, Ill.: Hospital Financial Management Association, 1975), p. 549.
5. David Novick, *Program Budgeting: Program Analysis and the Federal Budget* (Cambridge, Mass.: Harvard University Press, 1967), 2nd edition.

Chapter 13

Cash Forecasting and Management*

Cash forecasting and management are integral parts of the hospital's budgetary control system. The budgetary control system begins with the preparation of the operating budget and capital expenditure plans. Once they have been completed, cash forecasting and management can begin.

The first step in cash forecasting is to analyze the monthly income and expense statements to determine cash inflows and outflows. The time lag factors explained below are used in this analysis. In reality, cash forecasting turns the hospital's accrual system into a cash accounting statement.

Basically, two time lag factors must be computed and monitored:

1. cash inflow time lag factor: the amount of time between billing of the patient for services and receipt of payment of the hospital
2. cash outflow time lag factor: the amount of time between the incurring of an expense by the hospital and actual disbursement of cash to pay it

Management can control each time lag factor with any one of several methods, each of which features varying degrees of efficiency. Techniques for matching cash inflows and outflows for the most appropriate and profitable use of the hospital's resources will be discussed later in this chapter.

---

*Adapted from *Patient Account Management* by A.G. Herkimer, Jr., pp. 195–217, Aspen Publishers, Inc., © 1983.

301

PURPOSE

The primary purpose of cash forecasting and management is to assist management in determining whether there will be enough cash coming in to cover projected expenditures. The forecasting helps prepare management for the fact that additional funds may be needed to carry out the operating budget and the capital expenditure plan. The process also alerts management to the existence of surplus operating funds that can be invested, thus allowing the hospital to maximize its cash resources.

A secondary purpose of cash forecasting and management is to help the hospital satisfy the requirement of the Joint Commission on Accreditation of Hospitals (JCAH) that the hospital chief executive officer (CEO), consistent with governing board policy, maintain and safeguard appropriate physical resources and use them judiciously to implement hospital programs and meet patient needs. JCAH also prescribes that the CEO be responsible for implementing governing board policy covering the financial management of the hospital. This includes the development of cash inflow budgets.[1]

Effective cash forecasting and management will help ensure that the hospital has enough cash to:

- meet operating needs
- finance capital expenditures
- receive maximum earnings from investments

Basically, there are five ways to increase cash resources:

1. reduce the amount of current assets, for example, accounts receivable, inventories, and prepaid expenses
2. increase the amount of current liabilities, for example, accounts payable, notes payable, and taxes payable
3. increase operating revenues, that is, charges to patients, and reduce operating expenses (increase profits)
4. restrict capital expenditures
5. use bank float

These techniques can be used independently or combined. The first four are self-explanatory; use of bank float will be discussed later in this chapter.

If the hospital has a reasonably steady or even inflow of cash, its ideal operating cash balance is zero. A zero balance means that management is indeed using the hospital's resources judiciously.

MAJOR COMPONENTS

The cash forecasting and management process involves the control of four major components:

- cash inflows
- cash outflows
- borrowings and investments
- bank float

Cash inflows, cash outflows, and borrowings and investments are all shown in the cash forecast statement. Bank float, on the other hand, is not shown on the statement because it represents cash available only for a very limited time.

Cash Inflows

Patient accounts receivable usually represent a hospital's largest asset and its greatest source of cash inflows. There are two bases for forecasting cash from patient revenue:

1. gross charges to patients
2. net charges to patients

The basic distinction between the two is that the gross amount is determined before adjustments for deductions, for example, bad debts, contractual allowances, and courtesy discounts, have been applied. Net charges are determined after these deductions have been made. There are conflicting opinions about which method is better. In this book, the net charges method is preferred, and it will be the approach described in this chapter.

Borrowings, or outside financing, for example, loans, mortgages, bonds, and stock issues, constitute the hospital's second largest source of cash inflows. Short-term loan and investment accounts are frequently used in the cash inflow statement as balancing accounts to show additional funds generated from short-term loans or the investment of surplus cash. The cash inflows from borrowings and investments are entered in the master cash forecast statement as shown in Table 13–1, line 2c.

The remaining cash inflows to the hospital usually come from a variety of sources including:

Table 13–1 Master Cash Forecast Statement

Memorial Hospital, Anytown, U.S.A.
Master Cash Forecast Statement
For the Budget Year Ending December 31, 19x1
(in thousands of dollars)

| | Months | | | | | | | | | | | | |
---	1	2	3	4	5	6	7	8	9	10	11	12	Total
1. Beginning cash balance	$ 50	$ 0	$ 0	$ 0	$ 0	$ 0	$ 0	$ 0	$ 0	$ 0	$ 0	$ 0	$ 50
2. Cash Inflows:													
a. Net patient receivables	$227	$277	$287	$308	$316	$327	$326	$323	$316	$302	$313	$320	$3,642
b. Other operating sources	20	13	16	21	16	14	15	15	14	20	16	26	206
c. Borrowings (investments)	(28)	(39)	(26)	(51)	(50)	32	39	(9)	52	(33)	(38)	51	(100)
d. Total cash inflows	$219	$251	$277	$278	$282	$373	$380	$329	$382	$289	$291	$397	$3,748
3. Total cash-on-hand (line 1 + line 2 = line 3)	$269	$251	$277	$278	$282	$373	$380	$329	$382	$289	$291	$397	$3,798
4. Cash Outflows:													
a. Salary, wages, and related expenses	$190	$184	$196	$193	$198	$197	$201	$199	$203	$198	$204	$205	$2,368
b. Capital expenditures	5	0	10	0	5	100	100	50	100	10	5	110	495
c. Noncapital, nonsalary expenses	74	67	71	85	79	76	79	80	79	81	82	82	935
d. Total cash outflows	$269	$251	$277	$278	$282	$373	$380	$329	$382	$289	$291	$397	$3,798
5. Ending cash balance (line 3 – line 4 = line 5)	$-0-	$-0-	$-0-	$-0-	$-0-	$-0-	$-0-	$-0-	$-0-	$-0-	$-0-	$-0-	$-0-

- cafeteria sales
- medical record transcription
- investment income
- transfer from other hospital funds
- rentals
- vendors
- concessions
- gifts and donations
- owners' investments (sale of stock, etc.)
- other nonpatient revenue

It may be noted here that some hospitals have found fund-raising drives to be an excellent source of cash, while others have not. To gauge whether the hospital should undertake a fund-raising drive, hospital management must consider the community and its likely response to a campaign for gifts.

Cash Outflows

Basically, cash outflows can be divided into four major classifications:

1. salary, wages, and other related expenses
2. programmed nonsalary expenses
3. variable nonsalary expenses
4. capital expenditures

A hospital's largest cash outflow is for salary, wages, and related expenses, for example, social security taxes, retirement benefits, and group insurance premiums. Although these expenses are usually budgeted on a monthly basis, for cash management purposes, they must be planned according to the frequency of actual cash disbursement to the employee, whether it be weekly, biweekly, or monthly.

Programmed nonsalary expenses are those for which payment is scheduled or programmed for specific times throughout the year. Such expenses include:

- insurance premiums
- capital expenditures
- mortgage payments
- short-term loans

- rentals and leases
- utilities

Except for utilities, programmed expenses represent a fixed amount of money that does not vary regardless of volume of activity. Capital expenditures are handled as a separate line item direct from the capital budget.

Variable nonsalary expenses are operating expenses, for example, medical and surgical supplies and office supplies, that vary in direct proportion to the volume of work.

Capital expenditures represent the most manageable cash outflow in terms of time to disburse cash. Usually, capital expenditures can be delayed without jeopardizing operations. Consequently, management can place a "hold" on purchasing the capital asset until the cash position is more favorable. Conversely, if there is a cash surplus, capital expenditures can be acquired.

In one way or another, all the expenses or purchases in the hospital's revenue and expense statement and capital expenditure plan are recorded in its cash forecast, except the provision for depreciation. Depreciation is a noncash item that must be included in computing the hospital's total operating expenses. Since the provision for depreciation is an accounting procedure to recognize the amortization of a capital purchase, it is not included in the cash forecast. A capital expenditure is recorded in the cash forecast only when cash is actually paid out, or when the payment of that cash is planned.

Borrowings and Investments

Borrowings and/or investments may be accounted for as a balancing account in the cash forecast. For example, after all cash inflows and outflows have been computed for the month, the cash forecaster may find that cash inflows are not sufficient to cover cash outflows. In this case, the required cash must be borrowed to maintain the necessary bank balance. On the other hand, if the cash forecaster finds that cash available to the hospital after cash outflows have been taken into account is too great to remain in a noninterest-bearing checking account, the surplus will be invested.

There are two commonly used methods for recording these activities. In the first method, each activity is considered a separate function or account. Therefore, borrowings would be considered cash inflows and investments, or loan repayments, would be treated as cash outflows.

The second method considers these two activities as a single line item under cash inflows. If cash is borrowed, the amount would be recorded in the same manner as any other cash inflow. If cash is invested, the amount would be bracketed as illustrated below:

	January	February	March	Total
Borrowings (investments)	$10,000	$20,000	($15,000)	$15,000

An advantage of using one line item is that the balancing account can be identified quickly because it is netted out in the total column. Moreover, using two line items requires an additional computation.

Bank Float

Bank float represents an intangible and relatively uncontrollable amount of cash that the hospital can use by taking advantage of cash in transit. Bank float represents the portion of the bank balance created by the time interval between the drawing of checks on the hospital's account and the actual debiting of the account for those checks. Positive float allows the hospital to operate with a book balance that is actually less than the compensating balance the bank requires the hospital to maintain.[2] For example, if a hospital generally has $100,000 in outstanding checks at the time the bank account balance is reconciled to the hospital bank balance, this amount could be used for short-term investments or for payment of additional expenses. A word of caution about the use of bank float is absolutely necessary: it requires relatively constant and consistent cash flow, and electronic mail for banks is reducing the amount a hospital can float.

CASH FORECASTING METHODOLOGY

As stated earlier, the hospital's operating budget and capital expenditure plan must be completed before cash forecasting, that is, the analysis of time lag factors and amounts of cash inflows and outflows can begin. The two major analyses involved in cash forecasting are:

1. cash receipts analysis
2. cash disbursement analysis

Cash Receipts Analysis

The first step in cash forecasting is to analyze cash inflows from patient accounts receivable. This analysis involves determining:

- the type of paying agent
- the length of time before payment

Assume that the analysis of gross charges to patients indicates that the mix of paying agents corresponds to the one shown in Table 13–2. Historical cash receipts are then analyzed and time lag factors are established for each paying agent based on the amount of time it takes to collect cash from the agent for services rendered. Generally, the accounts of most patients are not paid in full with a single payment; rather the payment period may extend over time. For example, assume that a patient with commercial insurance has a $5,000 account. The payoff schedule might look like this:

Time of Payment	Source of Payment	Amount of Payment (Dollars)	(Percents)
Admissions day	Patient deposit	$ 500	10%
30 days after billing	Insurance	$3,600	72%
60 days after billing	Patient	$ 450	9%
90 days after billing	Patient	$ 450	9%
Total		$5,000	100%

The process of analyzing each paying agent's payment schedule is extremely time consuming. In addition, these schedules can vary according to outside economic factors such as inflation and interest rates. For this reason, management should conduct a statistical sam-

---

Table 13–2 Percent Analysis of Gross Charges to Patients by Paying Agent, Memorial Hospital, Anytown, U.S.A.

Paying Agent	% of Gross Charges
Blue Cross	30%
Medicare	40
Medicaid	10
Commercial Insurance	15
Self-Pay and Others	5
Total	100%

pling of the process instead of using a large amount of hours and resources to do a comprehensive study. The best approach is to do a periodic statistical sampling of payment schedules and time lag factors purely for verification and control.

The second step in cash forecasting is analysis of cash inflows from gross charges to patients according to the time cash is received. Table 13–3 shows a mix of payment schedules and time lag factors by paying agent. It should be noted that paying agents are classified into major groups in the table. However, some managers might find it beneficial to expand these classifications, especially if some categories include agents with widely different reimbursement systems or payment schedules. For example, a hospital may be a member of two Blue Cross plans, one of which pays the hospital prospectively based on patient gross charges, while the other pays the hospital based on costs with a retroactive adjustment based at the end of the fiscal period. Another good reason for a more detailed breakdown of paying agents would be the need for closer surveillance of cash inflows in situations in which one commercial insurance company or health maintenance organization (HMO) dominates its segment of the market.

After payment schedules and time lag factors have been analyzed by paying agent, the next step is to determine the net charges to patients by making provisions for contractual allowances and bad debts for each paying agent as illustrated in Table 13–4.

Basically, there are two different methods used to forecast cash inflows from paying agents. One is the weighted average monthly cash inflow percentage method, which relies on a weighted average such as the one illustrated in Table 13–5.[3]

Table 13–3 Percent Analysis of Cash Payment Schedules and Time Lag Factors of Gross Charges to Patients by Paying Agent, Memorial Hospital, Anytown, U.S.A.

	% of Payments Schedule Month After Charges Are Generated							
Paying Agent	*1*	*2*	*3*	*4*	*5*	*6*	*7*	*Total %*
Blue Cross	50	30	15	5	—	—	—	100%
Medicare	60	25	10	5	—	—	—	100
Medicaid	10	20	30	20	10	5	5	100
Commercial Insurance	30	40	15	10	5	—	—	100
Self-Pay and Others	15	25	25	15	10	5	5	100

Table 13–4 Percent Analysis of Net Patient Charges by Paying
Agent, Memorial Hospital, Anytown, U.S.A.

Paying Agent	Gross Charges	Less: Provision for Deductibles	Net Charges
Blue Cross	100%	10%	90%
Medicare	100	20	80
Medicaid	100	40	60
Commercial Insurance	100	5	95
Self-Pay and Others	100	15	85

The following formula is used in the weighted average computation:

Let:

MC = Monthly collection percentage
R = Revenue percentage
$(R \times MC^1)$ = Weighted percentage (first month)
$\Sigma(R \times MC^1)$ = Sum total of weighted percentage (first month)

In this illustration, the sum of the weighted averages $\Sigma(R \times MC^1)$ for the first month is computed as follows:

Paying Agent	(R	×	MC^1)		
Blue Cross	.30	×	50	=	15.0%
Medicare	.40	×	60	=	24.0
Medicaid	.10	×	10	=	1.0
Commercial insurance	.15	×	30	=	4.5
Self-Pay and others	.05	×	15	=	0.8
Total					45.3%

This means that 45.3 percent of total patient charges should be collected in cash during the first month after these charges are generated. A complete cash collection schedule of patient charges is shown in Table 13–6.

The second method used to forecast cash inflows from patient charges is to analyze the cash inflows by paying agent. If a computer is available, this method is recommended because of its greater accuracy. However, if the cash forecast is to be done manually, the weighted average method is preferable. Table 13–7 is an example of an application of the weighted average percentage developed in Table 13–6.

Table 13–5 Analysis and Computation of Weighted Collection Percentage of Patient Charges Collected, Memorial Hospital, Anytown, U.S.A.

	R % of Total Revenue	Month After Charges Are Generated												
		First		Second		Third		Fourth		Fifth		Sixth		Seventh	
Paying Agent		MC^1	$R \times MC^1$	MC^2	$R \times MC^2$	MC^3	$R \times MC^3$	MC^4	$R \times MC^4$	MC^5	$R \times MC^5$	MC^6	$R \times MC^6$	MC^7	$R \times MC^7$
Blue Cross	30%	50	15.0	30	9.0	15	4.5	5	1.5	—	—	—	—	—	—
Medicare	40	60	24.0	25	10.0	10	4.0	5	2.0	—	—	—	—	—	—
Medicaid	10	10	1.0	20	2.0	30	3.0	20	2.0	10	1.0	5	.5	5	.5
Commercial Insurance	15	30	4.5	40	6.0	15	2.3	10	1.5	5	.8	—	—	—	—
Self-Pay and Others	5	15	.8	25	1.2	25	1.2	15	.8	10	.5	5	.2	5	.2
Total Σ(R × MC)	100%		45.3		28.2		15.0		7.8		2.3		.7		.7

Table 13–6 Weighted Average Cash Collection Schedule of Patient Charges, Memorial Hospital, Anytown, U.S.A.

Month After Charges Are Generated	Weighted Average Collected
1	45.3%
2	28.2%
3	15.0%
4	7.8%
5	2.3%
6	.7%
7	.7%
Total	100.0%

Table 13–7 starts with the beginning patient accounts receivable balance of $500,000, which is distributed by the weighted average collection method. Net charges to patients are distributed on a monthly basis and totaled for each month as the cash inflows from net patient charges for that month. Any uncollected net charges are accumulated in the far right-hand column to determine the ending patient accounts receivable balance for the period.

The cash inflows from other operating sources, such as cafeteria sales and medical records transcriptions, are then analyzed as illustrated in Table 13–8, and the total is spread on the master cash flow statement (see Table 13–1, line 2b). The next step is to enter the cash inflows from net patient receivables in the master cash flow statement (see Table 13–1, line 2a). Once these inflows have been recorded, the analysis of cash outflows can begin.

Cash Disbursement Analysis

As stated earlier, cash outflows must be handled on a cash basis, even though the hospital uses the accrual accounting method. Generally, hospitals have a separate imprest fund for processing payroll checks. In that case, the hospital may transfer an amount equal to the net amount of the payroll from the general operating fund to the imprest payroll account. Separate checks to cover payroll taxes and related expenses are also drawn on the operating fund for deposit in the imprest payroll account.

Another way of handling an imprest payroll account is to deposit an amount equal to the total payroll, including the amount withheld from

Table 13–7 Cash Inflow Analysis of Net Patient Charges

Memorial Hospital, Anytown, U.S.A.
Cash Inflow Analysis of Net Patient Charges
For the Budget Year Ending December 31, 19x1
(in thousands of dollars)

Month	Beginning Patient Accounts Receivable Balance	\	Months												Ending Patient Accounts Receivable Balance
		1	2	3	4	5	6	7	8	9	10	11	12	
		(45.3)	(28.2)	(15.0)	(7.8)	(2.3)	(.7)	(.7)						
1	$500	$227	$141	$75	$39	$12	$3	$3							
2	300		136	85	45	23	7	2	$2					
3	280			127	79	42	22	6	2	$2				
4	320				145	90	48	25	8	2	$2			
5	330					149	93	49	27	8	2	$2		
6	340						154	96	51	27	8	2	$2	$2
7	320							145	90	48	25	8	2	4
8	315								143	89	47	25	7	12
9	310									140	87	47	24	33
10	290										131	82	44	86
11	325											147	92	181
12	330												149	310
Total net charges to patients	$3,770													
Cash inflow from net charges	$3,642	$227	$277	$287	$308	$316	$327	$326	$323	$316	$302	$313	$320	
Ending patient accounts receivable balance														$628

Note: Net charges were distributed using the weighted average collection in Table 13–6.

Table 13–8 Analysis of Monthly Cash Inflows from Other Operating
Sources

Memorial Hospital, Anytown, U.S.A.
Analysis of Monthly Cash Inflows from Other Operating Sources
For the Budget Year Ending December 31, 19x1
(in thousands of dollars)

Month	Source			Total
	Cafeteria	Medical Records	Other	
1	$ 10	$ 2	$ 8	$ 20
2	8	1	4	13
3	9	1	6	16
4	11	2	8	21
5	10	1	5	16
6	9	1	4	14
7	8	1	6	15
8	9	2	4	15
9	10	1	3	14
10	9	2	9	20
11	10	2	4	16
12	10	1	15	26
Total	$113	$17	$76	$206

employees for taxes and other withholding requirements, in the imprest
payroll account. There are many ways a hospital can use imprest
payroll accounts. However, some hospitals do not use imprest payroll
accounts at all, simply disbursing payroll from the general operating
fund. Nevertheless, salary, wages, and related expenses must be shown
on the cash forecast statement at the time payroll checks are disbursed.

Most hospitals disburse payroll and related expenses in the month in
which they are budgeted. Within that month, however, there is a time
lag between disbursement of the check to the employee and the cashing
of that check. A typical time lag factor is shown in Table 13–9. Note that
30 percent of the hospital's employees cash their payroll checks on
payday, while 5 percent of the employees cash their checks as long as 23
to 30 days after they are issued. The hospital can use the kind of
information shown in Table 13–9 to make short-term investments by
staggering payments from the general operating fund to the imprest
payroll account to cover payroll checks as they are cashed.

For illustration, assume that Memorial Hospital of Anytown, U.S.A.
pays its employees on the first and fifteenth of each month. Assume

Table 13–9 Analysis of Employee Payroll Cashing Process,
Memorial Hospital, Anytown, U.S.A.

Number of Days After Issuance	Amount		Employees	
	Dollar	%	Number	%
1	$21,375	25%	195	30%
2	12,825	15	130	20
3	8,550	10	98	15
4	8,550	10	65	10
5	6,840	8	52	8
6	1,710	2	13	2
7	8,550	10	39	6
8–14	4,275	5	13	2
15–22	4,275	5	13	2
23–30	8,550	10	32	5
Total	$85,500	100%	650	100%

further that the cash outflows for salary, wages, and related expenses for Memorial Hospital's budget year ending December 31, 19x1 are as shown in Table 13–10. (These cash outflows are shown on the master cash flow statement in Table 13–1, line 4a.)

Nonsalary cash outflows can be divided into two major categories of expenditure:

1. capital
2. noncapital

Cash outflows for capital expenditures come directly from the hospital's capital expenditure plan or capital budget. For illustration, Memorial Hospital's capital expenditure plan for the budget year ending December 31, 19x1, is shown in Table 13–11. (These totals are recorded on the master cash flow statement in Table 13–1, line 4b.)

Noncapital cash outflows can be classified by several methods. For purposes of this discussion, these expenditures are classified as either:

• programmed
• variable

Programmed expenditures are those noncapital, nonsalary cash flow requirements such as:

Table 13–10 Analysis of Cash Outflow for Salary, Wages, and Related Expenses

Memorial Hospital, Anytown, U.S.A.
Analysis of Cash Outflow for Salary, Wages, and Related Expenses
For the Budget Year Ending December 31, 19x1
(in thousands of dollars)

Month	Payroll Date	Monthly Payroll	Payroll Related Expense	Total Salary, Wages, and Related Expenses
1	1/1– 1/15	$ 165	$ 25	$ 190
2	2/1– 2/15	160	24	184
3	3/1– 3/15	170	26	196
4	4/1– 4/15	118	25	193
5	5/1– 5/15	172	26	198
6	6/1– 6/15	170	27	197
7	7/1– 7/15	175	26	201
8	8/1– 8/15	173	26	199
9	9/1– 9/15	176	27	203
10	10/1–10/15	172	26	198
11	11/1–11/15	177	27	204
12	12/1–12/15	178	27	205
Total		$2,056	$312	$2,368

- utilities
- rent and/or leases
- insurance
- mortgage payments

In short, these expenses are fixed payments that are essential in order to provide the facilities and equipment necessary to perform services to patients.

Variable noncapital, nonsalary expenses are those cash outflow requirements that usually vary in direct proportion to the volume of work, that is, patient days and outpatient visits.

Setting priorities for payment of individual expenses is a method used by some hospitals to schedule cash outflows. Table 13–12 shows the payment priority classification system Memorial Hospital uses for all cash outflows. Memorial Hospital has analyzed its noncapital, nonsalary cash outflows as shown in Table 13–13. The accumulated percent-

Table 13–11 Summary Analysis of Capital Expenditure Cash Flow Requirements

Memorial Hospital, Anytown, U.S.A.
Summary Analysis of Capital Expenditure Cash Flow Requirements
For the Budget Year Ending December 31, 19x1
(in thousands of dollars)

Month	Amount Needed
1	$ 5
2	-0-
3	10
4	-0-
5	5
6	100
7	100
8	50
9	100
10	10
11	5
12	110
Total	$495

Table 13–12 Payment Priority Classification for Cash Outflows, Memorial Hospital, Anytown, U.S.A.

Payment Priority	Description of Payment	Payment Schedules from Date of Receipt
A	Payroll, Commission, etc.	Current month
B	Mortgage, Rent, Leases, Utilities, Service Contracts	Current month
C	Foods, Medical and Surgical Supplies, Drugs	30 days (following month)
D	Discount Vendors	30 days (following month)
E	Funded Depreciation, Investments	30 days (following month)
F	Special Vendors	30–59 days (second month)
G	Other Vendors	60–90 days (third month)

ages in the right-hand column of Table 13–14 are then applied to the hospital's budgeted noncapital, nonsalary expenses shown in Table 13–15. The monthly cash outflows for these expenses are then recorded in the master cash flow statement (see Table 13–1, line 4c).

Table 13–13 Schedule of Noncapital, Nonsalary Cash Outflow Requirements

Memorial Hospital, Anytown, U.S.A.
Schedule of Noncapital, Nonsalary Cash Outflow Requirements
(in thousands of dollars)

| Month | Cash Require-ment | *Days After Receipt of Statement* | | | | |
		1–15 Days A, B = 55%	15–30 Days C = 10%	30 Days D, E = 10%	30–45 Days F = 10%	45–90 Days G = 15%
1	$ 70	$39	$7	$7	$7	$10
2	73	40	7	7	7	12
3	78	43	8	8	8	11
4	77	42	8	8	8	11
5	79	43	8	8	8	12
6	75	41	8	8	8	10
7	80	44	8	8	8	12
8	80	44	8	8	8	12
9	82	45	8	8	8	13
10	81	45	8	8	8	12
11	83	46	8	8	8	13
12	82	45	8	8	8	13
Total	$940					

Table 13–14 Analysis of Noncapital, Nonsalary Cash Outflows by Priority Classification, Memorial Hospital, Anytown, U.S.A.

Priority Classification	Payment Schedule from Date of Receipt	Percent of Cash Outflows	Monthly Accumulated Percentage
A	Current month	40	—
B	Current month	15	55
C	30 days	10	—
D	30 days	5	—
E	30 days	5	75
F	30–59 days	10	85
G	60–90 days	15	100%
Total		100%	

Table 13–15 Schedule of Noncapital, Nonsalary Cash Outflow Requirements

Memorial Hospital, Anytown, U.S.A.
Schedule of Noncapital, Nonsalary Cash Outflow Requirements
For the Budget Year Ending December 31, 19x1
(in thousands of dollars)

Month	Beginning Accounts Payable Balance	1	2	3	4	5	6	7	8	9	10	11	12	Ending Accounts Payable Balance
		(.55)	(.75)	(.85)	(1.00)									
1	$65	$35												
2	70	39	$13											
3	73		14	$7										
4	78		40	7	$10									
5	77			14	7	$12								
6	79			43	16	8	$11							
7	75				42	16	8	$11						
8	80					43	16	8	$12					
9	80						41	16	8	$10				
10	82							44	16	8	$12			$12
11	81								44	16	8	$12		21
12	83									45	16	8	$13	37
	82										45	16	8	
												46	16	
													45	
Total cash requirements	$1,005													
Cash outflow for expenses	$935	$74	$67	$71	$85	$79	$76	$79	$80	$79	$81	$82	$82	
Ending accounts payable balance														$70

At the beginning of the cash forecasting process, the cash balance was $50,000 (see Table 13–1, line 1). During the first month, the total cash inflows shown in Table 13–1 were

Line
2a	Net patient receivables	$227,000
2b	Other operating revenue	20,000
	Total cash inflows	$247,000

Thus, total cash on hand is $297,000.
Total cash outflows were:

Line
4a	Salary, wages, and related expenses	$190,000
4b	Capital expenditures	5,000
4c	Noncapital, nonsalary expenses	74,000
4d	Total cash outflows	$269,000

Hence there is a cash net difference or balance of $28,000. Since the hospital had adopted a "zero" cash balance policy, the $28,000 is invested in short-term instruments, leaving a net cash inflow of $219,000 (see Table 13–1, line 2d) and a total of $269,000 cash on hand for the month. Checking the borrowings/investment account (see Table 13–1, line 2c), the cash forecaster can project the need to either borrow or invest.

During the second month, $39,000 was deposited in the investment account, representing excess cash inflows. During the following three months, the following additions were added to the investment account, making a total of $194,000 in investments:

Month	Amount Deposited
3	$26,000
4	51,000
5	50,000
	$127,000

During the sixth month, the shortfall of cash inflows to cash outflows was $32,000; this amount was withdrawn from the investment account. During the seventh month, there was a $39,000 shortfall. The following is a recalculation of the borrowings/investment account at the end of the seventh month:

Month	Deposits	Withdrawals	Balance
1	$28,000		$ 28,000
2	39,000		67,000
3	26,000		93,000
4	51,000		144,000
5	50,000		194,000
6		$32,000	162,000
7		39,000	123,000

The subsequent months' cash flow forecasts were projected in the same manner, that is, using the borrowings/investment account as the "equalizer." The annual result was a total net cash investment of $100,000 (see Table 13–1, line 2c). A summary of the budgeted cash inflows and outflows is:

Beginning cash balance	$ 50,000
Plus:	
Cash inflows:	
Net patient accounts receivable	$3,642,000
Other operating services	206,000
Total cash inflows	$3,848,000
Cash on hand	$3,898,000
Less:	
Cash outflows:	
Salary, wages, and related expenses	$2,368,000
Capital expenditures	495,000
Noncapital, nonsalary expenses	935,000
Investments	100,000
Total cash outflows	$3,898,000
Ending cash balance	-0-

THE CASH MANAGEMENT PROCESS

The process of cash management is probably one of the most important functions in hospital financial management. If properly used, the process can be the instrument that will help keep the hospital solvent because it will be able to predict cash shortfalls and take corrective actions such as

• adjusting patient charges to meet expenses

- reducing expenses
- preparing for borrowings and/or investments

The following are some of the functions that should be performed:

Forecast Preparation:

1. Analyze patient accounts receivable by paying agent.
2. Identify the time lag factors for payments by paying agent.
3. Estimate the amount of bad debt writeoffs.
4. Calculate third party contractual allowances.
5. Estimate the amount of courtesy allowances and other similar deductions from gross patient charges.

Forecast Monitoring:

1. Assist in the preparation of the daily cash report (see Exhibit 13–1).

Exhibit 13–1 Daily Cash Report Form

Memorial Hospital, Anytown, U.S.A. Daily Cash Report as of _____, 19 ____	Today	Month-To-Date	
		Actual	Budget
1. Beginning Cash Balance	$ _____	$ _____	$ _____
2. Plus: Cash Inflows:			
a. Net Return Accounts Receivable	$ _____	$ _____	$ _____
b. Other Operating Sources	_____	_____	_____
c. Borrowings	_____	_____	_____
d. Total Cash Inflows	$ _____	$ _____	$ _____
3. Total Cash On Hand (line 1 + line 2d)	$ _____	$ _____	$ _____
4. Less: Cash Outflows:			
a. Salary, Wages, and Related Expenses	$ _____	$ _____	$ _____
b. Capital Expenditures	_____	_____	_____
c. Noncapital, Nonsalary Expenses	_____	_____	_____
d. Investments	_____	_____	_____
e. Total Cash Outflows	$ _____	$ _____	$ _____
5. Ending Cash Balance (line 3 − line 4e)	$ _____	$ _____	$ _____

2. Maintain close communication between the patient business services department and the chief financial officer (CFO) and alert CFO to any potential trouble spots.
3. Maintain close communication with all major third party payers in order to expedite payments.
4. Maintain constant awareness of new systems and procedures which might expedite cash payments from all types of payers.

In summary, even though the hospital's patient account manager has the ultimate responsibility for converting the hospital's largest single asset—accounts receivable—to cash, all department managers, whether the department generates revenue or not, should know the "cash impact" their respective department has upon the hospital's total cash flow. It requires a team effort to ensure the hospital a steady flow of cash.

REFERENCES

1. *Accreditation Manual for Hospitals* (Chicago: Joint Commission on Accreditation of Hospitals, 1981), p. 1.
2. Richard Baehr, *Cash Management* (Amherst, Mass.: Amherst Associates, Inc., 1979), pp. 79–82.
3. *Budgeting Manual*, 2nd ed. (Sacramento, Calif.: California Hospital Association, 1977), pp. 101–108.

Chapter 14

Facing the Future

THE SURVIVAL ISSUE

The DRG prospective payment and regulatory system and all of its implications have ushered in the most radical changes in the health care industry since the implementation of Medicare and Medicaid. The phase of change will be negotiated capitation rates. Survival within the present competitive environment must be examined from two aspects:

1. institutional
2. personal

Institutional Survival

It must be assumed that *the freestanding health care hospital and/or health delivery system is as obsolete as the dinosaur and the carrier pigeon.*

In order to survive, the organization has, but is not limited to, any or all of the following options:

1. joint venture (merge or consolidate with other health care organizations and insurance carriers)
2. horizontal and/or vertical diversification into an expanded alternative health care delivery system: HMO, PPO, surgicenter, urgent care, etc.
3. affiliation through shared services networks, with other health care organizations
4. acquisition of nonpatient-related businesses that can subsidize and/or complement the organization's financial viability

Usually, these alternative delivery systems will require some form of corporate restructuring. One word of caution to timid nontaxable hospitals—don't be hobbled and overly protective because of "not-for-profit" and tax-free status. This tax status can cause a defeatist syndrome. In all probability, tax-free status should be utilized as a structure, but should not prohibit management from exercising entrepreneurship and attempting profit-oriented ventures. However, corporate restructuring is only a partial solution. Institutional survival will require:

1. product (service) line cost-benefit accounting
2. visionary leadership and imaginary strategic planning
3. cost-effective and creative marketing
4. productivity-conscious employees and management
5. willingness to undertake risk-related ventures
6. competitive pricing
7. consumer-driven team management approach including management, medical staffs, and possibly insurance companies

To summarize, the health care organization must reevaluate and broaden its mission and adopt a responsible entrepreneurial attitude toward the marketplace. It must identify its market, know the market's needs, and then provide quality services and products to meet the market demands. It must be consumer driven.

Personal Survival

Gifford and Davidson state that hospital CEOs place the greatest emphasis on developing and strengthening the following skills and capabilities:

1. strategic planning
2. sales and marketing
3. business planning
4. risk taking
5. entrepreneurship
6. adaptability to change[1]

Further, they state that CEOs believe that building a stronger management team is a high priority. Significantly, more than one-fourth of the hospital CEOs surveyed believe they require additional formal training or schooling in these areas.[2] The data confirm a research study conducted by the author of California acute care hospital CEOs to

determine what master's degree courses they perceived as most important. The CEOs identified finance, finance-related courses, marketing,
and strategic planning as the most essential.[3]

According to the Gifford and Davidson study, the CEOs consider
changing the attitudes of the board and medical staff essential. They
stress the importance of becoming more competitive and more effective
with management and broadening the institution's mission.[4]

Alvin Toffler, in *Previews & Premises*, states that we are feeling the
first tremors of an economic earthquake and that we had better prepare
for it. Toffler believes that what is happening is unlike a hurricane that
sweeps across the landscape, leaving the earth itself unchanged. It is
more like the beginning of an earthquake, for the subterranean structure on which all our economics are based is now shifting and cracking.
In our efforts to prevent a major collapse, we are dealing with surface
phenomena rather than focusing on the deep structure, where really big
changes are occurring.[5]

In preparation for this economic upheaval, the answers to these
questions must be identified:

- What is the health care institution's mission?
- What is management's own professional mission?
- Do these two missions complement each other?
- Are the institution and management, as a whole, prepared to be on
  the cutting edge of the industry and the marketplace?
- Do they want to be on the cutting edge?
- Are they willing to innovate, to take a risk and occasionally to lose?

Survival in this new environment will depend on how well the institution and management have identified the marketplace, assessed its
needs, and prepared themselves to provide quality service and products
to meet the consumer's needs in a cost-effective manner. Toffler states
that we are all confronting an essentially new culture and have to learn
and to adapt a great deal.[6] The theories of hospital financial management are but one of many management tools available and necessary to
help meet future challenges. We all must learn how to use them.

REFERENCES

1. Richard D. Gifford and Nancy Davidson, "Executive Demand Highest in Marketing
   Information Systems," *Hospitals* 59 (April 16, 1985), pp. 106–112.
2. Ibid, p. 110.

3. Allen G. Herkimer, Jr., *What Kind of Graduate Courses and Degrees Do Future Acute-Care Hospital Administrators Need?* (La Verne, Calif.: University of La Verne, 1985), pp. 73–80.

4. Gifford and Davidson, p. 110.

5. Alvin Toffler, *Previews & Premises* (New York: Bantam Books, Inc., 1985), p. 11.

6. Ibid, p. 166.

Format of Laboratory Workload Recording Method

Section I Basic Concepts

Chapter 1 Basic Concepts

The CAP Laboratory Workload Recording Method is a management aid designed to effectively measure the productive time expended by technical, clerical, and aide staff performing procedures in the clinical laboratory. The generated data can assist in making decisions regarding space, staffing, equipment, and technical methodology selection.

The Method does not reflect time expended for other necessary nontesting activities performed by technical or support staff, or the time expended by pathologists, other laboratory physicians, and doctoral level clinical scientists, or students.

A unit value per procedure, the core of the Method, is a measure of the technical, clerical, and aide time expressed in minutes required to complete a defined procedure once. It is neither a relative value nor a measure of cost.

Management of the laboratory requires careful analysis of the productivity of resources (both capital and human) based on common comparable units measuring activity in the various sections of the laboratory. Uniform application of the Method provides the essential data base for comparison across laboratory sections and among similar laboratories.

Source: Reprinted from *Manual for Laboratory Workload Recording Method* by the College of American Pathologists Workload Recording Committee with permission of the College of American Pathologists, © 1986.

The Method is an established and validated system for providing essential management information. Personnel costs constitute a major fraction of total hospital costs, and the WLR Method can be used to identify staffing requirements, monitor personnel productivity, and provide a basis for selecting the most appropriate management strategies. It is now being used in several thousand hospitals and numerous independent laboratories in the United States. The Method is being used for interhospital comparisons by the American Hospital Association. It also is being used as a basis for establishing hospital reimbursement in several states.

DERIVATION OF THE UNIT VALUE PER PROCEDURE

The standardized unit value per procedure is the core of the Workload Method. The unit value per procedure represents the mean number of laboratory workload units (expressed in minutes) of technical, clerical, and aide time required to perform all the steps necessary to complete the defined procedure once.

The unit value per procedure does not include specimen collection, standards, quality controls, or repeats unless otherwise specified. All standards, quality controls, and repeats should be considered separate procedures and are assigned the same unit value as a patient specimen. Replicates (duplicates), in contrast to repeats, are not counted. Specimen collection and specific types of sample preparation are assigned separate unit values.

The statistics necessary for assigning permanent or temporary unit values are generated from time studies. The studies use a standardized time study format and are conducted in varied laboratory sites in the United States and Canada. The time studies must identify and measure all technical, clerical, and aide steps that routinely occur as part of the procedure. Time studies measure the time required for the following fields:

1. initial handling of the specimen
2. specimen testing
3. recording and reporting
4. daily preparation
5. maintenance and repair
6. solution preparation
7. glassware wash-up
8. direct technical supervision

1. Initial Handling of the Specimen. Initial handling includes the steps from the receipt of the specimen by the laboratory to completion of all preliminary preparation and recording normally required before testing can be started. Initial handling includes time stamping the requisition, sorting specimens, recording the patient's name, assigning a laboratory accession number, entering information on a worksheet, labeling the sample, placing the sample into and removing it from a centrifuge, removing the serum/plasma, and delivering the sample to the work area.

2. Specimen Testing. Specimen testing includes the steps required to perform the laboratory procedure up to and including the recording of results on the worksheet and/or completion of the required testing steps. Specimen testing includes diluting the specimen, adding reagents, adjusting the measuring instrument, placing the sample in the instrument, taking readings, recording the readings, and removing the sample from the instrument.

3. Recording and Reporting. Recording and reporting include the steps required to report the result(s), that is, the steps involved in converting the test results into a meaningful report that leaves the laboratory. These steps include calculating the result(s), recording them on the patient's report and in the laboratory's records, and checking, sorting, and filing the final reports. Incoming and outgoing telephone calls related to the initial report also are included.

4. Daily or Routine Preparation. Daily or routine preparation includes preparatory steps which must be done daily before the procedure can be performed. Daily preparation encompasses only those activities which are done occasionally and which need not be repeated for each sample or batch tested. Daily preparation may include preparation of quality control samples from lyophilized specimens and/or diluting stock standards. If an instrument is used, daily preparation includes instrument cleaning and warmup, calibration, and instrument cleaning prior to shut down.

5. Maintenance and Repair. Maintenance and repair includes all standard maintenance procedures performed by laboratory staff at set intervals (e.g., weekly or monthly). It also includes emergency repairs, part of which is defined as time spent identifying the defect. It does not include repair of major breakdowns.

6. Solution Preparation. Solution preparation includes all bulk preparation of reagents, solutions, and quality control materials required for the procedure.

7. Glassware Wash-up. Glassware wash-up includes all support activities performed by laboratory staff in relation to the preparation of reusable supplies for the procedure. Glassware wash-up includes washing, drying, and sterilization.

8. Direct Technical Supervision. Direct technical supervision includes the time required to directly supervise the procedure (e.g., reviewing quality control statistics, verifying and approving the reporting of results).

THE TIME STUDY PROCESS

Time studies include all technical, clerical, and aide time expended toward the completion of a procedure. Time studies involve more than one technologist performing the procedure and are performed several times in various locations. Each unit value per procedure represents an averaging of how the procedure is performed from a single STAT to varying sized batches in dissimilar facilities by different personnel.

Acceptable studies are then edited by the time study editors of the College of American Pathologists, Canadian Association of Pathologists, or American Association of Blood Banks. The resulting data are entered into the Master Log of Time Studies and presented to the International Workload Committee which consists of representatives from the College of American Pathologists' Workload Recording Committee and the Canadian Association of Pathologists' Unit Value Committee.

A *permanent (p) unit value per procedure* is established only after appropriate data are obtained from a statistically significant number of sites that have each completed an acceptable number of timings. Pending accumulation of sufficient time studies, an interim *temporary (t) unit value per procedure* may be published based on fewer time studies which meet the requirements established by the International Workload Committee. A temporary (t) unit value per procedure will not be assigned without a time study and may not be assigned by individual laboratories in the field.

If the user performs time studies, please follow the official CAP Time Study Format and submit your results so they may be edited and made available to all users through the International Committee.

An *extrapolated (e) unit value per procedure* may be assigned to a procedure or instrument before standard time studies have been performed. The extrapolated (e) unit value may be derived in part from components of previous time studies on similar procedures or instruments.

New instructions, clarifications, and new or altered unit values are published throughout the year in *Counterpoints,* a newsletter published six times per year for users of the CAP Workload Recording Method.

Specific time study formats have been developed to time procedures performed in the following departments: blood center, cytology, histology, microbiology, phlebotomy, transfusion service, and transmission electron microscopy.

PERSONAL, FATIGUE, AND DELAY (PFD) TIME

Delays are partially included in the time studies. For example, Field 3: Recording and Reporting allows for incoming and outgoing telephone calls related to the initial report. Therefore, the timings include brief interruptions and busy signals encountered when waiting for the appropriate staff person to accept a result. Field 5: Maintenance and Repair also incorporates some of the routine PFD time because it captures time for emergency repairs and routine scheduled maintenance.

CODING AND CLASSIFICATION

Each procedure is assigned a five-digit code generally based on the original *Current Procedural Terminology* (CPT) published by the AMA. Five-digit codes have not been changed to comply with CPT-4 and many others have been arbitrarily assigned.

Each procedure is classified in a *standard* section on the basis of the laboratory section in which it is most frequently performed. Abbreviations for the standard sections as they appear in the Procedure Lists are shown in parentheses.

01 Blood Bank (BANK)
02 Chemistry (CHEM)
03 Hematology (HEMA)
04 Histology (HIST)
05 Immunology (IMMU)
06 Microbiology (MICR)
09 Specimen Procurement, Preprocessing, Dispatch, and Report Delivery (SPEC)
10 Urine and Feces (URIN)

Chapter 2 Terminology

DEFINITION OF TERMS

Allocation   The process of distributing hours and/or workload units recorded in one area of activity to one or more other functional sections using an appropriate basis.

Counterpoints   A newsletter published six times annually, for users of the CAP Workload Recording Method. *Counterpoints* reviews components and concepts of the Method and highlights modifications. This publication is free to all CAP Computer Assisted Workload Recording participants. It is available on a subscription basis.

Extrapolated (e) Unit Value   A unit value assigned by the International Workload Committee to a procedure or instrument before standard time studies have been performed. The value may be derived from components of previous time studies on similar procedures or instruments.

Full-Time Equivalent (FTE)   Represents the time spent for each full time employee i.e., 40 employee hours paid per week or 2,080 hours (40 hours/week × 52 weeks/year) paid per year in most health care facilities. In other health care facilities one FTE may represent 37.5 or 35.0 employee hours paid per week.

Functional Section   A section organized and/or operating within the laboratory for which work output (CAP units) and manpower input (hours) can be identified.

Hours, nonspecified   All worked hours devoted to activities that do not produce CAP workload units.

Hours, paid   All paid time including vacation time, holiday time, sick time, education time away from the institution, actual overtime hours, and other paid time off (e.g., personal leave, jury duty). All personnel on the laboratory payroll (excluding pathologists, other laboratory physicians, doctoral level clinical scientists, and students) must be included in the paid hour total.

Hours, specified   Total worked hours minus all hours worked performing procedures or activities which have not been time studied and assigned unit values (non-specified hours).

Hours, worked   Total paid hours minus paid time off (paid vacation time, holiday time, sick time, education time away from the institution, personal leave, jury duty, etc.). Actual overtime hours are included on a one-for-one basis. Worked hours include the actual number of hours worked during a callback shift.

Item for Count Defines for each procedure what is to be counted to obtain the raw count. Abbreviations for the items for count, as they appear in the Procedure Lists, are shown in parentheses.

Absorption (ABSRP)—Used with antibody absorption procedures for each mixture and separation of serum and absorbing cells.

Antigen (ANTIG)—Generally used in blood bank and immunology to define qualitative or quantitative testing of a specimen for an antigen or its corresponding antibody. It refers to each individual antigen or corresponding antibody listed as applied to each individual specimen tested.

Antiserum (ANTISERA)—Used in microbiology for slide agglutination testing and refers to each serum containing antibodies against a specific antigen or group of antigens.

Application (APPL)—Used in chemistry for chromatographic procedures (e.g., thin layer, paper, column), and pertains to each application of specimen to the medium.

Aspirate (ASPIR)—Used for fine needle or other aspirated material in cytology to include all processing and preparation of slides from each aspiration performed.

Bag (BAG)—Used in microbiology and refers to a container used for the disposal of contaminated material.

Biobag (BIOBG)—Used in microbiology and refers to a plastic bag with a sealed closure containing a gaseous environment developed by flushing with an appropriate gas from a tank, or generated by chemical reactants placed in the container.

Batch (BATCH)—Used in antibody detection to represent a group of tubes processed at the same time in a single fixed-speed centrifuge head with no regard for the number of specimens tested. This is necessary because these tests are usually performed in batches, and an average value per specimen would be totally inadequate when only single specimens were run.

Note: To tally these determinations, each laboratory must develop its own system. It may be possible to tally each time a centrifuge head is run, or each laboratory may develop an average batch size for its operation and divide the total number of each type by this average batch size.

$$\frac{\text{number of specimens}}{\text{number of batches}} = \text{average batch size}$$

Block (BLOCK)—Used for each block where tissue or sedimented material is embedded for histologic processing. When specified, this includes cutting and staining one slide.

Bottle (BOTTLE)—Used in microbiology and refers to the container used in a blood culture procedure.

Case (CASE)—Used for anatomic pathology to describe a body for autopsy or all materials and reports referring to a surgical pathology, cytology, or cytogenetics specimen.

Cell Reagent (CELLRG)—Refers to the preparation of a cellular product (e.g., reagent red blood cells treated, preserved, or of a specific type; or lymphocytes).

Chart (CHART)—A book, binder, or clip board in which a patient's active medical history is stored on a nursing unit.

Constituent (CONST)—Pertains to the analyte or particle being assayed.

Delivery (DELIV)—Used for each delivery of blood or components by laboratory personnel to another location within the institution.

Dilution (DILUTION)—Used in some immunologic titrations to define the procedure as related to each dilution tested.

Disc (DISC)—Used in microbiology to describe a small piece of filter paper impregnated with material that assists in organism identification or susceptibility testing (e.g., bacitracin or optichin discs used for presumptive identification).

Donor (DONOR)—Used for procedures using a blood donor.

Filtrate (FILT)—Used for microporous membrane filtration in cytology to include all steps in the filtration and preparation of slides from the filter.

Function (FUNCT)—Used to describe an activity or task performed by laboratory personnel (e.g., recording temperature readings, washing bench tops).

Grid (GRID)—Used in electron microscopy to define the preparation or viewing and photography of one grid.

Injection (INJ)—Used in chemistry and microbiology for gas-liquid and high-pressure liquid chromatography procedures and pertains to each entry of a specimen into the portal of the instrument.

Jar (JAR)—A glass or plastic container fitted with a lid closure containing a controlled gaseous environment developed by flushing with appropriate gas from a tank or generated by chemical reactants placed in the container.

Karyotype (KARYO)—Used in cytogenetics for the identification of a satisfactory metaphase, necessary photography, enlarging, and preparation and analysis of the karyotype after the initial three per band.

Location (LOCATN)—A patient care or administrative department located outside the laboratory, within the institution (e.g., nursing unit, outpatient clinic, accounting department, medical records).

Organism (ORG)—Used in microbiology to represent one pure isolate.

Panel (PANEL)—Used for antibody identification where a panel of reagent red or white blood cells of known antigenicity is used. The unit value is based on the entire panel, usually eight to 12 cells. For a 13 to 24 cell panel, count as two panels.

Patient (PATNT)—Used when the presence of the patient is mandatory during the procedure, e.g., venipuncture.

Per 100 (PR100)—Pertains to counting 100 elements, e.g., bone marrow differential.

Plate (PLATE)—Used in immunology and chemistry for counter electrophoresis, immunoelectrophoresis, etc., to define the procedure related to one complete plate.

Plate, Bottle, and Tube (PBT)—Used as items for count in microbiology. (Note: a biplate counts as two plates, a quadrant plate counts as four plates.)

Print (PRINT)—Used for the making of one photographic print.

Round Trip (RTRIP)—Used when laboratory personnel travel to a location outside the laboratory but within the institution to render technical assistance or procure special specimens and return. Not to be used with other specimen collection values.

Row (ROW)—Represents one row of tubes in complement titration.

Slide (SLIDE)—Used when material is placed on a slide, e.g., tissue, bacteria.

Smear (SMEAR)—Used in microbiology and cytology and refers to the material placed on a microscopic slide. There may be more than one smear per slide.

Specimen (SPEC)—Is a biological sample for analysis. This item for count is used

a) when the procedure involves the production of several results or multiple procedures (e.g., urinalysis, ABO and $Rh_o(D)$ typing, animal inoculation),

b) to count the initial handling and clerical processing for surgical pathology and cytology,

c) when the procedure involves a specimen without producing a reportable result (e.g., centrifugation in cytology, elution in blood bank),

d) in histology to represent all the tissue removed at one time from a single anatomical site (e.g., multiple skin lesions are one specimen),

e) in microbiology when patient material from a single source (e.g., throat, wound) is submitted for culture or microscopic examination.

Substance (SUBST)—Used in chemistry and pertains to each substance for which the procedure is being performed, e.g., barbiturates, beryllium.

Test (TEST)—A defined activity leading to a result.

Tissue (TISS)—Used in cytogenetics for additional tissues cultured from a single tissue specimen.

Tray (TRAY)—Used for preparation of 60 or 72 well trays of test cells for lymphocytoxicity testing.

Unit (UNIT)—Used in blood bank for each aliquot of donor blood, component or derivative, or associated procedure.

Laboratory Workload Unit The basic measure of productive time in the Method. One unit is equal to one minute of technical, clerical, and aide time.

Permanent (p) Unit Value A value assigned by the International Workload Committee to a procedure or instrument after a statistically valid number of edited time studies have been performed.

Procedure A sequence of technical, clerical, and aide steps constituting a laboratory activity listed in the *Manual For Laboratory Workload Recording Method.* Each such procedure has a code number, an item for count, and may have a unit value per procedure. The procedure is arbitrarily assigned to a standard section.

Automated Procedure—A procedure in which most of the analytical steps are performed by an instrument.

Manual Procedure—A procedure in which most of the analytical steps are performed by hand.

Productivity A ratio of output [or workload done expressed in workload units (minutes)] to input (or resources consumed) expressed as either paid, worked, or specified hours:

$$\text{Productivity} = \frac{\text{total workload (minutes)}}{\text{hours}}$$

The above stated formula expresses productivity in minutes per hour, not percent. To convert to percent, simply multiply the quotient, obtained from the formula above, by 1.67.

Productivity, paid A ratio of output measured in workload units (minutes) to total technical, clerical, and aide time for which laboratory employees are being paid, whether or not the employees are on-site:

$$\text{Paid productivity} = \frac{\text{total workload (minutes)}}{\text{paid hours}}$$

Productivity, specified A ratio of output measured in workload units (minutes) to input expressed in hours used by personnel involved in time studied procedures:

$$\text{Specified productivity} = \frac{\text{total workload (minutes)}}{\text{specified hours}}$$

Productivity, worked A ratio of output measured in total workload units (minutes) to total technical, clerical, and aide time in hours on-site:

$$\text{Worked productivity} = \frac{\text{total workload (minutes)}}{\text{worked hours}}$$

Profile A profile is a group of procedures which is defined by the laboratory for convenience. It may be requested or performed as a group.

Raw Count Simple tally of items for count.

Repeat A procedure performed to solve a problem in a sample run. To qualify as a repeat, all of the analytical, data handling, and recording steps following the initial preparation of the specimen must have been performed.

The routine performance of duplicate procedures simply for quality assurance purposes without a reasonable probability of discrepant results is not considered to be a problem. Therefore, such procedures do not qualify as repeats. A repeat constitutes one raw count.

Replicate (duplicate, triplicate, etc.) The planned multiple performance of certain steps.

Replicated steps included in a specific methodology are already part of the unit value per procedure. Replicates are not counted. Routine performance of duplicate procedures for quality assurance purposes is replication and is not counted.

Step A well-defined single function such as logging, pipetting, inoculating, etc.

Suffix Code Three-digit codes used in conjunction with five-digit CAP procedure code numbers to indicate various concepts and/or procedures: automated instrumentation, microbiology specimen sources, histology stains, immunological antigens, etc.

Temporary (t) Unit Value A value assigned by the International Workload Committee to a procedure or instrument after a limited number of edited time studies have been performed and before enough data are available to calculate a permanent (p) unit value.

Unit Value per Procedure The number of laboratory workload units (minutes) of technical, clerical, and aide time required to perform all the activities to complete the defined procedure once [see extrapolated (e), permanent (p), and temporary (t)].

Workload The sum of all the products obtained by multiplying the raw count for each individual procedure by its unit value is the workload expressed in minutes.

Chapter 3 Suffix Codes

The addition of a three-digit suffix code to a five-digit CAP procedure code most often indicates that the procedure is performed on an automated instrument, but also may denote other concepts (e.g., specimen sources in microbiology, special stains in histology, specific antigens in immunology).

The resulting eight-digit code, consisting of a five-digit procedure code and a three-digit suffix code, denotes the procedure as well as the unit value.

SUFFIX CODES IN BLOOD BANK
(STANDARD SECTION NUMBER 01)

Eight-digit codes, consisting of five-digit blood bank procedure codes and three-digit suffix codes, are used in blood bank to indicate automated procedures.

To use the automated blood bank instrument list, select the appropriate five-digit CAP blood bank procedure code from the Procedure Lists contained in this Manual and enlarge that code by adding the three-digit suffix code assigned to the instrument used.

Example: The line item which describes the manual thaw and deglycerolization of frozen blood appears in the Procedure Lists as follows:

CAP Code No.	Procedure Name	Unit Value	Comments	Item for Count	Lab Sect
86276	Frozen Blood: Thaw and Deglycerolization	90.0	Auto BB UVs p. 19	UNIT	BANK

A unit value of 90 minutes per blood unit is tallied in a laboratory's workload for each raw count reported under CAP code number 86276. If this procedure is performed on the Haemonetics Model 17, the workload user should refer to the list of automated blood bank instruments in the Blood Bank Chapter of this Manual to identify the three-digit suffix code and unit value assigned to the instrument used. The combination of codes that should be used to indicate the thaw and deglycerolization of frozen blood using a Haemonetics Model 17 follows below.

CAP Code No.	Procedure Name	Unit Value	Item for Count	Lab Sect
86276.015	Frozen Blood: Thaw and Deglycerolization *Using a Haemonetics Model 17*	t 35.0	UNIT	BANK

A unit value of 35 minutes per blood unit is tallied as the laboratory's workload for each raw count reported under CAP code number 86276.015.

SUFFIX CODES IN CHEMISTRY
(STANDARD SECTION NUMBER 02)

Three-digit suffix codes are used in conjunction with five-digit CAP chemistry procedure codes to denote

1. A procedure performed using an automated chemistry instrument classified within a specific group

2. Several procedures included in an automated preset chemistry profile

3. An automated chemistry instrument which fits a group description but is not assigned a specific suffix code

4. A manual radioligand assay method group

Only one three-digit suffix code may be assigned per procedure per instrument in chemistry. The following examples will highlight some of the unique uses of three-digit suffix codes in chemistry:

Example 1A: A procedure performed using an automated chemistry instrument classified within a specific group. A blood gas analysis performed on a Corning 168 (a blood gas analyzer classified in Group 1) should be coded as follows:

CAP Code No.	Procedure Name	Unit Value	Item for Count	Lab Sect
82882.067	Blood Gas Analysis (Group 1 Analyzers only) *Corning 168*	4.0	SPEC	CHEM

Another example of a procedure performed using an automated chemistry instrument classified within a specific group appears below.

Example 1B: A glucose analysis performed on a Du Pont ACA (a chemical analyzer classified in the Batch or Single Test Mode Group) should be coded as follows:

82410.035	Automated Chemistry Specimen Setup *Du Pont ACA*	2.5	SPEC	CHEM
84330.035	Glucose *Du Pont ACA*	0.5	CONST	CHEM

In example 1B two line items are necessary to code one procedure. This is necessary for procedures performed using any of the instruments classified in the Batch or Single Test Mode Group of Chemical Analyzers.

Example 2: Several procedures included in an automated preset profile. A specimen analyzed for six constituents on the Technicon SMA 6/60 should be coded as follows:

82400.051	Chemistry Analysis Profile *Technicon SMA 6/60*	4.0	SPEC	CHEM

In example 2, only one line item is necessary to code six constituents because the item for count is specimen and not constituent or test. Only one line item is necessary to code procedures performed using any of the instruments classified in the Profile Mode Chemical Analyzer Group.

Example 3: An automated chemistry instrument which fits a group description but is not assigned a specific suffix code. If a blood gas analysis is performed on an instrument which fits the Group 1 Blood Gas Analyzers' description: Self-calibrating, self-calculating, and printed tape of results but no specific suffix code is assigned to the instrument used, then the following code should be used:

| 82882.001 | Blood Gas Analysis (Group 1 Analyzers only) NOS: Not Otherwise Specified | 4.0 | SPEC | CHEM |

Selection of the proper five-digit procedure code for suffix code expansion should be emphasized. A three-digit chemistry suffix code can be used only in conjunction with a five-digit chemistry procedure code where the phrase "Auto Chem UVs p. 22" appears in the line item.

Example 4: A digoxin analysis performed manually by direct [125] I radioligand assay without extraction should be coded as follows:

| 84756.501 | Digoxin/SA/Ligand
Radioligand Assay Group 1A indicated
by the three-digit suffix code .501 | 7.0 | TEST | CHEM |

SUFFIX CODES IN HEMATOLOGY
(STANDARD SECTION NUMBER 03)

Three-digit suffix codes are used in conjunction with five-digit CAP hematology procedure codes to denote automated hematology procedures. Only one three-digit suffix code is assigned per procedure per instrument in hematology.

Example 1A: A hemogram performed using an automated blood cell counting instrument. CAP code number 85015: Blood Cell Profile 1 represents a hemogram consisting of the following parameters: RBC, WBC, Hct, Hgb, and indices. If this procedure is performed using a Coulter Model S, it is coded as follows:

CAP Code No.	Procedure Name	Unit Value	Item for Count	Lab Sect
85015.070	Blood Cell Profile I *Coulter S*	3.0	SPEC	HEMA

Example 1B: A platelet count performed using the Ultra-Flo 100 should be coded as follows:

85570.068	Platelet Count: Whole Blood *Ultra-Flo 100 (RBC analysis tallied separately)*	t 5.0	TEST	HEMA

SUFFIX CODES IN HISTOLOGY
(STANDARD SECTION NUMBER 04)

Three-digit suffix codes are used in conjunction with five-digit CAP histology procedure codes to denote specific histologic stains or stain groups. Eight-digit codes consisting of a five-digit procedure code (representing a specific histology stain group) and a three-digit suffix code (representing the specific stains within the group) appear in the Procedure Lists in this Manual.

SUFFIX CODES IN IMMUNOLOGY
(STANDARD SECTION NUMBER 05)

Three-digit suffix codes are used in conjunction with five-digit CAP immunology procedure codes to denote the following concepts:

- an antigen or an antibody within a specific method group
- an automated instrument used to perform a procedure

Eight-digit codes consisting of five-digit codes (representing the specific method of analysis) and three-digit suffix codes (representing the specific antigen/antibody within the method group) appear in the Procedure Lists in this Manual.

Example 1: An antibody detection method group. A qualitative determination of an antibody by agglutination should be coded as follows if the specific antibody is not listed within the group:

CAP Code No.	Procedure Name	Unit Value	Item for Count	Lab Sect
86006.000	Antibody Determination by Agglutination (qual) Slide or Tube/Not Otherwise Specified (NOS)/Group 1	5.0	TEST	IMMU

Example 2: An antigen within a specific method group. A qualitative agglutination procedure to determine the presence of hCG should be coded as follows:

86006.018	hCG/Qual Group 1	5.0	TEST	IMMU

It is necessary to refer to the Immunology Chapter of this Manual to identify the appropriate suffix code and unit value when a procedure is performed using an automated instrument. A list of automated immunology instruments, complete with suffix codes and unit values listed for each, can be found in the Immunology Chapter of this Manual.

Example 3: An automated instrument used to perform a procedure. An analysis for Immunoglobulin (IgG) performed on an IDT FIAX Fluorometer should be coded as follows:

CAP Code No.	Procedure Name	Unit Value	Item for Count	Lab Sect
86318.051	Immunoglobulin (IgG) *IDT FIAX Fluorometer*	t 8.0	TEST	IMMU

Selection of the appropriate five-digit procedure code for suffix code expansion is extremely important. Three-digit immunology suffix codes, indicating the use of an automated instrument, can only be added to five-digit immunology procedure codes when the phrase "Auto Immu UVs p. 33" appears in the line item.

SUFFIX CODES IN MICROBIOLOGY
(STANDARD SECTION 06)

Three-digit suffix codes are used in conjunction with five-digit CAP microbiology procedure codes to denote various functions

- a procedure performed using an automated instrument
- a specific manual procedure within a general category
- to designate and track specimens received for routine bacteriology

A list of automated microbiology instruments, complete with their suffix codes and unit values, can be found in the Microbiology Chapter of this Manual. In the automated Chapter, each five-digit code indicating the procedure performed has been expanded with the appropriate three-digit suffix code.

The procedure codes can be found in the Procedure Lists, as well as in the Microbiology Chapter of this Manual.

Example 1: A procedure performed on an automated instrument. A blood culture performed using the Bactec 460 would be coded as follows:

CAP Code No.	Procedure Name	Unit Value	Item for Count	Lab Sect
87512.089	Blood Cultures—Automated *Bactec 460*	5.0	BOTTLE	MICR

The following codes should be used if the presence of Neisseria is being identified by the Bactec 460:

87514.089	Organism Identification *Bactec 460*	t 9.0	BOTTLE	MICR

Procedures in microbiology are listed in general categories represented by unique five-digit code numbers. Each procedure within a general category has an eight-digit code number consisting of the five-digit general category code and a unique three-digit suffix code which indicates the specific procedure performed. The complete eight-digit codes appear in the Procedure Lists of this Manual. Therefore, it is not necessary to refer to the Microbiology Chapter to identify the appropriate three-digit suffix codes for expansion.

Five-digit procedure codes and the general categories that they represent appear below.

CAP Code No.	General Category
87511	Blood Culture—Manual
87650	Organism Identification—Commercial Kit
87750	Organism ID/MIC Combo
87880	Digestion Decontamination Procedures Prior to Mycobacterial Culture
87885	Mycobacterial Stains
87920	Concentration Procedures Prior to Parasitic Examination
87925	Parasitology Examination
87930	Parasitology Stains
87954	Sensitivity Testing or MIC/Manual

Example 2: A specific procedure within a general category. To indicate the performance of an API 20E, a specific procedure within the general category entitled Organism Identification—Commercial Kit, use the following code:

87650.027	API 20E/Analytab Products Inc.	6.0	ORG

Example 3: Two pieces of media inoculated with a urine specimen for a bacterial culture. Three-digit suffix codes can be used in conjunction with a five-digit procedure code to indicate the source of a specimen which is planted on one or more pieces of media for a bacterial culture such as the following:

| 87532.626 | Planting of 2 Pieces of Media for a
Bacterial Culture
Specimen source indicated by the three-
digit suffix code (.626) is Urine. | 2.0 | SPEC |

Chapter 12   Implementation

FUNCTIONAL SECTIONS

Identification of the functional sections within a laboratory is the first step in setting up the workload recording method. The functional sections of each laboratory are those sections organized and/or operating within the laboratory for which work output and manpower input can be accurately identified. Functional sections should be created for the purpose of breaking down the laboratory into separate operational areas useful for effective analysis and management. Work units and personnel hours not counted in a defined functional section must be tabulated and allocated to the appropriate functional section. It is useful to discuss the number and type of functional sections with the payroll and billing departments of the institution. Coordination with other departments ensures that data compiled by the laboratory director will be better understood by individuals outside the laboratory involved in the fiscal viability of the institution.

Any one laboratory may actually consist of any combination of the standard sections designated by the CAP and any additional functional sections that the laboratory management deems appropriate. However, a small laboratory may consist of only one functional section (the laboratory as a whole) while a large laboratory may find it more effective to have numerous functional sections. For example, a large chemistry laboratory may prefer to establish automated, general, and special chemistry sections. Such decisions must be based on definable sections for which the workload units and hours of labor can be accurately counted.

USER PROCEDURE FILE DEVELOPMENT

After the functional sections of the laboratory are defined, a User Procedure File should be developed. Procedures performed in each section should be identified and coded by consulting the Procedure Lists in this Manual. A single procedure may be listed in only one section, or it may appear in several different sections. Specimens sent to reference laboratories should not be listed apart from the collection and dispatch including processing of specimens. The User Procedure File is the heart of the Method for the user laboratory and it must be amended whenever procedures are added or deleted.

PRESET PROFILES

Several preset profiles, describing procedures performed as a group, appear in this Manual as single line items and cannot be altered. CAP code number 85015: Blood Cell Profile I, is an example of a single line item designating several procedures performed as a group. Notice that the item for count is specimen rather than test or constituent. When CAP code number 85015 is expanded to 85015.070, it indicates that one specimen is being analyzed simultaneously on a Coulter Model S for five parameters: RBC, WBC, Hgb, Hct, and Indices.

It is unnecessary to identify and code each individual parameter included in Blood Cell Profile I when the analysis is performed on a multi-channel blood cell counting instrument such as the Coulter Model S.

Similarly, CAP code number 82420: Multiple Ion Analysis, describes the simultaneous analysis of both sodium and potassium on one specimen. When CAP code number 82420 is expanded to 82420.044, it indicates that one specimen is being analyzed simultaneously for sodium and potassium on an IL 143.

CAP code number 82400: Chemistry Analysis Profile, is expanded with three-digit suffix codes to indicate several procedures performed simultaneously on sequential multiple chemistry analyzers (e.g., Technicon 6/60, 12/60). When CAP code number 82400 is expanded to 82400.051, it indicates that a single specimen is being simultaneously analyzed for six analytes on the Technicon 6/60. One eight-digit code number designates several procedures.

CUSTOM PROFILES

In the CAP Workload Method, a profile is defined as a group of procedures identified by the laboratory for the convenience of reporting or tallying. Procedures contained in a profile may be requested or performed as a group. In setting up a profile, one should give each profile a number and a name, list its component procedures, then assign a total unit value based on the sum of the unit values for each of the component procedures.

Use of the profile concept is primarily a tallying aid. Caution must be taken to avoid the double counting of procedures performed as part of a profile, especially if a given procedure is sometimes performed as part of a profile and at other times as an independent procedure. Each procedure included in a custom profile should be tallied as a separate raw count.

The following are examples of possible profiles intended only to illustrate profile construction and not to recommend scope or standard of practice. Please note that these example profiles are not designed for Computer Assisted Workload Recording participants. CAP Computer Assisted Workload Recording participants should refer to the Computer Assisted Workload Recording Program Instruction Manual for specific directions.

Blood Bank—An *example* of a possible Transfusion Reaction Profile
(after one unit of packed red blood cells)

CAP Code No.	Procedure Name	Item for Count	Raw Count (RC)	Unit Value (UV)	Total Unit Value (RC × UV)
86166	Compatibility Test: Crossmatch (consists of saline and potentiating media phases, either or both of which are converted to an antiglobulin phase) *Two crossmatches: pretransfusion and postreaction specimens from patient*	TEST	2	7.0	14.0
86168	Antibody Detection (screen) Performed with a Crossmatch (consists of saline and potentiating media phases, either or both of which are converted to an antiglobulin phase) *Two antibody detections (screens): pretransfusion and postreaction specimens from patient*	TEST	2	10.0	20.0

Code	Description	Unit	Qty	Unit Value	Total
86082	ABO Cell, Serum and Rh$_o$(D) Typing, Slide or Tube (includes D^u typing when indicated) *Two cell typings: pretransfusion and postreaction specimens from patient*	SPEC	2	7.0	14.0
86081	ABO Cell and Rh$_o$(D) Typing, Slide or Tube (includes D^u typing when indicated) *Two cell typings: crossmatch segment from donor bag and remaining blood in returned blood container*	SPEC	2	5.0	10.0
86250	Antiglobulin Test, Direct *Two tests: pretransfusion and postreaction specimens from patient*	TEST	2	4.0	8.0
83032	Hemoglobin, Plasma *One test: postreaction blood specimen from patient*	TEST	1	15.0	15.0
82250	Bilirubin, Total *One test: postreaction blood specimen from patient*	TEST	1	15.0	15.0
81000	Urinalysis, Routine with Microscopic	SPEC	1	6.0	6.0
87511.055	Blood Culture *Two cultures: aerobic and anaerobic cultures of the remaining contents in the returned blood container*	BOTTLE	2	6.0	12.0
87718	Gram Stain: Direct from Specimen	SMEAR	1	t 5.1	5.1
	Totals		16		119.1

Chemistry—Creatinine Clearance Profile

Code	Description	Unit	Qty	Unit Value	Total
82565	Creatinine, Blood and Urine	TEST	2	10.0	20.0
81006	Urine, Volume Measurement	SPEC	1	2.0	2.0
82350	Calculation	TEST	1	3.0	3.0
	Totals		4		25.0

Chemistry—Five-Hour Glucose Tolerance Test Profile

84330	Glucose, Blood (analysis performed manually)	TEST	7	8.0	56.0
89343	Venipuncture (collection of a venous blood specimen by laboratory personnel from an outpatient)	PATNT	7	e 4.0	28.0
	Totals		14		84.0

Hematology—Coagulation Profile

85000	Bleeding Time	PATNT	1	e 8.0	8.0
85170	Clot Retraction, Qualitative	TEST	1	6.0	6.0
85613.084	Prothrombin Time (PT) and Thromboplastic Time, Partial (PTT) *Performed simultaneously on a Coag-a-mate*	SPEC	1	4.0	4.0
85016.075	Blood Cell Profile II *Performed on the Coulter S-Plus—analysis performed to obtain the platelet count*	SPEC	1	t 3.0	3.0
85581	Blood Film Screen (includes WBC estimate, RBC morphology, and platelet estimate)	SLIDE	1	5.0	5.0
	Totals		5		26.0

METHODS OF TALLYING RAW COUNTS

In general, tallying is performed by one of four methods or a combination of them. These methods are from billing reports, a master log, by computer, or manually.

The first method of tallying uses billing reports which are generated by the hospital's controller's office. A billing report generally lists the number of "billable" tests performed. Quality control specimens and standards, patient repeats, etc., are probably not tallied on the report since they are not billable items; they must, therefore, be tallied in another manner.

In addition, there are no provisions for tests such as blood bank, histology, and microbiology procedures which are counted by components rather than by test. A raw count of one would be inaccurate in these instances. Nonbillable procedures such as phlebotomies and urine volume measurements also are not captured on billing reports. If this type of report is to be used at all, it must be appropriately adjusted so that the entire workload is captured accurately.

While some management applications may require analysis of laboratory activity based on charged (billable) and noncharged workload units, it is essential to proper management of laboratory resources to capture the entire workload, billed or not.

Using a master log book is a second method. This contains some of the same flaws as the billing report, since it does not include standards, quality controls, and repeats, and usually lists only tests. The information is frequently disorganized and additional time would be required for assembling it into a usable form.

As a third method of tallying, laboratories with computer access can tally workload on the computer as the work is being performed. Once again, care must be taken to capture components rather than reportable tests only and also that the software tallying mechanism reflects the most current Manual.

For noncomputerized laboratories, the Workload Recording Committee recommends a fourth method, the "report-as-you-go" technique. With this method, the technologist manually records what has been done for each block of time worked on a tally sheet.

USING YOUR LABORATORY COMPUTER TO ACCUMULATE WORKLOAD STATISTICS

A laboratory computer is an excellent tool to accumulate workload statistics, but special programming is required to ensure that workload is properly tallied (e.g., documenting the specimen level workload in chemistry, ensuring that only specimens collected by laboratory personnel are tallied in specimen procurement, and accurately tallying slides in histology). Most laboratory computers will tabulate CAP workload units, but are relatively lacking in the calculation of productivity figures. Even the most sophisticated systems lack the comparative data necessary to judge your laboratory's performance against other comparable laboratories in the country.

For these reasons, all laboratories (even those with sophisticated in-house computers) will benefit from participation in the CAP Computer Assisted Workload Recording Program. (See Chapter 15: Computers and Workload Recording Method.)

DOCUMENTATION OF RAW COUNT ORIGINS

In the past, most governmental and some private insurance programs have reimbursed hospital laboratories on the basis of audited cost for inpatient work and have adjusted ("grossed up") referral or other outpatient work charged at lower levels. With the advent of prospective pricing much inpatient work will be covered by Diagnosis Related Groups (DRGs). Work generated from separate psychiatric sections or pediatric hospitals will still be reimbursed on an audited basis. Referral (nonpatient) testing must be treated separately. Outpatient testing will be reimbursed on a federal fee schedule.

As prospective payment evolves, it appears that administrators will focus on laboratory use and on the effort going into the production of services covered by prospective payment, services reimbursed under TEFRA cost reimbursement, and nonhospital outpatient (referral) activities, etc.

Most laboratory directors collect raw counts (procedure tallies) in at least three categories: inpatient (IP), outpatient (OP), and quality controls and standards (QC). Unfortunately, use of only these three categories may be too confining and insufficient for laboratory management. In keeping with the needs stated above, raw counts may be collected in nine categories as follows:

- Inpatient
- Outpatient
- Quality Controls and Standards
- Repeats
- Emergency Room (specimens)
- Referral (specimens received)
- Interstate (specimens received)
- Regional Laboratories
- Other

There are many areas of work that are difficult to classify by source, and the following guidelines are recommended:

Type of Activity	Three Category	Nine Category
Blood, donor, and component preparation and procedures	Inpatient	Inpatient or other
Blood bank inventory	Inpatient	Inpatient

Type of Activity	Three Category	Nine Category
Employee health testing procedures	Outpatient	Outpatient or other
Infection control/ epidemiology procedures	Quality control	Quality control or other
Phlebotomy or specimen procurement	Inpatient or outpatient	Inpatient, outpatient, or emergency room
Procedures performed on hospital inpatients or specimens obtained from hospital inpatients	Inpatient	Inpatient
Procedures performed on interstate specimens received	Outpatient	Interstate, regional, or referral
Procedures performed on referral specimens received from outside physicians or institutions	Outpatient	Referral
Procedures performed on specimens received from regional hospitals	Inpatient	Regional or interstate
Procedures performed on registered hospital outpatients or specimens obtained from hospital outpatients	Outpatient	Outpatient
Repeats	Prorate as inpatient and outpatient	Repeats

It will be crucial for laboratory directors to identify all types of activity in terms of workload. A simple listing of the number of procedures, such as would come from billing, is inadequate and misleading. Due to differences in reimbursement mechanisms, such data broken down by specimen sources may be invaluable when determining laboratory staffing and for evaluation of the advisability of performing or recruiting additional outside work. Similarly, decisions may be more rationally made as to what work should be forwarded to outside laboratories.

Each procedure included in a custom profile should be tallied as a separate raw count. Profiles consisting of several procedures should not be documented as one raw count. Counting a custom profile consisting of several procedures as one raw count will skew utilization and management indicators computed with the raw count figure (e.g., WLUs/RC).

QUALITY CONTROLS, STANDARDS, BLANKS, AND PRIMERS

Procedures performed for quality control are counted and given the same unit value per procedure as determinations on unknown specimens, unless otherwise specified. Quality control includes both internal (quality assurance) and external (proficiency survey) specimens.

While it is recognized that quality control and standard testing do not involve all accessioning and reporting steps, compensatory time is required for recording and statistical effort. Thus, assigning the same unit value per procedure as for a patient sample is appropriate.

Procedures performed on standards for the purpose of establishing calibration curves are counted and given the same unit value per procedure as the determination on an unknown specimen.

Reagent/serum blanks and primers are counted as an integral part of specimen testing when the unit values per procedure are computed and *must not* be counted as separate procedures.

Section II Management Applications

Chapter 13 Staffing and Productivity Analysis

Section I of this Manual is devoted to Basic Concepts which includes derivation of the unit value per procedure, the time study process, terminology, special directions for each section, and implementation of the Method. Section II is devoted to management applications including staffing and productivity analysis, quality control of the method, the management engineering approach to laboratory data, the CAP Computer Assisted Workload Recording Program, and other related topics.

TYPES OF HOURS

A standard definition of productivity is the ratio of output to input. In the CAP Workload Recording Method (WLR), output is the workload which is the sum of the mathematical products obtained by multiplying the raw count for each individual procedure by its unit value; this workload is expressed in units which represent minutes of personnel time. Input is quantified in terms of technical, clerical, and aide time. This time can be expressed in three ways:

1. total paid hours
2. total worked hours
3. total specified hours

Paid Hours

Paid hours are almost universally used to measure and monitor performance in any department. Paid hours constitute all paid time including vacation time, holiday time, sick time, educational time away from the institution, actual overtime hours, and other paid time off (e.g., personal leave, jury duty, death in family). In the WLR, paid hours are defined to include *all* laboratory personnel on the laboratory payroll *excluding* pathologists, other laboratory physicians, doctoral level clinical scientists, and students.

To provide comparability between hospital laboratories and freestanding outpatient laboratories, the following staff also may be excluded from total paid hours: accounts receivable staff, specimen delivery drivers, and report couriers (unless workload credit is claimed under CAP code number 89140: Report Delivery within the Institution).

Occasionally, it is necessary to include time generated by persons thought to be excluded from the paid hour total. Common sense is called for when including time expended by physicians, doctoral level clinical scientists, and students.

For example, if a student functions as, and is paid as an aide or phlebotomist during certain hours, that time is to be counted as paid hours. However, any time spent in a formal training program should not be included. If MDs or PhDs function exclusively as managers or as bench technologists, then their hours should be documented as paid time.

When determining whether or not physician, doctoral level clinical scientist, or student time should be included in the paid hour figure, consider the functional assignment rather than the educational background.

Paid hours reflect the total personnel burden. This burden also includes other costs such as healthcare benefits, insurance, and FICA, and will be affected by policy decisions (such as the length of the work day, the number of personal breaks per day, and the amount of vacation, holiday, and sick pay to grant).

Worked Hours

Total worked hours are total paid hours minus paid time off (paid vacation time, holiday time, sick time, education time away from the institution, personal leave, jury duty, death in family, etc.). Actual overtime hours are included on a one-for-one basis, regardless of the remuneration rate.

If the payroll system records worked hours on a holiday as 1.5 times the actual worked hours, worked and paid productivity would be slightly lower, particularly in the payroll period where the holiday occurs.

In a *typical* laboratory, the average full-time employee is paid for 15 to 20 vacation days, nine to 12 holidays and personal days, six to 10 sick days, and one to two other paid days off. This total of 31 to 44 paid days off is 12 percent to 17 percent of the total 260 paid days per year (52 weeks times five paid days per week).

Worked hours reflect the time available for performing all laboratory activities. For the *typical* employee, the majority of worked hours are spent doing procedures with assigned unit values. For some employees, most or all of their time is spent on activities without assigned unit values. This time was first identified in the 1980 Manual as non-specified time.

Paid and Worked Callback Hours

Ideally, hours to be documented for callback should be only the actual number of hours spent in the laboratory during each callback. However, the inclusion or exclusion of call hours depends on the institution's payroll system. There are two prevalent on call compensation practices:

1. If the employee is paid a flat fee for being on call, e.g., $20.00 for an eight-hour shift, the only hours which will show are those hours when the employee is actually called in (frequently including a two-hour minimum time regardless of the actual time spent in the laboratory). Therefore, the worked and paid hours when called in would be the same; and there would be no worked or paid hours if not called in.

2. If the employee is paid an hourly rate for part of a shift, e.g., two-hours pay for being on call for a shift, then, even if the employee is not called in, the two hours are included in paid hours. Institutions using this method of payment for call time will incur slightly more paid hours than institutions using the flat fee method, and will thereby slightly lower paid and worked productivity.

Whichever compensation method is used, compensation for the hours worked (including any minimum time) when called in is usually paid in addition to the on call pay.

Specified (Workloaded) Hours

Total specified hours are total worked hours minus all hours spent performing procedures or activities which have not been time studied or assigned an extrapolated (e) value. These procedures or activities that do not generate workload units are defined as non-specified activities. The terms specified hours and non-specified hours may cause some confusion as to whether one is specifying what is included or excluded. Therefore, the term "workloaded" is frequently substituted for specified, and the term "nonworkloaded" is frequently substituted for non-specified.

Many non-specified activities vary significantly between laboratories; therefore, some activities may never be time studied or assigned a unit value. Examples of non-specified activities are listed below and in Appendices II and III:

- accounting, billing, and related activities
- administrative activities such as budgeting, recruitment, orientation of new staff, counseling, discipline, performance appraisal, and employee scheduling. Also includes reading mail, professional society functions, time for employee to receive counseling, discipline, performance appraisal, etc.
- breaks and personal time including formal breaks mandated by law, contract, or policy, washup or other personal time
- CAP tally maintenance including time spent maintaining and updating the CAP workload tally—which includes daily manual tallies and monthly summarization
- clerical support including handling mail, photocopying, typing letters and administrative reports, screening telephone calls, payroll, setting up meetings, etc.
- computer activities including systems analysis, programming, and computer operations performed by laboratory staff. (Note: Not all time expended on computer activities is untimed. For example, time spent in preparation of drawing lists or recording test results are activities which are included in the unit value. Time spent on such activities should *not* be deleted when calculating specified hours.)
- decedent affairs (excluding autopsy attendant duties)

- in-hospital donor recruitment activities which include visits to patient care areas within the hospital to recruit family members of patients who have received blood components; and mobile donor draw activities which includes travel time to and from donor site, and time to set up and take down equipment
- education of others in formal programs such as residencies, schools of medical technology, newly hired nursing personnel, etc.
- in-service education within the institution
- laboratory procedures which have not yet been time studied or assigned an extrapolated unit value per procedure
- major repair of instruments (when performed by laboratory personnel)
- many IV team activities
- orientation including both the initial orientation of new laboratory employees and the orientation of existing laboratory employees to new equipment or procedures including computers
- purchasing and procurement functions
- research and development of new tests, or procedures to bring tests inhouse, evaluation of methods or equipment. Also includes preparing papers for publication
- tumor registry activities
- other untimed activities performed by personnel on the laboratory payroll

Standby or Idle Time

In addition to the three types of hours described above, there is a fourth component of the total staff time: *standby* or *idle time*. As shown in the illustration below, standby or idle time is the difference between the time spent on specified activities plus the time spent on non-specified activities and the total worked hours. In a *typical* laboratory, standby or idle time is five percent to 10 percent of the total worked hours.

Specified activities	Standby	Non-specified	Paid time off

——— Specified hours ———

——— Worked hours ———

——— Paid hours ———

While for an entire laboratory standby or idle time may average five percent to 10 percent, the percentage varies by laboratory section. A production-oriented section such as an automated chemistry or hematology section should have little standby time. An evening or night shift, STAT section, a phlebotomy section, or a section in any laboratory with only one or two staff members may have substantial standby time.

LABORATORY PRODUCTIVITY

Productivity Definitions

Based on the general definition of productivity—the ratio of output to input—the following formula can be used to determine the productivity of an individual section or of the laboratory as a whole:

$$\frac{\text{total workload units}}{\text{hours}} = \text{productivity (units/hour)}$$

Using the three types of hours which have been described, three types of productivity figures can be calculated: paid, worked, and specified productivity. The following formulas express productivity in units (minutes) per hour.

$$1.\ \text{Paid productivity (units/hour)} = \frac{\text{total workload units}}{\text{paid hours}}$$

$$2.\ \text{Worked productivity (units/hour)} = \frac{\text{total workload units}}{\text{worked hours}}$$

$$3.\ \text{Specified productivity (units/hour)} = \frac{\text{total workload units}}{\text{specified hours}}$$

1. Paid productivity is the ratio of output measured in workload units to total labor resources measured by the number of hours for which laboratory employees are being paid, whether or not the employee is on-site. This identifies the overall productivity of all employee resources required to produce the laboratory's workload. Paid productivity is therefore the lowest of the three types of productivity.
2. Worked productivity is the ratio of output to available labor resources. Comparison of worked and paid productivities illustrates the impact of vacation, holiday, sick time, and other paid time off. Laboratory management has little control over the institution's personnel benefits. However, these benefits can signif-

icantly reduce the number of hours that employees are available to do work. This difference represents the cost to the laboratory of having those employee resources available to do work.

3. Specified productivity most closely matches measured output (workload units) with testing-related personnel time. It is useful to assess the impact of non-specified activities on a laboratory's productivity. In theory, specified productivity is the only productivity figure which could be expected to approach 60 units (minutes) per hour. However, many factors such as delays between tasks (standby or idle time), equipment malfunctions, or much STAT work may decrease this figure.

Many individuals desire to see productivity expressed as a percent rather than as units per hour. To convert to percent, divide the productivity expressed as units per hour by 60 to eliminate the hours, then multiply by 100; a shortcut is to simply divide the productivity expressed as units per hour by 0.6 to get the productivity as a percentage.

Calculating Productivity

The following examples illustrate the calculation of the three forms of productivity figures:

1. paid productivity
2. worked productivity
3. specified productivity

Assume laboratory Section A has six full-time equivalents (each FTE equals 2,080 paid hours per year). Each employee in Section A uses 15 vacation days, 10 holidays, and six sick days annually. The section's workload is 500,000 units per year. Paid, worked, and specified productivity figures for Section A are illustrated in the calculations below:

1. Calculating Paid Hours and Paid Productivity Figures for Section A

Total Paid Hours per Year

$$\frac{8 \text{ hours}}{\text{day}} \times \frac{5 \text{ days}}{\text{week}} \times \frac{52 \text{ weeks}}{\text{year}} \times 6 \text{ FTEs} = \frac{12,480 \text{ paid hours}}{\text{year}}$$

OR

$$\frac{2080 \text{ hours}}{\text{year}} \times 6 \text{ FTEs} = \frac{12,480 \text{ paid hours}}{\text{year}}$$

Paid Productivity

$$\frac{500,000 \text{ units (minutes)/year}}{12,480 \text{ paid hours/year}} = \frac{40.1 \text{ units (minutes)}}{\text{paid hour}}$$

Conversion of Paid Productivity to a Percentage

$$40.1 \text{ units (minutes)/hour paid} \div 0.6 = 66.8\% \text{ Paid productivity}$$

One workload unit equals one minute of time, but no section within the laboratory or the laboratory as a whole should be expected to achieve a paid productivity of 60 units (minutes) per hour. Two general categories of activities typically consume 30 percent to 45 percent of paid hours: 1. paid but not worked time (e.g., vacation, holiday, sick time) typically accounts for 12 percent to 17 percent; 2. non-specified activities and standby time typically account for 20 percent to 30 percent.

2. Calculating Worked Hours and Worked Productivity Figures for Section A

Calculating the Nonworked but Paid Hours per Year for Section A

Vacation: $\dfrac{15 \text{ days}}{\text{year}} \times \dfrac{8 \text{ hours}}{\text{day}} \times 6 \text{ FTEs} = 720 \text{ hours/year}$

Holidays: $\dfrac{10 \text{ days}}{\text{year}} \times \dfrac{8 \text{ hours}}{\text{day}} \times 6 \text{ FTEs} = 480 \text{ hours/year}$

Sick Time: $\dfrac{6 \text{ days}}{\text{year}} \times \dfrac{8 \text{ hours}}{\text{day}} \times 6 \text{ FTEs} = 288 \text{ hours/year}$

Total number of nonworked but paid hours per year for Section A $\qquad$ 1,488 hours/year

The 1,488 total nonworked but paid hours per year for Section A represents 11.9 percent of the paid staff time.

$$\frac{1{,}488 \text{ nonworked hours/year}}{12{,}480 \text{ paid hours/year}} \times \quad 100 \quad = \quad \begin{array}{l} 11.9\% \text{ Paid} \\ \text{staff time} \end{array}$$

Total Worked Hours per Year

Total paid hours/year for Section A	=	12,480 paid hours/year
MINUS		
Total nonworked but paid hours/year for Section A	=	1,488 hours/year
EQUALS		
Total hours worked/year for Section A		10,992 worked hours/year

Worked Productivity

$$\frac{50{,}000 \text{ units (minutes)/year}}{10{,}992 \text{ worked hours/year}} = \frac{45.5 \text{ units (minutes)}}{\text{worked hour}}$$

Conversion of Worked Productivity to a Percentage

$$45.5 \text{ units (minutes) hours} \quad \div 0.6 \quad = \quad \begin{array}{l} 75.8\% \text{ Worked} \\ \text{productivity} \end{array}$$

The productivity of 45.5 units (minutes) per worked hours indicates that 14.5 minutes of each worked hour is dedicated to activities not measured in workload units or for standby capacity.

3. Calculating Specified Hours and Specified Productivity Figures for Section A

Untimed activities for each employee include one-half hour per week for group in-service education, and 30 minutes per (worked) day for breaks. One technologist spends one-half day per (nonvacation) week in research and development, and another averages five hours per month on purchasing functions. The supervisory technologist spends one quarter of the working day in administrative duties. The computation of specified hours and specified productivity is illustrated below:

Calculating the Hours Spent on Untimed Activities

Group Education:
$$\frac{0.5 \text{ hours}}{\text{week}} \times \frac{49 \text{ weeks}}{\text{year}} \times 6 \text{ FTEs} \quad = \quad 147 \text{ hours/year}$$

Breaks:
$$\frac{0.5 \text{ hours}}{\text{day}} \times \frac{260 - 31 \text{ paid but not worked days}}{\text{year}} \times 6 \text{ FTEs} = 687 \text{ hours/year}$$

R & D:

$$\frac{4 \text{ hours}}{\text{week}} \times \frac{49 \text{ weeks}}{\text{year}} \times 1 \text{ FTE} \qquad = \qquad 196 \text{ hours/year}$$

Purchasing:

$$\frac{5 \text{ hours}}{\text{month}} \times \frac{12 \text{ months}}{\text{year}} \times 1 \text{ FTE} \qquad = \qquad 60 \text{ hours/year}$$

Administration:

$$\frac{2 \text{ hours}}{\text{day}} \times \frac{260 - 31 \text{ paid but not worked days}}{\text{year}} \times 1 \text{ FTE} = 458 \text{ hours/year}$$

Total number of hours spent on untimed activities in Section A	1,548 hours/year

Total Specified Hours per Year

Total worked hours/year for Section A	=	10,992
MINUS		
Total hours spent on untimed activities	=	1,548
EQUALS		
Total specified hours/year for Section A		9,444

Specified Productivity

$$\frac{500,000 \text{ units (minutes)/year}}{9,444 \text{ specified hours/year}} = \frac{52.9 \text{ units (minutes)}}{\text{specified hour}}$$

Conversion of Specified Productivity to a Percentage

$$52.9 \text{ units (minutes)/hour} \div 0.6 \qquad = 88.2\% \text{ Specified productivity}$$

The 1,548 total hours per year spent on non-specified activities for Section A represents 12.4 percent of the paid staff time.

$$\frac{1,548 \text{ non-specified hours/year}}{12,480 \text{ paid hours/year}} \times 100 = 12.4\% \text{ Paid staff time}$$

The difference between the 9,444 total specified hours per year for Section A and the 8,333 workload hours (500,000 workload units (minutes) divided by 60 minutes per hour) or 1,111 hours per year, is due to standby or idle time or due to other unmeasured variations in workflow.

In Section A, the paid productivity of 40.1 units per hour (66.8 percent) is higher than the national median paid productivity for all laboratory sections. The median varies slightly from month to month but ranges from 34 to 36 units per hour for community hospital laboratories and one to three units per hour lower in university and other teaching hospitals.

It may be that the personnel in Section A are more productive than average or it may be that a portion of the work included in the unit values (i.e., initial handling) is performed by personnel assigned to other cost centers. If so, the Section A productivities, as calculated above, are artificially high. If this is the situation, the hours spent by other personnel performing work for Section A must be transferred to Section A in order to get a true productivity picture. This transfer process is called *allocation*. Allocation is discussed next.

Allocation

The objective of allocating overhead hours is to assign these hours fairly to the individual sections based on a reasonable measure of the degree of support provided to each section.

If any laboratory employee works in one functional section, and the workload units for the employee's activities are recorded in the same section productivity calculations are relatively straightforward. However, some laboratory personnel perform activities which constitute support services for more than one section of the laboratory, and many of these activities do not have assigned unit values. Activities such as supervision of quality control/proficiency testing, repetitive telephone result reporting, laboratory management, and secretarial support (excluding patient-related reports) are examples.

These activities generally involve support for more than one functional section and are not included in measurement of laboratory workload, but are essential for the laboratory's operation. The hours expended on such activities are referred to as laboratory overhead hours, or simply overhead hours.

In other instances, workload units for activities performed by employees in one section are recorded in another. An example might be specimen center personnel who are responsible for specimen procurement functions (for which unit values have been assigned and are recorded in the specimen center section), and are also responsible for centrifuging and aliquoting specimens (these activities are included in the workload units that are recorded in other functional sections, e.g., chemistry, hematology).

The laboratory may assign overhead hours by approximating the percentage of these hours which apply to each section. The following suggestions can be used to assign overhead hours:

1. percentage of paid hours
2. percentage of full-time equivalents (FTEs)
3. percentage of total unit values
4. best estimate which could include a sample time diary for each person.

Calculating Total Paid Hours (Paid Hours + Paid Allocated Overhead Hours) for Section A

Determining the allocation percentage

Total FTEs in the laboratory	=	33
Total overhead FTEs to be allocated	=	3
Total FTEs in Section A	=	6

Percentage of overhead hours to be allocated to Section A

$$\frac{6 \text{ FTEs}}{(33 - 3) = 30} \times 100 = 20\% \text{ overhead FTEs}$$

Calculating the number of overhead hours to be allocated to Section A

Total overhead hours paid for laboratory = 6,240 hours/year
   3 FTEs × 2,080 hours/FTE/year

Overhead hours allocated to Section A:
   6,240 hours/year × .20 = 1,248 hours/year

Calculating Total Paid Hours for Section A (including allocated overhead hours)

Paid hours for Section A	=	12,480 hours/year
PLUS		
Overhead hours allocated		
to Section A	=	1,248 hours/year
Total paid hours for		
Section A (including		
allocated overhead hours)		13,728 hours/year

Productivity Based on Total Paid Hours (Paid Hours + Paid Allocated Overhead Hours)

$$\frac{500,000 \text{ units (minutes)/year}}{13,728 \text{ total paid hours/year}} = \frac{36.4 \text{ units/(minutes)}}{\text{Total paid hours}}$$

Conversion to Percentage of Total Paid Hour Productivity

36.4 units (minutes)/hour ÷ 0.6 = 60.7% Total paid productivity

Compare with the calculated productivity of 40.1 units/paid hour.

The allocation methods listed above are examples of the approaches that might be used. However, there is no one correct allocation method; appropriate methods are those which result in meaningful data that can be used to analyze the laboratory's performance. Also, a single allocation method such as that used in the sample calculation need not be used for all component activities of laboratory overhead. Percentage of FTEs might be used to allocate administrative time, while percentage of unit values might be used to allocate time expended on supervision of quality control/proficiency testing, etc.

Also note that overhead allocations are only relevant when dealing with paid and worked hours. In general, overhead hours are excluded when computing specified hours. However, all laboratory overhead hours must be included in total paid and worked hours, before calculating the laboratory's paid and worked productivities, or inflated productivity values result. Furthermore, overhead hours *must* be assigned to individual laboratory sections *before* calculating section productivities.

The example of specimen center personnel who perform activities for which workload units are recorded in other functional sections poses a slightly different problem. In this case, the objective is to correctly relate the workload units recorded with the personnel hours that produced them. One method might be to estimate or time the number of hours spent on specimen procurement functions as opposed to the hours spent on initial handling of specimens. The hours spent on initial handling could then be allocated to the other functional sections, perhaps based on the percentage of requisitions for each section. Another alternative might be to allocate all hours for specimen center personnel to other functional sections and to allocate the specimen procurement workload units to the other functional sections in a similar manner. Again, the allocation method chosen will depend on the problem under study or the management decision being considered. However, it is essential to use consistent allocation methods over time to make valid comparisons of a given section's productivity over the same time period.

Another method for allocating hours for persons who do not work solely for one section is illustrated.

Functional		Percentage of Paid Hours		
		Wash and	Night	Specimen
Sections	Administration	Sterilize	Techs	Center
Microbiology	25%	25%	5%	15%
Chemistry	25%	25%	35%	20%
Urinalysis	7%	7%	5%	15%
Hematology	10%	10%	15%	20%
Histology/Morgue	5%	5%		5%
Cytology	5%	5%		5%
Blood Bank	15%	15%	37%	5%
Immunology	3%	3%		5%
Coagulation	2%	2%	3%	5%
Electrophoresis	3%	3%		5%
	100%	100%	100%	100%

Uses of Productivity Data

Once the paid, worked, and specified productivities have been calculated for a section or for the entire laboratory, it is possible to ask questions and analyze the data. The three productivity figures can be compared with similar figures from other laboratories. For example, if the paid and worked productivities are lower than at other facilities but the non-specified productivity is similar or higher than at other facilities, this means relatively more time is spent on non-specified activities.

Productivity data can be used to make staffing adjustments within cost centers or within the entire laboratory. If the staff in one cost center is overused and in another cost center underused, the workload data can be applied to quantify the imbalances, to identify specific activities that could be transferred, or to change the time of day selected activities are performed. The data can also be used to make skill-mix adjustments. If personnel in most sections participate in the early morning specimen procurement activity, the hours required per section can be determined. It may be possible to reduce costs by using lesser trained staff at lower salary levels.

ANALYSIS OF NON-SPECIFIED ACTIVITY

Why analyze or document this time? Third party payors are not interested in how time is spent in a laboratory, only in the total *price* for the services provided. Administrators are interested in reducing non-essential activities and in reducing the *cost* of laboratory services. In most laboratory analyses, the time required to document non-specified (non-workloaded) activity in detail, far exceeds the time required to document or verify specified (workloaded) activity.

Analysis Methods

There are several possible methods for analyzing and quantifying the time spent on non-specified activities. The decision on which method or methods to use should be based on the size of the laboratory staff and the degree of accuracy desired. The five most common methods are

1. interviews
2. employee diaries
3. direct observation
4. standard data
5. video taping

There are pros and cons to any method including the calendar time and staff time required, current status of employee relations, uniqueness of the section, and availability of special equipment.

A *trained interviewer* can conduct an interview in one to two hours depending on the section and the person being interviewed. Additional time is required for analysis and interpretation. The interviewees may give incorrect answers deliberately or may not be able to quantify the time spent by their employees, particularly personnel working other shifts or weekends. Relatively new supervisors also may have difficulty in knowing how the staff members actually spend their time.

Employee diaries are a common method of collecting data from a large staff, particularly if a section is staffed more than one shift or seven days a week. In some facilities, the forms have been developed to be routinely computer-processed and data are kept every week. A more common approach is to collect data for a short time frame, i.e., one or two weeks, and to use these results as an "average" for an extended time frame. These averages should be reviewed at least every six to 12 months.

Appendix II contains a Non-specified Hours Weekly Worksheet for continuous use. Appendix III contains a Glossary and a blank Employee Diary for a one-time data collection. Each employee completes one diary form per day worked. If the diary is kept for two weeks (14 days), most full-time employees will complete 10 forms (unless on vacation, holiday, or paid sick time). In a laboratory with 50 worked FTEs, 500 forms would have to be analyzed for a two week data collection. The keys to any worksheet or diary are thorough orientation and monitoring by trained personnel.

There are at least two dangers in using employee diaries: employees may expand the time spent on selected activities to show that they were diligently working the entire shift, and the time frame used for the one-time diary may not reflect an average situation. Employees may be hesitant to show standby or idle time. Instead they may record the time as performing laboratory procedures. Also, diaries reflect what is happening, not what should happen. If a section is short-staffed and the employees cannot attend an inservice class, the time for appropriate activity is lost.

In adjusting to average, the person reviewing the diaries should keep in mind activities which happen periodically. For example, if inservice or staff meetings are held monthly and the data collection is for two weeks, there is a 50 percent probability of allowing double the required time and a 50 percent probability of allowing zero time. Orientation is another factor which may or may not occur. For example, if one allowed four weeks nonproductive time per hire and if there were a 20 percent turnover rate in the section, the required orientation time would be 0.615 hours per FTE per week.

$$\frac{\begin{array}{c}4 \text{ weeks} \times 40 \text{ hours per week} \\ \times \ (20\% \ \times \ 0.01 \text{ turnover})\end{array}}{52 \text{ weeks per year}} = 0.615 \text{ Hours per FTE per Week}$$

If the section has 10 full-time staff, 6.15 hours per week would have to be allowed for orientation.

Direct observation requires a trained observer or observers who make enough observations so that the results are statistically valid. For activities which occur less than five percent of the time, it may be necessary to make a total of 1,000 or more observations in order to capture the correct percentage of time. Even a trained observer may not be able to accurately identify functions being performed. For example, the bench technologist observed using the telephone may be recording a STAT test request, giving a STAT result, giving the same result for the third time because someone on the nursing unit did not record the results or lost the report, or making a personal call. It is also difficult to get observers to work weekends, evenings, or nights.

Standard data are used in many departments. This CAP Manual is an example of standard data. The "e" value concept is another example. While there is a significant degree of consistency between laboratories for the specified activities, there is much less consistency for the non-specified activities. An average percentage of time for a given size or type laboratory provides a basis for comparing and validating the data for a given laboratory but should not be blindly used in lieu of a study.

Within a laboratory the results will also vary from section to section so that average percentages should not be used throughout. A laboratory administration section will have significantly more non-specified time than a functional section. Likewise, the percentage of time spent performing specified activity varies by skill level or job title. Section heads may spend less than 50 percent of their worked hours performing specified activities, a senior technologist may spend 75 percent, and a bench technologist may spend 85 percent.

Video taping has been used to develop standard times for specific functions or to analyze a given function. Few institutions and even fewer laboratories have the capability to video tape and convert the activity into standard times. If your organization has management engineering staff expertise available, they should be approached to see how they can be of assistance, be it for video taping or for more traditional studies.

As a result of conducting many laboratory staffing studies, consultants have developed expected operating ranges of the percentage of worked hours spent performing non-specified activities. Typical expected percentages for community hospital laboratories are shown below. Note: *these are for reference only* and are not to be blindly used as standards of performance.

EXPECTED PERCENTAGE OF WORKED HOURS
BY NON-SPECIFIED ACTIVITY
(Entire community hospital laboratory)

Accounting and billing	0-0.5%
Administrative activities	4.5-6.0%
Breaks and personal time	3.5-7.0%
CAP tally	0.5-1.0%
Clerical time	2.5-3.5%
Computer activities	0-2.0%
Education (no formal education program*)	0-0.5%
Education (formal education program*)	1.5-3.0%
In-service education	0.6-1.2%
Orientation	0.8-1.5%
Purchasing	0.5-1.0%
Research and development	0-1.0%

*MT, CT, HT, SBB, Residency, MLT

SUMMARY

Paid, worked, and specified hours and the productivity figures based on each are merely three different ways of representing the performance level of the laboratory. They are calculated using various measurements of personnel resources and are used for different types of analyses and management decisions.

Allocation methods are used to assign overhead hours to the functional sections for which support services are provided. These methods are also used to ensure that workload units and the corresponding personnel hours that produce the units match and are correctly recorded for each section.

Appropriate productivity levels should be defined by the laboratory director and manager in relation to the laboratory's multiple objectives. The primary objective of the clinical laboratory is to produce medical information in the form of test results. In the CAP Workload Recording Method, workload units are used as a measure of the time necessary for the laboratory to meet this objective.

However, there are a number of other objectives such as rapid turnaround time, decreasing hospital length of stay, education, and research and development which are not quantified as outputs in the Workload Recording Method.

In addition, the unit values are themselves averages and there should be no requirement to achieve an ideal productivity. The actual productivity figures for each laboratory may vary depending on differences in methods, facilities, test ordering patterns, patient populations being served, and other individual factors which characterize each laboratory. Target productivities or expected performance levels must be established on an individual basis for each laboratory section and institution. However, when a laboratory's or section's productivity differs substantially from the median derived from participant data in the CAP Computer Assisted Workload Recording Program, the factors which produced the differences should be identified.

Laboratory directors and managers finding that they consistently achieve very high or very low productivities should question their results, verify that they are allocating time correctly, and capturing units and hours correctly. Ultimately, they should examine their laboratory organization, level of service, turnaround time, employee turnover, and other factors.

Chapter 14 Other Management Indicators

The three calculations of productivity (units per paid hour, units per worked hour, and units per specified hour) can be used not only to assess productivity but also to identify problem areas. With appropriate calculations, laboratory managers can make intralaboratory and inter-laboratory comparisons. In addition, productivity on various shifts can be monitored to select among available alternatives for staffing, instrumentation, and other factors. Most hospitals experience a month-to-month fluctuation in census (e.g., December is usually low), and WLR Method permits assessment of the effects of such fluctuations on productivity. This, of course, may help in determining staffing needs.

The overall productivity and cost-effectiveness of the laboratory resources depend on two processes:

1. the efficient use of resources within the laboratory (e.g., technologists' time and skill mix, various equipment configurations, the physical layout of the benches, the recording and reporting systems in place)
2. the efficient use of the laboratory as a resource within the institution (e.g., the volume and scope of services per admission or Diagnosis Related Group (DRG), uneven demand for services, duplicative or inappropriate testing sequences)

The three types of productivity indicators discussed help management evaluate the efficiency of the laboratory resources used to produce laboratory services by section and as a whole. Monitoring these productivity indicators routinely, as well as comparing the trends and levels with similar laboratories and institutions provides management with an important tool to identify unusual/unacceptable patterns.

This analysis may guide management's investigation and reveal opportunities for productivity improvement. Tracking the relationship between the laboratory volume of activity (in workload units) relative to the institution's volume of activity may reveal trends and/or patterns in using the laboratory as a resource. For example, hospital laboratory management may review and monitor the following ratios:

$$\frac{\text{Total inpatient WLU}}{\text{Total patient days}} = \text{Average WLU per patient day}$$

$$\frac{\text{Total WLU}}{\substack{\text{Total discharges} \\ \text{or Total admissions}}} = \substack{\text{Average WLU per discharge} \\ \text{or admission}}$$

$$\frac{\text{Total WLU}}{\text{No. of physicians}} = \text{Average WLU per physician}$$

Trends found in these indicators also may suggest opportunities for further investigation. Hospital administration, accounting, and/or management engineering staff may provide useful guidance, ideas, and additional data that may provide insight into the underlying factors. It may be appropriate to conduct a special study, analysis, or data collection activity to get to the root of a problem/situation. For example, perhaps the laboratory's WLUs could be collected/analyzed on the basis of patient age (e.g., over 65), or DRG, or origin (e.g., zip code) for a limited period to provide additional data for analysis of the laboratory's use as a resource.

QUALITY EVALUATION OF WORKLOAD DATA

The CAP Workload Recording Method, when used in a consistent and uniform manner, is an excellent management tool. Those charged with administration of the laboratory *must* know the Method is being used appropriately since workload data can assist in making staffing, space, equipment, and technical methodology decisions.

Professionals constantly strive for excellence; therefore, it becomes extremely important to know that there exists a means for providing this reassurance. Unfortunately, workload data may not always be collected and used in the manner outlined in this Manual. This may be the result of legitimate error in data handling, lack of knowledge or understanding relating to the use of the Method, or deliberate misuse. Users must identify inappropriate use of the Method and institute corrective action.

One of the easiest ways to monitor the quality of workload data is through the use of graphs. When data is graphically displayed, it usually allows easier detection of trends as they emerge. Three graphs that can monitor the quality of CAP workload data are illustrated: 1) Graph number one plots CAP Workload Units versus Time, 2) Graph number two plots Raw Counts versus Time, and 3) Graph number three plots the Ratio of Workload Units/Raw Counts versus Time.

In a laboratory, the total unit values and raw counts produced will vary from month to month, especially on a seasonal basis. However, the ratio between these two values remains constant as long as major changes do not occur in the laboratory workload pattern. A major change in chemistry instrumentation, such as a significant increase in the level of automation, is an example of a change that would have an impact on the workload units/raw count ratio. When data suggests a significant change, management should investigate and understand reasons for the change.

This ratio will provide the average *unit value* for the section. Compare the average unit value for each section to quickly identify areas that have high labor requirements. A labor intensive section will be most sensitive to increases in test volume, scheduling changes, staffing freezes, etc. This can better prepare one to react to any new developments.

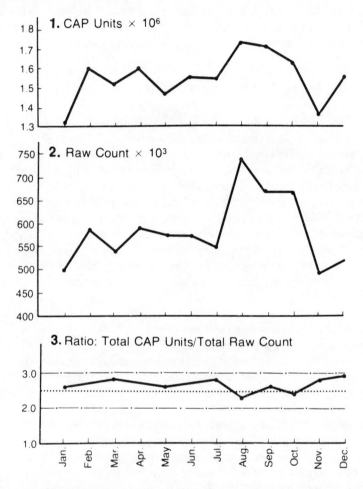

THE EFFECT OF BATCH SIZE AND STAT LOAD ON LABORATORY PRODUCTIVITY FIGURES

By its nature, the CAP Workload Recording Method averages out the effects of batch size and assumes an average STAT load. If a laboratory has an unusually large batch size (e.g., a large independent laboratory running thousands of specimens per day through an analyzer) or an unusually high STAT load (an intensive care unit laboratory where all specimens are run STAT), the expected productivity figures will be quite different from the average laboratory. A laboratory director or hospital administrator must take these variations into account when interpreting productivity figures. While the CAP does not yet have the data to recommend a specific conversion factor or formula to adjust these figures, the following general principles should be kept in mind:

- Unusually large batch sizes will spread the instrument setup, reagent preparation, and technical supervision components over a larger number of specimens, reducing the actual time input required per specimen. Accordingly, productivity will increase.
- High STAT percentages will require more in the way of instrument setup and specimen handling for each individual specimen. Therefore, productivity may decrease. Unfortunately, the degree to which it may decrease is volume- and machine-dependent, so that a general factor to be applied to one's STAT percentage to correct for this tendency cannot be recommended.

The CAP WLR Committee is considering several projects to enhance the WLR system. Included in these projects is one to quantitatively assess the effects of these unusual batch sizes. The Committee welcomes such laboratories as volunteers to perform time studies on these topics.

HOSPITAL ADMINISTRATION WORKLOAD INDICES

Laboratory directors should be aware that many hospital administrators submit management and financial information to their professional organizations in addition to the information required by regulatory and reimbursement agencies. The monthly *Monitrend* reports, offered by the Hospital Administrative Services (HAS) division of the American Hospital Association, are of prime interest. More than half of the hospitals in the United States subscribe to the *Monitrend* program. The Laboratory/Blood Bank section of the report is based upon CAP Workload Recording data. The *Monitrend* contains ratios relating laboratory expenses and revenues to workload, to total hospital expense by category, and to patient days or discharges. Some key laboratory ratios are

- WLUs/adjusted patient day
- percentage charged WLUs/total WLUs
- revenue/100 WLUs

- direct expense/adjusted patient day
- direct expense/100 WLUs
- salary expense/100 WLUs
- physician remuneration/100 WLUs
- ratio of total direct expenses/revenues
- direct expense percentage (of total hospital operating expense)
- outpatient revenue percentage
- paid hours/100 WLUs
- worked hours/100 WLUs

There are several other agencies, including many state regulatory commissions, which base their action on such reports. The important thing to remember is that the hospital submits the data. The laboratory director must ensure that the workload data are accurately generated by the laboratory. Hospital administration will usually extract hours and expenses from their own records and may try to derive total workload figures from billing records. Billing records usually do not include quality control, standard, or repeat tallies. The laboratory manager should ask to review the data before input and check it for accuracy (e.g., verify the hour totals, making sure that physicians, doctoral level scientists, and students are not included). Many hospital management decisions may be based on comparative data and if total workload is not accurately reported, inappropriate decisions may result.

THE MANAGEMENT ENGINEERING APPROACH TO LABORATORY DATA

Management engineers design operating systems to effectively use the resources assigned to achieve a set of tasks. They evaluate the nature of the tasks to be done, the flow of the work, the structure or layout of the work area, the productivity of the equipment and of the people, and the interrelationships of all these elements in the area under study. They evaluate opportunities for improving the overall productivity of the area by manipulating the components of these various elements that can be altered, such as:

- equipment configuration
- vacation schedules
- work distribution by shift
- methods for handling unusual or STAT requests

- increasing or decreasing volume by taking on or sending out reference work

These engineers also determine how to accommodate those components which cannot be altered over the short term, such as those listed.

- location of the sinks
- layout of the hospital complex or campus
- STAT demand due to emergency room activity

(Note: Over the long term, it may be a wise decision to adjust the above three more concrete elements if the benefits substantially outweigh the costs to the organization as a whole.)

Management engineers develop standards that help the management team evaluate the need for staff and capital equipment, and the productivity of the current resources. These can be compared to budgeted expectations, historical performance, or to an ideal performance level. These are developed based on a projected volume of total work to be done, and an expected or agreed on performance level or productivity goal.

The *total measured workload hours* are known as specified hours reflecting time spent on tests and procedures with assigned WLU values *specified* in the Manual. Management engineers often refer to this as the variable component of the laboratory's total work, because it varies directly with the volume of units of service. The CAP unit value per procedure represents one minute of time, which also can be expressed as .0167 hours. Management engineers often inflate the actual CAP WLU count by seven percent to 10 percent to more fully account for Personal, Fatigue, and Delay time.

The *additional hours* are referred to as the *non-specified* or *non-workloaded* hours. Management engineers may refer to this as the constant component, because it is often a constant amount of time added to the workload each day or period. The specific amount added may be an average based on actual measurement or observation, or it may be an estimate of the time spent by staff on the activities not captured in the CAP Workload Recording Method.

Theoretically, the sum of the total specified workload hours and the non-specified constant hours is the total working hours required to handle the laboratory's actual workload.

This total working hours figure is then modified by the target utilization, productivity, or performance goal for the work area. This target utilization is generally set between 90 percent and 95 percent of the total required working hours figure depending on the desired standby capacity, the type of facility, the number of shifts staffed per day, and the fluctuating workload. The resulting figure is an estimated worked staffing requirement for the area.

Dividing this figure by the number of hours a full-time staff person (or one FTE) has available to do the work will yield the working staff complement needed to handle the laboratory's activity. Because the benefit package includes paid time off (such as vacation, holiday, and sick time) the actual number of FTEs that must be hired to do this work will generally increase 12 percent to 18 percent, depending on the laboratory's specific policies.

Example: Computation of FTEs Required Using a Management Engineering Approach

1. Total measured workload adjusted for PFD =

$$\underset{\substack{\text{Actual specified} \\ \text{workload units}}}{} \times \underset{\substack{\text{Conversion factor} \\ \text{to hours/year}}}{} \times \underset{\substack{\text{PFD adjustment} \\ + 7\%}}{}$$

850,000 WLUs × 0.0167 hours/ × 1.07 = 15,189 hours/year
WLU

2. $\underset{\substack{\text{Total working hours} \\ \text{required}}}{} = \underset{\substack{\text{Total measured} \\ \text{workload adjusted} \\ \text{for PFD}}}{} + \underset{\substack{\text{Total additional work} \\ \left(\substack{\text{non-specified work} \\ \text{expressed in hours}}\right)}}{}$

18,000 hours/year = 15,189 hours/year + 2,811 hours/year

3. $\underset{\substack{\text{Actual worked hours} \\ \text{required}}}{} = \dfrac{\substack{\text{Total working} \\ \text{hours required}}}{\substack{\text{Target productivity} \\ \text{or utilization rate} \\ 90\%*}}$

$20{,}000 \text{ hours/year} = \dfrac{18{,}000 \text{ hours/year}}{.90*}$

4. $\underset{\substack{\text{Total working FTEs} \\ \text{required/year}}}{} = \dfrac{\substack{\text{Actual worked hours} \\ \text{required}}}{\text{Hours/FTE/year}}$

$\underset{\substack{\text{9.62 working FTEs} \\ \text{required/year}}}{} = \dfrac{20{,}000 \text{ hours/year}}{2{,}080 \text{ hours/FTE/year}}$

5. $\underset{\substack{\text{Total paid FTEs} \\ \text{required/year}}}{} = \underset{\substack{\text{Total working} \\ \text{FTEs required/year}}}{} \times \underset{\substack{\text{Benefit Package} \\ \text{(allowance for} \\ \text{paid time off)} \\ 14.5\%*}}{}$

$\underset{\substack{\text{11.0 paid FTEs} \\ \text{required/year}}}{} = 9.62 \times 1.145*$

*This figure may vary from institution to institution.

Chapter 15 Computers and the Workload Recording Method

Computers relate to the Workload Recording Method (WLR) in two principal ways—first, laboratory computers have a significant positive effect on productivity, as measured using the WLR Method. Secondly, both in-laboratory and remote (CAP) computers can be of considerable assistance in the use of the Method.

EFFECT OF LABORATORY COMPUTERIZATION ON PRODUCTIVITY

The numerous papers, books, etc. published to date on the effect of laboratory computerization on productivity support the contention that laboratory computerization markedly enhances productivity of laboratory personnel. This is especially true in the automation of clerical tasks, such as sorting, filing, and result inquiry. Certainly, a laboratory which desires to produce more work without adding staff would be well-advised to computerize its workflow and reporting system. Presently, the CAP Workload Recording Committee continues to recommend the same unit values be used in both types of laboratories. However, a valid argument can be made that the workload unit values which were developed in a laboratory using a manual reporting system are no longer appropriate in a computerized laboratory.

The CAP Workload Recording Committee has received several requests for assignment of unit values to data processing activities, such as daily computer backup, file maintenance, computer programming, systems analysis, etc. To date, the Committee has been impressed by the variability of these activities between different vendor's computer systems. Certain computer-related activities, such as daily backup, may eventually be sufficiently standardized to allow definition of values.

Personnel hours related to data processing should be handled as follows: those hours devoted to production of test results, including printing reports, result review logs, login of specimens, etc., should be allocated to sections as a part of specified hours. Activities not directly related to result production, including daily backup, production of billing reports, periodic maintenance of hardware and files, programming, systems analysis, etc., should be tabulated as non-specified hours.

Certain laboratory computer vendors claim, with some justification, that their systems are "more efficient" and result in greater productivity gains than other competitive systems. To date, it has not been possible to quantitate such findings. In the future, the Committee may undertake time studies and possibly even assign unit values to specimen login, result entry, etc., on various vendor-developed systems which would enable users of the Method to make such comparisons. The CAP welcomes your comments on this, please write us at the CAP Skokie Office.

CAP COMPUTER ASSISTED WORKLOAD RECORDING PROGRAM

The College of American Pathologists has for several years offered a Computer Assisted Workload Recording Program for the tabulation and calculation of workload data, and for the production of inter-laboratory comparative statistics.

This Program is now available in three forms:

1. manual input
2. microcomputer input
3. laboratory computer input (by compatible tape) and via modem in compatible format

The *Manual Input* (centralized data processing mainframe) *Program* provides the user laboratory with customized input forms for recording raw counts of individual procedures. Handwritten numbers, recorded on the Data Input Forms, are mailed to the CAP Computer Center and then entered into the laboratory's files. Hard copies of the *User Procedure File List* and *Comparative Analysis Report* are mailed monthly to the participant.

The *Microcomputer Input Program* maintains laboratory workload data on an in-laboratory microcomputer which allows daily in-laboratory workload management. The user can produce several reports on site, yet take advantage of peer comparisons, quality control, and the other unique features of the mainframe program by transmitting monthly data over telephone lines to the CAP Computer Center. The comparative data is generated and then transmitted back to the laboratory.

For those laboratories with large, vendor-supported laboratory computer systems, the *Laboratory Computer Input Program* has the capability of accepting accumulated data via telecommunication from the laboratory computer. Specifications are available from the CAP Computer Center. To participate in this Program, however, the laboratory computer software must properly count, accumulate, and transmit workload data. Any software modifications necessary in the laboratory's software are the responsibility of the laboratory and/or laboratory computer vendor, not the CAP. Comparative reports are transmitted back to the laboratory via telephone modem for printing.

Quality Control

One of the important advantages of submitting the laboratory's workload data to the CAP Computer Assisted Workload Recording Program, even if one has an in-house laboratory computer system, is the Program's extensive system of data quality control. Fifteen years of experience with the data from hundreds of laboratories has permitted the development of sophisticated error-detection algorithms. This capability helps to ensure that the calculated productivities may be relied on by both laboratory management and institution administration in making decisions on laboratory staffing and scheduling.

Reports

The Computer Assisted Workload Program generates a number of types of reports. The laboratory's *User Procedure File List* provides detail of the procedures performed in each functional section (as defined by the laboratory). Each entry reflects the current month's raw count and total workload for each of the nine standard input sources (e.g., inpatient, outpatient, emergency room, etc.). The *Monthly Comparative Analysis Report* lists (by section) total raw count, total unit value, total worked and paid hours, and the calculated productivity figures. The current month's paid productivity is also compared with the preceding six-, and 12-month averages. Median paid productivities for peer laboratories and all participating laboratories are provided for each standard section and for the total laboratory.

In the quarterly *Statistical Analysis Summary,* the laboratory's three-, six-, and 12-month productivities are calculated for each standard section. Three-month median productivity data for peer laboratories and for all participating laboratories also are computed for each section. The laboratory's data are summarized by reporting source, and various ratios and indices useful in laboratory management are displayed.

Periodic *Histograms* allow participants to easily compare and contrast themselves with institutions of similar bed size and type.

The reports are designed to organize the information needed to manage the laboratory. Six- and 12-month data averages highlight changes and trends within the laboratory. Overall laboratory and individual section productivities can be used for internal assessment of laboratory activities and comparison with peer institutions. These reports can serve as the basis for establishing methods for staffing and scheduling, and serve as an organized record of the laboratory's activities.

TABULATION OF WORKLOAD DATA WITH VENDOR-SUPPORTED LABORATORY COMPUTER SYSTEMS

Before the essential data elements and rules for tabulation of workload data using an in-laboratory computer can be described, the importance of submitting the laboratory's data to the CAP Workload Recording Program must be emphasized:

- The Method is not static. It is vitally important for every laboratory to have comparative productivity data, so that the laboratory's performance against appropriate peer groups can be judged on an on-going basis, particularly as the Method evolves from year to year.
- In-laboratory systems lack the quality control capabilities inherent in the CAP Program. Without this monthly checking, the laboratory runs a significantly increased risk of undetected erroneous tabulations and distorted productivity figures.
- The CAP Program is the largest and most accurate comparative data base of laboratory workload data in the United States. It is important for all users of the Method to help build and maintain this data base, both for their own use in comparing their productivity with other laboratories, and for providing a solid basis for updates in the Method over time.

WORKLOAD DATA TABULATION ON AN IN-LABORATORY COMPUTER

Workload data should be captured as a by-product of normal specimen login and result entry, rather than requiring the technologist to remember to separately enter a tally of items. Therefore, whenever a result is entered, a specimen is run on an automated instrument, etc., a raw count must be tallied. Special programming is required to ensure that the workload is properly tallied (e.g., documenting the chemistry specimen level workload, accurately tallying slides in histology).

Because the CAP Workload Method assigns different unit values to the same test depending on the method used, every result entered must be associated with the method required to produce that result before the workload can be tallied. For some methods (e.g., referral of specimens to an outside laboratory), a count can be accrued only once for an entire accession.

Statistics may include the number of times each test was performed (for the day, month, and year-to-date) broken down by method, with section and laboratory totals. Subdivision of these by ordering mode (panel versus individual order) and test priority (STAT, ASAP, routine) is helpful in determining laboratory capital equipment and staffing requirements. A breakdown by shift (with user-specified shift demarcations) is an essential tool for determination of staffing levels on evening and night shifts—ideally, one would be able to define the shift demarcations independently for different laboratory departments, or even workstation, but in any case the day shift technologist working overtime should be able to override the "default" shift allocation of the work units produced.

A useful comparative statistic is the *total number of specimens processed,* daily, monthly, and year-to-date. This is of particular importance in microbiology, where, for some applications, specimen per FTE per year is a more appropriate comparative statistic than worked productivity.

A detailed report might display both raw counts and CAP weighted workload units for each procedure performed by the laboratory staff (including phlebotomy, report delivery, blood bank QC, and other functions which may not be linked directly to a patient test result). Separate tabulations might be provided for each of the nine specimen sources (inpatient, outpatient, emergency room, etc.).

While some laboratory computer systems provide the capability to insert the number of worked and paid hours for each section and shift in the laboratory, the laboratory may be better off to interface the laboratory computer system with the Microcomputer Input Program of the CAP Computer Assisted Program.

In addition to paid and worked hours, the laboratory can tabulate and enter non-specified time for a more complete and accurate assessment of productivity. Laboratory computers can provide a convenient and reliable "notepad" for recording and tabulating such time.

A daily workstation report which lists numbers of patient tests, repeats, dilutions, QC samples, calibrations with weighted workload compares the hours of technologist time (from the security/signon system). It also may assist the laboratory manager in calculating an effective workstation productivity and in deciding on staffing reallocation.

Chapter 16 Other Factors

TEST PRICING

Caveat! The Method, by itself, is not adequate for price setting.
The Method incorporates only the labor component of testing; the cost of capital equipment, overhead, and reagents is not included. Therefore, use of the workload unit value as a *relative value,* to set a price, has serious pitfalls. Two possible examples are as follows.

Example 1: A laboratory determined that it produced 10 million workload units annually, at a cost (including overhead and margin) of $10 million. If the laboratory charged $1 per workload unit, this would result in a SMAC panel charge of $2.50, which totally overlooks the $350,000 capital cost of the instrument and the $100,000 annual reagent cost.

Example 2: In setting the price for a 10 minute test of fetal maturity, another laboratory discovered that the commercial kit for the test cost $50 per patient. Applying a blanket relative value approach would result in a loss of $40 on each test.

Obviously, factors such as test volume, numbers of quality control procedures, and overhead vary widely from one laboratory to another.

SCHEDULING OF STAFF BASED ON CAP WORKLOAD RECORDING STATISTICS

If a mechanism is developed to accumulate CAP workload statistics by day of week and by shift, this information can be used to staff according to procedure volume. However, one cannot short change the laboratory staff during usually slack times (e.g., Saturday evenings), because of the necessity of having adequate staff to handle the occasional heavy STAT load (e.g., when the victims of a multicar freeway accident arrive at the emergency room on a Saturday night). To balance these needs, it may be most cost-effective to schedule some infrequently performed routine work for the slack periods to justify having sufficient staff on duty to handle unexpected emergencies.

RESCHEDULING OF TESTING TO SHORTEN HOSPITAL LENGTH OF STAY

The advent of prospective pricing for Medicare patients radically changes the financial considerations in the hospital laboratory. One can no longer look at the cost of the laboratory in isolation. A policy that might improve efficiency of a laboratory, such as scheduling a given test to be run only once a week, could have a negative effect on total hospital cost by increasing length of stay. The CAP Workload Recording Method is an excellent tool to determine exactly what the cost of running an assay daily would be (as opposed to twice a week). This can then be balanced against the cost increase of length of stay resulting from a patient being held in the hospital awaiting test results.

SELECTION OF CAPITAL EQUIPMENT

A vital part of the evaluation of any proposed instrument should be assessment of the projected labor costs over five years. The only objective, unbiased measure available is the CAP Workload Recording unit value. Taking the projected test volume to calculate batch size, and adding necessary standards and quality control specimens, multiplied by the permanent or the temporary (t) unit value, it is possible to derive a precise measure of the labor cost of running the instrument. [The temporary (t) and extrapolated (e) values should be used cautiously for this purpose because of the relatively minimal timing data on which they are based.] Of course, one also must calculate the labor cost of the initial method evaluation and training.

Section III Procedure Lists

Chapter 17 Categories of Information Reflected in the Lists of Procedures

The following line items illustrate the information contained in the Procedure Lists. The Procedure Lists are arranged in three ways: numerically by code number, alphabetically by procedure name, and alphabetically by procedure name within each of the standard sections.

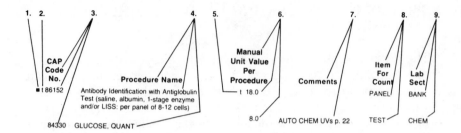

1. ■: indicates a major change in this edition.
2. t: indicates that a temporary unit value is assigned to this procedure.
   e: indicates that an extrapolated unit value has been assigned.
   No qualifiers before a value indicates that it is a permanent unit value.
3. CAP Code No.: the five-digit code identifying the procedure.
4. Procedure Name: describes a sequence of technical, clerical, and aide steps constituting a laboratory activity.
5. t: indicates that a temporary unit value is assigned to this procedure.
   e: indicates that an extrapolated unit value has been assigned.
   No qualifiers before a value indicates that it is a permanent unit value.
6. Manual Unit Value Per Procedure: the number of laboratory workload units (minutes) of technical, clerical, and aide time required to perform all the activities to complete the defined procedure once. Unit values for automated instruments can be found in the standard sections where they are used (e.g., blood bank, chemistry, hematology, histology, immunology, and microbiology).
7. Comments: Auto Chem UVs p. 22: refers the user to the Chemistry Chapter to identify the suffix code and unit value for the procedure if it is performed with an automated instrument. The same applies to procedures in other sections that are performed on automated instruments.
8. Item for Count: defines what is to be counted to obtain the raw count for each procedure.
9. Lab Sect.: indicates the CAP standard section in which this procedure is classified.

Chapter 20 Procedure List: Alphabetically by Procedure Name within Each Standard Section

CAP Code No.	Procedure Name	Manual Unit Value per Procedure	Comments	Item for Count	Lab Sect
		BLOOD BANK			
86081	ABO Cell and Rh$_o$(D) Typing, Slide or Tube (includes D^u typing when indicated)	5.0		SPEC	BANK
86080	ABO Cell and Serum Typing, Slide or Tube	5.0		SPEC	BANK
86082	ABO Cell, Serum, and Rh$_o$(D) Typing, Slide or Tube (includes D^u typing when indicated)	7.0	Auto BB UVs p. 19	SPEC	BANK
86084	ABO Cell Typing, Slide or Tube (e.g., retyping donor units, retyping recipient clots)	2.0		TEST	BANK
86083	ABO Hemolysin Test	5.0		SPEC	BANK
86086	ABO Serum Typing, Tube (e.g., typing plasma)	2.0		TEST	BANK
■ t 86196	Alarm Activation Blood Storage Refrigerator or Freezer [periodic (monthly) high-low temperature alarm activation check]	t 20.0		FUNCT	BANK
86135	Antibody Absorption	5.0		ABSRP	BANK
86167	Antibody Detection as Part of a Type and Screen (consists of saline and potentiating media phases, either or both of which are converted to an antiglobulin phase)	10.0		TEST	BANK
86148	Antibody Detection, Capillary Testing (saline, albumin, enzyme, or LISS)	*		TEST	BANK
86168	Antibody Detection (screen) Performed with a Crossmatch (consists of saline and potentiating media phases, either or both of which are converted to an antiglobulin phase)	10.0		TEST	BANK
86144	Antibody Detection (screen) with Antiglobulin Test (2-stage enzyme or LISS)	25.0		BATCH[1]	BANK
86139	Antibody Detection (screen) with Antiglobulin Test (saline, albumin, 1-stage enzyme and/or LISS)	20.0		BATCH[1]	BANK
86142	Antibody Detection (screen) without Antiglobulin Test (2-stage enzyme or LISS)	15.0		BATCH[1]	BANK
86140	Antibody Detection (screen) without Antiglobulin Test (saline, albumin, cold, 1-stage enzyme and/or LISS)	10.0		BATCH[1]	BANK
86150	Antibody Elution (heat, ether, alcohol, or chloroform)	20.0		SPEC	BANK
86156	Antibody Identification Capillary Testing (saline, albumin, enzyme or LISS)	*		PANEL	BANK
86160	Antibody Identification with Antiglobulin Test (2-stage enzyme or LISS: per panel of 8-12 cells)	32.0		PANEL	BANK

* = no unit value   [1]See Chapter 4 Blood Bank
t = temporary unit value
e = extrapolated unit value

CAP Code No.	Procedure Name	Manual Unit Value per Procedure	Comments	Item for Count	Lab Sect
t 86152	Antibody Identification with Antiglobulin Test (saline, albumin, 1-stage enzyme and/or LISS: per panel of 8-12 cells)	t 18.0		PANEL	BANK
86158	Antibody Indentification without Antiglobulin Test (2-stage enzyme or LISS: per panel of 8-12 cells)	30.0		PANEL	BANK
86154	Antibody Indentification without Antiglobulin Test (saline, albumin, cold, 1-stage enzyme and/or LISS: per panel of 8-12 cells)	15.0		PANEL	BANK
86161	Antibody Titration (with or without potentiating media, enzyme and/or antihuman globulin phase)	20.0		ANTIG	BANK
86120	Antigen Blood Type, Slide or Tube Direct Agglutination (e.g., Rh antigens, M, N)	2.0		ANTIG	BANK
86125	Antigen Blood Type with Antiglobulin Test (e.g., Fy^a, Jk^a)	4.0		ANTIG	BANK
86250	Antiglobulin Test, Direct	4.0		TEST	BANK
■ t 86199	Blood Bank Instrument Thermometer Reading and Temperature Recording, Daily (e.g,, reading a water bath's thermometer and recording the temperature, reading an incubator's thermometer and recording the temperature)	t 0.5		FUNCT	BANK
■e 86820	Blood Unit Credit Function, Clerical per Unit	e 3.0		UNIT	BANK
■ t 86129	Blood Unit Labeling (final product label on red cell unit)	t 2.5		UNIT	BANK
86131	Blood, Component or Derivative (delivery of blood or components by blood bank personnel to another location within the institution)	5.0		DELIV	BANK
86134	Blood, Component or Derivative (issue to or receive from other location in same hospital)	2.0		UNIT	BANK
86132	Blood, Component or Derivative (issue to or receive from outside blood bank or other hospital)	2.0		UNIT	BANK
■ t 86200	Blood Storage Refrigerator or Freezer Temperature Chart Change	t 3.0		FUNCT	BANK
■ t 86198	Blood Storage Refrigerator or Freezer Thermometer Reading and Temperature Recording, Daily (includes reading 3 thermometers and recording 3 temperatures per instrument)	t 1.10		FUNCT	BANK
t 86190	Calibrating Centrifuge	t 36.0		CENTFG	BANK
t 86192	Checking Tachometer on Centrifuge	t 3.0		CENTFG	BANK
t 86194	Checking Timer on Centrifuge	t 5.0		CENTFG	BANK
86166	Compatibility Test: Crossmatch (consists of saline and potentiating media phases, either or both of which are converted to an antiglobulin phase)	7.0		TEST	BANK
e 86164	Compatibility Test: Crossmatch (saline phase only)	e 5.0		TEST	BANK
86271	Cryoprecipitate Preparation	17.0		UNIT	BANK

* = no unit value
t = temporary unit value
e = extrapolated unit value

CAP Code No.	Procedure Name	Manual Unit Value per Procedure	Comments	Item for Count	Lab Sect
86269	Cryoprecipitate Preparation (applies when 4 or more units are prepared simultaneously)	*		UNIT	BANK
86272	Cryoprecipitate Thawing and Pooling (each unit, thawing and pooling into a single pool)	3.0		UNIT	BANK
■ t 86403	Decontamination of Lymphocyte Cell Preparation (e.g., platelets, granulocytes)	t 2.0		SPEC	BANK
86133	Donor, Blood Collection, 1 Unit (includes history, physical, and phlebotomy)	22.0		DONOR	BANK
■ t 86819	Donor Recruitment: In-Community (per donor drawn; includes all activities associated with recruitment)	t 7.8		DONOR	BANK
86818	Donor Recruitment: In-Hospital[1]	*		DONOR	BANK
86825	Donor Rejected (includes donor history and/ or physical prior to rejection)	11.0		DONOR	BANK
■ t 86206	Fetal Maternal Bleed Screening Test for Detection of Rh_o (D) Positive Cells Using a Commercial Rosette Technique Kit (e.g., Gamma Biologics, Ortho Diagnostics) Includes Positive and Negative Controls	t 6.9		TEST	BANK
86800	Fresh Frozen Plasma Preparation	10.0		UNIT	BANK
t 86801	Fresh Frozen Plasma Preparation (applies when 4 or more units are prepared simultaneously)	t 4.0		UNIT	BANK
86805	Fresh Frozen Plasma, Thawing	5.0		UNIT	BANK
86275	Frozen Blood Preparation	25.0		UNIT	BANK
86276	Frozen Blood: Thaw and Deglycerolization	90.0	Auto BB UVs p. 19	UNIT	BANK
86176	HBsAg Blood Donor Confirmation: ELISA	*		TEST	BANK
86172	HBsAg Blood Donor Confirmation: RIA	*		TEST	BANK
86174	HBsAg Blood Donor Confirmation: RPHA	*		TEST	BANK
t 86175	HBsAg Blood Donor: ELISA (batch processing)	t 1.6		SPEC	BANK
t 86171	HBsAg Blood Donor: RIA (batch processing)	t 1.3		TEST	BANK
86173	HBsAg Blood Donor: RPHA	*		TEST	BANK
86177	HLA Antibody Screen: by Lymphocytotoxicity	*		SPEC	BANK
86179	HLA Compatibility Testing (crossmatch) by Lymphocytotoxicity	*		TEST	BANK
■ t 86197	HLA Lymphocyte Cell Count after Lymphocyte Separation	t 1.5		SPEC	BANK
■ t 86202	HLA Lymphocyte Cell Count and Adjustment after Lymphocyte Separation	t 3.0		SPEC	BANK
■ t 86203	HLA Lymphocyte Viability after Lymphocyte Separation	t 2.0		SPEC	BANK
■ t 86182	HLA Phenotype: A,B,C Complete: by Lymphocytotoxicity (initial tray)	t 40.0		SPEC	BANK
■ t 86181	HLA Phenotype: A,B,C Complete: by Lymphocytotoxicity (each additional tray prepared simultaneously on same specimen)	t 23.0		SPEC	BANK
■ t 86188	HLA Phenotype Dr: by Lymphocytotoxicity (initial tray)	t 51.0		SPEC	BANK
■ t 86189	HLA Phenotype Dr: by Lymphocytotoxicity (each additional tray prepared simultaneously on same specimen)	t 25.0		SPEC	BANK

* = no unit value   [1]See Chapter 4 Blood Bank
t = temporary unit value
e = extrapolated unit value

CAP Code No.	Procedure Name	Manual Unit Value per Procedure	Comments	Item for Count	Lab Sect
86178	HLA Single Antigen Screening: by Lymphocytotoxicity (e.g., B27)	*		SPEC	BANK
86185	HLA Typing Tray Production for Lymphocytotoxicity (60 well)	*		TRAY	BANK
■e 86170	HTLV-III Antibody Blood Donor: Abbott EIA (batch processing)	e 2.0		TEST	BANK
t 86847	Inhibition/Neutralization (to include S_da, P_1, WBC, ABO)	t 6.0		TEST	BANK
86850	Inventory[1]	0.4		UNIT	BANK
86183	Irradiation of Blood Component	*		UNIT	BANK
86383	Leukapheresis	*	Auto BB UVs p. 19	DONOR	BANK
86180	Leukoagglutinin Compatibility Testing	*		TEST	BANK
86187	Leukoagglutinin Screen	*		SPEC	BANK
86382	Leukocyte Poor Blood Preparation (single wash)	10.0		UNIT	BANK
■ t 86186	Lymphocyte Separation from Blood Density Gradient (e.g., Ficoll)	t 18.0		SPEC	BANK
■ 86409	Lymphocyte Separation from Solid Tissue (e.g., lymph node, spleen)	*		SPEC	BANK
■ t 86184	Lymphocyte Separation: T and B Cell (by nylon wool)	t 22.0		SPEC	BANK
86384	Lymphocyte Storage, Liquid Nitrogen	10.0		CELLRG	BANK
■ 86195	Lymphocyte Thawing	*		CELLRG	BANK
86219	Lyophilized Coagulation Concentrate Reconstitution	5.0		UNIT	BANK
t 86848	Microplate Hemagglutination Technique— ABO and Rh_0(D) Typing (includes D^u typing when indicated)	t 1.2		SPEC	BANK
t 86849	Microplate Hemagglutination Technique— Serum Typing and Antibody Screen	t 1.5		SPEC	BANK
■ 86407	Mitogen Assay: Pulse, Harvest, and Counting	*		SPEC	BANK
■ 86406	Mitogen Assay: Setup	*		SPEC	BANK
■ 86405	Mixed Lymphocyte Culture: Pulse, Harvest, and Counting	*		SPEC	BANK
■ 86404	Mixed Lymphocyte Culture: Setup	*		SPEC	BANK
t 86796	Packed Red Blood Cells (applies when 4 or more units are prepared simultaneously by centrifugation; includes plasma disposition documentation)	t 2.0		UNIT	BANK
t 86795	Packed Red Blood Cells (preparation by centrifugation and removing plasma; includes plasma disposition documentation)	t 6.0		UNIT	BANK
86790	Packed Red Blood Cells (preparation by sedimentation and removing plasma; includes plasma disposition documentation)	5.0		UNIT	BANK
86840	Phlebotomy, Therapeutic	20.0		UNIT	BANK
86845	Phlebotomy, Therapeutic, Bedside	30.0		UNIT	BANK
86389	Plasmapheresis Additional Units (manual)	50.0		UNIT	BANK
86387	Plasmapheresis First Unit (manual)	70.0		UNIT	BANK
86388	Platelet Agglutinins	45.0		PANEL	BANK

* = no unit value   [1]See Chapter 4 Blood Bank
t = temporary unit value
e = extrapolated unit value

CAP Code No.	Procedure Name	Manual Unit Value per Procedure	Comments	Item for Count	Lab Sect
86393	Platelet Concentrate Pooling (each unit, pooling in a single pool for infusion)	3.0		UNIT	BANK
86392	Platelet Concentrate Preparation	25.0		UNIT	BANK
t 86390	Platelet Concentrate Preparation (applies when 4 or more units are prepared simultaneously)	t 3.0		UNIT	BANK
86395	Platelet Freezing, DMSO	*		UNIT	BANK
86391	Platelet Rich Plasma Preparation	20.0		UNIT	BANK
86396	Platelet Thawing and DE-DMSO	*		UNIT	BANK
86201	Reagent RBC, Freeze Glycerol Citrate	6.0		CELLRG	BANK
86204	Reagent RBC, Freeze Liquid Nitrogen	10.0		CELLRG	BANK
86211	Reagent RBC, Preparation, A, B, or O	10.0		CELLRG	BANK
86213	Reagent RBC, Preparation, Antiglobulin Test Control Cells	20.0		CELLRG	BANK
86216	Reagent RBC, Preparation, Enzyme or LISS	12.0		CELLRG	BANK
86207	Reagent RBC, Thawing	10.0		CELLRG	BANK
■ 86205	Red Blood Cell Removal from Lymphocyte Preparation (e.g., shocking, decontamination)	*		SPEC	BANK
86397	Red Cell Exchange	*		UNIT	BANK
86810	Separation of Blood Unit into Aliquots (tally the unit value each time the unit is aliquoted)	15.0		UNIT	BANK
86402	Separation of Red Cell Mixtures: Phthalate Ester	*		TEST	BANK
86401	Therapeutic Leukapheresis	*	Auto BB UVs p. 19	PATNT	BANK
86385	Therapeutic Plasma Exchange	*	Auto BB UVs p. 19	PATNT	BANK
86400	Therapeutic Thrombocytapheresis	*	Auto BB UVs p. 19	PATNT	BANK
86386	Thrombocytapheresis	*	Auto BB UVs p. 19	UNIT	BANK
86394	Thrombocyte and Leukapheresis	*	Auto BB UVs p. 19	DONOR	BANK
■ 86408	Transfusion: Outpatient	*		PATNT	BANK
t 86670	Washed RBCs, for Transfusion (single wash)	t 10.0	Auto BB UVs p. 19	UNIT	BANK

CHEMISTRY

81064	Acetaldehyde/Serum/Quant/GLC	*		SUBST	CHEM
81065	Acetaminophen/Serum/Quant/GLC	*		SUBST	CHEM
t 81067	Acetaminophen/Serum/Quant/HPLC	t 10.0		INJ	CHEM
84634	Acetaminophen/Serum/Quant/VIS	*		SUBST	CHEM
81068	Acetominophen	*	Auto Chem UVs p. 22	TEST	CHEM
82010	Acetone, Blood	10.0		TEST	CHEM
81070	Acetone/Serum/Quant/GLC	*		INJ	CHEM
81072	Acetone/Urine/Quant/GLC	*		INJ	CHEM
82925	Acid, Free QNT, DUOD, Gastric or Duodenal Analysis (acid titration, total; see also specimen procurement code 89130)	3.0		TEST	CHEM
82930	Acid, TOT, QNT, DUOD, Gastric or Duodenal Analysis (acid titration, total; see also specimen procurement code 89130)	3.0		TEST	CHEM
■ 82020	ACTH	*	SA/Ligand UVs p. 21	TEST	CHEM

* = no unit value
t = temporary unit value
e = extrapolated unit value

CAP Code No.	Procedure Name	Manual Unit Value per Procedure	Comments	Item for Count	Lab Sect
82030	Adenosine-5-Monophosphate	*		TEST	CHEM
82035	Adenosine-5-Triphosphate	*		TEST	CHEM
82040	Albumin	12.0	Auto Chem UVs p. 22	TEST	CHEM
84635	Alcohol/Ethyl/Serum/Quant	*	Auto Chem UVs p. 22	SUBST	CHEM
81090	Alcohol/Ethyl/Serum/Quant/ENZ	*		SUBST	CHEM
81094	Alcohol/Ethyl/Serum/Quant/GLC	*		INJ	CHEM
t 84637	Alcohol/Ethyl/Urine/Qual/Diff	t 7.0		SUBST	CHEM
84636	Alcohol/Ethyl/Urine/Quant	*	Auto Chem UVs p. 22	SUBST	CHEM
81092	Alcohol/Ethyl/Urine/Quant/ENZ	*		SUBST	CHEM
81096	Alcohol/Ethyl/Urine/Quant/GLC	*		INJ	CHEM
84638	Alcohol/Isopropyl/Serum/Quant/GLC	*		INJ	CHEM
84642	Alcohol/Methyl/Serum/Quant	*	Auto Chem UVs p. 22	SUBST	CHEM
84640	Alcohol/Methyl/Serum/Quant/GLC	*		INJ	CHEM
82090	Aldolase	*	Auto Chem UVs p. 22	TEST	CHEM
■ 83110	Aldosterone, Blood	*	SA/Ligand UVs p. 21	TEST	CHEM
■ 83115	Aldosterone, Urine	*	SA/Ligand UVs p. 21	TEST	CHEM
81098	Amikacin	*	Auto Chem UVs p. 22	SUBST	CHEM
■ 84643	Amikacin/Serum/Quant	*	SA/Ligand UVs p. 21	SUBST	CHEM
81100	Amikacin/Serum/Quant/Emit	*		SUBST	CHEM
■ t 81106	Amikacin/Serum/Quant/FIA	t 5.0		SUBST	CHEM
81104	Amikacin/Serum/Quant/HPLC	*		INJ	CHEM
82130	Amino Acid Chromatography/Quant	*		TEST	CHEM
82105	Amino Acids, Total/Urine	12.0		TEST	CHEM
82630	Amino Levulinic Acid, Delta/Urine	40.0		TEST	CHEM
84645	Amitriptyline/Serum/Qual/GLC	*		INJ	CHEM
■ 81112	Amitriptyline/Serum/Quant	*	Auto Chem UVs p. 22 SA/Ligand UVs p. 21	SUBST	CHEM
84646	Amitriptyline/Serum/Quant/GLC	*	*	INJ	CHEM
81110	Amitriptyline/Serum/Quant/HPLC	*		INJ	CHEM
84647	Amitriptyline/Urine/Quant/GLC	*		INJ	CHEM
82140	Ammonia, Blood	39.0	Auto Chem UVs p. 22	TEST	CHEM
82142	Amniotic Fluid Scan	20.0		SPEC	CHEM
84648	Amphetamine	*	Auto Chem UVs p. 22	SUBST	CHEM
84650	Amphetamine/Serum/Quant/GLC	*		INJ	CHEM
t 84651	Amphetamine/Urine/Qual/EMIT	t 3.0		SUBST	CHEM
84652	Amphetamine/Urine/Qual/GLC	*		INJ	CHEM
■ 84654	Amphetamine/Urine/Quant	*	SA/Ligand UVs p. 21	SUBST	CHEM
84653	Amphetamine/Urine/Quant/GLC	*		INJ	CHEM
82150	Amylase	10.0	Auto Chem UVs p. 22	TEST	CHEM
■ 82160	Androstenedione	*	SA/Ligand UVs p. 21	TEST	CHEM
83370	Angiotensin	*		TEST	CHEM
t 84655	Anticonvulsants/Serum/Quant/GLC	t 16.0		INJ	CHEM
t 81120	Anticonvulsants/Serum/Quant/HPLC	t 10.0		INJ	CHEM
84658	Antimony/Urine/Qual/HMS	*		SUBST	CHEM
84659	Antimony/Urine/Quant/AA	*		SUBST	CHEM
81130	Antimony/Whole Blood/Quant/AA	*		SUBST	CHEM
85005	Antithrombin III Assay	*	Auto Chem UVs p. 22	TEST	CHEM
81144	Arsenic/Serum/Quant/AA	*		SUBST	CHEM

* = no unit value
t = temporary unit value
● = extrapolated unit value

Appendix I Workload Recording Worksheet

NAME OF LABORATORY _____ MONTH _____ YEAR _____

	PROCEDURE NAME									PROCEDURE NAME									PROCEDURE NAME								
	CAP Code No.					Unit Value				CAP Code No.					Unit Value				CAP Code No.					Unit Value			
DAY	IP	OP	QC STD	REP	ER	REF	INT	REG	OTH	IP	OP	QC STD	REP	ER	REF	INT	REG	OTH	IP	OP	QC STD	REP	ER	REF	INT	REG	OTH
1																											
2																											
3																											
4																											
5																											
6																											
7																											
8																											
9																											
10																											
11																											
12																											
13																											
14																											
15																											
16																											
17																											
18																											
19																											
20																											
21																											
22																											
23																											
24																											
25																											
26																											
27																											
28																											
29																											
30																											
31																											
Sub Total RC																											
Total RC																											

IP = Inpatient Procedures, OP = Outpatient Procedures, QC STD = Quality Control and Standard Procedures,
REP = Repeat Procedures, ER = Emergency Room Procedures, REF = Referral Procedures, INT = Interstate Procedures,
REG = Regional Procedures, and OTH = Other Procedures

COLLEGE OF AMERICAN PATHOLOGISTS
© CAP 1985

Appendix II Non-specified Hours Weekly Worksheet

NAME _____   DEPARTMENT _____

DATES: From _____ To _____   SHIFT _____

ACTIVITY	DAYS OF THE WEEK						
I. Accounting/Billing Activities batch control							
charge generation							
other (please specify) _____							
II. Administrative Activities budget preparation							
counseling (preparation, delivery, or receipt)							
discipline (preparation, delivery, or receipt)							
employee schedule preparation							
management report preparation							
meeting							
orientation							
performance appraisal (preparation, delivery, or receipt)							
procedure manual review							
procedure preparation							
professional society functions							
reading mail/professional journals							
recruitment							
workload documentation (daily tallies, summaries, etc.)							
other (please specify) _____							
III. Breaks breaks/personal time							
IV. Clerical Support distribute/handle mail							
payroll							
schedule a meeting							
telephone calls *							
typing/word processing correspondence, management reports, manuscript for possible publication							
other (please specify) _____							
V. Computer Oriented Activities computer programming							
computer operations not related to an individual test or batch of tests*							
data base management							
systems analysis							
other (please specify) _____							
VI. Donor Recruitment and Mobile Drawing Activities equipment setup at mobile draw location							
in-house donor recruitment							
travel time to mobile draw location							
Totals (This Side Only)							

*CAUTION: Do not exclude time for activities included in a unit value

ACTIVITY	DAYS OF THE WEEK						
VII. Evaluation, Development, and Research							
publishable paper							
methods							
technical							
VIII. Formal Education (residency program, med tech school, new nursing personnel)							
attend class							
bench training							
lecture delivery							
lecture preparation							
meeting							
orientation (tour)							
other (please specify) _____							
IX. Laboratory Procedures Without Unit Values							
X. Other							
travel time to off-site patient location							
travel time to off-site location							
XI. Problem Solving							
instrumentation							
test request related							
other (please specify) _____							
XII. Quality Control							
review summaries							
other (please specify) _____							
XIII. Report Delivery							
tubing							
other (please specify) _____							
XIV. Supplies and Equipment							
delivery							
demonstration							
discussion with sales or tech rep							
ordering							
storage							
other (please specify) _____							
XV. Training							
coordination							
in-service education							
orientation to new equipment or procedures including computers							
phlebotomy							
Totals (Side A)							
Grand Totals							

Appendix III Glossary for Laboratory Employee Diary*

DIRECTIONS FOR USING THE EMPLOYEE DIARY

1. Complete the header information: name, date, shift, section, and position number.
2. Place a heavy squiggly line down the 15 minute column to the left of the part of the hour before you start to work if your shift does not start on the hour. Each hour is split into four 15 minute intervals labeled 00, 15, 30, and 45. 00 means on the hour until 15 minutes after, 15 means quarter past the hour until half past the hour, etc. If you start at 7:30 am, the line goes down through the 15 minute column.
3. Complete the hour heading by entering the one or two digits of each hour. For example, if you start at 7:30 am, the time headings would be 7, 8, 9, 10, 11, 12, 1, 2, 3, 4. You may use regular time after noon or military time so long as you indicate the shift.
4. Place *only one* X mark per 15 minute column on the line indicating how you spent the majority of each 15 minute interval. Most laboratorians fill out the form four times during their shift, at the first break, at the meal, at the second break, and at the end of the shift. If you moved frequently between two or more tasks, estimate the number of 15 minute intervals per task and place the correct number of X marks on each line. The diary is *not* designed to track your time throughout the shift, only to explain how much and what percentage of the time is spent on each major activity.
5. Place another squiggly line down the column immediately following the time you leave work, even if you only work part of your assigned shift, e.g., sent home due to a lack of work or due to illness or other personal reason. If you leave on the hour, the line goes down the 00 column.
6. In the left hand column, tally the number of marks for each activity. Total the marks at the bottom of that column. You can check that you have counted correctly by calculating the number of X marks for your shift. For example, if you work 7:30 am to 4:00 pm (8 hours paid plus an unpaid 30 minute meal break), there should be 34 marks total (8.5 hours times 4 marks per hour).

*Copyright © 1985, Applied Leadership Technologies, Inc.

7. If you stay overtime and need an additional sheet, please use one and staple it to the first sheet. If called back in, please use a second sheet.
8. Turn your completed diary in to your supervisor or the designated person. *Never* take the diary home if you have not had time to complete it at work. Completing the diary after work or the next day becomes an exercise in creative writing.

GLOSSARY FOR LABORATORY EMPLOYEE DIARY

Specified (Workloaded)

- *Specimen Collection*—Venipuncture, arterial puncture, etc., *when* performed by laboratory personnel.
- *Other Workloaded Activity*—All other activities for which you receive CAP workload recording units. This includes testing, recording and reporting, daily or routine preparation, maintenance and repair, solution preparation, glassware wash-up, and technical supervision.

Non-specified (Non-workloaded)

- *Accounting and Billing*—For patients or for outside organizations such as nursing homes; includes batch preparation and delivery of laboratory slips to the business office or other department.
- *Administrative*—Budgeting, recruitment, orientation of new staff, counseling, discipline, performance appraisal, and employee scheduling. This also includes reading mail, professional society functions, *informal* meetings, management report preparation, checking on this data collection, etc. Employees receiving counseling, discipline, performance appraisal, etc., should also record their time here. *Not* for employee orientation.
- *Breaks and Personal*—Coffee or other breaks according to policy or contract; toilet, wash-up, or other personal time including personal telephone calls.
- *CAP Tally Maintenance*—Time spent maintaining and updating the CAP workload tally; includes daily manual tallies and monthly

Note: The diary is designed to explain the majority of the activity performed in the laboratory. It is not designed to explain every minute of your day.

summarization. *Not* for preparation of monthly Productivity Monitoring Reports which are recorded as administrative time.

- *Clerical Support*—To pathologists and administrative staff. Includes handling and distributing mail, photocopying, typing letters and administrative reports or procedures; screening telephone calls (*not* for initial test requests), payroll, setting up meetings, typing minutes (*not* for taking minutes which is recorded under meetings). *Not* for reports receiving workload units (autopsies, cytology reports, surgical pathology, filing report slips); and *not* for delivery and charting which receive workload units.

- *Computer Activities*—Includes systems analysis, programming, editing of computer files, data base management, investigation of system malfunction and related items. Also, includes patient location queries. *Not* initial entry of test requests or test results. *Note:* the time spent in preparation of drawing lists or recording test results are activities included in the unit value.

- *Courier Activity*—Time spent by paid laboratory personnel picking up specimens drawn by other staff (nurses, doctors, etc.) from other hospitals, physicians, or commercial clients.

- *Decedent Affairs*—For placement of body in morgue or for release to undertaker. *Not* for the autopsy attendant duties.

- *Donor Recruitment*—Includes telephone calls to solicit donors, visits to meetings to explain the program, visits to patient care areas within the hospital to recruit family members of patients who have received blood, etc. Also includes mobile draw activities: travel time to and from donor site, and time to set up and take down equipment. *Not* for donor accounting when units are collected.

- *Education: Bench Training*—Time spent with students at the bench or similar location (drawing station, bedside, etc.). If part of the time is spent performing workloaded activities, include *only* the *additional* time required due to the education of the student, e.g., if four hours are used to do work that would have taken three hours, only count one hour as education.

- *Education: Lecture*—Time spent preparing lectures, setting up the classroom, giving the lecture or exam, correcting exams.

- *Education: Other*—Time spent with residents or performing other educational activities not covered in Education: Bench Training or Education: Lecture. Could include going to schools or colleges or other recruitment activities. Calculate as explained in bench training. *Explain* activity on back of diary.

- *Housekeeping/Infection Control*—Cleaning and disinfecting centrifuges, refrigerators, etc. *Not* for calibrating centrifuges, checking tachometers or timers, etc., which receive unit values; also *not* for preventive maintenance activities which are part of the workload values.
- *In-Service*—Within the institution and for which you are paid. *Note:* if the institution's payroll system records "away from the institution" education as worked hours, record such in-service or continuing education time here.
- *Laboratory Procedures*—Which have not yet been time studied and/ or assigned an extrapolated unit value per procedure. If the initial handling function is performed by others, verify that they are recording their time here also.
- *Liaison*—Includes problem-solving activities requiring laboratory personnel to respond to nursing or medical staff, administration, etc. May include time spent as a resource person for another department. If you *check* this block, you *must* use the back of the diary to explain the nature of the liaison.
- *Major Repairs*—Not for routine preventive maintenance.
- *Meetings: Not for In-Service or for Education*—For hospital, department, or sectional meetings. Use the back of the diary to explain which meeting attended.
- *Orientation*—For the employee being oriented to the laboratory or to a new piece of equipment or procedure.
- *Purchasing and Supplies*—Interviewing vendors, demonstrations within the institution, preparing weekly orders, receiving and putting supplies away on shelves or in storerooms, etc. *Record* site visits to evaluate equipment as administrative time.
- *Quality Control Activities*—May include use of computers or preparation of monthly reports. *Not* for running quality controls or tests for which you record CAP units.
- *Research and Development*—Development of new tests or procedures to bring tests in-house, evaluation of methods or equipment, test procedure writing, running in parallel on new equipment if the new equipment has no unit values, etc. Also includes preparing papers for publication (*clerical* personnel should record time for typing, mounting photos, etc. as clerical support).
- *Searching*—Searching for lost or missing specimens and/or reports. May include use and follow-up of incomplete, uncollected or other computer-generated lists or reports. *Do not* use this item for prepar-

Laboratory Staffing Analysis Employee Diary

Employee Name: _____ Number: _____ Section Number: _____

Day of Week: _____ Date: _____ Shift: _____ Section Name: _____

In each column to the right place an "X" for the one activity performed

Specified (Workloaded)
1. Specimen Collection
2. Other Workloaded Activity

Non-specified (Non-workloaded)
3. Accounting and Billing
4. Administrative
5. Breaks and Personal
6. CAP Tally Maintenance
7. Clerical Support
8. Computer Activities
9. Courier Activity
10. Decedent Affairs
11. Donor Recruitment
12. Education: Bench Training
13. Education: Lecture
14. Education: Other*
15. Housekeeping/Infection Control
16. In-service
17. Laboratory Procedures (Untimed)
18. Liaison*
19. Major Repairs
20. Meetings*
21. Orientation
22. Purchasing and Supplies
23. Quality Control Activities
24. Research and Development
25. Searching
26. Standby or Idle Time
27. Telephone
28. Unpaid Meal Time
29. Other*

Total number of "Xs"

*NOTE: For Meetings, Liaison, or Other explain below or use back for any remarks

Put your work hours above the minutes (00, 15, 30, or 45). Place one "X" in the block where you spent the majority of each 15 minutes. Turn in your diary at the end of your shift.

Copyright © 1985. Applied Leadership Technologies, Inc.

ing incident reports or other correspondence resulting from missing specimens or reports, use administrative time for that activity.

- *Standby or Idle Time*—When you have no item listed above or below to do during the majority of the 15 minutes. Could be evening or night shift waiting for work, any shift near the end of their tour when the work is completed or waiting for a frozen section or other work. *Note:* this is a legitimate activity, do not be afraid to use this item!

- *Telephone*—Calls relating to patient results and/or test status, *not* for initial calling of STATS. Also includes inquiries regarding specimen collection requirements, ordering procedures, turn-around time, etc. *Not* for administrative telephone calls recorded under Administrative.

- *Unpaid Meal Time*—Lunch or dinner break if not paid for the time. If paid for meal time, please include under Breaks.

- *Other*—If you spent the majority of the 15 minutes doing something that you do not believe is covered above, please check the *Other* block. You *must* explain below or on the back. Examples include employee health visits and responding to codes.

Appendix B

Listing of DRGs Weighting Factor and Related Data[1]

---

[1]From *Federal Register,* September 1, 1983. This information is required in all hospitals paid under PPS.

List of Diagnosis-Related Groups (DRGs), Relative Weighting Factors, Geometric Mean Length of Stay, and Length of Stay Outlier Cutoff Points Used in the Prospective Payment System

DRG	MDC	TITLE	Relative Weights	Geometric Mean LOS	Outlier Cutoffs
1	1 SURG	CRANIOTOMY AGE >17 EXCEPT FOR TRAUMA	3.3548	19.4	39
2	1 SURG	CRANIOTOMY FOR TRAUMA AGE >17	3.2829	15.8	36
3	1 SURG	*CRANIOTOMY AGE <18	2.9489	12.7	33
4	1 SURG	SPINAL PROCEDURES	2.2452	16.0	36
5	1 SURG	EXTRACRANIAL VASCULAR PROCEDURES	1.6780	9.8	30
6	1 SURG	CARPAL TUNNEL RELEASE	.3993	2.6	8
7	1 SURG	PERIPH + CRANIAL NERVE + OTHER NERV SYST PROC AGE >69 +/OR C.C.	1.0279	5.3	25
8	1 SURG	PERIPH + CRANIAL NERVE + OTHER NERV SYST PROC AGE <70 W/O C.C.	.7239	4.1	23
9	1 MED	SPINAL DISORDERS + INJURIES	1.3958	9.1	29
10	1 MED	NERVOUS SYSTEM NEOPLASMS AGE >69 AND/OR C.C.	1.3087	9.6	30
11	1 MED	NERVOUS SYSTEM NEOPLASMS AGE <70 W/O C.C.	1.2545	8.5	29
12	1 MED	DEGENERATIVE NERVOUS SYSTEM DISORDERS	1.1136	9.4	29
13	1 MED	MULTIPLE SCLEROSIS + CEREBELLAR ATAXIA	1.0150	8.9	29
14	1 MED	SPECIFIC CEREBROVASCULAR DISORDERS EXCEPT TIA	1.3527	9.9	30
15	1 MED	TRANSIENT ISCHEMIC ATTACKS	.6673	5.6	24
16	1 MED	NONSPECIFIC CEREBROVASCULAR DISORDERS WITH C.C.	.8592	7.4	27
17	1 MED	NONSPECIFIC CEREBROVASCULAR DISORDERS W/O C.C.	.8392	7.2	27
18	1 MED	CRANIAL + PERIPHERAL NERVE DISORDERS AGE >69 AND/OR C.C.	.7915	6.6	27
19	1 MED	CRANIAL + PERIPHERAL NERVE DISORDERS AGE <70 W/O C.C.	.6975	5.7	26
20	1 MED	NERVOUS SYSTEM INFECTION EXCEPT VIRAL MENINGITIS	1.3141	7.6	28
21	1 MED	*VIRAL MENINGITIS	.6301	4.5	15
22	1 MED	HYPERTENSIVE ENCEPHALOPATHY	.7869	6.4	26
23	1 MED	NONTRAUMATIC STUPOR + COMA	1.1568	5.9	26
24	1 MED	SEIZURE + HEADACHE AGE >69 AND/OR C.C.	.7279	5.6	26
25	1 MED	SEIZURE + HEADACHE AGE 18-69 W/O C.C.	.6392	4.9	25
26	1 MED	*SEIZURE + HEADACHE AGE 0-17	.4349	3.3	13
27	1 MED	*TRAUMATIC STUPOR + COMA, COMA >1 HR	1.1368	4.1	24
28	1 MED	TRAUMATIC STUPOR + COMA, COMA <1 HR AGE >69 AND/OR C.C.	1.0701	5.9	26
29	1 MED	*TRAUMATIC STUPOR + COMA <1 HR AGE 18-69 W/O C.C.	.7175	3.8	24
30	1 MED	*TRAUMATIC STUPOR + COMA <1 HR AGE 0-17	.3576	2.0	8
31	1 MED	CONCUSSION AGE >69 AND/OR C.C.	.6051	4.6	25

32	1 MED	CONCUSSION AGE 18-69 W/O C.C.	.4519	3.3	19
33	1 MED	*CONCUSSION AGE 0-17	.2483	1.6	5
34	1 MED	OTHER DISORDERS OF NERVOUS SYSTEM AGE >69 AND/OR C.C.	.9927	7.1	27
35	1 MED	OTHER DISORDERS OF NERVOUS SYSTEM AGE <70 W/O C.C.	.8460	6.2	26
36	2 SURG	RETINAL PROCEDURES	.7093	5.0	15
37	2 SURG	ORBITAL PROCEDURES	.5630	3.4	11
38	2 SURG	PRIMARY IRIS PROCEDURES	.4325	3.0	9
39	2 SURG	LENS PROCEDURES	.5010	2.8	6
40	2 SURG	EXTRAOCULAR PROCEDURES EXCEPT ORBIT AGE >17	.3977	2.4	7
41	2 SURG	*EXTRAOCULAR PROCEDURES EXCEPT ORBIT AGE 0-17	.3695	1.6	4
42	2 SURG	INTRAOCULAR PROCEDURES EXCEPT RETINA, IRIS + LENS	.5906	3.8	12
43	2 MED	*HYPHEMA	.3828	4.2	12
44	2 MED	ACUTE MAJOR EYE INFECTIONS	.6298	6.5	22
45	2 MED	NEUROLOGICAL EYE DISORDERS	.5641	4.3	18
46	2 MED	OTHER DISORDERS OF THE EYE AGE >17 WITH C.C.	.5964	4.1	23
47	2 MED	OTHER DISORDERS OF THE EYE AGE >17 W/O C.C.	.5064	3.0	12
48	2 MED	*OTHER DISORDERS OF THE EYE AGE 0-17	.4060	2.9	13
49	3 SURG	MAJOR HEAD + NECK PROCEDURES	2.5270	13.6	34
50	3 SURG	SIALOADENECTOMY	.7160	4.6	14
51	3 SURG	SALIVARY GLAND PROCEDURES EXCEPT SIALOADENECTOMY	.6702	4.2	15
52	3 SURG	*CLEFT LIP + PALATE REPAIR	.6488	3.8	11
53	3 SURG	SINUS + MASTOID PROCEDURES AGE >17	.5895	3.5	11
54	3 SURG	*SINUS + MASTOID PROCEDURES AGE 0-17	.6961	3.2	11
55	3 SURG	MISCELLANEOUS EAR, NOSE + THROAT PROCEDURES	.4153	2.5	7
56	3 SURG	RHINOPLASTY	.4144	2.8	8
57	3 SURG	*T + A PROC EXCEPT TONSILLECTOMY + /OR ADENOIDECTOMY AGE >17	.5251	2.7	9
58	3 SURG	*T + A PROC EXCEPT TONSILLECTOMY + /OR ADENOIDECTOMY AGE 0-17	.3130	1.5	3
59	3 SURG	*TONSILLECTOMY AND/OR ADENOIDECTOMY ONLY AGE >17	.3147	2.0	4
60	3 SURG	*TONSILLECTOMY AND/OR ADENOIDECTOMY ONLY AGE 0-17	.2643	1.5	3
61	3 SURG	*MYRINGOTOMY AGE >17	.4273	2.1	9
62	3 SURG	*MYRINGOTOMY AGE 0-17	.3121	1.3	3
63	3 SURG	OTHER EAR, NOSE + THROAT O.R. PROCEDURES	1.1090	5.8	26

* MEDPAR data have been supplemented by data from Maryland and Michigan for low volume DRGs.

** DRG categories combined (in pairs) in the calculation of the case mix index.

***DRGs 469 and 470 contain cases which could not be assigned to valid DRGs.

DRG	MDC	TITLE	Relative Weights	Geometric Mean LOS	Outlier Cutoffs
64	3 MED	EAR, NOSE + THROAT MALIGNANCY	1.0812	5.7	26
65	3 MED	DYSEQUILIBRIUM	.4857	4.6	17
66	3 MED	EPISTAXIS	.4116	3.7	15
67	3 MED	*EPIGLOTTITIS	.6762	4.3	17
68	3 MED	OTITIS MEDIA + URI AGE >69 AND/OR C.C.	.6289	6.0	22
69	3 MED	OTITIS MEDIA + URI AGE 18-69 W/O C.C.	.5417	4.8	19
70	3 MED	*OTITIS MEDIA + URI AGE 0-17	.3697	3.1	10
71	3 MED	*LARYNGOTRACHEITIS	.3589	2.9	9
72	3 MED	NASAL TRAUMA + DEFORMITY	.4857	3.8	18
73	3 MED	OTHER EAR, NOSE + THROAT DIAGNOSES AGE >17	.5217	3.5	17
74	3 MED	*OTHER EAR, NOSE + THROAT DIAGNOSES AGE 0-17	.3463	2.1	9
75	4 SURG	MAJOR CHEST PROCEDURES	2.6044	14.4	34
76	4 SURG	O.R. PROC ON THE RESP SYSTEM EXCEPT MAJOR CHEST WITH C.C.	1.8734	10.6	31
77	4 SURG	O.R. PROC ON THE RESP SYSTEM EXCEPT MAJOR CHEST W/O C.C.	1.8178	9.5	30
78	4 MED	PULMONARY EMBOLISM	1.4095	10.4	30
79	4 MED	RESPIRATORY INFECTIONS + INFLAMMATIONS AGE >69 AND/OR C.C.	1.7982	11.2	31
80	4 MED	RESPIRATORY INFECTIONS + INFLAMMATIONS AGE 18-69 W/O C.C.	1.7445	10.9	31
81	4 MED	*RESPIRATORY INFECTIONS + INFLAMMATIONS AGE 0-17	.8743	6.1	26
82	4 MED	RESPIRATORY NEOPLASMS	1.1400	7.4	27
83	4 MED	MAJOR CHEST TRAUMA AGE >69 AND/OR C.C.	.9809	8.1	28
84	4 MED	*MAJOR CHEST TRAUMA AGE <70 W/O C.C.	.7738	5.3	22
85	4 MED	PLEURAL EFFUSION AGE >69 AND/OR C.C.	1.1461	8.4	28
86	4 MED	PLEURAL EFFUSION AGE <70 W/O C.C.	1.1217	7.6	28
87	4 MED	PULMONARY EDEMA + RESPIRATORY FAILURE	1.5529	7.7	28
88	4 MED	CHRONIC OBSTRUCTIVE PULMONARY DISEASE	1.0412	7.5	28
89	4 MED	SIMPLE PNEUMONIA + PLEURISY AGE >69 AND/OR C.C.	1.1029	8.5	29
90	4 MED	SIMPLE PNEUMONIA + PLEURISY AGE 18-69 W/O C.C.	.9849	7.6	28
91	4 MED	*SIMPLE PNEUMONIA + PLEURISY AGE 0-17	.5131	4.6	14
92	4 MED	INTERSTITIAL LUNG DISEASE AGE >69 AND/OR C.C.	1.0370	7.8	28
93	4 MED	INTERSTITIAL LUNG DISEASE AGE <70 W/O C.C.	.9724	6.9	27
94	4 MED	PNEUMOTHORAX AGE >69 AND/OR C.C.	1.4374	9.2	29
95	4 MED	PNEUMOTHORAX AGE <70 W/O C.C.	1.1252	7.7	28
96	4 MED	BRONCHITIS + ASTHMA AGE >69 AND/OR C.C.	.7996	6.9	24
97	4 MED	BRONCHITIS + ASTHMA AGE 18-69 W/O C.C.	.7256	6.2	21

98	4 MED	*BRONCHITIS + ASTHMA AGE 0-17	.4275	3.7	11
99	4 MED	RESPIRATORY SIGNS + SYMPTOMS AGE >69 AND/OR C.C.	.8035	5.5	26
100	4 MED	RESPIRATORY SIGNS + SYMPTOMS AGE <70 W/O C.C.	.7730	5.1	24
101	4 MED	OTHER RESPIRATORY DIAGNOSES AGE >69 AND/OR C.C.	.9035	6.8	27
102	4 MED	OTHER RESPIRATORY DIAGNOSES AGE <70	.9024	6.1	26
103	5 SURG	*HEART TRANSPLANT	.0000	.0	0
104	5 SURG	**CARDIAC VALVE PROCEDURE WITH PUMP + WITH CARDIAC CATH	6.8527	20.9	41
105	5 SURG	**CARDIAC VALVE PROCEDURE WITH PUMP + W/O CARDIAC CATH	5.2308	16.2	36
106	5 SURG	**CORONARY BYPASS WITH CARDIAC CATH	5.2624	20.4	40
107	5 SURG	**CORONARY BYPASS W/O CARDIAC CATH	3.9891	13.5	34
108	5 SURG	CARDIOTHOR PROC, EXCEPT VALVE + CORONARY BYPASS, WITH PUMP	4.3756	13.3	33
109	5 SURG	CARDIOTHORACIC PROCEDURES W/O PUMP	3.6963	12.1	32
110	5 SURG	MAJOR RECONSTRUCTIVE VASCULAR PROCEDURES AGE >69 AND/OR C.C.	2.9328	14.3	34
111	5 SURG	MAJOR RECONSTRUCTIVE VASCULAR PROCEDURES AGE <70 W/O C.C.	2.5851	13.2	33
112	5 SURG	VASCULAR PROCEDURES EXCEPT MAJOR RECONSTRUCTION	2.3500	11.2	31
113	5 SURG	AMPUTATION FOR CIRC SYSTEM DISORDERS EXCEPT UPPER LIMB + TOE	2.6800	21.6	42
114	5 SURG	UPPER LIMB + TOE AMPUTATION FOR CIRC SYSTEM DISORDERS	2.1067	16.6	37
115	5 SURG	PERMANENT CARDIAC PACEMAKER IMPLANT WITH AMI OR CHF	3.9150	15.8	36
116	5 SURG	PERMANENT CARDIAC PACEMAKER IMPLANT W/O AMI OR CHF	2.8665	9.3	29
117	5 SURG	CARDIAC PACEMAKER REPLACE + REVIS EXC PULSE GEN REPL ONLY	1.8210	6.4	26
118	5 SURG	CARDIAC PACEMAKER PULSE GENERATOR REPLACEMENT ONLY	1.7809	4.2	18
119	5 SURG	VEIN LIGATION + STRIPPING	1.0610	7.2	27
120	5 SURG	OTHER O.R. PROCEDURES ON THE CIRCULATORY SYSTEM	2.5204	15.0	35
121	5 MED	**CIRCULATORY DISORDERS WITH AMI + C.V. COMP. DISCH. ALIVE	1.8648	11.9	32
122	5 MED	**CIRCULATORY DISORDERS WITH AMI, W/O C.V. COMP. DISCH. ALIVE	1.3651	9.8	30
123	5 MED	CIRCULATORY DISORDERS WITH AMI, EXPIRED	1.1360	3.1	23
124	5 MED	CIRCULATORY DISORDERS EXC AMI, WITH CARD CATH + COMPLEX DIAG	2.2200	8.4	28
125	5 MED	CIRCULATORY DISORDERS EXC AMI, WITH CARD CATH W/O COMPLEX DIAG	1.6455	5.0	25
126	5 MED	ACUTE + SUBACUTE ENDOCARDITIS	2.6645	18.4	38
127	5 MED	HEART FAILURE + SHOCK	1.0408	7.8	28
128	5 MED	DEEP VEIN THROMBOPHLEBITIS	.8639	9.6	28
129	5 MED	CARDIAC ARREST	1.5506	4.6	25
130	5 MED	PERIPHERAL VASCULAR DISORDERS AGE <69 AND/OR C.C.	.9645	7.1	27
131	5 MED	PERIPHERAL VASCULAR DISORDERS AGE <70 W/O C.C.	.9491	6.4	26
132	5 MED	ATHEROSCLEROSIS AGE >69 AND/OR C.C.	.9182	6.7	27
133	5 MED	ATHEROSCLEROSIS AGE <70 W/O C.C.	.8599	5.2	25

DRG	MDC	TITLE	Relative Weights	Geometric Mean LOS	Outlier Cutoffs
134	5 MED	HYPERTENSION	.7049	6.1	26
135	5 MED	CARDIAC CONGENITAL + VALVULAR DISORDERS AGE >69 AND/OR C.C.	.9922	6.1	26
136	5 MED	CARDIAC CONGENITAL + VALVULAR DISORDERS AGE 18-69 W/O C.C.	.9674	4.9	25
137	5 MED	*CARDIAC CONGENITAL + VALVULAR DISORDERS AGE 0-17	.6381	3.3	20
138	5 MED	CARDIAC ARRHYTHMIA + CONDUCTION DISORDERS AGE >69 AND/OR C.C.	.9297	5.7	26
139	5 MED	CARDIAC ARRHYTHMIA + CONDUCTION DISORDERS AGE <70 W/O C.C.	.8303	4.8	23
140	5 MED	ANGINA PECTORIS	.7548	5.5	21
141	5 MED	SYNCOPE + COLLAPSE AGE >69 AND/OR C.C.	.6475	5.0	21
142	5 MED	SYNCOPE + COLLAPSE AGE <70 W/O C.C.	.5680	4.3	18
143	5 MED	CHEST PAIN	.6814	4.4	19
144	5 MED	OTHER CIRCULATORY DIAGNOSES WITH C.C.	1.1267	7.0	27
145	5 MED	OTHER CIRCULATORY DIAGNOSES W/O C.C.	1.0020	6.4	26
146	6 SURG	RECTAL RESECTION AGE >69 AND/OR C.C.	2.7082	19.1	39
147	6 SURG	RECTAL RESECTION AGE <70 W/O C.C.	2.5087	17.9	38
148	6 SURG	MAJOR SMALL + LARGE BOWEL PROCEDURES AGE >69 AND/OR C.C.	2.5493	17.0	37
149	6 SURG	MAJOR SMALL + LARGE BOWEL PROCEDURES AGE <70 W/O C.C.	2.2154	15.2	35
150	6 SURG	PERITONEAL ADHESIOLYSIS AGE >69 AND/OR C.C.	2.3746	15.3	35
151	6 SURG	PERITONEAL ADHESIOLYSIS AGE <70 W/O C.C.	2.0274	13.4	33
152	6 SURG	MINOR SMALL + LARGE BOWEL PROCEDURES AGE >69 AND/OR C.C.	1.4851	10.6	31
153	6 SURG	MINOR SMALL + LARGE BOWEL PROCEDURES AGE >70 W/O C.C.	1.2599	9.3	29
154	6 SURG	STOMACH, ESOPHAGEAL + DUODENAL PROCEDURES AGE >69 AND/OR C.C.	2.6901	14.8	35
155	6 SURG	STOMACH, ESOPHAGEAL + DUODENAL PROCEDURES AGE 18-69 W/O C.C.	2.3336	13.0	33
156	6 SURG	*STOMACH, ESOPHAGEAL + DUODENAL PROCEDURES AGE 0-17	.8470	6.0	20
157	6 SURG	ANAL PROCEDURES AGE >69 AND/OR C.C.	.7985	6.0	25
158	6 SURG	ANAL PROCEDURES AGE <70 W/O C.C.	.6408	5.2	19
159	6 SURG	HERNIA PROCEDURES EXCEPT INGUINAL + FEMORAL AGE >69 AND/OR C.C.	.9297	7.1	23
160	6 SURG	HERNIA PROCEDURES EXCEPT INGUINAL + FEMORAL AGE 18-69 W/O C.C.	.7676	6.0	18
161	6 SURG	INGUINAL + FEMORAL HERNIA PROCEDURES AGE >69 AND/OR C.C.	.7068	5.7	16
162	6 SURG	INGUINAL + FEMORAL HERNIA PROCEDURES AGE 18-69 W/O C.C.	.5854	4.8	12
163	6 SURG	*HERNIA PROCEDURES AGE 0-17	.4358	2.1	6
164	6 SURG	APPENDECTOMY WITH COMPLICATED PRINC. DIAG AGE >69 AND/OR C.C.	1.8320	11.9	32
165	6 SURG	APPENDECTOMY WITH COMPLICATED PRINC. DIAG AGE <70 W/O C.C.	1.6154	11.3	29
166	6 SURG	APPENDECTOMY W/O COMPLICATED PRINC. DIAG AGE >69 AND/OR C.C.	1.4328	9.4	29
167	6 SURG	APPENDECTOMY W/O COMPLICATED PRINC. DIAG AGE <70 W/O C.C.	1.0818	7.4	22

168	6 SURG	PROCEDURES ON THE MOUTH AGE >69 AND/OR C.C.	.8631	4.3	24
169	6 SURG	PROCEDURES ON THE MOUTH AGE <70 W/O C.C.	.8992	4.2	24
170	6 SURG	OTHER DIGESTIVE SYSTEM PROCEDURES AGE >69 AND/OR C.C.	2.6602	14.6	35
171	6 SURG	OTHER DIGESTIVE SYSTEM PROCEDURES AGE <70 W/O C.C.	2.3976	13.3	33
172	6 MED	DIGESTIVE MALIGNANCY AGE >69 AND/OR C.C.	1.2268	8.2	28
173	6 MED	DIGESTIVE MALIGNANCY AGE <70 W/O C.C.	1.0517	6.7	27
174	6 MED	G.I. HEMORRHAGE AGE >69 AND/OR C.C.	.9281	6.7	27
175	6 MED	G.I. HEMORRHAGE AGE <70 W/O C.C.	.8236	5.8	24
176	6 MED	COMPLICATED PEPTIC ULCER	1.2438	8.1	28
177	6 MED	UNCOMPLICATED PEPTIC ULCER >69 AND/OR C.C.	.7422	6.6	24
178	6 MED	UNCOMPLICATED PEPTIC ULCER <70 W/O C.C.	.6141	5.5	20
179	6 MED	INFLAMMATORY BOWEL DISEASE	1.0153	8.0	28
180	6 MED	G.I. OBSTRUCTION AGE >69 AND/OR C.C.	.8197	6.2	26
181	6 MED	G.I. OBSTRUCTION AGE <70 W/O C.C.	.7845	5.9	26
182	6 MED	ESOPHAGITIS, GASTROENT. + MISC. DIGEST. DIS AGE >69 +/OR C.C.	.6185	5.4	22
183	6 MED	ESOPHAGITIS, GASTROENT. + MISC. DIGEST. DIS AGE 18-69 W/O C.C.	.5652	4.8	19
184	6 MED	*ESOPHAGITIS, GASTROENTERITIS + MISC. DIGEST. DISORDERS AGE 0-17	.3822	3.3	11
185	6 MED	*DENTAL + ORAL DIS. EXC EXTRACTIONS + RESTORATIONS, AGE >17	.6681	4.2	24
186	6 MED	*DENTAL + ORAL DIS. EXC EXTRACTIONS + RESTORATIONS, AGE 0-17	.4155	2.9	11
187	6 MED	DENTAL EXTRACTIONS + RESTORATIONS	.3990	2.7	8
188	6 MED	OTHER DIGESTIVE SYSTEM DIAGNOSES AGE >69 AND/OR C.C.	.7444	5.1	25
189	6 MED	OTHER DIGESTIVE SYSTEM DIAGNOSES AGE 18-69 W/O C.C.	.6576	4.5	23
190	6 MED	*OTHER DIGESTIVE SYSTEM DIAGNOSES AGE 0-17	.3379	2.1	8
191	7 SURG	MAJOR PANCREAS, LIVER + SHUNT PROCEDURES	4.1791	20.8	41
192	7 SURG	*MINOR PANCREAS, LIVER + SHUNT PROCEDURES	3.9197	20.1	40
193	7 SURG	BILIARY TRACT PROC EXC TOT CHOLECYSTECTOMY AGE >69 +/OR C.C.	2.4513	17.3	37
194	7 SURG	BILIARY TRACT PROC EXC TOT CHOLECYSTECTOMY AGE <70 W/O C.C.	1.9881	13.9	34
195	7 SURG	**TOTAL CHOLECYSTECTOMY WITH C.D.E. AGE >69 AND/OR C.C.	2.1690	16.0	36
196	7 SURG	**TOTAL CHOLECYSTECTOMY WITH C.D.E. AGE <70 W/O C.C.	2.0594	15.8	36
197	7 SURG	**TOTAL CHOLECYSTECTOMY W/O C.D.E. AGE >69 AND/OR C.C.	1.4868	11.5	29
198	7 SURG	**TOTAL CHOLECYSTECTOMY W/O C.D.E. AGE <70 W/O C.C.	1.2752	10.1	24
199	7 SURG	HEPATOBILIARY DIAGNOSTIC PROCEDURE FOR MALIGNANCY	2.4574	17.9	38
200	7 SURG	HEPATOBILIARY DIAGNOSTIC PROCEDURE FOR NON-MALIGNANCY	2.5818	15.1	35
201	7 SURG	OTHER HEPATOBILIARY OR PANCREAS O.R. PROCEDURES	2.7291	16.9	37
202	7 MED	CIRRHOSIS + ALCOHOLIC HEPATITIS	1.1965	9.3	29
203	7 MED	MALIGNANCY OF HEPATOBILIARY SYSTEM OR PANCREAS	1.0937	8.0	28

DRG	MDC	TITLE	Relative Weights	Geometric Mean LOS	Outlier Cutoffs
204	7 MED	DISORDERS OF PANCREAS EXCEPT MALIGNANCY	.9682	7.5	28
205	7 MED	DISORDERS OF LIVER EXC MALIG, CIRR, ALC HEPA AGE >69 AND/OR C.C.	1.0822	7.9	28
206	7 MED	DISORDERS OF LIVER EXC MALIG, CIRR, ALC HEPA AGE <70 W/O C.C.	.9247	6.8	27
207	7 MED	DISORDERS OF THE BILIARY TRACT AGE >69 AND/OR C.C.	.8492	6.6	27
208	7 MED	DISORDERS OF THE BILIARY TRACT AGE <70 W/O C.C.	.7315	5.5	24
209	8 SURG	MAJOR JOINT PROCEDURES	2.2912	17.1	37
210	8 SURG	HIP + FEMUR PROCEDURES EXCEPT MAJOR JOINT AGE >69 AND/OR C.C.	2.0833	17.8	38
211	8 SURG	HIP + FEMUR PROCEDURES EXCEPT MAJOR JOINT AGE 18-69 W/O C.C.	1.9530	15.9	36
212	8 SURG	*HIP + FEMUR PROCEDURES EXCEPT MAJOR JOINT AGE 0-17	1.7132	11.1	31
213	8 SURG	AMPUTATIONS FOR MUSCULOSKELETAL SYSTEM + CONN. TISSUE DISORDERS	2.1315	14.3	34
214	8 SURG	BACK + NECK PROCEDURES AGE >69 AND/OR C.C.	1.8427	15.6	36
215	8 SURG	BACK + NECK PROCEDURES AGE <70 W/O C.C.	1.4920	13.0	33
216	8 SURG	BIOPSIES OF MUSCULOSKELETAL SYSTEM + CONNECTIVE TISSUE	1.5596	11.3	31
217	8 SURG	WND DEBRID + SKN GRFT EXC HAND, FOR MUSCSKELETAL + CONN. TISS. DIS.	2.2824	13.1	33
218	8 SURG	LOWER EXTREM + HUMER PROC EXC HIP, FOOT, FEMUR AGE >69 +/OR C.C.	1.4250	10.9	31
219	8 SURG	LOWER EXTREM + HUMER PROC EXC HIP, FOOT, FEMUR AGE 18-69 W/O C.C.	1.0790	8.3	27
220	8 SURG	*LOWER EXTREM + HUMER PROC EXC HIP, FOOT, FEMUR AGE 0-17	.9339	5.3	25
221	8 SURG	KNEE PROCEDURES AGE >69 AND/OR C.C.	1.2727	8.3	28
222	8 SURG	KNEE PROCEDURES AGE <70 W/O C.C.	.9897	6.4	26
223	8 SURG	UPPER EXTREMITY PROC EXC HUMERUS + HAND AGE >69 AND/OR C.C.	1.0723	6.9	27
224	8 SURG	UPPER EXTREMITY PROC EXC HUMERUS + HAND AGE <70 W/O C.C.	.8952	5.6	24
225	8 SURG	FOOT PROCEDURES	.6476	4.8	15
226	8 SURG	SOFT TISSUE PROCEDURES AGE >69 AND/OR C.C.	.7984	5.1	25
227	8 SURG	SOFT TISSUE PROCEDURES AGE <70 W/O C.C.	.6337	4.2	18
228	8 SURG	GANGLION (HAND) PROCEDURES	.3626	2.2	7
229	8 SURG	HAND PROCEDURES EXCEPT GANGLION	.5998	3.4	14
230	8 SURG	LOCAL EXCISION + REMOVAL OF INT FIX DEVICES OF HIP + FEMUR	1.3594	8.9	29
231	8 SURG	LOCAL EXCISION + REMOVAL OF INT FIX DEVICES EXCEPT HIP + FEMUR	.9519	5.3	25
232	8 SURG	ARTHROSCOPY	.6063	3.6	15
233	8 SURG	OTHER MUSCULOSKELET SYS + CONN TISS O.R. PROC AGE >69 +/OR C.C.	1.7737	13.1	33
234	8 SURG	OTHER MUSCULOSKELET SYS + CONN TISS O.R. PROC AGE <70 W/O C.C.	1.2454	8.2	28
235	8 MED	FRACTURES OF FEMUR	1.7586	13.6	34
236	8 MED	FRACTURES OF HIP + PELVIS	1.3855	11.9	32
237	8 MED	SPRAINS, STRAINS, + DISLOCATIONS OF HIP, PELVIS + THIGH	.7929	6.4	26

238	8 MED	OSTEOMYELITIS	1.5511	12.3	32
239	8 MED	PATHOLOGICAL FRACTURES + MUSCULOSKELETAL + CONN. TISS. MALIGNANCY	1.0979	9.2	29
240	8 MED	CONNECTIVE TISSUE DISORDERS AGE >69 AND/OR C.C.	.9709	8.6	29
241	8 MED	CONNECTIVE TISSUE DISORDERS AGE <70 W/O C.C.	.9048	8.0	28
242	8 MED	SEPTIC ARTHRITIS	1.5880	11.2	31
243	8 MED	MEDICAL BACK PROBLEMS	.7551	7.5	28
244	8 MED	BONE DISEASES + SEPTIC ARTHROPATHY AGE >69 AND/OR C.C.	.7792	7.5	28
245	8 MED	BONE DISEASES + SEPTIC ARTHROPATHY AGE <70 W/O C.C.	.7177	6.3	26
246	8 MED	NON-SPECIFIC ARTHROPATHIES	.7147	6.8	27
247	8 MED	SIGNS + SYMPTOMS OF MUSCULOSKELETAL SYSTEM + CONN TISSUE	.6559	5.8	26
248	8 MED	TENDONITIS, MYOSITIS + BURSITIS	.6136	5.4	24
249	8 MED	AFTERCARE, MUSCULOSKELETAL SYSTEM + CONNECTIVE TISSUE	1.0203	7.6	28
250	8 MED	FX, SPRNS, STRNS + DISL OF FOREARM, HAND, FOOT AGE >69 +/OR C.C.	.7428	6.0	26
251	8 MED	FX, SPRNS, STRNS + DISL OF FOREARM, HAND, FOOT AGE 18-69 W/O C.C.	.5964	4.2	24
252	8 MED	*FX, SPRNS, STRNS + DISL OF FOREARM, HAND, FOOT AGE 0-17	.3533	1.8	7
253	8 MED	FX, SPRNS, STRNS + DISL OF UPARM, LOWLEG EX FOOT AGE >69 +/OR C.C.	.7466	6.6	27
254	8 MED	FX, SPRNS, STRNS + DISL OF UPARM, LOWLEG EX FOOT AGE 18-69 W/O C.C.	.6258	5.3	25
255	8 MED	*FX, SPRNS, STRNS + DISL OF UPARM, LOWLEG AGE 0-17	.4687	2.9	15
256	8 MED	OTHER DIAGNOSES OF MUSCULOSKELETAL SYSTEM + CONNECTIVE TISSUE	.8706	6.5	27
257	9 SURG	TOTAL MASTECTOMY FOR MALIGNANCY AGE >69 AND/OR C.C.	1.1085	9.3	23
258	9 SURG	TOTAL MASTECTOMY FOR MALIGNANCY AGE <70 W/O C.C.	1.0729	8.9	21
259	9 SURG	SUBTOTAL MASTECTOMY FOR MALIGNANCY AGE >69 AND/OR C.C.	1.0141	7.4	27
260	9 SURG	SUBTOTAL MASTECTOMY FOR MALIGNANCY AGE <70	.9325	6.4	26
261	9 SURG	BREAST PROC FOR NON-MALIG EXCEPT BIOPSY + LOC EXC	.7329	4.8	19
262	9 SURG	BREAST BIOPSY + LOCAL EXCISION FOR NON-MALIGNANCY	.4617	3.0	10
263	9 SURG	SKIN GRAFTS FOR SKIN ULCER OR CELLULITIS AGE >69 AND/OR C.C.	2.4737	21.3	41
264	9 SURG	SKIN GRAFTS FOR SKIN ULCER OR CELLULITIS AGE <70 W/O C.C.	2.2031	18.2	38
265	9 SURG	*SKIN GRAFTS EXCEPT FOR SKIN ULCER OR CELLULITIS WITH C.C.	1.4959	8.6	29
266	9 SURG	SKIN GRAFTS EXCEPT FOR SKIN ULCER OR CELLULITIS W/O C.C.	.9485	5.9	26
267	9 SURG	PERIANAL + PILONIDAL PROCEDURES	.6113	5.0	18
268	9 SURG	SKIN, SUBCUTANEOUS TISSUE + BREAST PLASTIC PROCEDURES	.5388	3.0	15
269	9 SURG	OTHER SKIN, SUBCUT TISS + BREAST O.R. PROC AGE >69 +/OR C.C.	.9947	5.7	26
270	9 SURG	OTHER SKIN, SUBCUT TISS + BREAST O.R. PROC AGE <70 W/O C.C.	.8123	4.5	25
271	9 MED	SKIN ULCERS	1.3802	12.1	32
272	9 MED	MAJOR SKIN DISORDERS AGE >69 AND/OR C.C.	.8620	7.8	28
273	9 MED	MAJOR SKIN DISORDERS AGE <70 W/O C.C.	.8286	7.3	27

DRG	MDC	TITLE	Relative Weights	Geometric Mean LOS	Outlier Cutoffs
274	9 MED	MALIGNANT BREAST DISORDERS AGE >69 AND/OR C.C.	1.0108	7.5	28
275	9 MED	MALIGNANT BREAST DISORDERS AGE <70 W/O C.C.	.9014	6.4	26
276	9 MED	NON-MALIGNANT BREAST DISORDERS	.6066	4.2	22
277	9 MED	CELLULITIS AGE >69 AND/OR C.C.	.8863	8.3	28
278	9 MED	CELLULITIS AGE 18-60 W/O C.C.	.8096	7.2	27
279	9 MED	*CELLULITIS AGE 0-17	.4789	4.2	13
280	9 MED	TRAUMA TO THE SKIN, SUBCUT TISS + BREAST AGE >69 +/OR C.C.	.6201	5.4	25
281	9 MED	TRAUMA TO THE SKIN, SUBCUT TISS + BREAST AGE 18-69 W/O C.C.	.5377	4.2	23
282	9 MED	*TRAUMA TO THE SKIN, SUBCUT TISS + BREAST AGE 0-17	.3460	2.2	9
283	9 MED	MINOR SKIN DISORDERS AGE >69 AND/OR C.C.	.6394	5.3	25
284	9 MED	MINOR SKIN DISORDERS AGE <70 W/O C.C.	.5971	4.4	24
285	10 SURG	AMPUTATIONS FOR ENDOCRINE, NUTRITIONAL + METABOLIC DISORDERS	2.8658	24.0	44
286	10 SURG	*ADRENAL + PITUITARY PROCEDURES	2.8952	16.1	36
287	10 SURG	SKIN GRAFTS + WOUND DEBRIDE FOR ENDOC, NUTRIT + METAB DISORDERS	2.8143	22.8	43
288	10 SURG	*C.R. PROCEDURES FOR OBESITY	1.5695	10.0	24
289	10 SURG	PARATHYROID PROCEDURES	1.3736	8.3	28
290	10 SURG	THYROID PROCEDURES	.8549	6.0	17
291	10 SURG	*THYROGLOSSAL PROCEDURES	.4909	2.9	8
292	10 SURG	OTHER ENDOCRINE, NUTRIT + METAB O.R. PROC AGE >69 +/OR C.C.	2.0307	10.8	31
293	10 SURG	*OTHER ENDOCRINE, NUTRIT + METAB O.R. PROC AGE <70 W/O C.C.	1.4951	8.0	28
294	10 MED	DIABETES AGE = >36	.8087	7.7	28
295	10 MED	DIABETES AGE 0-35	.7457	5.6	26
296	10 MED	NUTRITIONAL + MISC. METABOLIC DISORDERS AGE >69 AND/OR C.C.	.8979	7.3	27
297	10 MED	NUTRITIONAL + MISC. METABOLIC DISORDERS AGE 18-69 W/O C.C.	.7923	6.0	26
298	10 MED	*NUTRITIONAL + MISC. METABOLIC DISORDERS AGE 0-17	.7538	5.4	25
299	10 MED	INBORN ERRORS OF METABOLISM	.9407	6.8	27
300	10 MED	ENDOCRINE DISORDERS AGE >69 AND/OR C.C.	.9731	7.8	28
301	10 MED	ENDOCRINE DISORDERS AGE <70 W/O C.C.	.8143	6.4	26
302	11 SURG	KIDNEY TRANSPLANT	6.6322	24.1	44
303	11 SURG	KIDNEY, URETER + MAJOR BLADDER PROCEDURE FOR NEOPLASM	2.5397	16.2	36
304	11 SURG	KIDNEY, URETER + MAJ BLDR PROC FOR NON-MALIG AGE >69 +/OR C.C.	1.7952	12.8	33
305	11 SURG	KIDNEY, URETER + MAJ BLDR PROC FOR NON-MALIG AGE <70 W/O C.C.	1.7043	11.9	32
306	11 SURG	PROSTATECTOMY AGE >69 AND/OR C.C.	1.1399	8.6	29
307	11 SURG	PROSTATECTOMY AGE <70 W/O C.C.	.9513	7.2	26

308	11 SURG	MINOR BLADDER PROCEDURES AGE >69 AND/OR C.C.	1.0441	7.1	27
309	11 SURG	MINOR BLADDER PROCEDURES AGE <70 W/O C.C.	.9290	5.7	26
310	11 SURG	TRANSURETHRAL PROCEDURES AGE >69 AND/OR C.C.	.7071	4.9	20
311	11 SURG	TRANSURETHRAL PROCEDURES AGE <70 W/O C.C.	.5871	4.1	15
312	11 SURG	URETHRAL PROCEDURES, AGE >69 AND/OR C.C.	.7424	5.2	22
313	11 SURG	URETHRAL PROCEDURES, AGE 18-69 W/O C.C.	.6897	5.1	21
314	11 SURG	*URETHRAL PROCEDURES, AGE 0-17	.4368	2.3	11
315	11 SURG	OTHER KIDNEY + URINARY TRACT O.R. PROCEDURES	2.4884	9.8	30
316	11 MED	RENAL FAILURE W/O DIALYSIS	1.3314	6.7	27
317	11 MED	*RENAL FAILURE WITH DIALYSIS	.2385	1.2	3
318	11 MED	KIDNEY + URINARY TRACT NEOPLASMS AGE >69 AND/OR C.C.	.9142	5.5	26
319	11 MED	KIDNEY + URINARY TRACT NEOPLASMS AGE <70 W/O C.C.	.7942	4.2	24
320	11 MED	KIDNEY + URINARY TRACT INFECTIONS AGE >69 AND/OR C.C.	.8123	7.0	27
321	11 MED	KIDNEY + URINARY TRACT INFECTIONS AGE 18-69 W/O C.C.	.6803	5.6	23
322	11 MED	*KIDNEY + URINARY TRACT INFECTIONS AGE 0-17	.4553	3.7	13
323	11 MED	URINARY STONES AGE >69 AND/OR C.C.	.7131	4.9	25
324	11 MED	URINARY STONES AGE <70 W/O C.C.	.5472	3.9	19
325	11 MED	KIDNEY + URINARY TRACT SIGNS + SYMPTOMS AGE >69 AND/OR C.C.	.7247	5.4	25
326	11 MED	KIDNEY + URINARY TRACT SIGNS + SYMPTOMS AGE 18-69 W/O C.C.	.5875	4.3	21
327	11 MED	*KIDNEY + URINARY TRACT SIGNS + SYMPTOMS AGE 0-17	.5027	3.1	14
328	11 MED	URETHRAL STRICTURE AGE >69 AND/OR C.C.	.6508	4.8	22
329	11 MED	URETHRAL STRICTURE AGE 18-69 W/O C.C.	.5326	3.9	17
330	11 MED	*URETHRAL STRICTURE AGE 0-17	.2817	1.6	5
331	11 MED	OTHER KIDNEY + URINARY TRACT DIAGNOSES AGE >69 AND/OR C.C.	.8919	6.3	26
332	11 MED	OTHER KIDNEY + URINARY TRACT DIAGNOSES AGE 18-69 W/O C.C.	.7763	5.0	25
333	11 MED	*OTHER KIDNEY + URINARY TRACT DIAGNOSES AGE 0-17	.5146	3.2	18
334	12 SURG	MAJOR MALE PELVIC PROCEDURES WITH C.C.	1.5612	12.7	30
335	12 SURG	MAJOR MALE PELVIC PROCEDURES W/O C.C.	1.3590	11.8	29
336	12 SURG	TRANSURETHRAL PROSTATECTOMY AGE >69 AND/OR C.C.	1.0079	8.4	22
337	12 SURG	TRANSURETHRAL PROSTATECTOMY AGE <70 W/O C.C.	.8491	7.2	17
338	12 SURG	TESTES PROCEDURES, FOR MALIGNANCY	.9069	6.3	26
339	12 SURG	TESTES PROCEDURES, NON-MALIGNANT AGE >17	.6093	4.5	15
340	12 SURG	*TESTES PROCEDURES, NON-MALIGNANT AGE 0-17	.4381	2.4	7
341	12 SURG	PENIS PROCEDURES	.9983	6.0	23
342	12 SURG	CIRCUMCISION AGE >17	.4228	2.8	10
343	12 SURG	*CIRCUMCISION AGE 0-17	.3828	1.7	4

DRG	MDC	TITLE	Relative Weights	Geometric Mean LOS	Outlier Cutoffs
344	12 SURG	OTHER MALE REPRODUCTIVE SYSTEM O.R. PROCEDURES FOR MALIGNANCY	1.1204	7.4	27
345	12 SURG	OTHER MALE REPRODUCTIVE SYSTEM O.R. PROC EXCEPT FOR MALIG	.8334	5.6	26
346	12 MED	MALIGNANCY, MALE REPRODUCTIVE SYSTEM, AGE >69 AND/OR C.C.	.9395	6.9	27
347	12 MED	MALIGNANCY, MALE REPRODUCTIVE SYSTEM, AGE <70 W/O C.C.	.8304	5.7	26
348	12 MED	BENIGN PROSTATIC HYPERTROPHY AGE >69 AND/OR C.C.	.8864	6.2	26
349	12 MED	BENIGN PROSTATIC HYPERTROPHY AGE <70 W/O C.C.	.6998	4.9	22
350	12 MED	INFLAMMATION OF THE MALE REPRODUCTIVE SYSTEM	.6096	5.2	20
351	12 MED	*STERILIZATION, MALE	.2655	1.3	3
352	12 MED	OTHER MALE REPRODUCTIVE SYSTEM DIAGNOSES	.6385	4.4	20
353	13 SURG	PELVIC EVISCERATION, RADICAL HYSTERECTOMY + VULVECTOMY	1.9376	12.4	32
354	13 SURG	NON-RADICAL HYSTERECTOMY AGE >69 AND/OR C.C.	1.1108	9.6	20
355	13 SURG	NON-RADICAL HYSTERECTOMY AGE <70 W/O C.C.	1.0156	8.8	17
356	13 SURG	FEMALE REPRODUCTIVE SYSTEM RECONSTRUCTIVE PROCEDURES	.8460	8.1	18
357	13 SURG	UTERUS + ADENEXA PROCEDURES, FOR MALIGNANCY	1.9188	13.9	34
358	13 SURG	UTERUS + ADENEXA PROC FOR NON-MALIGNANCY EXCEPT TUBAL INTERRUPT	1.0890	8.0	28
359	13 SURG	*TUBAL INTERRUPTION FOR NON-MALIGNANCY	.4279	2.3	7
360	13 SURG	VAGINA, CERVIX + VULVA PROCEDURES	.5985	4.2	19
361	13 SURG	*LAPAROSCOPY + ENDOSCOPY (FEMALE) EXCEPT TUBAL INTERRUPTION	.4864	2.6	10
362	13 SURG	*LAPAROSCOPIC TUBAL INTERRUPTION	.3126	1.4	3
363	13 SURG	D+C, CONIZATION + RADIO-IMPLANT, FOR MALIGNANCY	.6516	4.3	18
364	13 SURG	D+C, CONIZATION EXCEPT FOR MALIGNANCY	.4028	2.6	9
365	13 SURG	OTHER FEMALE REPRODUCTIVE SYSTEM O.R. PROCEDURES	1.7965	12.7	33
366	13 MED	MALIGNANCY, FEMALE REPRODUCTIVE SYSTEM AGE >69 AND/OR C.C.	.8444	5.2	25
367	13 MED	MALIGNANCY, FEMALE REPRODUCTIVE SYSTEM AGE <70 W/O C.C.	.5786	3.5	24
368	13 MED	INFECTIONS, FEMALE REPRODUCTIVE SYSTEM	.7944	6.7	27
369	13 MED	MENSTRUAL + OTHER FEMALE REPRODUCTIVE SYSTEM DISORDERS	.6959	5.1	25
370	14 SURG	*CESAREAN SECTION WITH C.C.	.9912	7.6	15
371	14 SURG	*CESAREAN SECTION W/O C.C.	.7535	6.1	10
372	14 MED	*VAGINAL DELIVERY WITH COMPLICATING DIAGNOSES	.5534	3.8	9
373	14 MED	VAGINAL DELIVERY W/O COMPLICATING DIAGNOSES	.4063	3.2	9
374	14 MED	*VAGINAL DELIVERY WITH STERILIZATION AND/OR D+C	.5492	3.6	7
375	14 SURG	*VAGINAL DELIVERY WITH O.R. PROC EXCEPT STERIL AND/OR D+C	.6889	4.4	15
376	14 MED	*POSTPARTUM DIAGNOSES W/O O.R. PROCEDURE	.4158	2.9	10
377	14 SURG	*POSTPARTUM DIAGNOSES WITH O.R. PROCEDURE	.4761	2.2	8

378	14 MED	*ECTOPIC PREGNANCY	.8094	5.5	11
379	14 MED	*THREATENED ABORTION	.3169	2.2	8
380	14 MED	*ABORTION W/O D+C	.2705	1.5	4
381	14 MED	*ABORTION WITH D+C	.3602	1.4	4
382	14 MED	*FALSE LABOR	.1842	1.2	2
383	14 MED	*OTHER ANTEPARTUM DIAGNOSES WITH MEDICAL COMPLICATIONS	.4317	3.4	14
384	14 MED	*OTHER ANTEPARTUM DIAGNOSES W/O MEDICAL COMPLICATIONS	.3245	2.2	9
385	15	*NEONATES, DIED OR TRANSFERRED	.6883	1.8	14
386	15	*EXTREME IMMATURITY, NEONATE	3.6863	17.9	38
387	15	**PREMATURITY WITH MAJOR PROBLEMS	1.8459	13.3	33
388	15	**PREMATURITY W/O MAJOR PROBLEMS	1.1693	8.6	29
389	15	*FULL TERM NEONATE WITH MAJOR PROBLEMS	.5482	4.7	16
390	15	*NEONATES WITH OTHER SIGNIFICANT PROBLEMS	.3523	3.4	9
391	15	*NORMAL NEWBORNS	.2241	3.1	7
392	16 SURG	SPLENECTOMY AGE >17	2.7746	16.4	36
393	16 SURG	SPLENECTOMY AGE 0-17	1.5366	9.1	29
394	16 SURG	OTHER O.R. PROCEDURES OF THE BLOOD + BLOOD FORMING ORGANS	1.1146	6.1	26
395	16 MED	RED BLOOD CELL DISORDERS AGE >17	.7839	6.1	26
396	16 MED	*RED BLOOD CELL DISORDERS AGE 0-17	.6295	4.1	18
397	16 MED	COAGULATION DISORDERS	.9863	6.7	27
398	16 MED	RETICULOENDOTHELIAL + IMMUNITY DISORDERS AGE >69 AND/OR C.C.	.8900	6.1	26
399	16 MED	RETICULOENDOTHELIAL + IMMUNITY DISORDERS AGE <70 W/O C.C.	.8459	5.6	26
400	17 SURG	LYMPHOMA OR LEUKEMIA WITH MAJOR O.R. PROCEDURE	2.8272	16.9	37
401	17 SURG	LYMPHOMA OR LEUKEMIA WITH MINOR O.R. PROC AGE >69 AND/OR C.C.	1.2409	8.9	29
402	17 SURG	*LYMPHOMA OR LEUKEMIA WITH MINOR O.R. PROCEDURE AGE <70 W/O C.C.	1.1316	7.1	27
403	17 MED	LYMPHOMA OR LEUKEMIA AGE >69 AND/OR C.C.	1.1715	7.1	27
404	17 MED	LYMPHOMA OR LEUKEMIA AGE 18-69 W/O C.C.	1.1787	6.4	26
405	17 MED	*LYMPHOMA OR LEUKEMIA AGE 0-17	1.0517	4.9	25
406	17 SURG	MYELOPROLIF DISORD OR POORLY DIFF NEOPLASM W MAJ O.R. PROC + C.C.	2.2671	15.0	35
407	17 SURG	MYELOPROLIF DISORD OR POORLY DIFF NEOPL W MAJ O.R. PROC W/O C.C.	2.1366	13.3	33
408	17 SURG	MYELOPROLIF DISORD OR POORLY DIFF NEOPL WITH MINOR O.R. PROC	1.1389	7.1	27
409	17 MED	*RADIOTHERAPY	.8134	5.7	26
410	17 MED	CHEMOTHERAPY	.3527	2.6	12
411	17 MED	HISTORY OF MALIGNANCY W/O ENDOSCOPY	.7221	4.7	25
412	17 MED	HISTORY OF MALIGNANCY WITH ENDOSCOPY	.3400	2.0	8
413	17 MED	OTHR MYELOPROLIF DISORD OR POORLY DIFF NEOPL DX AGE >69 +/OR C.C.	1.0975	7.3	27

DRG	MDC	TITLE	Relative Weights	Geometric Mean LOS	Outlier Cutoffs
414	17 MED	OTHR MYELOPROLIF DISORD OR POORLY DIFF NEOPL DX AGE<70 W/O C.C.	1.0359	6.4	26
415	18 SURG	O.R. PROCEDURE FOR INFECTIOUS + PARASITIC DISEASES	3.0027	15.1	35
416	18 MED	SEPTICEMIA AGE >17	1.5504	9.2	29
417	18 MED	*SEPTICEMIA AGE 0-17	.7152	5.2	20
418	18 MED	POSTOPERATIVE + POST-TRAUMATIC INFECTIONS	.9968	8.4	28
419	18 MED	FEVER OF UNKNOWN ORIGIN AGE >69 AND/OR C.C.	.8628	6.9	27
420	18 MED	FEVER OF UNKNOWN ORIGIN AGE 18-69 W/O C.C.	.8022	6.2	26
421	18 MED	VIRAL ILLNESS AGE >17	.6045	5.4	21
422	18 MED	*VIRAL ILLNESS + FEVER OF UNKNOWN ORIGIN AGE 0-17	.4360	3.2	10
423	18 MED	OTHER INFECTIOUS + PARASITIC DISEASES DIAGNOSES	1.2107	8.8	29
424	19 SURG	O.R. PROCEDURES WITH PRINCIPAL DIAGNOSES OF MENTAL ILLNESS	2.1938	14.2	34
425	19 MED	ACUTE ADJUST REACT + DISTURBANCES OF PSYCHOSOCIAL DYSFUNCTION	.6812	5.8	26
426	19 MED	DEPRESSIVE NEUROSES	.9495	9.4	29
427	19 MED	NEUROSES EXCEPT DEPRESSIVE	.7678	6.9	27
428	19 MED	DISORDERS OF PERSONALITY + IMPULSE CONTROL	.9741	8.3	28
429	19 MED	ORGANIC DISTURBANCES + MENTAL RETARDATION	.9523	8.8	29
430	19 MED	PSYCHOSES	1.0934	10.8	31
431	19 MED	*CHILDHOOD MENTAL DISORDERS	2.2519	15.4	35
432	19 MED	**OTHER DIAGNOSES OF MENTAL DISORDERS	1.0525	7.2	27
433	20	**SUBSTANCE USE + SUBST INDUCED ORGANIC MENTAL DISORDERS, LEFT AMA	.4457	2.5	17
434	20	**DRUG DEPENDENCE	1.0404	9.1	29
435	20	**DRUG USE EXCEPT DEPENDENCE	1.0738	8.0	28
436	20	**ALCOHOL DEPENDENCE	.8853	8.1	28
437	20	**ALCOHOL USE EXCEPT DEPENDENCE	.6183	3.5	24
438	20	**ALCOHOL + SUBSTANCE INDUCED ORGANIC MENTAL SNYDROME	.8420	6.9	27
439	21 SURG	*SKIN GRAFTS FOR INJURIES	1.8219	8.9	29
440	21 SURG	*WOUND DEBRIDEMENTS FOR INJURIES	1.4807	7.2	27
441	21 SURG	*HAND PROCEDURES FOR INJURIES	.7180	3.0	16
442	21 SURG	OTHER O.R. PROCEDURES FOR INJURIES AGE >69 AND/OR C.C.	1.9026	9.1	29
443	21 SURG	OTHER O.R. PROCEDURES FOR INJURIES AGE <70 W/O C.C.	1.5211	6.6	27
444	21 MED	MULTIPLE TRAUMA AGE >69 AND/OR C.C.	.8830	6.7	27
445	21 MED	MULTIPLE TRAUMA AGE 18-69 W/O C.C.	.7530	5.2	25
446	21 MED	*MULTIPLE TRAUMA AGE 0-17	.4846	2.4	10
447	21 MED	ALLERGIC REACTIONS AGE >17	.4785	3.7	19

448	21 MED	*ALLERGIC REACTIONS AGE 0-17	.3505	2.9	9
449	21 MED	TOXIC EFFECTS OF DRUGS AGE >69 AND/OR C.C.	.7331	5.6	26
450	21 MED	TOXIC EFFECTS OF DRUGS AGE 18-69 W/O C.C.	.5957	3.9	23
451	21 MED	*TOXIC EFFECTS OF DRUGS AGE 0-17	.2912	2.1	8
452	21 MED	COMPLICATIONS OF TREATMENT AGE >69 AND/OR C.C.	.8492	5.5	26
453	21 MED	COMPLICATIONS OF TREATMENT AGE <70 W/O C.C.	.9020	5.1	25
454	21 MED	OTHER INJURIES, POISONINGS + TOXIC EFF DIAG AGE >69 AND/OR C.C.	.8224	5.3	25
455	21 MED	*OTHER INJURIES, POISONINGS + TOXIC EFF DIAG AGE <70 W/O C.C.	.6185	3.5	22
456	22	**BURNS, TRANSFERRED TO ANOTHER ACUTE CARE FACILITY	2.0902	11.6	32
457	22	**EXTENSIVE BURNS	6.8631	12.6	33
458	22 SURG	**NON-EXTENSIVE BURNS WITH SKIN GRAFTS	2.8572	18.3	38
459	22 SURG	**NON-EXTENSIVE BURNS WITH WOUND DEBRIDEMENT + OTHER O.R. PROC	2.7568	12.7	33
460	22 SURG	**NON-EXTENSIVE BURNS W/O O.R. PROCEDURE	1.4225	9.0	29
461	23 SURG	O.R. PROC WITH DIAGNOSES OF OTHER CONTACT WITH HEALTH SERVICES	1.6507	8.0	28
462	23 MED	*REHABILITATION	1.8268	13.5	34
463	23 MED	SIGNS + SYMPTOMS WITH C.C.	.7702	6.3	26
464	23 MED	SIGNS + SYMPTOMS W/O C.C.	.7322	6.0	26
465	23 MED	**AFTERCARE WITH HISTORY OF MALIGNANCY AS SECONDARY DX	.2071	1.5	4
466	23 MED	**AFTERCARE W/O HISTORY OF MALIGNANCY AS SECONDARY DX	.6377	3.7	24
467	23 MED	OTHER FACTORS INFLUENCING HEALTH STATUS	.9799	6.1	26
468		UNRELATED O.R. PROCEDURE	2.1037	11.2	31
469		***PDX INVALID AS DISCHARGE DIAGNOSIS	.0000	.0	0
470		***UNGROUPABLE	.0000	.0	0

The Impact of Third Party Payers on Hospital Rates and the Bottom Line*

A private entrepreneur would not tolerate the pressures that some of the major third party payers for hospital services are applying to this nation's hospital rates and bottom-line operating results. If an individual had no third party insurance coverage, or if he or she subscribed to a commercial health insurance plan, the individual would object vehemently to these pressures and in time would likely rebel against the system. There are not, however, enough persons speaking out about the financial impact Medicare, Medicaid and some Blue Cross plans have on the general, acute care hospitals in this country.

TWO PARTY PAYERS

In health care, as in most businesses, there is a producer and a consumer. In the provision of hospital care, the hospital is the producer, and the patient is usually the consumer (two party payer). In some views of the system, the physician is considered to be the consumer.

The producer must determine the rate or selling price to charge the consumer for the services or product. The producer knows that there are certain direct expenses (i.e., salaries, supplies, depreciation, etc.) that must be reimbursed for by the consumer. There are also indirect or overhead expenses that must be recovered, such as utilities, plant maintenance, plant operations, housekeeping, administration, and other general services. Furthermore, to stay in business, the producer must take in enough surplus income to compensate for inflation and for technological advancements.

---

*Reprinted from *The Health Care Supervisor*, Vol. 1, No. 2, pp. 1–10, Aspen Publishers, Inc., © January 1983.

A hospital has an absolute need to provide for a reasonable profit margin. The hospital must plan to pay for growth and development and must also provide for some income that will eventually be lost because of bad debts. All of a hospital's necessary costs of doing business are identified in the following summary:

Operating expenses
- direct expenses
    salaries and wages
    supplies and other expenses
    depreciation
- indirect expenses
    utilities
    plant operations
    plant maintenance
    administrative and general expenses

Other financial requirements
- provision for bad debts
- provision for growth and development (profit)

Once the hospital identifies the total budgeted operating expenses and all financial requirements, it apportions them over the anticipated units of service to be produced to arrive at the rate to charge the consumer. The following example illustrates this process.

The Memorial Hospital of Anytown, U.S.A. is using the following budgeted statistics and accompanying financial data:

Number of beds	250
Patient days	77,560
Direct expenses	$11,634,000
Indirect expenses	$7,756,000
Total operating expenses	$19,390,000

The hospital wants to allow 1.5 percent of gross revenue for bad debts and also wishes to realize approximately 10 percent net profit margin on its total operating expenses. The rate paid by the two party purchaser of services would be computed as follows:

1. total operating expenses	$19,390,000
2. provision for profit	1,939,000
3. provision for bad debts	319,935

4. total financial requirements
(sum of lines 1, 2, and 3) $21,648,935
5. total patient days   77,560
6. average rate or selling price
per patient day (line 4 divided by
line 5 rounded to nearest dollar) $279

In a traditional two party transaction, as in this example, the producer would provide the service and charge the consumer the computed average rate of $279. In exchange, the consumer would pay the producer at this rate for each unit of service received. However, this straightforward approach is no longer used in hospitals.

THIRD PARTY PAYERS

A third party payer is one who pays for a service or product on behalf of another individual or subscriber. For example, Medicare pays a hospital for services rendered to its subscribers. The catch is that Medicare agrees to pay the hospital only *allowable* costs, not published rates. The difference between published rate and allowable cost is called *contractual allowance,* and it is without recourse to the patient (the hospital cannot collect from the patient).

Nonallowable costs for Medicare payments are those operating expenses that Medicare determines are not necessary for good patient care, such as luxury accommodations, televisions, telephones, malpractice insurance and fund-raising costs (with the exception of interest expenses on loans). By the time Medicare has sifted out all of the nonallowable expenses, the net allowable expenses may represent 96 percent of total operating expenses or less. No provision for other financial requirements is allowed.

Someone has to make up the cost of nonallowable expenses and enable the hospital to meet its full financial requirements. The only persons able (or left) to do so are the self-pay and commercial insurance (private) patients. These patients are called on to make up the difference between the hospital's total financial requirements and the amount paid by Medicare and the other third party payers.

PATIENT MIX BY PAYING AGENT

Patient mix by paying agent refers to the percentage or numeric distribution of the hospital's total patient days. A hospital having a high proportion of self-pay and commercial insurance patients has what is termed a "rich mix" of patients. Conversely, a hospital that has a high proportion of cost-based patients (i.e., Medicare, Medicaid, etc.) is considered to have a "lean mix" of patients. Classification of patient mix is based on the proportion of self-pay and commercial insurance patients. In Table C–1, three patient mix conditions are considered.

Under the two party payer system (condition A), every patient pays the hospital's published charges. Under the third party payer, cost-based system (conditions B and C), the hospital negotiates—or has imposed upon it—a payment rate that is based on either the hospital's historical costs or its budgeted costs. (The patient's hospital bill, however, usually indicates the published charge. This is misleading to the patient.) Medicare and Medicaid reimburse hospitals on a *retrospective* basis based on historical costs. Some Blue Cross plans pay hospitals on a retrospective basis, similar to the way Medicare payments are made, requiring a year-end adjustment of payments to meet allowable costs once they are completely known.

What is the financial impact of these payment systems and their retrospective patient mix conditions on the hospital's bottom line?

THIRD PARTY PAYERS' IMPACT ON BOTTOM LINE

Under patient mix A, 100 percent of the hospital's 77,560 patient days are reimbursed by self-pay and commercial insurance. This condition gives the hospital its desired 10 percent operating profit of $1,939,000. (See Table C–2.)

Under patient mix conditions B and C, the third party payers reimburse the hospital for its services on the following basis:

Table C–1 Patient Mix by Type of Payer

		Percentage of patient mix	
Type of payer	A	B	C
Self-pay and commercial insurance	100	23	15
Medicare	—	35	39
Medicaid	—	12	14
Blue Cross	—	30	32
Total	100	100	100

Table C–2 Comparative Analysis of Patient Mix Impact on Bottom Line while Maintaining a Constant Rate

	Patient mix A		Patient mix B		Patient mix C	
	Total	Percent-age	Total	Percent-age	Total	Percent-age
Patient days						
Self-pay and commercial insurance	77,560	100	17,839	23	11,634	15
Medicare			27,146	35	30,248	39
Medicaid			9,307	12	10,858	14
Blue Cross			23,268	30	24,820	32
Total	77,560	100%	77,560	100%	77,560	100%

	Total	Rate	Total	Rate	Total	Rate
Gross revenue						
Self-pay and commercial insurance	$21,648,935	$279	$4,979,311	$279	$3,247,340	$279
Medicare			7,577,127	279	8,442,973	279
Medicaid			2,597,816	279	3,030,739	279
Blue Cross			6,494,681	279	6,927,883	279
Total	$21,648,935	279	$21,648,935	279	$21,648,935	279
Deductions						
Bad debts	319,935	4	74,690	4	48,710	4
Medicare			1,062,087	39	1,183,453	39
Medicaid			503,741	54	587,689	54
Blue Cross			677,681	29	722,883	29
Total	$ 319,935	4	$2,318,199	30	$2,542,735	33
Net revenue						
Self-pay and commercial insurance	21,329,000	275	4,904,621	275	3,198,630	275
Medicare			6,515,040	240	7,259,520	240
Medicaid			2,094,075	225	2,443,050	225
Blue Cross			5,817,000	250	6,205,000	250
Total	$21,329,000	275	$19,330,736	249	$19,106,200	246
Expenses						
Direct expenses	11,634,000	150	11,634,000	150	11,634,000	150
Indirect expenses	7,756,000	100	7,756,000	100	7,756,000	100
Total	$19,390,000	$250	$19,390,000	$250	$19,390,000	$250
Net profit or (loss)	$ 1,939,000	$ 25	$ (59,264)	$ (1)	$ (283,800)	$ (4)

- Medicare, 96% of total operating expenses;
- Medicaid, 90% of total operating expenses;
- Blue Cross, 100% of total operating expenses.

(Note: This is an example only; the rates presented here are for illustrative purposes and should not be construed as representative of rates actually paid. Most third party payers limit their payments to the lesser of costs or charges.)

In Table C–2 the average expense per patient day is $250. Payment rates and amounts for patient mix B are calculated in Table C–3.

Net revenue from self-pay and commercial insurance payers is computed as follows:

Gross revenue	$4,979,311
(17,839 patient days × $279)	
Less bad debts	74,690
Net revenue from self-pay and commercial insurance	$4,904,621

In this illustration the total net revenue has been reduced from $21,329,000 for patient mix A to $19,330,736 for patient mix B. Following the same analysis, the net revenue for patient mix C has been further reduced to $19,106,200. The hospital's total operating expenses remain the same at $19,390,000. The comparative summary of the financial impact of the third party patient mix on the bottom line is as follows:

Patient mix condition	Bottom line results—profit or (loss)
A—Rich mix	$1,939,000
B—Moderate mix	($59,264)
C—Lean mix	($283,800)

Throughout this example the average daily gross charge to patients has remained the same at $279. What will happen to the average daily

Table C–3 Payment Rates and Amounts for Patient Mix B

Paying agent	Cost per patient day	Percentage rate	Dollar rate	Number of patient days	Total payment
Medicare	$250	96	$240	27,146	$ 6,515,040
Medicaid	250	90	225	9,307	2,094,075
Blue Cross	250	100	250	23,268	5,817,000
Total third party payments					$14,426,115

rate if the hospital attempts to maintain its desired profit line and meet all other financial requirements?

THIRD PARTY PAYER'S IMPACT ON RATES

For the hospital to maintain its desired profit line, the self-pay and commercial insurance patients will be required to make up the shortage. The amount of payments from third party payers will remain the same regardless of the rate charged. This process is called "cost shifting." In the example presented, the hospital's total financial requirements were identified as $21,648,935. Table C–4 illustrates how the adjustment of rates is computed.

The movement of cost from the cost-based payers of hospital care to the full-charge payers has not only artificially inflated the hospital's room rates; it has also boosted all other published charges for ancillary services. Table C–5 is a comparative analysis of the impact of patient mix on rates if a constant bottom line is maintained. It was computed using the average daily charge per patient day for services. This was done to simplify the computation while demonstrating the financial impact of third party payers' practices on the hospital's rates. The artificially inflated average daily room rate is one of the indices by which the government evaluates the increase or decrease in the cost of hospital care. This may be a very misleading figure, but it is one that the average patient cannot question because he or she is generally uninformed.

Table C–4 Adjustment of Rates

	Patient mix condition		
	A	B	C
Total financial requirements	$21,648,935	$21,648,935	$21,648,935
Less amount received from third parties	—	14,426,115	15,907,570
Amount needed to meet total financial requirements (line 1 minus line 2)	21,648,935	7,222,820	5,741,365
Number of self-pay and commercial insurance patient days	77,560	17,839	11,634
Average rate per patient day (line 3 divided by line 4)	279	405	493
Percentage increase	—	45%	76%

Table C–5 Comparative Analysis of the Impact of Patient Mix Rates while Maintaining a Constant Bottom Line

	Patient mix A		Patient mix B		Patient mix C	
	Total	Percent-age	Total	Percent-age	Total	Percent-age
Patient days						
Self-pay and commercial insurance	77,560	100	17,839	23	11,634	15
Medicare			27,146	35	30,248	39
Medicaid			9,307	12	10,858	14
Blue Cross			23,268	30	24,820	32
Total	77,560	100%	77,560	100%	77,560	100%
	Total	Rate	Total	Rate	Total	Rate
Gross revenue						
Self-pay and commercial insurance	$21,648,935	$279	$7,224,795	$405	$5,735,562	$493
Medicare			10,994,130	405	14,912,264	493
Medicaid			3,769,335	405	5,352,994	493
Blue Cross			9,423,540	405	12,236,260	493
Total	$21,648,935	279	$31,411,800	405	$38,237,080	493
Deductions						
Bad debts	319,935	4	108,370	6	86,033	7
Medicare			4,479,090	165	7,652,744	253
Medicaid			1,675,260	180	2,909,944	268
Blue Cross			3,606,540	155	6,031,260	243
Total	$ 319,935	4	$9,869,260	127	$16,679,981	215
Net revenue						
Self-pay and commercial insurance	21,329,000	275	7,116,425	399	5,649,529	486
Medicare			6,515,040	240	7,259,520	240
Medicaid			2,094,075	225	2,443,050	225
Blue Cross			5,817,000	250	6,205,000	250
Total	$21,329,000	275	$21,542,540	278	$21,557,099	278
Expenses						
Direct expenses	11,634,000	150	11,634,000	150	11,634,000	150
Indirect expenses	7,756,000	100	7,756,000	100	7,756,000	100
Total	$19,390,000	$250	$19,390,000	$250	$19,390,000	$250
Net profit or (loss)	$ 1,939,000	$ 25	$ 2,152,540	$ 28	$ 2,167,099	$ 28

FROM THE PRIVATE PATIENT'S PERSPECTIVE

In all probability, most patients are not aware of the cost-shifting process, primarily because it does not directly affect their pocketbooks and also because the hospitals have not informed them of it.

Most self-pay and commercial insurance patients (private), as well as Medicare and Medicaid patients, have their insurance premiums either partially or totally paid by another (i.e., employer, government, etc.). Consequently, they are not directly aware of their premium costs and of hospital costs in general.

The Health Insurance Association of America (HIAA) has labeled the cost-shifting process a "hidden tax." HIAA contends that since the federal government pays only part of the hospital expenses incurred by Medicare and Medicaid patients, the self-pay and commercial patients and their employers are unknowingly subsidizing government patients. To continue this thought process further, the private patients are also supporting the Medicare and Medicaid programs with their tax dollars—thus there is double taxation and a "hidden tax."

In 1981, average daily Medicare and Medicaid payments were $41 less than what the self-pay and commercial insurance patients were charged. Such underpayments shifted to the self-pay and commercial insurance patients an estimated $4.8 billion in 1981, and this burden could continue to grow if the government cuts back further in its programs.

There is consensus among those affected by the hospital industry—government, business, labor, hospitals, patients, insurance companies, and others—to reduce or at least contain hospital costs. This goal is noble; however, cost shifting does not solve the problem. Rather, cost shifting compounds the problem by simply shifting the responsibility to the private-pay patient.

FROM THE HOSPITAL'S PERSPECTIVE

Hospitals, physicians, insurance companies and even government have identified, experimented with and implemented numerous cost-saving techniques, such as the following:

- utilization review committees to reduce overuse of hospital services
- second opinions to reduce unnecessary surgery
- health planning and certificate of need to reduce duplication of services and prevent overexpansion of capital expenditures
- employee incentive plans to improve productivity
- preventive medicine, ambulatory care, same-day surgery and home care services to reduce the utilization of the more costly inpatient hospital services

- government-sponsored experiments in incentive and prospective reimbursement to improve productivity and reduce cost per unit of hospital service

Unfortunately, cost shifting undermines all of these efforts. The fact remains unaltered: rates are higher because of the need to subsidize Medicare and Medicaid programs.

THE SOLUTION: A COMMON RATE FOR ALL PAYERS

What are the possible consequences of today's inequitable distribution of hospital costs? The following results are conceivable:

- Medicare and Medicaid patients will eventually be denied ready access to all the hospital benefits they have become accustomed to.
- Self-pay and commercial insurance patients will continue to pay hospital rates that escalate in disproportionate relation to the cost of living.
- Commercial insurance premiums will continue to rise in direct porportion to hospital charges.
- Employers will continue to pay higher insurance premiums.
- Employees' net fringe benefit packages will shrink in value.
- The government may eventually discontinue some health care programs that have become priced beyond the financial capacity of the population.

A reasonable solution would call for all patients to pay the same rates for the same services. This is not just theory; it is reality in two states. In Maryland and New Jersey, strong incentives are provided for hospitals to cut costs wherever possible. As a result, Medicare and Medicaid have agreed to pay for hospital services on the same basis as everyone else. By removing the hidden tax in hospital bills, hospitals can help to eliminate cost shifting and concentrate on true cost containment.

Together with their commercial insurers, hospitals must publicize the facts of reimbursement to their patients, employers, subscribers and legislators. They must advocate the kind of change that will be equitable to all participants in the system: a common rate for all payers.

Index

About the Author

Allen G. Herkimer, Jr., Ed.D., FHFMA, CMPA, is an associate professor of Health Administration at Southwest Texas State University, San Marcos, Texas. In addition, he is a partner of Alfa Management Services, an Austin, Texas consulting firm that specializes in health care financial management, systems analysis, management development, and in-service education.

Dr. Herkimer has nearly 30 years of experience within the nontaxable and taxable segments of the health care industry as hospital controller, corporate controller, vice president, educator, author, and consultant.

After 12 years as a hospital chief financial officer, Dr. Herkimer served from 1969 through 1972 as project director of the nation's first Incentive Reimbursement Experiment, funded by the Social Security Administration and Connecticut Blue Cross. For two years, 1973–1975, he served as co-chairperson of the President's Cost of Living Council, National Commission on Productivity's Panel on Hospital Financial Management. In 1974, he created and directed the Hospital Resource Unit (HRU) project. The objective of this research project was to develop a quantitative productivity measurement of hospital services. From 1973 through 1980, he was a principal with a major international accounting and consulting firm and a vice president of a national health care management company. In 1980, he joined the faculty of California State University, Northridge. In 1985–1986 he served as president of the Southern California Chapter of the Healthcare Financial Management Association (HFMA), which has over 1,200 members.

He has authored numerous trade journal articles and published four books. The first edition of *Understanding Hospital Financial Management*, published by Aspen Publishers, Inc., was selected by the *Ameri-*

can Journal of Nursing as its Book of the Year in 1979. Presently he is writing a book on budgeting for health care organizations.

Dr. Herkimer is a Fellow (FHFMA), National Life Member, Certified Patient Account Manager (CMPA), and a past national director of HFMA, and in 1975 received HFMA's Frederick C. Morgan Award to an individual who has made an outstanding contribution to the field of health care financial management. In addition, he is a member of the American College of Healthcare Executives and a national lifetime member of the American Guild of Patient Account Managers (AGPAM). He received a Bachelor of Science degree from Syracuse University, New York, in 1949, a Master's of Business Administration degree from the University of Bridgeport, Connecticut, in 1972, and a Doctorate of Education degree from the University of La Verne, California, in 1985.